FOR DUMMIES

The fun and easy way™ to travel!

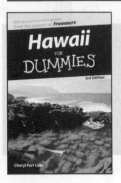
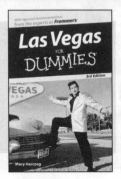

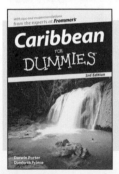

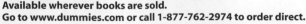

Montréal & Québec City

FOR

DUMMIES®

2ND EDITION

by Austin Macdonald

WILEY

Wiley Publishing, Inc.

Montréal & Québec City For Dummies, 2nd Edition

Published by
Wiley Publishing, Inc.
111 River St.
Hoboken, NJ 07030-5774
www.wiley.com

WILEY

About the Author

Austin Macdonald (austin_macdonald@yahoo.com) first came to Montréal for school. For three summers, while studying English Literature at McGill University, he worked as a tour guide in both Montréal and Québec City. Since teaching English in Tokyo, counting down the millennium in Rio, and having a series of misadventures in the dot-com world, Austin has been working as a freelance writer concerned with urban affairs at large. His work has been published in magazines such as *Art and Antiques*, *Toronto Life*, and *Azure* and in newspapers, including *Globe and Mail*, the *National Post*, and the *Montréal Gazette*.

Publisher's Acknowledgments

We're proud of this book; please send us your comments through our Dummies online registration form located at www.dummies.com/register/.

Some of the people who helped bring this book to market include the following:

Editorial

Editors: M. Faunette Johnston, Production Editor; Elizabeth Kuball, Development Editor; Naomi Kraus, Project Editor

Copy Editor: Doreen Russo

Cartographer: Anton Crane

Senior Photo Editor: Richard Fox

Front Cover Photo: © Philip Gould/ Corbis. Description: Quebec City market.

Back Cover Photo: © Mark Downey/ Masterfile. Description: Notre Dame Basilica, Quebec City.

Cartoons: Rich Tennant (www.the5thwave.com)

Composition Services

Project Coordinator: Michael Kruzil

Layout and Graphics: Carl Byers, Joyce Haughey, Barbara Moore, Heather Ryan, Julie Trippetti

Proofreaders: Laura Albert, Leeann Harney, Jessica Kramer, Techbooks

Indexer: Techbooks

Publishing and Editorial for Consumer Dummies

Diane Graves Steele, Vice President and Publisher, Consumer Dummies

Joyce Pepple, Acquisitions Director, Consumer Dummies

Kristin A. Cocks, Product Development Director, Consumer Dummies

Michael Spring, Vice President and Publisher, Travel

Kelly Regan, Editorial Director, Travel

Publishing for Technology Dummies

Andy Cummings, Vice President and Publisher, Dummies Technology/General User

Composition Services

Gerry Fahey, Vice President of Production Services

Debbie Stailey, Director of Composition Services

Contents at a Glance

Introduction 1

Part 1: Introducing Montréal and Québec City 7
  Chapter 1: Discovering the Best of Montréal and Québec City....9
  Chapter 2: Digging Deeper into Montréal and Québec City 13
  Chapter 3: Deciding When to Go 19

Part 11: Planning Your Trip to Montréal
and Québec City 31
  Chapter 4: Managing Your Money 33
  Chapter 5: Getting to Montréal and Québec City 43
  Chapter 6: Catering to Special Travel Needs or Interests 51
  Chapter 7: Taking Care of the Remaining Details 59

Part 111: Settling Into and Exploring Montréal 73
  Chapter 8: Arriving and Getting Oriented in Montréal 75
  Chapter 9: Checking In at Montréal's Best Hotels 89
  Chapter 10: Dining and Snacking in Montréal............................108
  Chapter 11: Discovering Montréal's Best Attractions 132
  Chapter 12: Shopping the Montréal Stores 152
  Chapter 13: Following an Itinerary: Five Great Options 161
  Chapter 14: Going Beyond Montréal: Three Day-trips 177
  Chapter 15: Living It Up after Dark: Montréal Nightlife...........188

Part 1V: Settling Into and Exploring
Québec City 205
  Chapter 16: Arriving and Getting Oriented in Québec City 207
  Chapter 17: Checking in at Québec City's Best Hotels 214
  Chapter 18: Dining and Snacking in Québec City 227
  Chapter 19: Exploring Québec City 241
  Chapter 20: Shopping the Québec City Stores 257
  Chapter 21: Living It Up after Dark: Québec City Nightlife 266

Part V: The Part of Tens 275
  Chapter 22: Ten Terroir Ingredients and Local
    Specialties to Look for on Your Plate 277
  Chapter 23: Ten (or So) T-Shirts with Tons
    of Montréal Street-Cred...281

Appendix: Quick Concierge 285

Index 295

Maps at a Glance

Greater Montréal 76
Vieux-Montréal Accommodations 95
Downtown Montréal Accommodations 96
Downtown and Vieux-Montréal Dining and Snacking 112
Plateau and Mile End Dining 115
Downtown Montréal Attractions 134
Vieux-Montréal Attractions 137
East Montréal Attractions 139
Underground City 157
Connecting with Your French Roots 169
The English Establishment 172
Brunch, Tam-tams, and Beyond 174
Downtown Ottawa 179
The Laurentian Mountains 183
The Eastern Townships 186
Downtown Montréal Nightlife...192
Plateau, Mile End, and Gay Village Nightlife 194
Québec City Orientation 210
Québec City Accommodations 216
Québec City Dining and Snacking......................................228
Québec City Attractions 242
Historical Highlights of Vieux-Québec 254
Québec City Nightlife 270

Table of Contents

Introduction *1*

    About This Book...1
    Conventions Used in This Book 2
    Foolish Assumptions 4
    How This Book Is Organized....................................4
        Part I: Introducing Montréal and Québec City 4
        Part II: Planning Your Trip to Montréal
           and Québec City 5
        Part III: Settling Into and Exploring Montréal............5
        Part IV: Settling Into and Exploring Québec City......5
        Part V: The Part of Tens 5
    Icons Used in This Book..5
    Where to Go from Here...6

Part 1: Introducing Montréal and Québec City *7*

    Chapter 1: Discovering the Best of Montréal
    and Québec City **9**
        Montreal's Best Neighborhoods 10
        Québec City's Best Neighborhoods 10
        The Best Hotels 11
        The Best Restaurants 11
        The Best Attractions...12
        The Best Nightlife...12

    Chapter 2: Digging Deeper into Montréal
    and Québec City **13**
        History 101: The Main Events................................13
        The French discovered Québec 13
        . . . and then Montréal 14
        . . . and then Québeckers took over 14
        Parlez-Vous?...14
        Soaking Up That European Flavor 15
        Following Your Stomach....................................15
        Experiencing the Festival Frenzy 15
        Living It Up After Hours....................................15
        Checking Out the Many Faces of Montréal.....................16
        Walking (and Skiing and Eating)
           in a Winter Wonderland....................................16

Eyeing Recommended Books and Movies 17
Turning the pages 17
Screening films 18

Chapter 3: Deciding When to Go 19

Revealing the Two Faces of Montréal
and Québec City 19
Experiencing the Secret of the Seasons 20
Spring 21
Summer 22
Fall 22
Winter 23
Viewing Montréal's Calendar of Events...........................23
January/February 23
March 24
April..24
May 25
June...25
July..26
August 26
September/October 27
November 28
Checking Out Québec City's Calendar of Events 29
January/February 29
March/April 29
May 29
June..29
July..30
August 30
September/October...30

**Part II: Planning Your Trip to Montréal
and Québec City 31**

Chapter 4: Managing Your Money...............................33

Planning a Budget 33
Lodging...33
Transportation 34
Dining 34
Attractions 35
Shopping 35
Nightlife..35
Watching Out for Hidden Expenses 35
Taking taxes into account 35
Tipping 36

Cutting Costs — But Not the Fun............................36
Handling Money 37
    Understanding the Loonie 37
    Converting your greenbacks 38
    Using ATMs and carrying cash....................39
    Charging ahead with credit cards..............40
    Toting traveler's checks 41
Dealing with a Lost or Stolen Wallet.................41

Chapter 5: Getting to Montréal and Québec City........43
Flying to Montréal or Québec City......................43
    Finding out which airlines fly there...........43
    Getting the best deal on your airfare 44
Driving to Montréal or Québec City 46
Arriving by Other Means.....................................46
Joining an Escorted Tour 47
Choosing a Package Tour 48
    Finding escorted and package tours 49
    Package deals to Montréal and Québec City..........50

**Chapter 6: Catering to Special Travel Needs
or Interests 51**
Traveling with the Brood: Advice for Families..................51
Making Age Work for You: Tips for Seniors 53
Advice for Travelers with Disabilities 54
    Worldwide resources...................................54
    Canadian resources 54
    Local resources 54
    Support while traveling to either city 55
    Support while traveling within cities 55
Out and About: Advice for Gay and Lesbian Travelers....56
    The Montréal scene......................................57
    The Québec City scene 57

Chapter 7: Taking Care of the Remaining Details........59
Getting a Passport...59
    Applying for a U.S. passport.......................60
Renting a Car — and Understanding Why You Shouldn't ...62
    Finding the car you need at the price you want 62
Playing It Safe with Travel and Medical Insurance 64
    Trip-cancellation insurance........................64
    Medical insurance.......................................65
    Lost-luggage insurance 65
Staying Healthy When You Travel.......................66
Staying Connected by Cellphone or E-Mail........................66
Keeping Up with Airline Security Measures 69

Making Dinner Reservations in Advance 70
Surfing ahead of time...70
Reserving a table for dinner 71
Getting a Few Packing Tips 71
What not to bring..71
What to bring..72

Part III: Settling Into and Exploring Montréal 73

Chapter 8: Arriving and Getting Oriented in Montréal 75

Navigating Your Way through Passport Control
and Customs 75
Making Your Way to Your Hotel...78
If you arrive by plane 78
If you arrive by car 79
If you arrive by train...80
Traveling between Montréal and Québec City.................80
By rental car 80
By bus...80
By train 81
Figuring Out Montréal's Neighborhoods.........................81
Vieux-Montréal 81
Downtown...81
Chinatown..82
Quartier Latin 82
Gay Village 82
Plateau..82
Mile End 83
Little Italy 83
Finding Information after You Arrive...............................83
Getting Around Montréal 84
By foot 85
By public transportation (Métro and bus) 85
By bicycle...86
By car 86
By taxi..88

Chapter 9: Checking In at Montréal's Best Hotels 89

Getting to Know Your Options 89
Boutique hotels...89
Luxury hotels 89
Chain hotels...90
Independent hotels...90
Bed-and-breakfasts 90

Finding the Best Room at the Best Rate............................90
  Finding the best rate 91
  Reserving the best room...92
Arriving without a Reservation 93
Montréal's Best Hotels from A to Z.............................93

Chapter 10: Dining and Snacking in Montréal.........108

Getting the Dish on the Local Scene................................108
  Your terroir is my local ingredient 108
  The brunch bunch 109
  Tasty tapas for fast friends 109
  Super-fun supper clubs 109
Trimming the Fat from Your Budget 110
Homing In on Dining Etiquette 110
Montréal's Best Restaurants from A to Z........................111
Dining and Snacking on the Go.................................125
  Pizza and burgers 125
  The best bagels 126
  Sandwich, anyone? 126
  The big breakfast bonanza 127
  Picnicking and markets 128
  Eating like a local 129
  The vegetarian scene 129
  BYOB 130
  Coffee and pastries 131

Chapter 11: Discovering Montréal's
Best Attractions...132

Montréal's Top Sights from A to Z 132
Finding More Cool Things to See and Do 143
  Kid-pleasers 143
  Best city parks 145
  Museums...................................145
  Churches 147
  Spectator sports 148
Seeing Montréal by Guided Tour 149
  Walking it...149
  Riding it..................................150
  Boating it.................................150
  Hoofing it................................151

Chapter 12: Shopping the Montréal Stores................152

Surveying the Scene 152
Checking Out the Big Names 154
Discovering the Best Shopping Neighborhoods 155
  Downtown.......................................155
  Mile End/Outremont (avenue Laurier)................158

The Plateau 158
St-Henri (rue Notre-Dame) 159
Vieux-Montréal (rue St-Paul) 160
Westmount (rue Sherbrooke Ouest) 160

Chapter 13: Following an Itinerary: Five Great Options 161

Montréal in Three Days 161
Day 1 162
Day 2 164
Day 3 165
Montréal in Five Days 166
Day 4 166
Day 5 167
Connecting with Your French Roots 168
The English Establishment 171
Brunch, Tam-tams, and Beyond 173

Chapter 14: Going Beyond Montréal: Three Day-trips 177

Ottawa, the Nation's Capital 178
Getting there 178
Seeing the sights 178
Where to stay 181
Where to dine 181
The Laurentian Mountains 182
Getting there 182
Seeing the sights 182
Where to stay 184
Where to dine 184
The Eastern Townships 185
Getting there 185
Seeing the sights 185
Where to stay 187
Where to dine 187

Chapter 15: Living It Up after Dark: Montréal Nightlife 188

Applauding the Cultural Scene 188
Getting the inside scoop 188
Raising the curtain on the performing arts 189
Hitting the Clubs and Bars 190
Shaking your groove thing: The best
dance clubs 195
Grooving to live music 197

Hopping between hot spots: Montréal's
cafes and bars 199
Lounging like lizards................................201
Dropping into neighborhood bars.........................202
What's brewing in Montréal?....................203
Racking up in a pool hall.........................203
Yucking it up at comedy clubs 204
Being out and proud in Gay Village 204

Part IV: Settling Into and Exploring Québec City.................................205

Chapter 16: Arriving and Getting Oriented in Québec City...............................207
Making Your Way to Your Hotel..................207
If you arrive by plane 207
If you arrive by car 208
If you arrive by train or bus................208
Figuring Out Québec City's Neighborhoods 208
Haute-Ville (Upper City)...................209
Basse-Ville (Lower City)....................209
Grande-Allée 209
Finding Information after You Arrive............209
Getting Around Québec City.........................212
By foot 212
By public transportation 212
By taxi...212
By car 213
By bicycle..213

Chapter 17: Checking in at Québec City's Best Hotels 214
Québec City Hotels from A to Z................215

Chapter 18: Dining and Snacking in Québec City.....227
Getting the Dish on the Local Scene................227
The Old City....................................227
Grande-Allée 230
Québec City's Best Restaurants 230
Québec City's Best Snacks 238
Cafes for coffee and more....................238
Pizza and burgers 239
For chocolate lovers..........................240
All crêpes, all the time........................240
A vegetarian outpost 240

Chapter 19: Exploring Québec City...........................241

Exploring Québec City's Top Sights from A to Z.............241
Finding More Cool Things to See and Do.........................247
  Kid-pleasing places...247
  For military and history buffs.................................249
  Teen-tempting areas..250
  The best strolling streets.......................................251
  Seeing Québec City by guided tour........................252
Hitting the Historical Highlights of Vieux-Québec..........253

Chapter 20: Shopping the Québec City Stores 257

Surveying the Scene 257
Checking Out the Big Names 258
Going to Shopping Malls 258
Discovering the Best Shopping Neighborhoods 259
  Rue St-Paul..260
  Rue St-Jean...261
  Le Petit-Champlain/Place-Royale...........................261
  Château Frontenac..262
  Avenue Cartier 262
  Rue St-Joseph...263

**Chapter 21: Living It Up after Dark:
Québec City Nightlife 266**

Finding Out What's Going On 267
Checking Out the Scene 268
Dancing the Night Away: Québec City's Best Clubs 268
Grooving to Live Music: Where to Catch
  Québec City's Best Acts 269
Drinking In the Local Flavor: Québec City's
  Neighborhood Bars and Pubs..................................273
Being Out and Proud in Québec City............................274

Part V: The Part of Tens 275

**Chapter 22: Ten *Terroir* Ingredients and Local
Specialties to Look for on Your Plate.....................277**

Maple Syrup...278
Unpasteurized Cheese...278
Microbrewery Beer..278
Cidre de Glace 278
Duck from Lac Brôme..279
Lamb 279
Blueberries from Lac St. Jean....................................279

Strawberries from Île d'Orléans 279
Tourtière...280
Poutine 280

**Chapter 23: Ten (or So) T-Shirts with Tons
of Montréal Street-Cred 281**
Fidel Clothing...281
Plateau...282
Nordiques/Expos..282
McGill/Concordia 282
Piknic Electronik 282
Bily Kun 283
Wolf Parade 283
St-Viateur Bagels 283
Onetop.ca...283
Montrealite.com 284
Three Monkeys..284

Appendix: Quick Concierge 285
Fast Facts 285
Toll-Free Numbers and Web Sites 291
Where to Get More Information 293

Index 295

Introduction

● ●

*E*uropean flair and French *joie de vivre* — you'll definitely find these elusive old-world qualities in Montréal and Québec City.

Visiting Montréal is like escaping into a little corner of Europe, except that you don't have to cross the Atlantic to get here. And Montréal doesn't feel European only because life and business is carried out mostly in French. Things are really different here. People eat later (and, may I add, better), they party differently (ditto), and life is infused with a touch of European style. Montréalers seem to keep one eye on Paris all the time.

Visiting Québec City is like slipping into the past without actually leaving the present. One of the oldest, most picturesque cities in North America, Québec City has preserved all its historic charm while hanging on to its vibrant and distinct culture.

To give you a better idea, the whole province (state) of Québec consumes half the wine sold in all of Canada. Yet Québec is only about 20 percent of the country's total population. Although the rest of Canada's colonial roots are English, Protestant, and Anglo-Saxon, in Québec, the French arrived first, making its roots Catholic and Latin. So, life's bound to be a little different in many ways in this, still-predominantly-French-speaking corner of the world.

Yet make no mistake. Both cities have their feet firmly planted in North America. Distinct as they are, Montréal and Québec City feel familiar, too: The road system looks similar, telephones work the same way, and people here smile at strangers. You'll feel a *je ne sais quoi* about both cities, but people here won't seem as foreign as the people you meet when traveling to another part of the world.

About This Book

By no means is *Montréal & Québec City For Dummies,* 2nd Edition, an encyclopedia about the two cities. Although I've scoured both cities, this book highlights the *best* — not the *most* — of each. It's the insider information and street knowledge you need to know to make savvy decisions during your trip. I assume you have only so much time and need to cut to the chase. With that in mind, I've organized the chapters in this book to answer your questions roughly in the order they pop up — from figuring out whether you really want to visit these cities to knowing when to go, planning a budget, deciding where to stay and eat, and figuring out what to see and do.

Of course, you may not have the same questions in the same order, so feel free to jump ahead and read the chapters in any order you want. Who am I to judge? In these pages, you find a fair bit more information about Montréal than Québec City, but that's not because I'm choosing favorites. Montréal is a much bigger city, with much more to see and do (and many more places to eat!). To give you the best of Montréal, I have to give you more. However, if you decide to skip Montréal, don't worry, because I cover all the bases in Québec City, too.

Remember: Travel information is a dicey game — things change — particularly prices. So, take heed; be sure to call ahead for confirmation, especially of essential matters like your travel and lodging reservations. Once on-site, you have a little more leeway to improvise. Please keep in mind: the authors, editors, and publisher can't be held responsible for the experiences of readers while traveling. Your safety is important to us, however, so I encourage you to stay alert and be aware of your surroundings. Generally, keep a close eye on cameras, purses, and wallets — all favorite targets of thieves and pickpockets in cities worldwide.

Conventions Used in This Book

Montréal & Québec City For Dummies, 2nd Edition, uses a few conventions to help you find information quickly.

All prices in this book are shown first in Canadian dollars, then in U.S. dollars. The dollar signs are preceded by *C* or *US* so that you know which is which. (At the time of this writing, C$1 is worth US85¢, and all prices are converted at that rate. That may change by the time you read this and when you travel to these cities.)

In the hotel sections, the prices I give are the *rack rates* (the official rates the hotel publicizes) for one night for a double room, during the high season of tourism: May to October. The price you end up paying may be significantly lower if you travel off season or with a package deal.

In the restaurant sections, I give you the price range of a main course at each establishment. In most cases, these are the prices of dinner entrees, but if a restaurant doesn't serve dinner, I give you the price of a lunch entree.

I also use dollar-sign symbols ($) in both the hotel and restaurant sections. These signs give you the price range of a night's stay at a hotel (non-discounted, standard rates) or a restaurant meal (including drinks and tips). Check out the following table to decipher the dollar signs:

Cost	Hotels	Restaurants
$	Less than C$100 (US$85)	Less than C$20 (US$17)
$$	C$100–C$199 (US$85–US$169)	C$20–C$39 (US$17–US$33)

Cost	Hotels	Restaurants
$$$	C$200–C$299 (US$170–US$254)	C$40–C$59 (US$34–US$50)
$$$$	C$300 (US$255) or above	C$60 (US$51) or above

I also use abbreviations for credit cards, so that you can quickly see how you can pay for hotels and restaurants. They are as follows:

AE: American Express

DC: Diner's Club

DISC: Discover

MC: MasterCard

V: Visa

In addition, I keep the addresses of hotels, restaurants, and attractions in French, because that's what you'll see on street signs — I hope this simplifies finding your way around. Here's the rundown of French street terminology:

French Term	U.S. Equivalent
Rue	Street
Bd.	Boulevard
Av.	Avenue
Est	East
Ouest	West
Nord	North
Sud	South

You may sometimes see the odd street name starting with *place*. Some street names also start with *côte*, which means hill, so at least you know what to expect before you get there. (Don't worry, though, most hills are just gentle slopes.) Also, many streets are named for saints, whose given names are preceded by *Ste* (for female saints) or *St* (for male saints). *Vieux* means "old," as in *Vieux-Montréal* and *Vieux-Québec*, the older sections of the cities, which are loaded with history and character.

I also keep names of buildings and sites in French, except where they are very frequently referred to in English.

Otherwise, I translate French words and expressions into English as much as possible. However, some terms just don't translate very well, and when that happens, I leave the words in French and put them in italics. For a list of handy French expressions, see the Cheat Sheet at the front of this book.

For those hotels, restaurants, and attractions that are plotted on a map, a page reference is provided in the listing information. If a hotel, restaurant, or attraction is outside the city limits or in an out-of-the-way area, it may not be mapped.

Foolish Assumptions

I make a few assumptions about you, dear reader. You probably fall into one or more of these categories:

- ✔ **You're a first time visitor to Montréal or Québec City.** Or you stopped here briefly, say, on business, got a taste of it, and want to go back for more. I don't want to give you a comprehensive course on these cities. I simply show you how to enjoy them best with the least amount of planning and painstaking research possible.

- ✔ **You're busy.** Perhaps you're an experienced traveler, but you don't have a ton of time to spend planning a trip, or you don't have loads of time to spend in Montréal and Québec City after you get there. You want expert advice on how to maximize your time and enjoy a hassle-free trip.

- ✔ **You don't want to spend your whole trip reading a guidebook.** This book is a quick and easy read, focusing on the very best that Montréal and Québec City have to offer. It's also a reliable reference for a quick recommendation while on-the-fly, booting around town.

How This Book Is Organized

Montréal & Québec City For Dummies, 2nd Edition, is both a planning guide to help you prepare for your trip and a travel guide that gives you all the information you need to have an interesting and fun stay that doesn't break the bank. As such, this book is organized into five parts.

Part 1: Introducing Montréal and Québec City

Right out of the gate I introduce you to the very best of Montréal and Québec City. I describe the main attractions for each city, tell you what the weather is like, and give you ideas of what's going on throughout the year.

Part II: Planning Your Trip to Montréal and Québec City

I tell you how much everything costs, give you tips on how to plan a budget, and help you decide whether to use cash, credit, traveler's checks, or ATMs. From the advice in this chapter, you'll be able to decide on the best way to travel to Montréal and Québec City. Finally, I give specialized advice for gay and lesbian travelers, people traveling with kids, travelers with disabilities, and senior citizens.

Part III: Settling Into and Exploring Montréal

I start this part by explaining what to do when you arrive in Montréal and where to get the information you need to visit the city. Here is where you'll begin to familiarize yourself with the different Montréal neighborhoods. The chapters in this part also list the best hotels, restaurants, attractions, and shopping in the city. I then cover the best nightspots in Montréal and also describe the best daytrips, in case you want to get out of the city for an afternoon.

Part IV: Settling Into and Exploring Québec City

Here, I describe the Québec City neighborhoods you want to spend time exploring. I also give you a list of my top hotel picks, recommend what to see and do, and direct you to the best food in town — whether you want fine French cuisine or just pizza. Finally, I suggest some sample itineraries that let you explore different themes in the city.

Part V: The Part of Tens

One thing to never forget when you travel is your sense of humor. In this part, I tell you how to have fun in Montréal and Québec City. Some of my advice is practical. Some of it is whimsical — just an indirect way of poking fun at the cities and their inhabitants. You be the judge.

Icons Used in This Book

To help you find information as quickly and easily as possible, every *For Dummies* book includes a series of icons that serve as little road signs, alerting you to pleasures and dangers ahead — or just alerting you, period. In this book, I add an icon of my own to tell you what's really, truly, unique about this French-speaking corner of the continent.

 Traveling in Canada used to be a real steal for Americans, thanks to the weak Canadian dollar. Those days are over — at least in the short term — so you have work a little harder to cut corners off your travel budget. I use this icon to make that job easier for you.

Best of the Best highlights the best Montréal and Québec City have to offer in all categories — hotels, restaurants, attractions, activities, shopping, and nightlife.

Watch for the Heads Up icon to identify annoying or potentially dangerous situations such as tourist traps, unsafe neighborhoods, budgetary rip-offs, and other things to beware.

Think traveling with kids is hard work? Okay, you're right. Nevertheless, I try to make the process easier by using this icon when a hotel, restaurant, or attraction happens to be particularly well-suited for your pint-size companions.

Some of the sites, foods, and activities in Montréal and Québec City wrap up what's unique about Québec. I don't want you to miss out on these or accidentally overlook them, so I flag them with this icon. *Vive le Québec!*

This icon alerts you to special, insider advice on everything from dealing with Québec's extreme weather to exchanging money and finding the best rate on accommodations.

Where to Go from Here

Time to dig in and do some reading. You won't find any fixed rule about which chapters to read first. I've organized them in what I thought was a logical sequence, but you're free to wander in and out of them to your heart's content, in whatever order suits you. You may actually want to read about attractions and restaurants before you dig into the nitty-gritty about planning a trip and buying air tickets — just to see what fun stuff is in store for you.

Don't worry, though. Regardless of the order in which you plan this trip, you'll be amply rewarded when you arrive. So start reading!

Part I
Introducing Montréal and Québec City

The 5th Wave   By Rich Tennant

"Here's something. It's a language school that will teach you to speak French for $500, or for $200 they'll just give you an accent."

In this part . . .

This part will help you get a first taste of Montréal and Québec City. Dive right in and discover the best about each city, some background information on life in this French-speaking corner of North America, and what highlights you can expect over the course of a year. These are two wonderful destinations, which will leave you with two different impressions of New France. Don't feel that one is a replacement for the other. Ideally, you should try to experience both.

Chapter 1

Discovering the Best of Montréal and Québec City

In This Chapter

▶ Walking through the best neighborhoods

▶ Staying at the best hotels — or at least checking out their lobbies!

▶ Finding fantastic ways to spend your time in Québec

*M*ontréal is fun, sexy, and sophisticated. It's a city with charisma, a place with flair. Even the people who live here think so. Is it the mix of French and North American cultures that is so appealing? Is it Montréal's tumultuous past as a battleground between English and French? Or is it just the great food and pulsing night and the generally hedonistic ways of modern Montréalers? Actually, it's the combination of these and other qualities that give the city its unique beat.

Montréal has seen some dark days. A little over a decade ago, the economy was in a slump, political tensions were at their peak, and morale hit rock bottom. It wasn't pretty. But the city made an amazing about-face — which means now is a great time to visit Montréal. The economy has seen a remarkable upturn in the last five years, so the city boasts more great restaurants, clubs, and attractions than ever. The city's festivals are getting bigger and more glamorous every year, attracting an amazing array of talent. Tensions between English and French feel like ancient history now. And, best of all, this cultural and economic germination is really putting Montréalers in a good mood.

Québec City, with its quaint cobblestone streets, top-notch restaurants, beautiful vistas, and old-world charm, never goes out of style. In 2003, *Travel + Leisure* magazine ranked Québec City as one of the top five destinations in North America. In 2005, it took the seventh spot. And the city is in no danger of losing the title of North America's most romantic holiday destination. Just being in this fortified, cliff-top, port city is enough — although you can find plenty more to do than just soak up the view. For a small city, it offers an impressive roster of cultural events, exhibitions, performances, festivals, and more. The booming economy through Québec province hasn't done its capital city any harm, either.

In the following pages I introduce you to the choicest parts of both.

Montreal's Best Neighborhoods

Vieux-Montréal is a "must-see" for its yesteryear architecture and cobblestone streets. During the day, this bustling neighborhood is home to many businesses, boutiques, restaurants, and cafes. **Rue St-Paul** is the main shopping street. The establishments on **Place Jacques Cartier** have terraces that spill out onto the square where there's always a busker shilling for the large crowds. The **Old-Port,** a boardwalk and green space along the riverfront, has many attractions and hosts special events throughout the year. By dark, Vieux-Montréal empties out somewhat, which makes it *very* romantic for strolling couples, whose steps echo down the streets. Increasingly, though, bars and lounges are setting up there, and it is in the early stages of becoming an exciting nightlife destination.

The Plateau is Montréal's trendiest neighborhood and the epicenter of its pulse. Strut up **boulevard St-Laurent,** across **avenue Mont-Royal,** and down **avenue St-Denis** and you will have covered the Plateau's main commercial drags and seen some of what it's all about. You'll have difficulty passing yourself off as a local, at first, but you, too, will immediately wish you were a *Plateauzard,* the name for the indigenous hipsters from this 'hood.

Little Italy is northeast of downtown, just beyond the Plateau neighborhood. The main attraction here is **Marché Jean Talon.** It's worth getting up early to catch all the morning hubbub of merchants setting up their stalls and haggling with shoppers over fresh produce and other local ingredients. (*Note:* See Chapter 10 for a brief discussion on the importance of *terroir,* locally grown specialty ingredients, on Montréal's restaurant scene.) The **Marché Atwater** is at the opposite end of the city but is not as action-packed.

Québec City's Best Neighborhoods

Québec City is much smaller than Montréal. In fact, at first glance, the whole seems happily contained in the **Haute-Ville** and **Basse-Ville,** the upper and lower parts of the **Vieux-Québec.**

Step beyond the fortified walls to experience a more everyday version of Québec City, the province's capital. Exit the gate on **rue St-Jean.** Beyond, this street becomes a long commercial strip with many independent boutiques, cafes, and bars — fewer tourists and more locals going about their daily errands. Also outside the walls, **rue St-Louis** becomes **La Grande Allée,** which is Québec City's nightlife hub.

Several blocks farther in the same direction lies a cross-street, **avenue Cartier,** which is another charming district and somewhat hidden from the tourists buzzing between sights. In the Basse-Ville, if you go past Place Royale, you'll come to a narrow sliver of land between the cliff and the river, the 3 or 4 blocks in here are fun to troll. **Rue St-Paul** is Québec City's **"Antique Alley."** Hidden away in the up-and-coming district of **St. Roch,** don't miss the shopping on rue St-Joseph. Once an undesirable part of town, this strip is now lined with destination boutiques, bustling bistros, and happening pubs.

The Best Hotels

The most exciting development in Québec's hotel industry is the ever-multiplying number of boutique hotels. In Montréal, the **W Hotel** and the **Hôtel Godin** are the latest additions to an already crowded roster. Some of the first boutique hotels that started the trend here are **Hôtel Le Germain, Hôtel Nelligan, Hôtel Gault,** and **Hôtel St. Paul.** Many located in Vieux-Montréal took over 18th-century buildings that had fallen into disuse.

The **Dominion 1912** and the **Royal William** are the boutique hotels in Québec City. Even if you don't stay in one this time, it's definitely worth sticking your head in and taking a look around.

The Best Restaurants

Eating well will be a major theme for your trip to Québec. In the French tradition, food, drink, and merrymaking are major concerns of the people here.

Au Pied de Cochon, which opened in 2002, remains one of the most exciting destinations on Montréal's culinary landscape. **Toqué!, Beaver Club,** and **Moishe's** are top-dollar places serving the very best. However, Montréal's restaurant scene is so varied that there's plenty of feasting for any budget. Bistros **L'Express** and **Le Continental** are longtime favorites among foodies.

Montréal's restaurant scene reflects the many ethnic communities that make up its population. There are tons of restaurant specializing in different cuisines from around the globe. Some of the most popular are also great values, like **Taquéria Mexicaine, Rôtisserie Italienne,** and **Pushap Sweets** (Indian). **Schwartz's,** a Hebrew deli, is a must for the city's best "smoked meat" (Montréal's way better version of corned beef or pastrami).

Also, don't miss stopping in at **Cobalt, Le Cartet,** or **Le Reservoir** for snazzy brunches on weekends.

Québec city is heavy on French food with lots of small bistros doing escargot, steak frites, crème brûlée, and other brasserie-type staples. **Café du Monde** and **L'Ardoise** are two notables among them. Québec City's finest tables include **Le Paris-Brest, Le Saint-Amour,** and **Initiale.** A great spot for a casual meal is **Chez Victor,** which has the best burgers in town.

The Best Attractions

The **Musée d'Archeologie et d'Historie de Montréal** and the **Canadian Centre for Architecture** are two of the city's best museums. By regular museum standards, both are quite unusual and reveal lots about Montréal. Of course, the **Musée des Beaux-Arts de Montréal** is the spot for culture vultures to get their fine-arts fix. Many visitors can't resist the temptation of winning big money at the **Casino de Montréal,** so they go there instead. Winter or summer, **Parc Mont-Royal** attracts the fitness- or leisure-conscious. Visitors to Montréal should hike up to the lookout atop the "Mountain," just because it's there. It's not that high or that steep. The penguins at the **Biodome** are always a favorite with the kids.

In Québec City, locals call the **Château Frontenac,** atop the cliff overlooking the St. Lawrence River, **"Québec's Eiffel Tower,"** and indeed, it is — everyone goes to see it. Behind this famous hotel is **La Citadel,** a fortress that defended this hotly contested port city over the course of its history. Weather permitting, you can witness the **Changing of the Guard,** a procession of expressionless redcoat soldiers in tall fur hats — oddly enough, just like the ones in England. Behind it lie the **Parc des Champs-de-Bataille** and the **Plains of Abraham** where the decisive battle between the French and English took place. In the Basse-Ville at the bottom of the cliff is the **Musée de la Civilisation,** featuring engaging exhibits on the first settlers and the Native American people who were already here. Beyond the Plains of Abraham is the **Musée du Québec,** which, along with its permanent collection, hosts temporary exhibits of a surprisingly high caliber.

The Best Nightlife

Montréal's just hitting its stride when the sun goes down. Kick off your evening at a brewpub like **Le Reservoir** or a martini lounge, like **Jello Bar,** for after-work drinks — called the *cinq a sept* in local lingo. Step it up another notch or two after dinner by hitting places like **Mile End** or **Newtown.** After midnight, if you're looking to dance, **Club 1234** qualifies as Montréal's most crowded dance floor of the moment. The **Society of Art and Technology** and **Casa del Popolo** provide other good options for a more alternative crowd.

Nights in Québec City aren't necessarily more sedate, just smaller in scale. Pubs and other intimate settings with lots of live music are what dominate the scene. The two exceptions are the mega-clubs on the Grand Allée, **Chez Dagobert** and **Chez Maurice.** Many spend their night hopping between the two. **Les Salons Edgar, Bistro Scanner Multimedia,** and **Bal du Lezard** are three good alternatives in the St. Roch neighborhood just beyond the Basse-Ville.

Chapter 2

Digging Deeper into Montréal and Québec City

In This Chapter

▶ Uncovering the distinct European flair of French North America

▶ Diving into Montréal's and Québec City's cultural and linguistic experiences

▶ Experiencing dining, nightlife, and festivals in both cities — winter or summer

▶ Reading up on novels by homegrown writers and viewing films by local directors

*I*n this chapter, I provide some background information. The aim of these easily digestible bites is to steady your footing, open your eyes, and prime your senses to discover the different possibilities that Montréal and Québec City offer.

History 101: The Main Events

The cities of Montréal and Québec City boast fascinating histories. The following are some highlights from the annals of two of the oldest cities in North America.

The French discovered Québec . . .

Looking for a quick passage to Asia, French explorer Jacques Cartier landed at the future site of Québec City in 1535. For some reason, he thought the ground was rich with diamonds. It wasn't, so he went back to France.

In 1608, another French explorer, Samuel de Champlain, founded a fur trading post in Québec, which attracted French settlers. The British captured the colony from France in 1759 and began to settle it with Irish, Scottish, and English immigrants and American Loyalists.

In the 19th century, when railroads began cutting into Québec's port business and economic prospects looked grim, the English-speaking population moved to Montréal, leaving Québec City almost entirely to French speakers.

. . . and then Montréal

Jacques Cartier also discovered Montréal in 1535, but again, he left without making much of an impression. In 1641, the French explorer Paul de Chomedey Maisonneuve founded a mission on the site and set out to convert natives to Christianity. Then, of course, the French ceded Montréal to the English in 1760.

By the early 1800s, Montréal was the cultural and commercial capital of Canada, with a booming port business and a wealthy English population running the show, while the Catholic French-speaking majority did the grunt work for them.

. . . and then Québeckers took over

In the 1960s, Québec's French-speaking majority decided to become their own bosses and shake off the influence of the Catholic Church in one shot. The period is known as the *Quiet Revolution*. Practically overnight, French-speaking Québeckers went from being mostly farmers and working poor dominated by the Catholic Church to being a modern, secular society.

Parlez-Vous?

The question on most people's minds when they visit either city is: "Can I get by without French?" To be honest, you can have more fun if you master a few words of French, but you can get by just fine without it. Although once upon a time, the English and the French were throwing rocks at each other in the streets of both cities, today, young Montréalers are often as comfortable speaking English as they are French — or Spanish or Italian, for that matter. In Québec City, the booming tourism industry has done its work in making English widely used and understood. You can always expect warmth and cordiality from Québeckers, but especially if you make an effort to speak their native tongue.

Savoring the language

Before taking your trip, why not take some time to brush up on your French? Québec City is almost entirely French-speaking, and in Montréal, some of the most interesting parts of the city are predominantly French. Although you don't need to speak French to get around either city, knowing when to drop the occasional civility, such as *bonjour* and *au revoir,* or *s'il vous plait* and *merçi,* endears you to the locals. They may answer you in English anyway, but they'll be flattered by your effort. (The words and expressions I provide on the Cheat Sheet at the front of this book can definitely get you out of any tight spot.)

Soaking Up That European Flavor

That Québec and Montréal have so much European flair isn't surprising. These are two of the oldest cities in North America — and definitely among the best preserved. In both, you can stroll cobblestone streets and gaze at stone buildings and churches that date back to the 1700s. The relaxed pace, late hours, and abundance of cafes only add to the illusion that you're somewhere in Europe. For maximum old-world impact, visit the port areas of both cities. In Vieux-Québec, don't miss **Le Petit Champlain.** In Montréal, la **rue Notre-Dame** or la **rue St-Paul** transport you back in time.

Following Your Stomach

Thanks to the ongoing French influence on local cuisine, Montréal and Québec City are both renowned for excellent restaurants and a refined approach to dining. And trust me, it's getting better every day. That said, Québeckers also eat their share of fast food, so you want to be selective about where you eat. Chapters 10 and 18 give you the lowdown on the best food for every budget in both cities.

 Excellent eateries can be found everywhere, but in some neighborhoods, you just can't get a bad meal. Québec's Old City houses many fine choices, such as the **Café du Monde.** Montréal's Old Port area is actually not the best place to eat, but **rue St-Denis** and **boulevard St-Laurent** offer impressive dining choices.

Experiencing the Festival Frenzy

Other cities may have summer festivals, but Montréal is famous for its festivals. Unlike elsewhere, this city shuts down large portions of downtown for a string of festivals lasting practically all summer long. An intoxicating mix of English and French permeates these widely attended events. The fact that party-hearty Montréalers attend the festivals in droves, not to mention various states of intoxication, certainly doesn't hurt. There's definitely a *je ne sais quoi* about the dozens of summer events here, whether it's the **Montréal International Jazz Festival,** the **Just for Laughs Comedy Festival,** the **International Film Festival,** the **Nuits d'Afrique** African-music festival, or the **FrancoFolies** (the largest French-language music festival in the world).

 See Chapter 3 for a calendar of the major festivals in Montréal and Québec City.

Living It Up After Hours

Back in the 1920s, when the rest of North America was in the grips of Prohibition, Montréal was known as the "City of Sin" for its freewheeling, immoral ways. Among modern-day Canadians, the city is still revered for late bar closings (last call is at 3 a.m.), public affection (couples get very cozy on benches in public parks), and general lack of political correctness — all of which can create a carnival-like atmosphere after dark. If you want to let your hair down or stay out all night, Montréal offers endless opportunities for entertainment. You can roam the hopping club scenes, which are concentrated along **boulevard St-Laurent, rue Crescent,** and **rue St-Denis.**

Checking Out the Many Faces of Montréal

France isn't the only culture you taste in Montréal — and I mean that literally. Dozens of other nationalities have marked out distinct corners of the city and filled them with great restaurants. In sheer numbers of immigrants, Montréal doesn't compare to multicultural havens like Toronto and Vancouver, but Montréal's long-established ethnic neighborhoods have left a lasting mark, and they continue to play a vital role on the urban landscape.

Have a cappuccino at **Café Italia** in Little Italy, pick up some bagels on **rue St-Viateur** in the heart of Montréal's Orthodox Jewish neighborhood, or grab a souvlaki along **avenue du Parc,** with its concentration of Greek restaurants, and you'll see what I mean.

Many of these areas boast interesting architecture as well, such as the famous winding staircases of the Plateau and Little Italy; winding cobblestone streets and graceful, stone buildings of Vieux-Montréal; and the beautiful churches, basilicas, and cathedrals throughout the city.

Walking (and Skiing and Eating) in a Winter Wonderland

There's no denying winter in Montréal and Québec City, where temperatures can regularly dip to −5°F (−20°C) or lower for weeks on end. However, while many North Americans live in denial of their semi-Nordic surroundings, Québeckers embrace winter. By April, locals have had enough of snow, slush, and those speeding sidewalk plows that terrorize pedestrians. But from November to March, locals whisk away the winter blues by dressing properly — and plenty stylishly — and then skiing, snowboarding, skating, snowshoeing, and, let's be honest, eating and drinking to their heart's content.

Join the fun and dive right into the season by taking your trip during Québec City's **Winter Carnival** or Montréal's **Fête des Neiges** (Snow Festival), both in February. In either city, you're less than an hour from great skiing and snowboarding destinations, such as **Mont Tremblant** or **Mont Ste-Anne.** If you really can't take the cold, you can always retreat to Montréal's **underground city,** where you never have to leave the safety of central heating to visit a number of museums, shopping centers, skyscraper lobbies, and major hotels.

Eyeing Recommended Books and Movies

Complement your hard-nosed research about the nuts-and-bolts of your trip to Montréal and Québec City with some lighter fare. From the following novels and films you'll gain a better picture of life in Québec. I've limited most of my recommendations to English movies and books; however, it's a minority perspective. *Remember:* Most media in Québec is in French, so, if you took French immersion or if you like foreign films with subtitles, there's a whole other vast world of titles to explore.

Turning the pages

Montréalers Leonard Cohen and the late Mordecai Richler were both English-speaking Québec's literary lions of the 20th century. Cohen's *The Favourite Game* and *Beautiful Losers* are set in Montréal and emblematic of life in the 1960s and '70s. Richler's *The Apprenticeship of Duddy Kravitz* and *Barney's Version* reveal much about the different facets of Montréal that may not be apparent to the naked eye of a first-time visitor. *Barney's Version* won the Giller Prize in 1997, one of Canada's most prestigious book awards.

Though not a Montréal native, Hugh MacLennan wrote a novel, *Two Solitudes,* that won the 1945 Governor General's Award for Literature and coined a term that's still used to describe the collectively imagined abyss between the lives of English- and French-speaking co-inhabitants of Montréal and the province at large.

Though Québec's independence may seem like a distant issue today, during the most recent bout of separatist unrest in the early 1990s, which prompted a referendum in 1995, Richler penned a satirical essay entitled *Oh Canada! Oh Québec!* — his commentary on the mounting political tension of the time. William Weintraub's novel *The Underdogs* speculates about life in Québec after separation.

The Anglo Guide to Survival in Québec by Josh Freed and Jon Kalina has become a cult classic among expats of all stripes wanting the lowdown on the hidden codes of *la belle province* — rife with humor, some of what it reveals would possibly take years to learn otherwise.

In 1983, reviewers heralded Ken Dryden's *The Game* as the best book on hockey and, perhaps, the greatest sports book ever. It can also be enjoyed by someone who has never seen the game. This memoir tells of day-to-day life on the Montréal Canadiens, Stanley Cup dynasty team of the '70s — at a time when hockey and *les glorieux* were everything in Québec. They won six league championships during Dryden's eight years playing. It reveals what the whole era was like, beyond hockey, including his experiences as an Anglophone in French-speaking Québec.

Screening films

Like Toronto and Vancouver, Montréal is a popular destination for Hollywood movie productions — which seems to ensure the presence of at least one A-list celebrity in town at any time. Montréal's varied architecture offers many different looks, making it a great place to shoot "on location." By and large, the scenes shot in Montréal are for movies set elsewhere. Montréal rarely gets to play itself. This is particularly true of Vieux Montréal, which regularly stands in for European cities: Today it's Paris, tomorrow Prague.

Nonetheless, there are several movies actually set in Montréal. A young Richard Dreyfuss plays the lead in *The Apprenticeship of Duddy Kravitz* (1974), a coming-of-age story adapted from Mordecai Richler's novel. In 1989, Québécois director Denys Arcand received an Oscar nomination for *Jesus of Montréal,* which follows a troupe of actors through the consequences arising from their avant-garde update of a "passion play" for a local parish. Another homegrown movie is *Eldorado* (1995), where streetscapes from Montréal's Plateau neighborhood are the backdrop for several days in the lives of an odd cast of characters during a summer heat wave. In *Afterglow* (1997), Nick Nolte and Julie Christie star in this drama about two Montréal couples cheating on each other.

The Score (2001), with Robert De Niro and Edward Norton, is a heist flick, with a brief cameo by Marlon Brando. Almost the entire movie takes place in Vieux Montréal, along rue St-Paul, Est, in front of the Marché Bonsecours and near the Canada Customs House, on the western edge of this historic district. (They're trying to break in.)

Mambo Italiano (2003) is a comedy arising from the fuss caused by Angelo and Nino, two first-generation Italian-Canadians, who are a gay couple and must come out to their somewhat more traditional families. Denys Arcand's *The Barbarian Invasions* (2003) won an Oscar for Best Foreign-language Film. It's the sequel to Arcand's *Decline of the American Empire* (1986), which also received an Oscar nomination, but, alas, didn't win.

C.R.A.Z.Y. (2005) is the latest film out of Québec to make a stir. It won the audience award at the festival in Venice and Best Canadian Feature Film at the Toronto International Film Festival in the fall of 2005. It's Canada's Foreign-Language hopeful for the 2006 Academy Awards.

Chapter 3

Deciding When to Go

In This Chapter

▶ Choosing a steamy urban jungle or winter wonderland
▶ Examining the four seasons of each city
▶ Scanning Montréal and Québec City's cultural calendars
▶ Timing your trip with your favorite event

*M*ontréal is always hopping — no matter when you decide to visit — but the weather is always an issue. During the year, Montréal's climate swerves between scorching summer heat waves and icy winter cold snaps. Between these extremes, spring and fall are as unpredictable as they are short.

Québec City is 250km (155 miles) down the St. Lawrence River from Montréal, and 1 degree of latitude to the north, so the winters tend to be a couple of degrees Fahrenheit colder. Snowfalls are heavier and more consistent than in Montréal. In fact, by the end of the winter, the accumulated snow in the streets can reach as high as the rooftops. Summers are a little cooler than those in Montréal, but they can still be surprisingly hot and humid. During summer evenings, a wind off the river can make you feel a bit chilly.

Be aware when making travel plans that weather extremes and unpredictability are the general rules. The heat — or cold — can hit when you least expect it. Bring a sweater, even in July.

Revealing the Two Faces of Montréal and Québec City

Freezing temperatures, snowy conditions, and icy roads may intimidate some travelers, but for residents of Montréal and Québec City, winter's harsh conditions are merely facts of life. We simply don more layers, tread carefully over icy patches, and spend more time indoors. As soon as we have enough snow and the temperatures are low enough, we swing into hardy outdoor pursuits, such as ice hockey, cross-country skiing, skating, snowboarding, snowshoeing, snowmobiling — and even ice fishing, which is incredibly popular in Québec.

Fortunately, all these activities can be done within an hour's drive of either Montréal or Québec City. If you're tempted by the idea of trekking into the wilderness in winter, just remember that daylight hours are extremely short from November until March.

Quiet, midnight snowfalls and pristine snowbanks never seem to lose their magic. Fresh snow turns Québec City, with its fortifications, cannons, French colonial architecture, and cliff-top setting next to the river, into a winter wonderland. For the first two weeks in February, the provincial capital celebrates its Nordic spirit with the **Québec City Winter Carnival,** the world's largest outdoor winter festival. In 2003, this *Carnaval de Québec* celebrated its 50th anniversary.

Come March, however, all that snow turns into salty, gray-brown slush that coats both cities and drives everyone nuts. Navigating through slush ponds is an arduous, nerve-jangling task, whether you're driving or walking, and the salt that city officials dump on the roads to thaw the ice stains pant legs and ruins shoes.

When spring comes, it's short; this is partly because Montréalers interpret any warm weather as proof that summer has begun. At the first sign of a parasol on a terrace, locals hit the streets and start tearing off their clothing. Really.

From the grease, glitz, and green light of the **Formula One Canadian Grand Prix** in early June to the last curtain of the **Montréal World Film Festival** in September, outdoor events and festivals jam this city's summer schedule. By the end of June, Montréal is a steamy urban jungle, where throngs of locals and visitors flock the streets for free outdoor concerts, stand-up comedy shows, open-air film screenings, and more. Summer in Montréal is one long party.

Experiencing the Secret of the Seasons

Your tolerance for cold — or heat — is probably the first aspect to consider when planning your trip to Montréal and Québec City. In the following sections, I tell you what to expect from the seasons. Table 3-1 provides the average temperatures and precipitations for Montréal, and Table 3-2 provides the information for Québec City.

Table 3-1   Montréal's Average Temperatures and Precipitation

	Jan	Feb	Mar	Apr	May	June	July	Aug	Sep	Oct	Nov	Dec
High (°F/°C)	22/ −5.8	24/ −4.3	36/ 2.1	51/ 10.7	66/ 18.9	74/ 23.3	79/ 26.3	76/ 24.7	67/ 19.5	55/ 12.5	42/ 5.3	28/ −2.4
Low (°F/°C)	5/ −14.9	8/ −13.4	20/ −6.9	33/ 0.7	46/ 7.6	52/ 12.4	60/ 15.5	58/ 14.2	49/ 9.2	38/ 3.1	28/ −2.2	13/ −10.8
Rainfall (in./cm.)	2.77/ 7.04	2.35/ 5.97	2.84/ 7.22	3/ 7.61	2.97/ 7.55	3.32/ 8.44	3.54/ 9.01	3.7/ 9.42	3.6/ 9.13	3.05/ 7.76	3.66/ 9.3	3.24/ 8.23

Table 3-2   Québec City's Average Temperatures and Precipitation

	Jan	Feb	Mar	Apr	May	June	July	Aug	Sep	Oct	Nov	Dec
High (°F/°C)	18/ −7.9	21/ −6.1	32/ 0.1	46/ 7.8	63/ 17.1	72/ 22.2	77/ 25	74/ 23.4	64/ 17.7	51/ 10.7	37/ 2.9	23/ −4.8
Low (°F/°C)	0/ −17.6	3/ −16	15/ −9.4	29.66/ −1.3	42/ 5.3	51/ 10.6	56/ 13.4	54/ 12.4	45/ 7.2	35/ 1.7	24/ −4.3	8/ −13.4
Rainfall (in./cm.)	3.54/ 8.98	2.77/ 7.06	3.55/ 9.03	3.19/ 8.12	4.17/ 10.61	4.49/ 11.42	5.03/ 12.78	4.59/ 11.67	4/ 10.17	4.94/ 12.55	4.01/ 10.2	4.11/ 10.44

Spring

With the annual great thaw, excitement in both cities builds as snow and ice melt away:

- ✔ Days are longer, particularly during daylight saving time.
- ✔ You encounter less snow, sleet, and cold.
- ✔ After a barren winter, life returns to the streets.

The dicey weather of the short transition between winter and summer, however, comes with its drawbacks:

- ✔ You usually can't put away your coat, hat, and gloves until the middle or end of April.
- ✔ As temperatures warm and the snow melts, expect a bit of everything, weather-wise. Definitely be prepared for some rain.

✔ Enormous slush ponds form at every street corner. Be prepared by wearing waterproof footwear or risk spending some of your stay with cold, wet feet.

Summer

After the heat of a summer day, when the sun goes down, the city's nightlife comes alive:

✔ Expect festivals galore. Both in Montréal and Québec City, the summer season brings many special events.

✔ People in the streets bask in the glorious weather.

✔ Eating and drinking moves outdoors. People dine on their balconies. Restaurants open their patios, and the parks are filled with picnicking families (a popular option for travelers, too, because drinking wine and beer in parks is perfectly legal, as long as you accompany your drink with a meal).

On the downside, the heat and the crowds can get unbearable, so you may want to seek refuge in your air-conditioned hotel room — if you can find one, that is. Here are some other drawbacks:

✔ The crowds of tourists and festival-goers, although loads of fun, can be enough to give you a mild fit of agoraphobia.

✔ The heat can be brutal — and it's not just the temperature. Montréal and Québec City can be unbearably humid in the summer.

✔ Booking a room, particularly during the major festivals, can be difficult.

✔ Rates at hotels and attractions are high.

✔ During the Construction Holidays, in the last two weeks of July, many Québeckers take their summer vacations. It's a major holiday; so, many out-of-town accommodations can be booked solid at this time. Québec City also gets a major influx of visitors from around the province during these two weeks.

Fall

Brisk fall days are glorious, with the brilliantly colored leaves, harvest bounty at the markets, and temperatures that are typically ideal:

✔ The leaves change color.

✔ Temperatures are cooler and usually remain pleasantly warm until the end of September.

✔ You have an easier time finding accommodations.

✔ Restaurants keep their terraces open practically until the first frost, when people eventually make their way inside.

✔ The cultural calendar kicks up again with the start of the seasons at the theater, opera, ballet, symphony, and arts in general.

However, as winter begins, autumn can start to turn nasty:

✔ Cold, unpredictable weather can set in as early as October. First you see frost, then the ground freezes, and then you get snow.

✔ Most of the outdoor festivals are over, and the winter activities haven't begun yet, so on overcast days the cities can feel a tad drab.

Winter

Instead of seeing the snow and ice as impediments, your best bet is to regard them as opportunities for seasonal recreation and leisure. By braving the extreme conditions in the name of fun, or, *le fun* as locals are likely to say, you're taking part in Québec's Nordic spirit:

✔ It's sunny almost all the time, and the days can be really exhilarating, even if your hands and feet are numb, your glasses are fogged, and you have hat-head all the time.

✔ By the end of December, both cities usually offer enough snow and ice for all winter sports. Skaters at the artificially frozen rink in the **Bonsecours Basin** (Montréal's Old Port) are usually the first to hit the ice outdoors.

✔ Good food, not to mention drink, goes down that much better when you've worked up an appetite by braving the elements all day.

Lots of layers and defensive driving are the winter's watchwords:

✔ You need a hat, mittens, and a scarf — and not just as fashion accessories.

✔ Driving can be difficult. When it snows, roads become slippery or icy and visibility is poor.

Viewing Montréal's Calendar of Events

Montréal is definitely a four-season town — although one of its seasons can be brutally cold — so you get plenty of reasons to celebrate all year 'round.

January/February

In January, bundled-up kids celebrate the annual *Fête des Neiges* (literally, Snow Party). The festival takes place on Île Ste-Hélène and features ice skating, ice sculptures, tube slides, dogsleds, mitten-making workshops, and more. Most activities are free of charge. For more information, visit www.fetedesneiges.com. Three weekends in late January and early February.

The **Montréal High Lights Festival** (www.montrealhighlights.com) is an adult version of the snow party, combining multimedia light shows, a performing arts program, and guest appearances by world-renowned chefs at the trendier downtown eateries. Eleven days in mid- to late February.

March

The **International Festival of Films on Art** (www.artfifa.com) is the only festival of its kind in the Americas. The screenings happen at different venues around town; the programming also includes conferences and seminars on the topic. Ten days in mid-March.

When the sap in Québec's maple trees starts to drip, it's **Sugaring-Off** time; groups of friends and families flock to the countryside to visit sugar shacks where maple farmers boil the sap and make syrup. The main event on these excursions is a traditional meal in a mess hall where fresh maple syrup is used as a topping for everything — gulp, even fried pork fat. Back in town, outdoor stands at markets and on sidewalks sell *tire* (pronounced *teer*), which is maple taffy that's made by ladling thick, hot, unrefined syrup from a steaming caldron onto a bed of snow. When the syrup cools, you wrap the gooey stuff on a Popsicle stick and watch salivating kids devour it. The fun starts in early March and lasts until mid-April.

Everyone in Montréal is Irish on St. Patrick's Day, despite historic tensions between the English and the French. Beginning at noon, thousands of onlookers line rue Ste-Catherine for Montréal's **St. Patrick's Day Parade,** a procession of floats, marching bands, and folk dancing. After the parade, the crowds get a little rowdy and roam the streets in search of green beer. The parade is the oldest and longest-running one of its kind in North America. For more info, not beer, visit Tourisme Montréal on the Web (www.tourisme-montreal.org). March 17.

April

In 2005, UNESCO proclaimed Montréal as the World Book Capital. During that time, the city was responsible for leading the world in promoting books and reading. Alas, the honor lasts but a year. However, for five days early in the month on an annual basis, **Blue Metropolis** (www.blue-met-bleu.com) is Montréal's international literary festival. From its quiet beginnings in 1999, it has since grown into a significant event on the cultural calendar. Early April.

At the end of the month, the *Festival de théâtre des amériques* (www.fta.qc.ca) begins. This critically acclaimed biennial offers two weeks of French-language theater productions from the Americas and Europe in odd-numbered years. Plays tend toward the edgy, and many make their North American debuts here. The programming lasts for a week into May.

May

Bikes are popular here. **Féria du vélo de Montréal** (www.velo.qc.ca), or **Bike Fest,** is a weeklong event near the end of the month celebrating this two-wheeled, environmentally sound, and health-inducing form of transportation. In fact, this is a unique event in North America. One of the high points is the **Tour de l'Ile,** which draws over 30,000 participants. The course, which changes annually, winds through a number of Montréal neighborhoods, making for a fun group or family outing.

If you're in Montréal this time of year, take advantage of **Museum Day,** when entry to select museums is free, as is a shuttle service running among them. For more, check out www.museesmontreal.org. Last Sunday in May.

June

Start the month off at the **Mondial de la bière** (www.festivalmondial biere.qc.ca), or **World Beer Festival,** where visitors sample 250 liquid products, including beer, scotch, cider, and port, from around the world. It's one of the largest festivals of its kind on the continent.

Though there are several electronic music events over the course of a year, **MUTEK** (www.mutek.ca) is Montréal's premier happening. It takes place early in June and draws acts from all over the world: new music producers brandishing their high-tech gear — and making suitably far-out sounds. Some of the performances are simultaneously broadcast via the Web site.

Les FrancoFolies de Montréal (www.francofolies.com) is a festival that features a bevy of French-language musicians from across the planet. It takes place on the city's main festival site which closes to car traffic and opens to hordes of music lovers and people watchers throughout the summer. Les FrancoFolies kicks off the action for ten days in mid-June.

The **Montréal Fringe Festival** (www.montrealfringe.ca) offers off-off-Broadway-type drama on boulevard St-Laurent. Ten days in mid-June.

Late in the month, the **Formula One Grand Prix** (www.grandprix.ca) makes its only Canadian stop at *Circuit Gilles Villeneuve* on Île Notre-Dame, where, at press time, homegrown F-1 hero Jacques Villeneuve has not finished a race on the track named after his father since his second place debut in 1996. In the weeklong festivities leading up to Sunday's race, fumes of motor oil and champagne mix freely on the main drags downtown.

The **Montréal International Jazz Festival** (www.montrealjazzfest. com) is the summer's main event. For two weeks, a boatload of international acts plays free outdoor shows and world-class headliners top the bills at ticketed venues. Each year, well over 1.5 million people swarm the downtown site of the festival, which takes place on the streets and in parks surrounding Place des Arts, Montréal's main performing arts center. Like clockwork, every year, you can count on the bands to strike up in the last week of June and carry on for a week into July.

At this time of year, after dark, it's always tough to choose between an evening at the Jazz Fest or catching the **Montréal International Fireworks Competition** (www.lemondialsaq.com). The riverfront in Vieux-Montréal is an ideal place to watch the pyrotechnics, which go off at 10 p.m. Every Saturday, mid-June to late July.

July

For just a month, a local theater troupe gives free outdoor presentations of the Bard's original plays during the annual **Shakespeare-in-the-Park** (www.shakespeareinthepark.ca) tour. Visit its Web site for the schedule. Mid-June to mid-August.

Right after the Jazz Fest, the *Festival International Nuits d'Afrique* (www.festivalnuitsdafrique.com), or **Nights of Africa Festival,** showcases African and Caribbean musicians at paid venues downtown. *Nuits d'Afrique* is nearly two decades old, and by now, many of the greatest names in world music have participated. Ten days in early July.

Gory B-movies and improbable sci-fi action are the hallmarks of the **Fantasia Film Festival** (www.fantasiafest.com), held in a state-of-the-art theater at Concordia University's downtown campus. The screenings start in mid-July, and for about three weeks, these are some of the hottest tickets in town.

Beach volleyball in Montréal? Yes! As strange as it may sound, mid-month, the women of the **International Volleyball Federation World Cup** (www.fivb.org) make a stop here for a five-day beach-volleyball tournament. The action is riveting. It's mid-season and between two Grand Slam events, so the competitors are in top form. The action goes down at the Uniprix Stadium in the northern reaches of the city.

The **Just For Laughs Comedy Festival** (www.hahaha.com) is another roaring success with locals and visitors alike. This outdoor festival has launched the likes of Jim Carrey, Ray Romano, and Tim Allen. It takes place on rue St-Denis south of rue Sherbrooke, where the scene turns into a veritable freak show, with clowns, street acts, and circus-school students all vying for the attention of passersby. Do your best not to end up as the victim of a gag on the festival's spin-off, candid-camera TV show. By all accounts, it's a hysterical two weeks in mid-July.

August

The **Divers/Cité Festival** (www.diverscite.org) starts off the month with a weeklong celebration thrown by Montréal's gay community. It's capped off by the lesbian, gay, bisexual, and transgendered **Pride**

Parade on a Sunday. It's an absolutely fab party, which has attracted 800,000 people in past years.

Join the caber-toss at the **Montréal Highland Games** (www.montreal highlandgames.qc.ca), a sporting event that could best be described as the pole vault's distant, cross-dressing cousin. Men in kilts should not be vaulting over anything. Thankfully, here, it's the caber that goes over the bar atop the uprights. Also: bag pipes, drumming, and highland dancers over the course of a fun-filled Sunday, Celtic style; early in the month.

Tennis, anyone? Mid-month, Montréal hosts one-half of the **Tennis Masters Canada** (www.masters-series.com), sharing it with Toronto. Each year, the women's and men's tournaments alternate between the cities. The eight-day tournament is a warm-up for the U.S. Open; so, many top-ranked players make a show here.

Park Maisonneuve, next to the Olympic Stadium, hosts *La Fête des enfants de Montréal* — a weekend festival for Montréal's kids. Mid-August.

Then, near the end of the month, the **Montréal Indy** (www.molsonindy. com) brings another class of screaming race cars back to the Gilles Villeneuve track (also discussed in the "June" section).

And, if that's not fast-track enough, movie stars and paparazzi descend on the city for the **World Film Festival** (www.ffm-montreal.org). Screenings, premieres, and parties abound. "What, I'm not on the list? Do you *know* who I am?" Late August through second week in September.

September/October
Warmly anticipated by Montréalers, cooler weather brings the **Magic of Lanterns** (www.ville.montreal.qc.ca/jardin) to the Botanical Gardens, a dazzling annual display of over 700 handcrafted lanterns of silk and bamboo from Shanghai. The show's theme changes annually and it lasts from the beginning of September until the end of October.

Every second year, it's *Mois de la photo* (www.moisdelaphoto.com), or **Image and Imagination,** and for a month, the city stands still just long enough to play host to a variety of exhibits and events related to photography, including several outdoor galleries along major streets. Early September to early October.

At the beginning of October, over the course of a weekend, Québec's arts community holds an open house of sorts, called *Les journées de la culture* (www.journeesdelaculture.qc.ca). Across the province, artists from every métier open the doors to their workshops, studios, cooperatives, and other creative spaces to the general public. The three days offer a variety of demonstrations, guided tours, and discussion forums. From architecture, to circus arts, to electronic art, to pluridisciplinary art — it's all encompassing. The 2006 edition marks the event's tenth anniversary. Three days in early October.

Slated at the beginning of October, **Pop Montréal** (www.popmontreal. com) is a relative newcomer to the city's festival circuit. It's a weeklong bender staging a variety of alt-rock shows, reflective of the local live-music scene and focusing on innovative and independent artists both homegrown and from abroad. It's a thriving event and Montréal seems to have become a hotbed for producing this kind of breakout talent as of late, so there's lots of buzz. (Think: Rufus Wainwright, The Sam Roberts Band, Arcade Fire, The Dears, and Wolf Parade — just to name a few.)

Also, early in October, over 12,000 people of all persuasions attend the **Black and Blue Festival's Main Event** (www.bbcm.org), an extravagant, mega-dance party with DJs and choreographed live performances, making it one of the largest AIDS benefit events in the world. Everyone's there to dance into the wee hours of the morning for a good cause.

The **Montréal International Festival of New Cinema and New Media** (www.nouveaucinema.ca) pushes the frontiers of high-tech art a little more each year, with its eclectic mix of provocative film and other digital arts. Mid-October.

The Botanical Gardens' **Great Pumpkin Ball** is as close as Montréal gets to the Peanuts gang's *It's the Great Pumpkin, Charlie Brown.* Literally hundreds of decorated pumpkins are on display in the main greenhouse during most of October. It's actually a contest. There's a resident witch, who hosts the proceedings. Throughout October.

The ***Grand Masquerade*** (www.grandemascarade.com) is a Halloween-themed celebration that takes place on Place Jaques Cartier and at the Marché Bonsecours in Vieux-Montréal. The historic part of the city is an ideal location for scaring up ghosts of yore with a costumed ball. You don't have to be in costume to join the fun, but dressing up is encouraged. Several evenings leading up to Halloween.

November

During the **Santa Claus Parade,** Montréalers bid *adieu* to the big guy just before he leaves for work in the North Pole. Yes, Santa spends his off season in Montréal. Kids line up to watch the procession down rue Ste-Catherine, shivering with excitement until the very last float. For information, call ☎ 514-937-7754. Mid-November.

Montréal's documentary film festival, ***Rencontres internationales du documentaire de Montréal*** (www.ridm.qc.ca), features the work of local, Canadian, and international documentary filmmakers. Ten days in mid-November.

Checking Out Québec City's Calendar of Events

The fun doesn't end just because the temperatures are frigid. Some of the city's best events take place in the beginning of the year. But great events occur in the other seasons, too.

January/February

A red-sashed snowman known as the *Bonhomme du Carnaval* leads the festivities at the **Carnaval de Québec** (☎ 418-626-3716; www. carnaval.qc.ca). More than a million people brave the cold to join parades, concerts, and nightly winter balls in an ice palace. Many fortify themselves against the cold with *caribou,* a Québec specialty consisting of red wine and pure alcohol, which in colonial times contained actual caribou blood. Two weeks in late January and early February.

March/April

Slurp up as much maple syrup as you can at the **cabanes à sucre (sugar shacks)** surrounding the city, from the beginning of March to mid-April.

Festival de la Gastronomie de Québec/Coupe des nations (www. festivalgastronomiequebec.com) is a food-and-drink extravaganza and competition that showcases Québec's regional specialties. Three days in late April.

Over the course of five days at the end of March and at the beginning of April, the **Festival de cinéma des 3 Amériques** (www.fc3a.com), a pan-American film festival, screens over 100 short and feature-length films in Saint-Roch, a neighborhood just outside the Old City.

May

The *Manifestation international d'art de Québec* (www.manifdart. org), a biennial exhibition taking place in the odd years (the next one is in 2007), showcases the newest and the best contemporary and multi-disciplinary artists in Québec City. First two weeks of May.

During the last half of May, the **Carrefour international de theatre** (www.carrefourtheatre.qc.ca) is a festival that stages nearly 100 contemporary theater performances from the world-over.

June

St-Jean-Baptiste Day (☎ 418-640-0799; www.snqc.qc.ca), Québec's so-called national holiday, was named in honor of the province's patron saint, this holiday is taken very seriously in Québec City, which many Québeckers consider their "national" capital. June 24.

Daredevils ride iron horses at Mt. Ste. Anne, Eastern Canada's highest peak, during **Velirium** (www.velirium.com), a mountain biking festival and competition. Three weekends during the middle of the month.

July

The *Festival d'été de Québec* (www.infofestival.com) is one of the world's largest French-speaking cultural events, featuring more than 600 performers from 22 countries. First two weeks of July.

Les grands feux (www.lesgrandsfeux.com), a fireworks display choreographed to music, starts at the end of the month. Wednesday and Saturday nights for three weeks from mid-July to early August.

August

At the beginning of the month, the **New France Festival** (www.nouvelle france.qc.ca) reproduces colonial life of Québec City, as it was in the 17th and 18th centuries.

The biennial *Festival des Troubadours et Saltimbanques* (www. lefestival.info) is early in the month over a weekend. This medieval festival is a tip of the hat to the popular origins of street performance and public spectacle.

For five days in the middle of August, it's the **Québec City International Festival of Military Bands** (www.fimmq.com). This annual *tattoo* (military exhibition), gives marching bands a chance to perform somewhere other than parades and college football-game half times.

September/October

Envol et Macadam (www.envoletmacadam.com) is a weekend at the beginning of September jam packed with alt-rock, punk, techno, and hip-hop acts, including international headliners. In 2005, the event celebrated its tenth year of hell raising.

When Québec's colorful autumn leaves start to fall, visitors lift their spirits with inspirational music at the **Québec Festival of Devotional Music** (www.festivalmusiquesacree.ca), ten days at the end of October, which features internationally known gospel singers, Gregorian chanters, and a cappella groups.

Part II

Planning Your Trip to Montréal and Québec City

In this part . . .

Planning your trip in advance will help you hit the ground running, and save you from learning while on vacation when your time's most precious. While in either Montréal or Québec City, you want to be out and about on the town experiencing the street life, yakking with locals, shopping for gear, tasting different foods from around the world, and drinking it all in. It's a balancing act — of course, you'll have to refer to this book and your other material throughout, but the more you know beforehand the better equipped you'll be to enjoy these cities to their fullest. This part focuses on the essential steps of setting a budget for your trip, figuring out how to get to Québec, and other important matters to consider before you take off.

Chapter 4

Managing Your Money

● ●

In This Chapter

▶ Gauging how you'll spend your money

▶ Avoiding hidden expenses and finding ways to cut costs

▶ Understanding the Canadian dollar, or "Loonie"

▶ Considering different ways to carry cash and pay

▶ Dealing with a lost or stolen wallet

● ●

*O*n the whole, the living is easy in Montréal and Québec City. Like the French, Québeckers tend to consider eating at restaurants and going out more like a basic human right than a luxury. That attitude somehow keeps prices affordable. Plus, you can find plenty to do for free — strolling quaint streets, gazing at stunning architecture, gawking at beautiful people. Factor in the still-favorable exchange rate for the U.S. dollar, and you have yourself a pretty amazing vacation for the money.

Planning a Budget

Planning a budget is a little bit like performing a juggling act. You have six vacation pins: lodging, transportation, dining, attractions, shopping, and nightlife. You can't really afford to drop any of them (that is, unless you want to be truly spartan), but you may want to throw some pins higher than others. First, decide ahead of time what's most important to you: Staying in a fine hotel? Eating gourmet meals? Hitting the chicest shops? After you set your priorities, look for ways to cut costs in other areas. To get you started, the following sections show you what to expect — and expect to pay — from each category of basic travel expenses.

Lodging

Whether you like it or not, accommodations are your biggest expense. Before leaving on your trip, do your homework to find bargains and reserve rooms. Plan ahead, and you may save enough to stay another night! (See Chapter 9 for details on getting the best hotel deals.)

The minimum you want to spend on accommodations per night is around C$100 (US$85). Sure you can get better deals, but your comfort may be compromised.

Transportation

Here's an area where you can save. You don't need a car unless you want to take day trips around Montréal and Québec City. Driving in either city can be a nightmare, and you don't need to put yourself through it. Québec's Old City is so small and compact you can walk everywhere. Montréal has a great **public-transportation system,** with a subway that serves all major attractions, even the ones outside the city. A booklet of six tickets (valid for both buses and the subway) costs C$11.25 (US$9.60) — less than the price of a single taxi ride across downtown.

If you're bent on **renting a car,** check Chapter 7 for details on getting a good rental deal. When you're doing your calculations, remember that gas is expensive in Canada. At press time, the price of gas was hovering around the C$1 mark (per liter), or the equivalent of US$3.21/gallon. Nothing on the nightly news suggests prices will be dropping any time this century.

 Montréal and Québec City (outside of the old cities) have an abundance of **taxis** that are easy to flag in case you're too tired to walk back to your hotel. Just find a busy street and raise your arm.

See Chapter 5 for ways to save on your trip to and from Montréal or Québec City. Booking your travel arrangements well in advance is one sure way to save money. Researching and comparing the prices of lots of different fare options, like discount airlines, seat-sales, courier fares, or flying standby, is another. Usually both of these factor into what you end up paying.

Dining

Dining is probably not the place to trim the fat in your budget. Look at it this way: Eating out in Montréal and Québec City is an entertaining, potentially evening-long activity. Splurge at the dinner table, and you won't need to spend money on entertainment for the rest of the night. With a little planning, you won't need to bust the bank to satisfy your palate, either. I suggest eating a big breakfast, and then cutting back on lunch, either by grabbing a sandwich at a cafe or picnicking in a park.

 You can get inexpensive lunches at many ethnic eateries for, usually, C$10 (US$8.50) per person. Prices at fast food restaurants are comparable to U.S. prices, so just factor in the exchange rate. See Chapters 10 and 18 for recommendations. In the evening, most fine restaurants offer a *table d'hôte* (also called a *menu*) that's usually a good deal with prices ranging from C$20 to C$65 (US$17–US$55.25) for a meal, not including drinks. For the higher-end places, expect to spend from C$30 to C$100 (US$25.50–US$85) per person for a complete dinner, including drinks.

Attractions

The adult admission price for most museums and attractions is between C$10 and C$12 (US$8.50–US$10.25). Pricier attractions, such as La Ronde, set you back about C$28 (US$24) for adults and C$17 (US$14.50) for kids under 12. Kids under 6 get into most attractions for free. See Chapters 11 and 19 for exact prices in each city.

Shopping

Shopping in Montréal and Québec City can be hazardous to your budget. With so much great stuff to buy — from clothes to art to home decorations — the abundance of merchandise may make you lose your perspective, not to mention your senses. I recommend that you give yourself a shopping allowance before you leave home, either a daily one, a weekly one, or one that's for the whole trip (if you're disciplined and do your accounting regularly). If shopping isn't your thing, you can save big bucks in this department.

Nightlife

Nightlife is another area where money can disappear before you know it. But you can indulge inexpensively. The cheapest time to visit a bar is during happy hour, or *cinq à sept*, as it's called in Québec. (The expression "five to seven" refers to the early evening hours, not the number of drinks you get for one price!) Drinks usually range between C$5 and C$8 (US$4.25–US$6.75).

Tickets for shows seem to start around C$10 (US$8.50) and go up to C$100 (US$85), or more, for prime seats. The cabaret show (without dinner) at the Montréal casino starts at C$43 (US$36.50). Movie prices range from C$9 to C$13 (US$7.75–US$11). For details on the prices of outings, see Chapters 15 and 21.

Watching Out for Hidden Expenses

Planning a travel budget is like renovating a house. It always ends up costing more than you think. Both endeavors are laden with temptations. Trust me, if you're setting out to be a spartan traveler, Montréal and Québec City will test your willpower. To help you stick to your budget, keep in mind the tips in the following sections.

Taking taxes into account

There's a price to easy living throughout Québec: **steep taxes on sales and services.** Whenever you see a price, except on alcoholic beverages, add 15 percent.

You can still live it up here with limited damage to your pocketbook. The secret? Make a travel budget and stick to it.

Non-Canadians can get a refund on the federal Goods and Services Tax, GST, or *Tax Produits et Services* (TPS) in French, if it adds up to more than C$14 (US$12) in tax or C$200 (US$170) in hotel bills. However, unless you're an amateur accountant, the paperwork may prove to be more of a hassle than it's worth. Just make sure you keep original receipts. If you want to go after the refund, pick up a copy of the booklet "Tax Refund for Visitors to Canada" at duty-free shops, hotels, and tourist offices. Complete and submit the forms with your original receipts within a year of the purchases. Note that you have to attach your original boarding pass or travel ticket to the application. Complete instructions are available on the Canada Customs Web site (www. ccra-adrc.gc.ca/tax/nonresidents/visitors).

Tipping

To tip or not to tip, and how much? These are the eternal questions when you find yourself in a strange land. In Québec, tipping waiters 15 percent is the norm. You can go higher or lower if you'd like to make a statement about the quality of the service. Taxi drivers usually expect 10 percent. For bellhops, C$1 or C$2 (US85¢–US$1.75) per bag does the trick. For hotel housekeeping, count C$1 (US85¢) per person per day. For valet parking, plan on C$1 or C$2 (US85¢–US$1.75).

In restaurants, remember that you're tipping on the total price *before* taxes, not the total on the bottom of the bill. There's an easy trick to calculate a 15 percent tip. Just add up the two taxes, federal and provincial, that appear above the total on the bill — they equal 15 percent of the bill's subtotal, which is how much you should tip.

Cutting Costs — But Not the Fun

A little foresight and planning are all you need to cut down on your basic travel expenses. Follow these tips so that you can free up some extra funds for a shopping spree or a wild night on the town.

- ✔ **Go in the off season.** You get better deals when you travel at non-peak times between November and April. For winter trips, avoid the Christmas season, New Year's Eve, and the school March break.

- ✔ **Travel midweek.** Flights are cheaper on Tuesdays, Wednesdays, and Thursdays. When you book your flight, ask which days have the best rates.

- ✔ **Check out package tours.** You may get airfare, hotel, and even ground transportation and attractions for less if you buy them all at once, through a packager. See Chapter 5 for details on finding package deals.

✔ **Reserve a room with a kitchen.** Doing a bit of cooking is an easy way to save on your food budget. Grab some basic food items, cereal, coffee, bread, and milk at a *dépanneur* (corner store) near your hotel. Make some sandwiches before you leave in the morning so that you can afford to splurge on some serious gastronomy in the evening.

✔ **Ask for discounts.** You may be eligible for deals and not know it. Membership in AAA, frequent-flier plans, trade unions, AARP, or other groups may qualify you for savings on hotels, airfare, car rentals, and meals. It never hurts to ask.

✔ **Bunk with your kids.** A room with two double beds usually doesn't cost more than one with a queen-size bed. Many hotels won't charge you extra if you put your little angels (usually under age 12) in the extra bed. If they do charge a surplus, it's still cheaper than renting another room. Fees for rollaway beds are usually C$10 to C$15 (US$8.50–US$12.75) per day.

✔ **Try expensive restaurants at lunch rather than dinner.** Lunch tabs usually are a fraction of what dinner costs at top restaurants, and the menu often boasts many of the same specialties. Chapters 10 and 18 suggest a number of cheap eats — some of the best meals are at inexpensive ethnic joints.

✔ **Walk.** A good pair of walking shoes can save you plenty of money getting around. Montréal and Québec City were meant for walking — particularly the historic districts. Both are old cities, so car culture isn't as entrenched. Walking — combined with the Métro (subway), city buses, and the occasional taxi ride — is an unbeatable way to see either place.

Handling Money

Should you spend cash? Credit? Traveler's checks? This section explains the pros and con of the various options.

You're the best judge of how much cash you feel comfortable carrying or what alternative form of currency is your favorite. That's not going to change much on your vacation. True, you'll probably be moving around more and incurring more expenses than you generally do (unless you happen to eat out every meal when you're at home). But, that aside, the only type of payment that won't be quite as available to you away from home is your personal checkbook.

Understanding the Loonie

The tail-side of the Canadian-dollar coin has an image of a loon, a bird common to the Canadian north — therefore, it's called a "Loonie." It seems natural that the two-dollar coin would be called a "Twonie" — and it is. In Canada, coins come in denominations of $1 (Loonie), $2 (Twonie), and 1¢, 5¢, 10¢, and 25¢.

Canadian bills are all sorts of different colors, prompting many Americans to joke about them looking like Monopoly money — and until recently, there was a lot of truth to that. They come in $5 (blue), $10 (purple), $20 (green), $50 (red), and $100 (brown) denominations.

Converting your greenbacks

As a currency, the Canadian dollar has always lagged behind the U.S. dollar in terms of its value on the world market. However, as of late, the Canadian currency has gained on the American; in fact, the Loonie is at an all-time high against the greenback. This means that Canada is still a deal — but less so than before.

The Bank of Canada, the country's central bank, has a currency-converter feature on their Web site (www.bankofcanada.ca). But Table 4-1 provides a rough estimate for you.

Table 4-1	Simple Currency Conversions		
Canadian $	*U.S. $*	*British £*	*Euro €*
1	0.85	0.5	0.7
2	1.7	1	1.4
3	2.55	1.5	2.1
4	3.4	2	2.8
5	4.25	2.5	3.5
6	5.1	3	4.2
7	5.95	3.5	4.9
8	6.8	4	5.6
9	7.65	4.5	6.3
10	8.5	5	7
15	12.75	7.5	10.5
20	17	10	14
25	21.25	12.5	17.5
50	42.5	25	35

Canadian $	U.S. $	British £	Euro €
75	63.75	37.5	52.5
100	85	50	70
125	106.25	62.5	87.5
150	127.5	75	105
175	148.75	87.5	122.5
200	170	100	140
225	191.25	112.5	157.5
250	212.5	125	175
275	233.75	137.5	192.5
300	255	150	210
350	297.5	175	245
400	340	200	280
500	425	250	350
1,000	850	500	700

The figures in Table 4-1 were accurate at the time of writing this guide, they may no longer be valid by the time of your departure. Check with your local bank, if you have any doubts. Don't fret if you can't score any Canadian dollars before you leave — there's an ATM at the airport that will dispense them at your request.

Using ATMs and carrying cash

The easiest and best way to get cash when you're away from home is from an ATM. The Cirrus (☎ 800-424-7787; www.mastercard.com) and PLUS (☎ 800-843-7587; www.visa.com) networks span the globe; look at the back of your bank card to see which network you're on, and then call or check online for ATM locations at your destination.

The major Canadian banks in Montréal and Québec City and the bankcard system they honor are as follows:

- **Bank of Montréal:** Cirrus
- **Banque Nationale du Canada:** Cirrus
- **Caisse populaire Desjardins:** PLUS

✓ **CIBC:** PLUS

✓ **Royal Bank of Canada:** Cirrus and PLUS

✓ **Scotia Bank:** Cirrus

Be sure you know your personal identification number (PIN) and your daily withdrawal limit before you leave home. You'll also want to keep in mind that many banks impose a fee every time your card is used at a different bank's ATM, and that fee can be higher for international transactions (up to $5 or more) than for domestic ones (where they're rarely more than $3). On top of these fees, the bank from which you withdraw cash may charge its own fee. With your bank, check the fees for withdrawals from foreign ATMs before you leave.

Is there a place on Earth that doesn't accept or exchange U.S. dollars? If there is, I've never seen it. But use them only if you're in a pinch. You get less bang for your buck when doing a cash exchange in a retail shop, because on most cash transactions, the exchange rate can be up to 10 percent higher.

Charging ahead with credit cards

Credit cards are a safe way to carry money. They also provide a convenient record of all your expenses and generally offer relatively good exchange rates. You can also withdraw cash advances from your credit cards at banks or ATMs, provided you know your PIN. If you've forgotten yours, or didn't know you had one, call the number on the back of your credit card and ask the bank to send it to you. It usually takes five to seven business days, though some banks will provide you the number over the phone if you tell them your mother's maiden name or some other personal information. If you do opt for a cash advance, remember that you're charged interest from the moment of the transaction, rather than only after your account's billing date.

Keep in mind that when you use your credit card abroad, most banks assess a 2 percent fee above the 1 percent fee charged by Visa, MasterCard, or American Express for currency conversion on credit-card charges. But credit cards still may be the smart way to go when you factor in things like exorbitant ATM fees and higher traveler's check exchange rates and service fees.

Some credit-card companies recommend that you notify them of any impending trip abroad so they don't become suspicious when the card is used numerous times in a foreign location and end up blocking your card. Even if you don't call you credit-card company in advance, you can always call the card's toll-free emergency number if a charge is refused. But perhaps the most important tip is to carry more than one card with you on your trip. For any number of reasons, a card may not work, so having a backup is the smart way to go.

Toting traveler's checks

These days, traveler's checks are less necessary because most cities have 24-hour ATMs that enable you to withdraw small amounts of cash as needed. However, keep in mind that you probably will be charged an ATM withdrawal fee if the bank is not your own. So if you're withdrawing money every day, you may be better off with traveler's checks — provided that you don't mind showing the required identification every time you want to cash one.

You can get traveler's checks at almost any bank. **American Express** offers denominations of $20, $50, $100, $500, and (for cardholders only) $1,000. You pay a service charge ranging from 1 to 4 percent. You can also get American Express traveler's checks over the phone by calling ☎ **800-221-7282;** Amex gold and platinum cardholders who use this number are exempt from the 1 percent fee.

Visa offers traveler's checks at Citibank locations nationwide, as well as several other banks. The service charge ranges between 1.5 and 2 percent; checks come in denominations of $20, $50, $100, $500, and $1,000. Call ☎ **800-732-1322** for more information. AAA members can obtain Visa checks without a fee at most AAA offices or by calling ☎ **866-339-3378.** MasterCard also offers traveler's checks. Call ☎ **800-223-9920** for a location near you.

 If you choose to carry traveler's checks, be sure to keep a record of their serial numbers separate from your checks in the event they are stolen or lost. You'll get a refund faster if you know the numbers.

Dealing with a Lost or Stolen Wallet

Be sure to contact your credit-card companies the minute you discover your wallet has been lost or stolen and file a report at the nearest police precinct. Your credit-card company or insurer may require a police-report number or record of the loss. Most credit-card companies have an emergency toll-free number to call if your card is lost or stolen; they may be able to wire you cash immediately or deliver an emergency credit card within a day or two.

See the appendix for the major credit-card companies' Canadian toll-free numbers.

 If you need emergency cash over the weekend when all banks and American Express offices are closed, you can have money wired to you via Western Union (☎ **800-325-6000;** www.westernunion.com).

Identity theft or fraud is a potential complication of losing your wallet, especially if you've lost your driver's license along with your cash and credit cards. Notify the major credit-reporting bureaus immediately; placing a fraud alert on your records may protect you against liability for criminal activity. The three major U.S. credit-reporting agencies are Equifax (☎ 800-766-0008; www.equifax.com), Experian (☎ 888-397-3742; www.experian.com), and TransUnion (☎ 800-680-7289; www.transunion.com). Finally, if you've lost all forms of photo ID, call your airline and explain the situation; they might allow you to board the plane if you can produce a copy of your passport or birth certificate and a copy of the police report you filed. (Make copies of all such documentation and give them to someone you trust before you leave.)

Chapter 5

Getting to Montréal and Québec City

In This Chapter
▶ Making your travel arrangements
▶ Getting the best airfare
▶ Traveling to Montréal and Québec City
▶ Choosing the best package deal

So you're ready to chill in Montréal and Québec City. Even if you've been to another part of Canada before, you're in for a big surprise, because, it's a whole different kind of place. Brush up on your French pronunciation and get ready to plunge into a distinctive culture. But, first, you'll have to decide how to get to either of these great cities. Are you coming by land, sea, or air?

Flying to Montréal or Québec City

If you're traveling to Montréal, you'll arrive at Montréal's **Pierre Elliott Trudeau International Airport** (☎ 800-465-1213 or 514-394-7377; www. admtl.com), YUL in airline-speak, in the suburb of Dorval, a 20-minute drive from downtown.

A number of major airlines serve Québec City's **Jean-Lesage International Airport** (☎ 418-640-2700), or YQB, but most of the traffic passes through Montréal first.

Finding out which airlines fly there

In Montréal, passenger airline flights land at **Pierre Elliot Trudeau International Airport.** For Québec City, airplanes touch-down at **Jean Lesage Airport.** Here's a brief description of each. For the contact information of specific airlines mentioned, see the Quick Concierge at the back of the book. For how to make your way to downtown Montréal and Québec City from each airport, see Chapters 8 and 16, respectively.

✔ Montréal's **Trudeau** airport is 20.4km (12¾ miles) from downtown. Getting from the airport to downtown takes about 30 minutes from door to door — if there's no traffic. Many North American airline carriers fly there nonstop from the United States: **Air Canada** (from Boston, Chicago, Fort Lauderdale, Fort Myers, Las Vegas, Los Angeles, Miami, New York, Philadelphia, and Washington), **American Airlines** (from Chicago, Dallas, Miami, and New York), **Atlantic Southeast** (from Atlanta), **Continental** (from Cleveland and New York), **Delta** (from Atlanta), **Northwest** (from Detroit), **United** (from Chicago, Minneapolis, and Washington), and **US Airways** (from Philadelphia). Some international airlines also fly to Montreal nonstop, including **Air Canada** (from Frankfurt, London, and Paris), **British Airways** (from London), **Czech Airlines** (from Prague), **KLM** (from Amsterdam), **Olympic Airlines** (from Athens), and **Royal Maroc Airlines** (from Casablanca).

✔ Québec City's **Jean Lesage Airport** is somewhat smaller. It's served nonstop by: **Air Canada** (from Montréal, Ottawa, and Toronto), **Northwest** (from Detroit), and **Continental** (from New York). Throughout the year, charter companies like **Air Transat** offer nonstop transatlantic flights from London and Paris.

Getting the best deal on your airfare

Competition among the major U.S. airlines is unlike that of any other industry. Every airline offers virtually the same product (basically, a coach seat is a coach seat is a coach seat), yet prices can vary by hundreds of dollars.

Business travelers who need the flexibility to buy their tickets at the last minute and change their itineraries at a moment's notice — and want to get home before the weekend — pay (or at least their companies pay) the premium rate, known as the *full fare.* But if you can book your ticket far in advance, stay over Saturday night, and are willing to travel midweek (Tues, Wed, or Thurs), you can qualify for the least expensive price — usually a fraction of the full fare. On most flights, even the shortest hops within the United States, the full fare is close to $1,000 or more, but a 7- or 14-day advance-purchase ticket might cost less than half of that amount. Obviously, planning ahead pays.

The airlines also periodically hold sales, in which they lower the prices on their most popular routes. These fares have advance-purchase requirements and date-of-travel restrictions, but you can't beat the prices. As you plan your vacation, keep your eyes open for sales, usually in seasons of low travel volume. You almost never see a sale around the peak summer vacation months of July and August, or around Thanksgiving or Christmas.

Consolidators, also known as bucket shops, are great sources for international tickets, although they usually can't beat the Internet on fares within North America. Start by looking in weekend newspaper travel sections; U.S. travelers should focus on the *New York Times, Los Angeles Times,* and *Miami Herald.*

 Bucket-shop tickets are usually nonrefundable or rigged with stiff cancellation penalties, often as high as 50 to 75 percent of the ticket price, and some put you on charter airlines with questionable safety records.

Several reliable consolidators are worldwide and available on the Web. STA Travel (☎ 800-781-4040; www.statravel.com), the world's leader in student travel, offers good fares for travelers of all ages. ELTExpress (☎ 800-TRAV-800; www.flights.com) started in Europe and has excellent fares worldwide but particularly to that continent. Flights.com also has "local" Web sites in 12 countries. FlyCheap (☎ 800-FLY-CHEAP; www.1800flycheap.com) is owned by package-holiday megalith MyTravel and has especially good access to fares for sunny destinations. Air Tickets Direct (☎ 800-778-3447; www.airticketsdirect.com) is based in Montréal and leverages the currently weak Canadian dollar for low fares; it'll also book trips to places that U.S. travel agents won't touch, such as Cuba.

Booking your flight online

The "big three" online travel agencies, **Expedia** (www.expedia.com), **Travelocity** (www.travelocity.com), and **Orbitz** (www.orbitz.com) sell most of the air tickets bought on the Internet. (Canadian travelers should try www.expedia.ca and www.travelocity.ca; U.K. residents can go for www.expedia.co.uk and opodo.co.uk.) Each has different business deals with the airlines and may offer different fares on the same flights, so shopping around is wise. Expedia and Travelocity will also send you a notification when a cheap fare becomes available to your favorite destination. Of the smaller travel agency Web sites, **SideStep** (www.sidestep.com) receives good reviews from users. It's a browser add-on that purports to "search 140 sites at once" but, in reality, only beats competitors' fares as often as other sites do.

Great last-minute deals are available through free weekly services provided directly by the airlines. Most of the deals are announced Tuesday or Wednesday and must be purchased online. Most are only valid for travel that weekend, but some can be booked weeks or months in advance. Sign up for weekly alerts at airline Web sites or check megasites that compile comprehensive lists of last-minute specials, such as **Smarter Living** (www.smarterliving.com). For last-minute trips, www.site59.com in the United States and www.lastminute.com in Europe often have better deals than the major-label sites.

If you're willing to give up some control over your flight details, use an *opaque fare service,* like **Priceline** (www.priceline.com) or **Hotwire** (www.hotwire.com). Both offer rock-bottom prices in exchange for travel on a "mystery airline" at a mysterious time of day, often with a mysterious change of planes en route. The mystery airlines are all major, well-known carriers — and the possibility of being sent from Montréal to

Québec City via Ottawa is remote. But your chances of getting a 6 a.m. or 11 p.m. flight are pretty high. Hotwire tells you flight prices before you buy; Priceline usually has better deals than Hotwire, but you have to play their "name your price" game. See **Bidding for Travel** (www.biddingfortravel.com) for tips on playing the opaque-fare game. *Note:* In 2004, Priceline added non-opaque service to its roster. You now have the option to pick exact flights, times, and airlines from a list of offers — or opt to bid on opaque fares as before.

Great last-minute deals are also available directly from the airlines through a free E-mail service called E-Savers. Each week, the airline sends you a list of discounted flights, usually leaving the upcoming Friday or Saturday and returning the following Monday or Tuesday. You can sign up for all the major airlines at one time by logging onto **Smarter Living** (www.smarterliving.com), or you can go to each individual airline's Web site. Airline sites also offer schedules, flight booking, and information on late-breaking bargains.

One more Web site: I'm a bit biased, but I think **Frommer's** (www.frommers.com) is an excellent and comprehensive travel-planning resource, with daily travel tips and bargains, reviews, monthly vacation giveaways, and a popular message-board section where readers post queries and share advice.

Driving to Montréal or Québec City

From the south, you'll either approach Montréal on Highway 10 or 15; at the border, these highways are 87 from New York and 89 from Vermont. When you hit the city limits, follow signs for downtown, or "Centre-ville." From both the east and west, you drive into Montréal on Highways 20 or 40. You're also looking for "Centre-ville."

Unless you're crossing the border in Maine, where you'd eventually hit Highway 73 to Québec City, cars from the United States should drive to Montréal first, and then follow either highway 20 or 40 east to Québec City.

Arriving by Other Means

If flying isn't an option, or if you're in the mood to see some countryside panoramas, you can always take the train. It's slower, but it's more romantic than air travel and not terribly stressful. Take a book along (we recommend the one you're reading now), spend hours talking to perfect strangers, or stare out the window like a 6-year-old on a car trip with his parents. Montréal's **Central Station** is located at 895 rue de la Gauchetière Ouest (☎ 514-989-2626). Québec's **Gare du Palais** is located at 450 rue de la Gare-du-Palais (☎ 418-692-3940).

VIA Rail (☎ 888-842-7245; www.viarail.ca), Canada's national passenger rail network, offers significant discounts if you book at least five days ahead of time. Since there are a limited number of discounted seats per train, they can sell out before advance offers expire. If you know that you're taking the train, try to book early.

Amtrak (☎ 800-872-7245; www.amtrak.com) offers daily departures to Montréal from New York City, departing in the morning and arriving in the early evening.

Another option is traveling by bus. **Greyhound Lines, Inc.** (☎ 800-661-8747; www.greyhound.com), travels to Montréal from the United States and Ottawa. Another bus line operates the route from Toronto. Yet another company takes care of busing people to and from Québec City. Regardless, in Montréal, all buses arrive at the **Station Centrale,** 505 bd. de Maisonneuve (☎ 888-999-3977 or 514-842-2281), in the Quartier Latin neighborhood. In Québec City, the bus station, the **Terminus Gare du Palais,** is located at 320 rue Abraham-Martin (☎ 418-525-3000).

Both Montréal and Québec City are increasingly popular ports for eastern seaboard boat cruises. The two cities are usually on St. Lawrence River and Great Lakes itineraries. Conveniently, the historic districts of both, Vieux Montréal and Vieux Québec, both "must-sees" of any stopover, are on the water, adjacent to the ports.

In Montréal, cruise ships dock in the commercial port. Travelers disembark at the **Iberville Passenger Terminal.** It's a short cab ride into town. Check out the **Port of Montréal's** Web site (www.port-montreal.com) for more info, including a schedule of cruise vessels. Or, call ☎ 514-283-7011.

Cruise-ship visitors stopping in Québec City arrive at the **Port de Québec's** new terminal (☎ 418-648-3640; www.portquebec.ca). It's located beside the Basse-Ville, but I suggest taking a taxi uphill to the front of the Chateau Frontenac to start your visit. You can walk down on your way back.

Joining an Escorted Tour

You may be one of the many people who love escorted tours. The tour company takes care of all the details and tells you what to expect at each leg of your journey. You know your costs up front, and, in the case of the tamer tours, you don't get many surprises. Escorted tours can take you to the maximum number of sights in the minimum amount of time with the least amount of hassle. Many escorted tours to Montréal and Québec City also include other Canadian cities, such as Toronto and Ottawa, or other regions, such as Eastern Canada.

If you decide to go with an escorted tour, I strongly recommend purchasing travel insurance, especially if the tour operator asks you to pay up front. But don't buy insurance from the tour operator! If the tour operator doesn't fulfill its obligation to provide you with the vacation you paid for, you have no reason to believe that the operator will fulfill its insurance obligations, either. Get travel insurance through an independent agency. (I tell you more about the ins and outs of travel insurance in Chapter 7.)

When choosing an escorted tour, along with finding out whether you have to put down a deposit and when final payment is due, ask a few simple questions before you buy:

- ✔ **What is the cancellation policy?** Can the tour company cancel the trip if it doesn't get enough people? How late can you cancel if you're unable to go? Do you get a refund if you cancel? What if the tour group cancels?

- ✔ **How jam-packed is the schedule?** Does the tour schedule try to fit 25 hours into a 24-hour day, or does it give you ample time to relax by the pool or shop? If getting up at 7 a.m. every day and not returning to your hotel until 6 or 7 at night sounds like a grind, certain escorted tours may not be for you.

- ✔ **How large is the group?** The smaller the group, the less time you spend waiting for people to get on and off the bus. Tour operators may be evasive about this, because they may not know the exact size of the group until everybody has made reservations, but they should be able to give you a rough estimate.

- ✔ **Is there a minimum group size?** Some tours have a minimum group size and may cancel the tour if it doesn't book enough people. If a quota exists, find out what it is and how close the tour company is to reaching it. Again, tour operators may be evasive in their answers, but the information may help you select a tour that's sure to happen.

- ✔ **What exactly is included?** Don't assume anything. You may have to pay to get yourself to and from the airport. A box lunch may be included in an excursion, but drinks may be extra. Beer may be included but not wine. How much flexibility do you have? Can you opt out of certain activities, or does the bus leave once a day, with no exceptions? Are all your meals planned in advance? Can you choose your entree at dinner, or does everybody get the same chicken cutlet?

Choosing a Package Tour

Package tours are not the same thing as escorted tours. *Package tours* are simply a way to buy airfare, accommodations, and other elements of your vacation (such as car rentals and airport transfers). Some companies bundle every aspect of your trip, including tours to various sights.

But most deal only with selected aspects, which allows you to get good deals by putting together an airfare and hotel arrangement, say, or an airfare and greens fee (golf) package. Packages tend to leave you a lot of leeway, while saving you a lot of money.

 Follow these tips for doing your due diligence and weeding out the packagers that are duds:

- **Do your homework.** Read through this guide and decide what attractions you want to visit and what type of accommodations you think you'll like. Compare the rack rates that I list in Chapters 9 and 17 against the discounted rates being offered by the packagers to see whether you're actually being given a substantial savings.

- **Read the fine print.** Make sure you know exactly what's included in the price you're being quoted and what's not. Some packagers include airfare plus lots of extra discounts on restaurants and activities, but others don't even include airfare in the price.

- **Know what you're getting yourself into — and if you can get yourself out.** Before you commit to a package, make sure that you know how much flexibility you have. Some packagers require non-refundable binding commitments, whereas others charge minimal fees for changes or cancellations. Ask about the packager's restrictions and cancellations policies up front.

- **Ask questions.** If you're unsure about the pedigree of a smaller packager, check with the Better Business Bureau in the city where the company is based, or go online to www.bbb.org. If a packager won't tell you where it's based, don't fly with it.

Finding escorted and package tours

How do you find these deals? Well, every city is different; the tour operators I mention may not offer deals convenient from your city. If that's the case, check with local travel agents: They generally know the most options close to home and know how best to put together escorted tours and airline packages.

The travel section of your local Sunday paper lists many of the deals available. Check ads in national travel magazines like *Travel + Leisure, National Geographic Traveler,* and *Condé Nast Traveler.* Then call a few escorted- or package-tour companies and ask them to send you their brochures.

Big hotel chains and airlines also offer packages. If you already know where you'd like to stay, call the hotel and ask if it offers land/air packages. Or contact the airlines themselves — most major airlines offer air/land packages.

The online travel sites (Expedia, Travelocity, Orbitz, and so on) also do brisk business in package travel.

Package deals to Montréal and Québec City

Some of the following companies offer both package and escorted tours. Normally, a travel agent books these packages, but you can call or visit the company Web sites on your own, too. Remember that some agencies have better reputations than others; your travel agent, if you have one, can guide you. Transportation to and from airports is often included but is sometimes optional.

- ✔ **Air Canada Vacations** (☎ 800-254-1000; www.aircanada vacations.com) is the largest carrier flying into Montréal. It offers lots of options for visiting both cities, separately or together, including escorted tours, independent packages, fly/drive tours, ski holidays, and more. This is a great place to start.

- ✔ **Collette Tours** (☎ 800-340-5158; www.collettetours.com) offers three-, four-, and five-day getaways to Québec City, Montréal, or both cities, including accommodations, dinner at local restaurants, and city tours. Longer city tours of Eastern Canada also offer stops in Montréal and Québec City.

- ✔ **Continental Airlines Vacations** (☎ 800-301-3800; www.covacations.com) offers separate packages to Montréal and Québec City, with hotel and airfare included and car rental optional. This is a good option if you like fancy hotels, because its packages include accommodations in upscale hotels.

- ✔ **Gogo Worldwide Vacations** (☎ 800-299-2999 or 702-457-1615; www.gogowwv.com) offers two- or three-night stays in Montréal and Québec City and cruises that pass through one or both ports. The short-stay packages do not include airfare, but they offer a good choice of hotels. Most of the packages are targeted to specific tastes and preferences, including casino admission, sightseeing, and admission to historical and cultural attractions, depending on what you're into. This company accepts reservations from U.S. and Canadian travel agents only.

- ✔ **Yankee Holidays** (☎ 800-225-2550 or 978-922-4819; www.yankee-holidays.com) offers vacation packages of mainly the two-day/three-night variety to both cities. Packages are targeted toward specific interests and can include museum passes, show tickets, gourmet meals, sightseeing tours, and festival admissions. The activity options are more limited in Québec City. Airfare is not included.

Chapter 6

Catering to Special Travel Needs or Interests

● ●

In This Chapter

▶ Surviving the trip with your pint-sized travelers

▶ Savoring refined pleasures if you're a senior traveler

▶ Overcoming disabilities on the road

▶ Living it up in gay Québec

● ●

Montréal and Québec City are about as open-minded and welcoming as cities get. The fun factor is spread out across all groups, whether you're traveling with a family, you qualify for senior discounts, you travel with a disability, or you're a gay or lesbian traveler.

Traveling with the Brood: Advice for Families

Montréal is a safe, clean, relatively inexpensive city full of fun things for kids to do. While Québec City is hardly Disney World, you can find plenty of activities and sights that interest kids, and the city is well organized to accommodate families.

Here are a few tips to keep in mind when you're planning your kid-friendly trip:

✔ **Find out what your kids want to do.** Look for kid-friendly activities before you travel, and let the kids get in on the action by having them check Web sites, read brochures, and, well, dream of adventures to come.

✔ **Surf the Web for ideas.** Check out www.montreal.com for lists of kids' activities. The Montréal-based site www.yikeskids.com has an "Ask the Experts" link, where you can ask a local expert about entertaining little ones. Québec City's tourism site (www.quebec region.com) doesn't have a specific kids section, but ask your kids to let you know what appeals to them.

✔ **Play up the history.** From bayonets and epic battles to fancy frocks and horse-drawn carriages, Montréal and Québec City have plenty of historical aspects that set kids' imaginations on fire.

✔ **Locate kid-friendly establishments.** Throughout this book, I identify kid-friendly hotels, restaurants, and attractions with the Kid Friendly icon.

✔ **Visit tourism centers.** In Montréal, the **Infotouriste Centre** is downtown at 1000 Square-Dorchester (☎ 800-266-5687 or 514-873-2015). In Québec City, the **Bureau d'information touristique** is in the Old City at 835 av. Wilfrid-Laurier (☎ 418-649-2608). Both centers distribute free **Official Tourist Guides** with special sections on activities for kids.

✔ **Have a Plan B.** As far as the weather goes, the only certainty is uncertainty. Abrupt rain cancellations can definitely send kids into a tailspin, so plan activities for rain, shine, heat, and cold. Plan indoor activities, like museums, on rainy days, for relief from the cold in winter, or when you need to avoid the noonday heat in summer. Outdoor activities, such as inline skating or amusement parks, are best in late afternoon or early evening.

✔ **Have a little talk about language before you leave.** Older kids may be miffed when they don't understand what people around them are saying. Explain that most people in Québec speak French, and teach them a few words. *Bonjour* and *au revoir* will probably do (or check out the Cheat Sheet at the front of this book). You can turn it into a game and pick up a few words yourself.

Traveling with kids can be a riot, but sometimes it actually turns into one. If you want to leave the kids behind for a day — in trustworthy hands — some hotels offer babysitting services. Ask at the front desk. The **Montréal YMCA,** downtown on rue Stanley, offers educational day care for kids 18 months to 5 years (☎ 514-849-8393; www.ymca.ca).

The books *Family Travel* (Lanier Publishing International) and *How to Take Great Trips with Your Kids* (The Harvard Common Press) are full of good general advice that can apply to travel anywhere. Another reliable tome with a worldwide focus is *Adventuring with Children* (Foghorn Press).

You can also check out *Family Travel Times,* published six times a year by Travel with Your Children, 40 Fifth Ave., 7th Floor, New York, NY 10011 (☎ 888-822-4FTT or 212-477-5524; www.familytraveltimes.com). It includes a weekly call-in service for subscribers. Subscriptions are US$39 a year. A free publication list and a sample issue are available upon request.

Familyhostel (☎ 800-733-9753; www.learn.unh.edu/familyhostel) takes the whole family, including the kids ages 8 to 15, on moderately priced international learning vacations, with lectures, field trips, and sightseeing guided by a team of academics.

You can find good family-oriented vacation advice on the Internet from sites such as **Family Travel Forum** (www.familytravelforum.com), a comprehensive site that offers customized trip planning; **Family Travel Network** (www.familytravelnetwork.com), an award-winning site that offers features, deals, and trips; **Traveling Internationally with Your Kids** (www.travelwithyourkids.com); and **Family Travel Files** (www.thefamilytravelfiles.com), which offers an online magazine and a directory of off-the-beaten-path tours and tour operators for families.

Making Age Work for You: Tips for Seniors

Montréal and Québec City are both great cities for refined pleasures like fine dining and visiting museums and galleries. And, of course, if you're not in the mood for culture, you can always head to the Montréal Casino.

Several Canadian tour companies offer organized holidays for seniors. In Montréal, **Prométour Cultural Tours** is located in Vieux-Montréal (☎ 514-848-0766). In Québec City, **Groupe Voyages Québec** is located right in the thick of it on Grande Allée (☎ 800-463-1598 or 418-525-4585).

If you need help or advice finding senior services, contact the **Fédération de l'age d'or du Québec (Québec Golden Age Federation)** in Montréal (☎ 514-252-3154).

Most attractions in the city offer senior discounts, as do public transportation and movie theaters. Members of **AARP** (formerly the American Association of Retired Persons), 601 E St. NW, Washington, DC 20049 (☎ 888-687-2277 or 202-434-2277; www.aarp.org), get discounts on hotels, airfares, and car rentals. AARP offers members a wide range of benefits, including *AARP: The Magazine* and a monthly newsletter. Anyone over 50 can join.

Many reliable agencies and organizations target the over-50 market. **Elderhostel** (☎ 877-426-8056; www.elderhostel.org) arranges study programs for those aged 55 and over (and a spouse or companion of any age) in the United States and in more that 80 countries around the world. Most courses last five to seven days in the United States (two to four weeks abroad), and may include airfare, accommodation in university dormitories or modest inns, meals, and tuition. **ElderTreks** (☎ 800-741-7956; www.eldertreks.com) offers small-group tours to off-the-beaten-path adventure-travel locations, restricted to travelers 50 and older. **INTRAV** (☎ 800-456-8100; wwwintrav.com) is a high-end tour operator that caters to the mature, discerning traveler—not specifically for seniors—with trips around the world that include guided safaris, polar expeditions, private-jet adventures, and small-boat cruises down jungle rivers.

Recommended publications offering travel resources and discounts for seniors include the quarterly magazine *Travel 50 & Beyond* (www.travel50andbeyond.com); *Travel Unlimited: Uncommon Adventures for the Mature Traveler* (Avalon); *101 Tips for Mature Travelers,* available from Grand Circle Travel (☎ **800-221-2610** or 617-350-7500); and *Unbelievably Good Deals and Great Adventures That You Absolutely Can't Get Unless You're Over 50* by Joan Rattner Heilman (McGraw-Hill).

Advice for Travelers with Disabilities

Canada is a world leader in promoting the rights of people with disabilities. If you or someone in your party is traveling with a disability, you can find loads of resources and services to make your trip as hassle-free and fun as possible.

Worldwide resources

Check out *A World of Options,* a 658-page book with resources for disabled travelers. It is available from **Mobility International USA,** P.O. Box 19767, Eugene, OR 97440 (☎ **541-343-1284** voice and TTY; www.miusa.org).

Visit the Web site of **Access-Able Travel Source** (www.access-able.com), which provides names and addresses of travel agents who specialize in disabled travel, as well as information on accessible destinations around the world. The Web site www.disabilitytravelexperts.com also has recommendations.

Vision-impaired travelers should contact the **American Foundation for the Blind,** 11 Penn Plaza, Suite 300, New York, NY 10001 (☎ **800-232-5463**).

Canadian resources

While visiting Montréal and Québec City, you may also seek the support of or information from these national sources:

- ✔ *Abilities Magazine* is Canada's best magazine on disability lifestyle issues. The magazine's Web site (www.enablelink.org) offers links to a wide range of services in Canada for persons with disabilities.

- ✔ **The Active Living Alliance for Canadians with a Disability** can direct you to resources and services in Canada (☎ **800-771-0663** or 613-244-0052).

Local resources

The best resource for accessible travel in Québec is an organization called **Kéroul.** Check out its tourism guide, *Accessible Québec,* for lists of accessible attractions. The group also provides travel packages for travelers with disabilities and a database of accessible places in the province (☎ **514-252-3104;** www.keroul.qc.ca).

Québec's **Recreation Association for People with Disabilities** *(Association Québécoise pour le Loisir des Personnes Handicappées)* also provides information on accessible leisure activities (☎ 514-252-3144; www.aqlph.qc.ca).

Most large hotels in both cities have some accessible rooms, so call around. The **Hyatt Regency Montréal** (formerly the Wyndam Hotel), 1255 Jeanne-Mance (☎ 514-285-1450), in downtown Montréal, provides information on its facilities for disabled travelers.

Also consider:

- ✔ **Montréal Association for the Blind** (☎ 514-488-0043).

- ✔ **Office for Persons with Disabilities** (Montréal: ☎ 888-873-3905; Québec City: ☎ 800-567-1465).

- ✔ **West Island Association for the Intellectually Handicapped** (☎ 514-694-7722).

- ✔ **Québec Society for Disabled Children** (☎ 514-937-6171).

- ✔ **Access to Travel** (www.accesstotravel.gc.ca): This organization provides information on wheelchair-accessible transport in Québec.

Support while traveling to either city

In this section, I include the organizations to call while traveling to and from Montréal and Québec City:

- ✔ **Air Canada** (☎ 899-247-2262) and **Air Transat** (☎ 877-872-6782) offer wheelchair-accessible service.

- ✔ **Greyhound** (☎ 800-661-8747) and **Orléans Express** (☎ 514-395-4000) offer wheelchair-accessible bus service between Montréal and Québec City.

- ✔ **Via Rail** offers wheelchair-accessible service on some of its routes, but you have to reserve in advance (☎ 888-842-7245).

Support while traveling within cities

Montréal's transit commission has 456 low-floor, wheelchair-accessible buses on over 40 routes in the city (☎ 514-280-5100). Despite the good intentions of the public-transport system, however, the buses are not actually that accessible, especially during peak periods.

 Paratransit in Montréal offers free wheelchair-accessible minivan service, but you have to apply for the right to use it (☎ 514-280-8211). You can get the application from its Web site at www.stcum.qc.ca/English/t-adapte/a-index.htm. Apply two months in advance. For wheelchair-accessible taxis, call **Taxi Boisjoli** (☎ 514-255-2815).

In Québec City, **Paratransit** (☎ 418-687-2641) also offers free wheelchair-accessible minibus service, but, as in Montréal, you need to reserve in advance. Call several days before your departure to register for services. Note that these are public transportation services, and you may wait up to eight hours for your minibus.

Many travel agencies offer customized tours and itineraries for travelers with disabilities. **Flying Wheels Travel** (☎ 507-451-5005; www.flying wheelstravel.com) offers escorted tours and cruises that emphasize sports and private tours in minivans with lifts. **Access-Able Travel Source** (☎ 303-232-2979; www.access-able.com) offers extensive access information and advice for traveling around the world with disabilities. **Accessible Journeys** (☎ 800-846-4537 or 610-521-0339) offers trips for wheelchair travelers and their families and friends.

Organizations that offer assistance to disabled travelers include **MossRehab** (www.mossresourcenet.org), which provides a library of accessible-travel resources online; **SATH (Society for Accessible Travel and Hospitality)** (☎ 212-447-7284; www.sath.org; annual membership fees: US$45 adults, US$30 seniors and students), which offers a wealth of travel resources for all types of disabilities and informed recommendations on destinations, access guides, travel agents, tour operators, vehicle rentals, and companion services; and the **American Foundation for the Blind (AFB)** (☎ 800-232-5463; www.afb.org), a referral resource for the blind or visually impaired that includes information on traveling with Seeing Eye dogs.

For more information specifically targeted to travelers with disabilities, the community Web site **iCan** (www.icanonline.net) has destination guides and several regular columns on accessible travel. Also check out the quarterly magazine *Emerging Horizons* (www.emerginghorizons.com; US$14.59 per year, US$19.95 outside the United States); **Twin Peaks Press** (☎ 360-694-2462), offering travel-related books for travelers with special needs; and *Open World Magazine,* published by SATH (subscription: US$13 per year, US$21 outside the United States).

Out and About: Advice for Gay and Lesbian Travelers

Québeckers have an extremely tolerant attitude toward gay and lesbian travelers. This is a country where gays and lesbians can legally marry, after all. The gay community in Montréal is one of the largest in the world, and the city even has its own Gay Chamber of Commerce and a Gay Village Merchants Association. For a list of gaycentric activities, events, and accommodations, go to www.montrealplus.ca. In Québec City, you find fewer services and resources for the gay and lesbian communities, but that's because it's a smaller city, not because people are uptight.

The Montréal scene

According to Tourism Québec, Montréal's gay tourism industry is the third biggest draw to the city, after the Grand Prix and the Jazz Festival. With its circuit of bars, clubs, restaurants, boutiques, antiques shops, discos, bathhouses, and more, there's plenty of action. Montréal's Gay Village runs along rue Ste-Catherine between rue Berri and rue Papineau, in gritty-but-vibrant south-central downtown.

Places to stay

Gay Village offers plenty of gay-friendly hotels and inns. For lesbians, there's **Pension Vallières,** 6562 rue de Lorimier (☎ 514-729-9552), an all-women hotel. For men, there's the **Auberge Cosy,** 1274 rue Ste-Catherine Est (☎ 514-525-2151; www.aubergecosy.com), **Bed & Breakfast du Village,** 1281 rue Montcalm (☎ 888-228-8455 or 514-522-4771; www.bbv.qc.ca), or **Le Chasseur B&B,** 1567 rue St-André (☎ 514-521-2238; www.lechasseur.com).

Places to eat

Gay Village also has no shortage of great restaurants. I recommend **Area,** 1429 rue Amherst (☎ 514-890-6691), for fine French cuisine, and **Bazou,** 1310 bd. de Maisonneuve Est (☎ 514-526-4940), for refined fare in a quirky "haute" flea-market setting, where you can bring your own wine. Check out **La Piazzetta,** 1101 rue Ste-Catherine Est (☎ 514-526-2244), for good thin-crust pizza.

Bars and clubs

The hot spots of the moment in the Gay Village are **Unity II,** 1171 rue Ste-Catherine Est (☎ 514-529-6969); **Club Parking,** 1296 Amherst (☎ 514-282-1199); and **Stereo,** 858 rue Ste-Catherine Est (☎ 514-286-0300), which opens late and carries on until the next morning. You can also find dozens of clubs and bars just by walking around the Village at night.

Special events

The big yearly events in the gay and lesbian community are Montréal's **Gay Pride Parade** (☎ 514-285-4011; www.diverscite.org/anglais/index.htm), which takes place at the beginning of August; the gay and lesbian film festival, **Image+Nation** (www.image-nation.org), in September; and the **Black and Blue Festival** (www.bbcm.org), the world's largest gay and lesbian benefit event, in October.

The Québec City scene

In Québec City, the gay community is centered on rue St-Jean, between rue Dufferin and rue St-Augustin, just outside the walls of the Old City. For accommodations, the most famous inn is **Le 253,** 253 rue de la Reine (☎ 418-647-0590). Other good options are **Le Coureur des Bois,** 15 rue Ste-Ursule (☎ 418-692-1117), and **Guest House 727,** 727 rue d'Aiguillon (☎ 418-648-6766).

For more general travel information and packages, the **International Gay and Lesbian Travel Association (IGLTA)** (☎ **800-448-8550** or 954-776-2626; www.iglta.org) is the trade association for the gay and lesbian travel industry and offers an online directory of gay- and lesbian-friendly travel businesses; go to the Web site and click on "Members."

The following travel guides are available at most travel bookstores and gay and lesbian bookstores, or you can order them from **Giovanni's Room,** 1145 Pine St., Philadelphia, PA 19107 (☎ **215-923-2960;** www. giovannisroom.com): *Out and About* (☎ **800-929-2268** or 415-644-8044; www.outandabout.com), which offers guidebooks and a newsletter (US$20/year; ten issues) packed with solid information on the global gay and lesbian scene; *Spartacus International Gay Guide* (Bruno Gmünder Verlag; www.spartacusworld.com/gayguide) and *Odysseus,* both good, annual, English-language guidebooks focused on gay men; the *Damron* guides (www.damron.com), with separate, annual books for gay men and lesbians; and *Gay Travel A to Z: The World of Gay & Lesbian Travel Options at Your Fingertips* by Marianne Ferrari (Ferrari International, Box 35575, Phoenix, AZ 85069), a very good gay and lesbian guidebook series.

Chapter 7

Taking Care of the Remaining Details

In This Chapter

▶ Dealing with Customs

▶ Understanding the ins and outs of renting a car

▶ Figuring out what travel insurance you need

▶ Making advance reservations for meals and special events

▶ Mastering the art of packing

*T*ime is especially precious when you're traveling, so you don't want to learn on the job. This chapter explains all the things you need to know *before* you leave.

Getting a Passport

In this day and age, a valid passport is best when traveling to international destinations. Having one means that you can pick up and go at a moment's notice, which is really exciting, very jet-set. What's more, some airlines now require you to present a valid passport at check-in for international flights — which goes above and beyond the actual entry requirements.

A valid passport is the only legal form of identification accepted around the world. In most cases, you can't cross an international border without one. Until December 31, 2007, Americans don't need a passport to come to Canada — still Canadian border officials strongly recommend having one (and starting 2008, they'll be required). Otherwise, you will need proof of citizenship and a government-issued photo ID, such as a birth certificate and driver's license combo. If you're not a U.S. citizen, but are a permanent resident of the United States, bring your green card.

 Getting a passport is easy, but the process takes some time. For an up-to-date country-by-country listing of passport requirements around the world, go to the "Foreign Entry Requirements" Web page of the U.S. Department of State at `http://travel.state.gov/visa/americans1. html`.

Applying for a U.S. passport

If you're applying for a first-time passport, follow these steps:

1. Complete a **passport application** in person at a U.S. passport office; a federal, state, or probate court; or a major post office. To find your regional passport office, either check the U.S. Department of State Web site, http://travel.state.gov, or call the National Passport Information Center (☎ **877-487-2778**) for automated information.

2. Present a **certified birth certificate** as proof of citizenship. (Bringing along your driver's license, state or military ID, or Social Security card also is a good idea.)

3. Submit **two identical passport-sized photos,** measuring 2 x 2 inches in size. You often find businesses that take these photos near a passport office. *Note:* You can't use a strip from a photo-vending machine because the pictures aren't identical.

4. Pay a **fee.** For people 16 and older, a passport is valid for ten years and costs US$97. For those 15 and younger, a passport is valid for five years and costs US$82.

Dealing with a lost passport

Always pack a photocopy of the inside photo page of your passport separate from your wallet or purse. In the event your passport is lost or stolen, the photocopy can help speed up the replacement process. While traveling in a group, never let one person carry all the passports. If the passports are stolen, obtaining new ones can be much more difficult, because at least one person in the group needs to be able to prove his or her identity so the others can be identified.

If you're a U.S. citizen and you either lose your passport or have it stolen, go to the **Consulate General of the United States of America**, 1155 rue St-Alexandre, Montréal (☎ **514-398-9695;** http://montreal.usconsulate.gov). Australians need to contact the **Australian High Commission,** in Ottawa (☎ **888-990-8888** or 613-236-0841; www.ahc-ottawa.org). New Zealanders should contact the **New Zealand High Commission,** also in Ottawa (☎ **613-238-5991;** www.nzembassy.com/canada).

U.K citizens should contact the **British Consulate-General,** 1000 rue De La Gauchetière Ouest, Suite 4200, Montréal (☎ **514-866-5863;** www.britainincanada.com). In Québec City, an **Honorary Consulate,** Le Complexe St-Amable, 1150 Claire-Fontaine, Suite 700 (☎ **418-521-3000;** www.britainincanada.com), provides a more limited array of services for British Nationals, but it is still the first call to make upon losing your passport in Québec City.

Traveling with minors

Having plenty of documentation always is wise when traveling with children in today's world. Keep up to date on details of the changing entry requirements for children traveling abroad by going to the U.S. Department of State Web site (http://travel.state.gov/visa/americans1.html).

To prevent international child abduction, governments in some countries require documented evidence of your relationship with your children and permission for their travel from any parent or legal guardian who isn't present. Having such documentation in hand, even if not required, facilitates entries and exits. All children must have their own passports. To obtain a passport, the child must be present — that is, in person — at the center issuing the passport. Both parents must be present as well if the child is younger than 14. If one or both parents cannot be present, then a notarized statement from the absent parent is required.

For more information about passport requirements for your children, call the **National Passport Information Center** (☎ 877-487-2778) Monday to Friday 8 a.m. to 8 p.m. eastern standard time.

Make sure that you allow plenty of time before your trip to apply for a passport; processing normally takes three weeks, but it can take longer during busy periods (especially spring).

If you have a passport in your current name and issued within the past 15 years (and you were older than 16 when it was issued), you can renew the passport by mail for $67. Whether you're applying in person or by mail, you can download passport applications from the U.S. Department of State Web site at http://travel.state.gov. For general information, call the **National Passport Agency** (☎ 202-647-0518). To find your regional passport office, either check the U.S. Department of State Web site or call the **National Passport Information Center's** toll-free number (☎ 877-487-2778) for automated information.

Applying for other passports

The following list offers more information for citizens of Australia, New Zealand, and the United Kingdom:

- ✔ **Australians** can visit a local post office or passport office, call the **Australia Passport Information Service** (☎ 131-232 toll-free from Australia), or log on to www.passports.gov.au for details on how and where to apply.

- ✔ **New Zealanders** can pick up a passport application at any New Zealand Passports Office or download one from its Web site. For information, contact the **Passports Office** (☎ 0800-225-050 toll-free in New Zealand or 04-474-8100; www.passports.govt.nz).

✔ **United Kingdom** residents can pick up applications for a standard ten-year passport (five-year passport for children younger than 16) at passport offices or travel agencies. For information, contact the **United Kingdom Passport Service** (☎ **0870-521-0410;** www.ukpa. gov.uk).

Renting a Car — and Understanding Why You Shouldn't

If you plan to spend most of your time visiting Montréal within city limits, a car is probably more trouble than it's worth. In Québec City, driving is even less advisable. And Vieux-Québec is so small that you can walk anywhere you want to go.

Parking in either city can be tough. Although you find lots of metered parking in downtown areas, competition for those spaces is fierce. In Montréal's residential neighborhoods, a system of reserved parking zones still has many locals baffled; you get the added handicap of trying to figure out the signs in French. To get out of the downtown core of Montréal, take the subway (known as the **Métro**) or any number of bus lines. Ask for a public transportation map at your hotel or at the ticket booth of any Métro station. You can also easily flag taxis in both cities.

Still want to drive? Well, the truth is, finding your way around Montréal is easy in a car, and renting one is a snap (see the appendix for agencies in both cities). Just remember that traffic signs are in French. Some other peculiarities to keep in mind are as follows:

✔ It's legal to turn right on a red light everywhere in Québec except in Montréal.

✔ At many lights in both cities, the greens start out as green pointing arrows. For their duration, you can travel through the intersection only in the directions they are pointing.

✔ Gas is more expensive in Canada than the United States. You'll pay around C$50 (US$42.50) to fill the tank of a midsize car.

Finding the car you need at the price you want

The rates at most major car rental companies are about the same in both cities, but the rates among local competitors can vary some. The following tips may help you save a significant amount of money:

✔ **Weekend rates are cheaper.** This may mean picking up the car Thursday afternoon or Friday morning and returning it Monday morning. If you rent for five days or more, the daily rate is cheaper.

✔ **Drop-off charges may apply.** There's often a fee for returning the car to a different location than where you rented it. Allegedly, they're the ones who have to drive it back. Ask if this is the case when you're shopping around.

✔ **At the airport, check if the rates are cheaper downtown.** There may be a difference at some car rental agencies between the rates they offer at the airport and those at other locations. Investigate whether this is the case and whether you can save by picking up your vehicle downtown.

✔ **Mention who you are.** Be up front about the fact that you have a membership with AAA, AARP, a trade union, professional association, or anything else that may seem relevant. It could land you discounts ranging from 5 to 30 percent.

✔ **Check your frequent-flier accounts.** Often, frequent-flier programs offer discounts with certain car rental companies. In addition, most car rentals add 500 miles to your account.

✔ **Check your car-insurance policy at home.** You're probably insured for rental cars, so you don't need to buy extra insurance when you rent — just make sure you take your policy number with you.

✔ **Shop around.** Even within one company, rates vary between agencies. Rates are higher during the tourist season (May–Sept). Local rental agencies may offer better rates than national chains. Ask at the front desk of your hotel.

✔ **Estimate your driving distance.** When you rent, the rates for unlimited mileage are higher. Plan where you're going — if your mileage will be low, don't pay any extra for unlimited mileage.

Using the Internet to find deals

As with other aspects of planning your trip, using the Internet can make comparison-shopping for a car rental much easier. You can check rates at most of the major agencies' Web sites. (Double-check to make sure you are on the Canadian [.ca] versions of the car-rental company's Web site.) Plus, all the major travel sites — **Travelocity** (www.travelocity.com), **Expedia** (www.expedia.com), **Orbitz** (www.orbitz.com), and **Smarter Living** (www.smarterliving.com), for example — have search engines that can dig up discounted car-rental rates. Just enter the car size you want, the pickup and return dates, and the location, and the engine returns a price. You can even make the reservation through any of these sites.

Understanding additional charges

In addition to the standard rental prices (C$30–C$50/US$25.50–US$42.50 a day in Montréal and Québec City), other optional charges, discussed in the two following sections, can add up.

The **Collision Damage Waiver (CDW),** which requires you to pay for damage to the car in a collision, costs up to US$15 a day. Many credit-card companies cover this fee; ask your credit card company before you sign up.

Car rental companies also offer **liability insurance** (if you harm others in an accident), **personal accident insurance** (if you harm yourself or your passengers), and **personal effects insurance** (if your possessions are stolen from the car). Your car insurance policy at home probably covers these situations as well, so check before you leave. You can probably safely skip the personal effects insurance (unless you're driving around with a stack of CDs, which petty thieves in Montréal love to steal), but you should definitely be covered for harm to yourself and others.

Some companies also offer **refueling packages,** in which you pay for your initial full tank of gas up front and can return the car with an empty gas tank. The prices can be competitive with local gas prices, but you don't get credit for any gas remaining in the tank. If you reject this option, you pay only for the gas you use, but you have to return the car with a full tank or face charges of $3 to $4 a gallon (C$1 per liter) for any shortfall. If you usually run late, and a fueling stop may make you miss your plane, you're a perfect candidate for this refueling option.

 Taxes on purchases are steep in Québec. The General Sales Tax (on your bill, in French, this shows up as the TPS) is 7 percent. Then, the Provincial Sales Tax (TVQ) is 7.5 percent. Québec squeezes an extra bit of provincial sales tax out of each purchase by calculating the TVQ on the total of the original price *plus* the TPS. I'm not sure how they get away with it, but no one seems to complain.

Playing It Safe with Travel and Medical Insurance

Three kinds of travel insurance are available: trip-cancellation insurance, medical insurance, and lost-luggage insurance. The cost of travel insurance varies widely, depending on the cost and length of your trip, your age and health, and the type of trip you're taking, but expect to pay between 5 and 8 percent of the vacation itself. Here's my advice on all three.

Trip-cancellation insurance

Trip-cancellation insurance helps you get your money back if you have to back out of a trip, if you have to go home early, or if your travel supplier goes bankrupt. Allowed reasons for cancellation can range from sickness to natural disasters to the U.S. Department of State declaring your destination unsafe for travel.

A good resource is **Travel Guard Alerts,** which supplies a list of companies considered high risk by Travel Guard International (www.travel guard.com). Protect yourself further by paying for your trip with a credit card. By law, consumers can get their money back on goods and services not received if they report the loss within 60 days after the charge is listed on their credit-card statement.

Note: Many tour operators, particularly those offering trips to remote or high-risk areas, include insurance in the cost of the trip or can arrange insurance policies through a partnering provider, a convenient and often cost-effective way for the traveler to obtain insurance. Make sure the tour company is a reputable one. Some experts suggest you avoid buying insurance from the tour or cruise company you're traveling with. They say buying from a third-party insurer is better than putting all your money in one place.

Medical insurance

For international travel, most medical-insurance health plans (including Medicare and Medicaid) don't provide coverage, and the ones that do often require you to pay for services up front, reimbursing you only after you return home. Even if your plan covers overseas treatment, most out-of-country hospitals make you pay your bills up front and send you a refund only after you've returned home and filed the necessary paper-work with your insurance company. As a safety net, you may want to buy travel medical insurance, particularly if you're traveling to a remote or high-risk area where emergency evacuation is a possible scenario. If you require additional medical insurance, try **MEDEX Assistance** (☎ **888-MEDEX-00**; www.medexassist.com), **Travel Assistance International** (☎ **800-821-2828**; www.travelassistance.com), or **Worldwide Assistance Services, Inc.** (☎ **800-777-8710**; www.world wideassistance.com).

Lost-luggage insurance

Lost-luggage insurance isn't necessary for most travelers. On domestic flights, checked baggage is covered up to US$2,500 per ticketed passenger. On international flights (including U.S. portions of international trips), baggage coverage is limited to approximately US$9.07 per pound, up to approximately US$635 per checked bag. If you plan to check items more valuable than the standard liability, see if your homeowner's policy covers your valuables, get baggage insurance as part of your comprehensive travel-insurance package, or buy Travel Guard's "Bag Trak" product. Don't buy insurance at the airport — it's usually overpriced. Be sure to take any valuable or irreplaceable items with you in your carry-on luggage because many valuables (including books, money, and electronics) aren't covered by airline policies.

If your luggage is lost, immediately file a lost-luggage claim at the airport detailing the luggage contents. For most airlines, you must report delayed, damaged, or lost baggage within four hours of arrival. The airlines are required to deliver luggage, once found, directly to your house or destination free of charge.

For more information, contact one of the following recommended insurers: **Access America** (☎ **866-807-3982**; www.accessamerica.com), **Travel Guard International** (☎ **800-826-4919**; www.travelguard.com),

Travel Insured International (☎ 800-243-3174; www.travelinsured.
com), or **Travelex Insurance Services** (☎ 888-457-4602; www.
travelex-insurance.com).

Staying Healthy When You Travel

Getting sick will ruin your vacation, so I strongly advise against it, of
course.

Talk to your doctor before leaving on a trip if you have a serious and/or
chronic illness. For conditions such as epilepsy, diabetes, or heart problems, wear a **MedicAlert identification tag** (☎ 888-633-4298; www.
medicalert.org), which immediately alerts doctors to your condition
and gives them access to your records through MedicAlert's 24-hour
hot line.

Contact the **International Association for Medical Assistance to
Travelers (IAMAT)** (☎ 716-754-4883 or, in Canada, 416-652-0137; www.
iamat.org) for tips on travel and health concerns in the countries
you're visiting, and lists of local, English-speaking doctors.

The **United States Centers for Disease Control and Prevention** (☎ 800-
311-3435; www.cdc.gov) provides up-to-date information on health
hazards by region or country and offers tips on food safety.

Staying Connected by Cellphone or E-Mail

Just because your cellphone works at home, doesn't mean it will work
elsewhere on the continent — due to North America's fragmented cellphone system. Canadian cellphone networks support the following standards: GSM, TDMA, and CDMA. Chances are, if you're in a city and your
phone's compatible, you'll pick up a signal.

If you're not from North America, you'll be appalled at the poor reach of
the GSM (Global System for Mobiles) wireless network, which is used by
much of the world. Your phone will probably work in most major cities,
but it definitely won't work in many rural areas. And you may or may
not be able to send text messages home — something North Americans
do less of anyway for various cultural and technological reasons.
(International travelers like to send text messages home because it's
much cheaper than making overseas calls.)

Some cellphone companies offer an "international roaming" package
that reduces the per-minute rate of your calls while abroad. Savings
range between 25 and 50 percent. Of course, this feature comes at a
price, a monthly fee on your bill. It's usually under $5, and you can
remove it from your plan upon your return. Depending on whether your

phone will work and how much you actually plan to use it while traveling, temporarily opting in for this feature could be a worthwhile move.

Assume nothing. Call your cellphone provider to get the full scoop on picking up a signal, current rates, and possible discounts.

For many, renting a phone is a good idea. (Even world-phone owners have to rent new phones whenever they're traveling to non-GSM regions.) Although you can rent a phone from any number of usual spots in foreign countries, including kiosks at airports and at car-rental agencies, consider renting the phone before you leave home. That way, you can give loved ones and business associates your new number, make sure the phone works, and take the phone wherever you go. Phone rental isn't cheap. You'll usually pay $40 to $50 per week, plus airtime fees of at least a dollar a minute.

Two good wireless rental companies are **InTouch USA** (☎ **800-290-1606;** www.intouchusa.com) and **RoadPost** (☎ **888-290-1601** or 905-272-5665; www.roadpost.com). Give them your itinerary, and they'll tell you what wireless products you need.

Travelers have any number of ways to check their E-mail and access the Internet on the road. Of course, using your own laptop — or even a personal digital assistant (PDA) or electronic organizer with a modem — gives you the most flexibility. But even if you don't have a computer, you can still access your E-mail, and even your office computer, from cybercafes.

It's hard nowadays to find a city that *doesn't* have a few cybercafes. Although no definitive directory exists for cybercafes — these are independent businesses, after all — two places to start looking are www.cybercaptive.com and www.cybercafe.com.

Aside from formal cybercafes, most **youth hostels** nowadays have at least one computer you can use to get to the Internet. And most **public libraries** across the world offer Internet access free or for a small charge. Avoid **hotel business centers** unless you're willing to pay exorbitant rates.

Most major airports have **Internet kiosks** scattered throughout their gates. These kiosks, which you'll also see in shopping malls, hotel lobbies, and tourist information offices around the world, give you basic Web access for a per-minute fee that's usually higher than cybercafe prices. The clunkiness and high price mean these kiosks should be a last resort.

To retrieve your E-mail, ask you Internet service provider (ISP) whether it has a Web-based interface tied to your existing E-mail account. If your ISP doesn't have such an interface, you can use the free **mail2web** service (www.mail2web.com) to view and reply to your home E-mail. For more flexibility, you may want to open a free, Web-based E-mail account with **Yahoo! Mail** (http://mail.yahoo.com). (Microsoft's Hotmail is another popular option, but Hotmail has severe spam problems.) Your home ISP may be able to forward your E-mail to the Web-based account automatically.

If you need to access files on your office computer, look into a service called **GoToMyPC** (www.gotomypc.com). The service provides a Web-based interface for you to access and manipulate a distant PC from anywhere — even a cybercafe — provided your "target" PC is on and has an always-on connection to the Internet. The service offers top-quality security, but if you're worried about hackers, use your own laptop rather than a cybercafe computer to access the GoToMyPC system.

If you're bringing your own computer, the buzzword in computer access to familiarize yourself with is **Wi-Fi** (wireless fidelity), and more and more hotels, cafes, and retailers are signing on as wireless "hotspots" where you can get a high-speed connection without cable wires, networking hardware, or a phone line. You can get a Wi-Fi connection one of several ways. Many laptops sold in the last year have built-in Wi-Fi capability (an 802.11b wireless Ethernet connection). Mac owners have their own networking technology called Apple AirPort. For those with older computers, an 802.11b/Wi-Fi card (around $50) can be plugged into your laptop.

You sign up for wireless access service much as you do cellphone service, through a plan offered by one of several commercial companies that have made wireless service available in airports, hotel lobbies, and coffee shops. **T-Mobile Hotspot** (www.t-mobile.com/hotspot) serves up wireless connections at more than 1,000 Starbucks coffee shops in the United States. **Boingo** (www.boingo.com) and **Wayport** (www.wayport.com) have set up networks in airports and high-class hotel lobbies. IPass providers also give you access to a few hundred wireless hotel-lobby setups. Best of all, you don't need to be staying at the Four Seasons to use the hotel's network — just set yourself up on a nice couch in the lobby. The companies' pricing policies can be complex, with a variety of monthly per-connection and per-minute plans, but in general, you pay around $30 a month for limited access — and as many more companies jump on the wireless bandwagon, prices are likely to get even more competitive.

You can also find places that provide free wireless networks in cities around the world. To locate these free hotspots, go to www.personaltelco.net/index.cgi/WirelessCommunities.

If Wi-Fi isn't available at your destination, most business-class hotels throughout the world offer dataports for laptop modems, and a good number now offer free high-speed Internet access using an Ethernet network cable. You can bring your own cables, but most hotels rent them from around $10. Call your hotel in advance to see what your options are.

In addition, major ISPs have local access numbers around the world, enabling you to go online simply by placing a local call. Check your ISP's

Web site or call its toll-free number, and ask how you can use your current account away from home and how much it will cost. If you're traveling outside the reach of your ISP, the iPass network has a dial-up number in most of the world's countries. You'll have to sign up with an iPass provider, which then tells you how to set up your computer for your destination. For a list of iPass providers, go to www.ipass.com and click "Individuals Buy Now." One solid provider is **i2roam** (☎ **866-811-6209** or 920-235-0475; www.i2roam.com).

Wherever you go, bring a connection kit of the right power and phone adapters, a spare phone cord, and a spare Ethernet network cable — or find out whether your hotel supplies them to guests.

Keeping Up with Airline Security Measures

With the federalization of airport security, security procedures at U.S. airports are more stable and consistent than ever. Generally, you'll be fine if you arrive at the airport **one hour** before a domestic flight and **two hours** before an international flight. If you show up late, alert an airline employee and he'll probably whisk you to the front of the line.

Bring a current, **government-issued photo ID** such as a driver's license or passport. Keep your ID ready to show at check-in, the security checkpoint, and sometimes even the gate. (Children under 18 don't need government-issued photo IDs for domestic flights, but they do for international flights to most countries.)

In 2003, the Transportation Security Administration (TSA) phased out **gate check-in** at all U.S. airports. And **E-tickets** have made paper tickets nearly obsolete. Passengers with E-tickets can beat the ticket-counter lines by using the airport's **electronic kiosks** or even **online check-in** from a home computer. Online check-in involves logging on to your airline's Web site, accessing your reservation, and printing out your boarding pass — and the airline may even offer you bonus miles to do so. If you're using an airport kiosk, bring the credit card you used to book the ticket or your frequent-flier card. Print out your boarding pass from the kiosk and simply proceed to the security checkpoint with your pass and a photo ID. If you're checking bags or looking to snag an exit-row seat, you will be able to do so from most airline kiosks. Even the smaller airlines are employing the kiosk system, but always call your airline to make sure these alternatives are available. **Curbside check-in** is also a good way to avoid lines, although a few airlines still ban curbside check-in; again, call before you go.

Security checkpoint lines are getting shorter, but some doozies still remain. If you have trouble standing for long periods of time, tell an airline employee; the airline will provide a wheelchair. Speed up security by **not wearing metal objects** such as big belt buckles. If you've got metallic body parts, a note from your doctor can prevent a long chat with security screeners. Keep in mind, only **ticketed passengers** are allowed past security except for folks escorting disabled passengers or children.

Federalization has stabilized **what you can carry on** and **what you can't.** The general rule is that sharp things are out, nail clippers are okay, and food and beverages must be passed through the X-ray machine — however, security screeners can't make you drink from your coffee cup. Bring food in your carryon rather than checking it because explosive-detection machines used on checked luggage have been known to mistake food (especially chocolate, for some reason) for bombs. Travelers in the United States are allowed one carry-on bag, plus a "personal item" such as a purse, briefcase, or laptop bag; as long as it has a laptop in it, it's still considered a personal item. The TSA has issued a list of restricted items; check its Web site (www.tsa.gov/public/index.jsp) for details.

Look for Travel Sentry certified **luggage locks** at luggage or travel shops and Brookstone stores (you can buy them online at www.brookstone.com). These locks, approved by the TSA, can be opened by luggage inspectors with a special code or key. For more information on the locks visit www.travelsentry.org. If you use something other than TSA-approved locks, your lock will be cut off your suitcase if a TSA agent needs to hand-search your luggage.

Making Dinner Reservations in Advance

If you're counting on attending any of the big shows at festivals — particularly the **Jazz Festival** or the **Just for Laughs Festival** — purchase your tickets in advance. In the summer, try to book your room at least several weeks in advance — on the weekend of Montréal's Gay Pride Parade (early Aug), for example, there isn't a room to be had in town. The following sections give you some tips for advance planning.

Surfing ahead of time

The Web is the best and cheapest way to find out what's going on in Montréal and Québec City, make reservations, and buy tickets before you leave home. Here are my favorite sources for Montréal:

- ✔ **Events:** To find out what's going on in Montréal, visit the Montréal Plus Web site (www.montreal-plus.com) or Tourism Montréal (www.tourism-montreal.org).

- ✔ **Sports:** Get schedules and reserve tickets for Montréal Alouettes, Canadiens, or Impact, through the Admission Network (www.admission.com).

- ✔ **Entertainment:** The best sources are the sites of Montréal's weekly cultural magazines, the Montréal *Mirror* (www.montrealmirror.com) and *Hour* (www.hour.ca), and Montréal's English-language daily paper, *The Gazette* (www.montrealgazette.com).

And for Québec City:

- ✔ **Culture:** *Voir* (voir.ca) is a free weekly cultural magazine, with a Québec City edition. The site covers special events and concerts, as well as film and dining.

- ✔ **A little bit of everything: Québec Plus** (www.quebecplus.ca), operated by the phone company's Internet arm, has directories of entertainment, accommodations, shopping, dining, and nightlife, bolstered with profiles and seasonal features. **Bonjour Québec** (www.bonjourquebec.com), operated by the Province's Ministry of Tourism, contains pages on the entire province but has a section devoted to Québec City and the surrounding area. Québec City's official site, www.quebecregion.com, is run by the Québec City and Area Tourism and Convention Bureau.

Reserving a table for dinner

Québeckers eat late. In the summer, restaurants in Montréal and Québec City fill up at 9 p.m. and serve until 11 p.m. or later. If you want to be in the thick of the eating action, don't make dinner reservations before 7:30 p.m. On the flip side, if you want to get a table at a popular restaurant at the last minute, tables are almost always available at 6 p.m. or earlier.

Weekends are the only time you have trouble making same-day reservations at most restaurants. In Chapters 10 and 18, I tell you which restaurants require reservations. If all my suggestions are booked, don't despair. Ask for alternatives at the front desk of your hotel. Neither city suffers from a shortage of culinary choices.

Getting a Few Packing Tips

Think you can visit Montréal and Québec City in a sweat suit and sneakers? Think again. Both cities are slightly more stylish and formal than the North American norm; you really won't feel comfortable walking around in a jogging suit. Make sure you have at least a decent pair of slacks, a nice shirt, and clean shoes.

After you set your style standards, think practically. The weather is always unpredictable, so make sure you have at least one warm sweater, plus sunscreen, a sun hat, and an umbrella. For winter, bring a warm coat, mitts, hats, gloves, and boots — sorry, there's no way around it.

 Travel lightly. I know I just told you to be stylish and prepare for rain or shine, but don't break your back over it. One large, preferably wheeled, suitcase and a carry-on bag is the way to go.

What not to bring

You probably don't need formalwear, so don't bog down your bags with fancy suits or satin pumps. For women, one dressy — preferably a knit — outfit will do. For men, one jacket and tie combo will suffice. The best idea is always to have something versatile.

What to bring

Your airline can tell you how much luggage you can bring. Usually you are allowed to check two pieces and carry one small bag with you, but many charter airlines allow only one checked piece of luggage and a carry-on bag. Airlines have become fairly strict about baggage limitations in the last couple of years, so if you plan to take a lot with you, call the airline for specific weight and size limitations. You don't want any unpleasant surprises at check-in.

Your carry-on bag should contain whatever you can't afford to lose, and whatever you need to get by for a day in case your luggage gets lost (if they lose your bag, most airlines locate it quickly). Return tickets, vital documents, toiletries, an extra pair of underwear, something to read, a small bottle of water, and a light sweater or jacket does the trick.

Don't pack any sharp objects (scissors, tweezers, and so on) in your carry-on bag. These items are strictly prohibited. Pack them in your checked luggage, instead, or leave them at home.

In addition, think about the following when packing:

✔ **Leave your new shoes at home.** Even if your old ones are a little scuffed, you'll be far happier walking around in them instead of nursing bruises and blisters.

✔ **Find a color scheme.** When packing, choose colors that complement each other. Black, white, gray, and navy work wonders, as do beige and brown. *Remember:* Most of the people who see you while traveling will probably never see you again.

✔ **Stick to knits.** They don't wrinkle. Leave your linen shirts at home. They're not worth it.

✔ **Bring along a little laundry soap.** A small bottle of laundry detergent weighs a lot less than those three extra shirts you were going to bring along just in case you dribble truffle juice down your collar. Do a little hand washing in the hotel sink.

✔ **Save up small bottles.** Pour into them only as much shampoo or shower gel as you need for your stay. You won't believe how much space and weight you save. Pharmacies also sell miniature travel versions of everything from toothpaste to hand cream.

✔ **Find an itsy-bitsy, teeny-weeny, yellow polka-dot . . . umbrella.** These days they make umbrellas that practically fit into your fist. An umbrella is a must for any trip to Montréal or Québec City; a compact version takes some weight off your shoulders.

Part III
Settling Into and Exploring Montréal

"Montréal is wonderful. We spent the morning at Vieux Port, the afternoon at Vieux Mont-Royal, and right now we're at Vieux hotel room."

In this part . . .

Now comes the fun part. Here's where I tell you about Montréal and guide you through its highlights, its best hotels and restaurants, and its hottest attractions. You can follow one of my itineraries for visiting the city on foot. And in case you want to swap urban landscapes for mountains, lakes, and rivers, I offer a few recommended daytrips around Montréal.

Chapter 8

Arriving and Getting Oriented in Montréal

. . . .

In This Chapter

▶ Finding your way into town

▶ Discovering Montréal's neighborhoods

▶ Knowing where to find tourist information

▶ Getting around on foot, by bicycle, or in a car

. . . .

*M*ontréal is an island with a mountain in the middle. Well, sort of. Mont Royal is a 761-foot-high hill, topped by a crucifix, that everyone calls "the Mountain." It looms large over several Montréal neighborhoods. And unless you're near the water, like in Vieux-Montréal, it's not obvious that you're on an island in the mighty St. Lawrence River. Suburban Montréalers who creep over the bridges and snake through the tunnels on their daily commutes never forget it, though. This chapter explains how to get to Montréal and how to get around after you arrive.

Navigating Your Way through Passport Control and Customs

Canadians are such welcoming folks. We're well known for being particularly nice, saying "sorry" all the time, and, generally, not wanting to offend. Our Customs officials, thankfully, are sterner individuals, charged with protecting our borders. The drill here, as at any border crossing, is to answer the officer's questions: no more, no less. If you think about it, this usually brief exchange just before beginning your vacation is like the opposite of a job interview, but you should treat it seriously just the same.

Customs officers usually ask where you're from, how long you plan to stay, and maybe, whether you have anything to declare. Your answer to this last question is "no," unless you're importing goods or an incredibly large sum of cash. Just answer politely and don't take the interrogation personally.

Greater Montréal

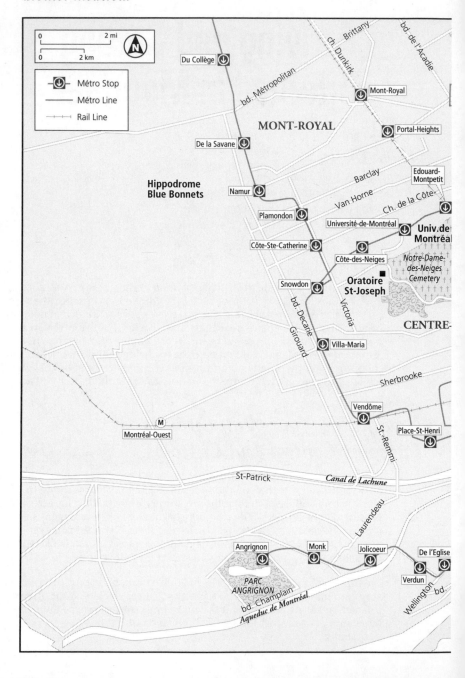

0   2 mi
0   2 km

N

—⊕— Métro Stop
——— Métro Line
—+—+— Rail Line

Du Collège ⊕

bd. Métropolitan

ch. Dunkirk

Brittany

bd. de l'Acadie

Mont-Royal ⊕

MONT-ROYAL

Portal-Heights ⊕

De la Savane ⊕

Hippodrome
Blue Bonnets

Namur ⊕

Barclay

Van Horne

Edouard-
Montpetit ⊕

Ch. de la Côte-

Plamondon ⊕

Université-de-Montréal ⊕

**Univ. de
Montréal**

Côte-Ste-Catherine ⊕

Côte-des-Neiges ⊕

*Notre-Dame-
des-Neiges
Cemetery*

Snowdon ⊕

**Oratoire
St-Joseph** ■

bd. Decarie

Victoria

Girouard

CENTRE-

Villa-Maria ⊕

Sherbrooke

Vendôme ⊕

M
Montréal-Ouest

Place-St-Henri ⊕

St-Remmi

St-Patrick

Canal de Lachune

Laurendeau

Angrignon ⊕

Monk ⊕

Jolicoeur ⊕

De l'Eglise ⊕

*PARC
ANGRIGNON*

bd. Champlain
Aqueduc de Montréal

Verdun ⊕

Wellington bd.

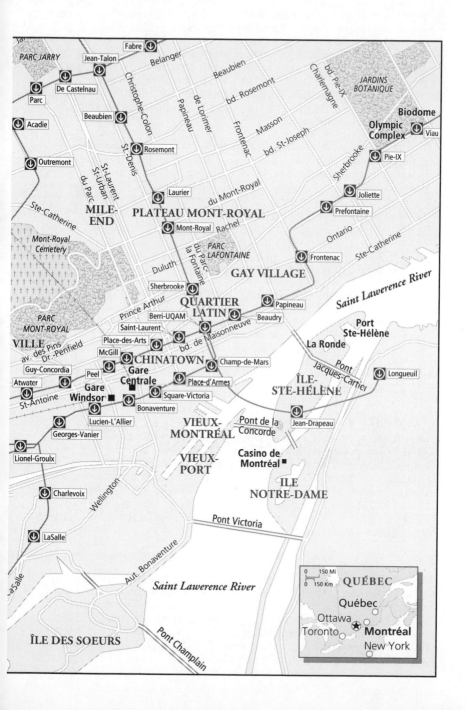

In this day and age, you should really have a valid passport for any international travel. See Chapter 7 for how to go about getting one.

However, U.S. citizens and permanent residents don't require passports or visas to enter Canada. Americans can provide proof of citizenship and a government-issued photo ID (a citizenship or naturalization card, or a birth certificate with a valid photo identification, like a driver's license). If you're not a U.S. citizen, but are a permanent resident of the United States, also bring your green card.

All other foreign travelers visiting Canada need at least a passport — and maybe a visa. Before you go, find out what you need to enter Canada by visiting the **Canada Border Services Agency** Web site at www. cbsa-asfc.gc.ca.

See Chapter 12 for Customs regulations regarding how much loot you can take home.

Making Your Way to Your Hotel

After you make it through Customs (see the preceding section), you're almost there. Now you have to drop your bags where you'll be staying. A good, hot shower can be worth several hours of sleep for weary travelers. Changing your socks is the next best thing. (Don't believe me? Try it.)

Depending on how you traveled to Montréal, these are the different options for finding your way downtown to your hotel room. After you're settled, your visit can begin.

If you arrive by plane

You will arrive at Montréal's recently renovated and renamed **Pierre Elliott Trudeau International Airport** (☎ 800-465-1213 or 514-394-7377; www.admtl.com), formerly known as Dorval. After clearing Customs and claiming your checked baggage, you may want to exchange money. A currency exchange counter, open between 4:30 p.m. and 12:30 a.m., and a 24-hour ATM are located on the Arrivals level of the airport — which is where you'll be. Car-rental agencies are also located at this level, but you have plenty of other ways to get downtown.

Getting to your hotel by taxi

Taxis and limousines are available curbside, immediately upon exiting the Arrivals level of the terminal. Airport limousines are not the stretch brand favored by Paris Hilton and Co., but black, tinted-window, leather-interior sedans of the type used for whisking around international dignitaries. The cabs are metered, and a trip downtown costs about C$30 (US$26); limousines charge a flat fee of C$70 (US$60) plus tip (10 to 15 percent is customary) from Trudeau.

Getting to your hotel by shuttle

The Aérobus (☎ 514-399-9877) is a **shuttle bus** that runs frequently between the airport and downtown. This is the best value for getting downtown as quickly and hassle-free as possible, at C$12 (US$10) from Trudeau. However the coach service isn't door to door. It makes two stops, first downtown at 777 rue de la Gauchetière, behind the Fairmount Queen Elizabeth Hotel, and then at Montréal's bus station, **Station Central,** in the Quartier Latin, adjacent to the Berri-UQAM Métro stop. From de la Gauchetière, a free minivan takes travelers to any hotel. If you're not staying in a hotel, you may try asking for a lift anyway. You're bending the rules, but it's worth a try.

Getting to your hotel by public transportation

For a mere C$2.50 (US$2.25) you can get downtown by **public transportation,** but it's a bit of a schlep, requiring two buses and a subway (Métro) ride. To me, it's worth the extra bucks for the shuttle, especially if you have lots of luggage. If you arrive with only a carry-on bag, however, you can save some money going this route. Catch the city-bound bus No. 204 on the island across the first lane of traffic on the lower level in front of the terminal. It takes you on a short ride to Dorval Station, where you transfer to a second bus, No. 211, that goes directly to the Lionel-Groulx Métro (Orange Line). Hold on to your transfer stub — which the first driver extends in exchange for your fare — because you'll need it to get on the second bus and then onto the subway.

Getting to your hotel by rental car

I discourage **renting a car,** mainly because Montréal is such a great walking city and because its traffic, one-way streets, and scarce parking are maddening. However, at Trudeau airport, a gauntlet of booths belonging to the usual suspects of car-rental agencies are near domestic arrivals on the lower level. After you have your keys in hand, you can drive into town.

From Trudeau Airport, follow the signs for Autoroute 20 Est (Highway 20 East). You encounter many sharp turns exiting the airport, so be careful. Eventually, you come to a light and a traffic circle going through an overpass. Follow it around and get on the highway ramp on the other side — going eastbound. Follow the signs for Montréal, and **Centre-Ville,** and this highway takes you right into the heart of the city.

For tips on getting the best car-rental rates and information on car-rental insurance options, see Chapter 7. For names and contact information for car-rental agencies see the appendix.

If you arrive by car

From the Canada–U.S. border, allow an hour to get to Montréal. Depending on where you crossed, you approach Montréal's South Shore on either Autoroute 15 or Autoroute 10. To get to Montréal proper, you must traverse the river onto the island via one of the bridges; look for the Pont Jacques-Cartier.

From Ontario, you're about an hour away, depending on traffic, after you cross into the province of Québec going east along the Trans-Canada Highway. To remind you that you're no longer in Ontario, an extravagant, three-dimensional, illuminated sign-cum-monument stands on the border. You'll find an **Infotouriste Centre** at the first rest area, but you can always wait until you get to town. Eventually, the highway splits, so take Autoroute 20 and follow it straight into downtown, or *Centre-ville,* in French. At one point, Autoroute 20 breaks down into a slower road with a series of traffic lights and strip malls on either side. Do not despair, the highway starts again, after a mile or two.

From Québec City, travel west along Autoroute 20 or 40; either takes you through Montréal. Autoroute 40 runs along the top of the island, and Autoroute 20 along the bottom.

If you arrive by train

In these ultra-fast times, rail travel has an undeniable romance. All trains bound for Montréal arrive at the downtown **Gare Centrale,** 895 rue de la Gauchetière Ouest (☎ 514-989-2626). After you disembark and claim your luggage, you have several options. The Gare Centrale connects to the Bonaventure Métro station through a twisting network of store-lined corridors, part of the city's fabled "underground city." Follow the signs for the Métro. The subway system's logo is an eye-catching blue circle with a downward pointing arrow. Closer at hand, you'll find a taxi stand on the same level as the main hall. In addition, several excellent, though pricey, hotels are within walking distance. The Infotouriste Centre, a good place to begin your visit, is at the north end of nearby Square Dorchester. See the "Finding Information after You Arrive" section for hours.

 If you've ever wanted to know the words to Canada's national anthem, they are inscribed along the bottom of the bas-relief sculpture on the upper walls around Gare Centrale's main hall.

Traveling between Montréal and Québec City

You have several options to get to Québec City from Montréal's main airport.

By rental car

All of Québec's major car-rental companies have counters in the arrivals area of Trudeau Airport. For tips on getting the best rental deals, see Chapter 7. For telephone numbers of rental companies, see the appendix.

By bus

Autocars Orléans Express (☎ 514-842-2281) serves the Montréal-Québec City corridor. Express buses leave every hour on the hour from Montréal's **Central Bus Station** (☎ 514-842-2281), located at 505 bd. de

Maisonneuve Est, to Québec City. The trip takes about three hours, and a round-trip ticket costs C$71 (US$60.25) plus taxes. See earlier in this chapter for details on how to get from Trudeau Airport to the Central Bus Station in Montréal.

By train

Trains leave four times daily from Montréal's **Central Station,** 895 rue de la Gauchetière Ouest (☎ **514-989-2626**), to Québec City's **Gare du Palais,** 450 rue Gare-du-Palais (☎ **418-692-3940**). If you reserve five days ahead of time, a round-trip ticket costs C$124 (US$105). The trip takes a little over three hours.

See Chapter 16 for more information on arriving in Québec City.

Figuring Out Montréal's Neighborhoods

Although a map comes in handy, Montréal's central neighborhoods are so different from each other that you can orient yourself just by looking around. You can walk them all in a single day, if you're an athlete. If you're a normal person, take your time. Depending on your interests, you can walk through each neighborhood in a matter of minutes, spend an afternoon visiting, or take the whole day exploring its different parts.

Vieux-Montréal

This is the oldest part of the city and the crown jewel of Montréal's neighborhoods. Travelers flock here to soak up the European flavor from the well-preserved remains of the French and English colonial periods. Just exploring the neighborhood's nooks and crannies is a treat. Walk down an interesting-looking street and then another; find a secret courtyard, fountain, or square; ride in a horse-drawn carriage; or stop for drinks in the heart of it all: at an outdoor terrace along Place Jacques-Cartier.

Montréal boasts plenty of historic sites, museums, tours, shops, galleries, cafes, and other attractions, but just being here is the real trip. You can fancy yourself in a European capital or on the back lot of a Hollywood studio. In fact, Vieux-Montréal often passes as Paris in television and film productions shooting on location.

Downtown

Rue Ste-Catherine is the downtown main commercial artery. It is crowded all day long with businesspeople, tourists, shoppers, and all varieties of Montréal street creatures. In the morning, office types wielding aluminum mugs of caffeine dodge delivery trucks. After lunch, the shoppers are out in full force, hitting the street's boutiques, department stores, and shops. The foot traffic is especially heavy after work as the two crowds mingle. By dark, the mobs thin, leaving behind couples rushing to catch a movie or packs of friends carrying on into the night.

There's plenty more to downtown than the bright lights of rue Ste-Catherine. If you're a culture vulture, you can get your fix at the **Centre Canadien de L'architecture (Canadian Center for Architecture)**, the **Musée des Beaux Arts (Fine Arts Museum)**, and **McGill University**'s gated campus.

Chinatown

Dim sum, dragon-beard candy, bubble tea, exotic fruits, herbal remedies, and curio shops — Montréal's Chinatown reveals many treasures to the adventurous traveler. The red, imperial arches along boulevard St-Laurent mark the neighborhood's northern and southern borders. Halfway in between and to the west, you can stroll along rue de la Gauchetière, which is closed to cars and has a good concentration of Chinese shops and restaurants.

Quartier Latin

Rue St-Denis, south of rue Sherbrooke, spills into Montréal's lively Latin Quarter. Serviced by the city's largest Métro station, Berri-UQAM, and squeezed between downtown, the Plateau, the Gay Village, and Chinatown, this neighborhood's central location makes it a crossroads of sorts. By evening, it fills with friends looking for a spot to rendezvous over drinks. During the warmer months, the same friends are hanging out on the numerous terraces that run the length of the street. The **Bar St-Sulpice** is a choice destination for such occasions, with its huge beer garden that's extremely popular among university students.

Gay Village

Montréal is an extremely gay-positive city. The stretch of rue Ste-Catherine, east of rue Amherst and as far east as avenue Papineau, is the epicenter of Montréal's vibrant and colorful gay community. Gay couples wander along the restaurant- and boutique-lined street hand-in-hand, and life goes on in a perfectly banal way.

Plateau

For a long time, this has been Montréal's trendiest neighborhood. In the early '90s, the low rents of this formerly working-class neighborhood attracted artists and other creative types, and hip boutiques, restaurants, bars, and cafes soon followed. Now the very people who made the Plateau what it is are fighting tooth and nail to keep their rent-controlled apartments, as the Plateau's absentee landlords look to cash in with the condo crowd.

Despite the recent gentrification, everyone here still has their look and plenty of swagger. It's a great neighborhood for people-watching, shopping, and eating. The main streets with all the action include avenue Mont-Royal, boulevard St-Laurent, and rue St-Denis.

Mile End

 Mainly a residential area, a mix of artists, writers, students, young couples, and immigrant families — predominantly Greek, Orthodox Jew, and Italian — inhabit this idyllic neighborhood. The shops along rue St-Viateur reflect the community's varied tastes and backgrounds. For several blocks, between avenue du Parc and boulevard St-Laurent, rue St-Viateur is full of appealing, yet quaint, health-food stores, cafes, restaurants, booksellers, gourmet shops, and the like. **Café Olympico** is the neighborhood hangout, with some of the best coffee in town.

One block north, on rue Bernard, you find a similar scene, but everything becomes decidedly more upscale west of avenue du Parc, which is the neighborhood of **Outremont.** Although only open seasonally, **Bilboquet,** at the westernmost point on this commercial strip, serves up scoops of homemade ice cream in a wide variety of interesting flavors, including maple taffy, or *tire* (pronounced *teer*), which is available only for a few fleeting days in the spring.

Mile End is also bagel country. Montréal's bagels are even better than those in New York City; some say that they're the best in the world! Scrawnier and chewier than their Big Apple cousins, the dough of a Montréal bagel is thinner, so the inner circle is much bigger, making it more difficult to schmear with your favorite topping. **St-Viateur Bagel** and **Fairmout Bagel,** a block south on rue Fairmount, are the city's two most famous factories, churning out the bagels 24/7, and Montréalers keep up a perennial debate as to which bagel is best.

Little Italy

Boulevard St-Laurent north, way north, is the heart of Montréal's Italian community. This is where to go to catch up on European soccer league scores, challenge elderly men to bocce ball games in **Parc Martel,** or sip cappuccino and munch on biscotti at a sidewalk cafe. The loyal patrons of the '50s-style **Café Italia** claim that the coffee here is the best in Montréal.

At the strip's northern end, and a couple of blocks east of the intersection of boulevard St-Laurent and avenue Jean Talon, the immense **Marché Jean Talon (Jean Talon Market)** is at the geographical center of the city. It's packed on weekends. Formerly filled with new Canadians foraging for deals on produce, the crowd these days consists also of culinary highbrows searching for *terroir* items — quality local ingredients — and frugal gourmets of all stripes shopping for produce, cheeses, meats, and specialty items from Québec's bountiful regions, like ostrich meat from Salaberry de Valleyfield.

Finding Information after You Arrive

Québec's Ministry of Tourism runs Montréal's **Infotouriste Centre,** 1001 Square Dorchester (www.bonjourquebec.com), a block south of rue

Ste-Catherine, between rue Peel and rue Metcalf, and at the north end of Square Dorchester. It's the city's main resource for travel information on Montréal and the surrounding regions, and it's chock-full of free flyers and booklets. The keen and knowledgeable staff can answer almost any query you can muster. During the high tourist season, from the beginning of June through early September, the center is open daily from 8:30 a.m. to 7:30 p.m. After Labour Day until the end of May, it operates daily from 9 a.m. to 6 p.m. You can also reach the center by phone (☎ 877-266-5687 or 514-873-2015), should you need some roadside assistance while out and about. With different hours from the actual information center, lines are open April through September, Monday to Friday 8 a.m. to 10 p.m. (except for Wed, when they don't open until 10 a.m.), and from October through March Monday through Friday 9 a.m. to 7 p.m. (except for Wed, when they don't open until 10 a.m.). On weekends, all year round, you can reach the center from 9 a.m. to 5 p.m.

The **Tourist Information Centre of Vieux-Montréal** (www.tourism-montreal.org) is at 174 rue Notre-Dame Est, at the northwest corner of Place Jacques-Cartier, an immense sloping square in honor of the city's founder. This is an excellent resource with a helpful staff, maps, and brochures.

Directory Assistance is free from Bell pay phones. If you're looking to find a local number, dial ☎ 411, just like in the United States. Doing so from a hotel room isn't such a hot idea. The usual charge from a land line is 75¢ but it's common practice for hotels to add on a hefty premium for connecting you to directory assistance. If you're looking for an address or a number and have access to the Internet, go to www.canada411.ca.

Getting Around Montréal

However you choose to get around Montréal, keep in mind that it's a large city with all the modern conveniences and headaches caused by the sheer volume of people on the move. In other words, getting around the city has its pros and cons.

On the plus side:

✔ The city's central neighborhoods are compact and well served by bike paths and an extensive public transport system that includes four subway lines and a network of buses.

✔ Taxis are plentiful and reasonably priced.

On the minus side:

✔ Driving in the city can be a hassle, because of an inordinate number of narrow, one-way streets. Chances are, you'll spend some of your time in a taxi stuck behind a garbage or recycling truck, with only

Montréal's mediocre English-language radio programming to help you pass the time.

✔ Parking and rush hours are the same nightmares you get in any big city.

By foot

Walking is one of the best ways to travel in Montréal (see Chapter 13 for suggested walking itineraries). With the occasional support of public transportation and taxis, you can get everywhere you need to go on foot. Along the way, you experience much more of what Montréal has to offer. Even in the cold weather, a couple layers of clothing and a brisk pace go a long way toward combating the elements. So, don gloves, a warm hat, and a scarf.

Compared to most of the continent, where suburban attitudes are the rule, Montréal *feels* urban. Montréal's spirit is on the sidewalks of the neighborhoods, not in malls in the outlying areas. The sights and smells of the rapidly changing streetscapes are a feast for the senses.

The city's streets are inordinately safe by North American standards. Although a modicum of street smarts is a must, there's no mood of fear and imminent danger on Montréal's streets. In fact, it's quite the contrary. The general population of stylish pedestrians is laid back, friendly, and usually glad to offer directions.

By public transportation (Métro and bus)

Completed for Expo '67, Montréal's Métro stations were built with a futuristic vision that has yet to materialize above ground. Today, the look is retro, maybe a little kitschy. Even the orange interiors of the trains are reminiscent of something out of Stanley Kubrick's film *2001: A Space Odyssey.*

Run by the *Sociéte de Transport de Montréal,* or STM (☎ 514-288-6287; www.stcum.qc.ca), the Métro has 65 stops. The lines extend to the farthest reaches of the city. The downtown core is serviced by the Green and Orange lines, between Lionel-Groulx in the west and Berri-UQAM in the east. The trains run from 5:30 a.m. until about 12:30 a.m. See the Cheat Sheet in the front of this book for a tear-out map.

Ask the ticket collector at any Métro station for a free map of the Island of Montréal's entire transit system, which includes all the bus routes. (The map is very handy, even if you never board public transport during your stay.) Near the ticket booths, schedules and routes of individual buses departing from that station are available. Most bus stops around the city have a departure schedule. The buses on some of the city's major arteries run 24 hours a day; other schedules vary. During the day, the service, both above and below ground, is regular, so you won't need to plan around it, but just in case, you can also get transit schedules by calling the STM or visiting its Web site. (See Chapter 6 for information on public transportation for the disabled.)

A single fare is good for one transfer, or *correspondence,* between the Métro and the buses. The rule is that you have to take a transfer at your point of origin, not ask for one later. In the Métro stations, silver mechanized dispensers just beyond the turnstiles spit transfers out at the press of a button. Bus drivers automatically extend one to you when you pay the fare, and they're valid for an hour and a half. Should you forget to grab one before getting on the subway, you can get it on your way out, and buses usually accept them. If the driver questions you, tell him you're a tourist and he'll probably let you on. You must also produce a valid transfer when switching between buses.

The STM charges C$2.50 (US$2.25) for a single ride, but if you plan to use public transit several times while in Montréal, buying in bulk may prove more economical. A strip of six tickets costs C$11.25 (US$9.50), a single-day pass is C$8 (US$6.75), a three-day pass is C$16 (US$14), and a weekly pass (from Mon–Sun) runs you C$18 (US$15). Monthly passes are also available for C$61 (US$52). You can buy any of these at a Métro station's ticket booth and at some *dépanneurs* (convenience stores) and drugstores throughout the city.

By bicycle

Montréal is North America's bicycling capital. Despite the harsh winter climate that sends most cyclists into hibernation for four months, *Bicycling Magazine* rated Montréal tops in North America for its cycling infrastructure and culture.

A bike is great way to get around Montréal when the weather's not too nasty, although doing battle in traffic with aggressive drivers can be a hair-raising experience. Luckily, the city has an extensive network of bike paths, 240 miles in all, which provides a less harrowing ride through much of the city, including stretches through parks and along the waterfront.

You can rent a bicycle at several places in Montréal. These are the best:

- ✔ **Cycle Pop et Pop Tours,** 1000 rue Rachel Est (☎ 514-526-2525; www.cyclepop.ca)

- ✔ **La Cordee Plein-Air,** 2159 rue Ste-Catherine Est (☎ 800-567-1106 or 514-524-1106; www.lacordee.com)

- ✔ **Montréal on Wheels,** 27 rue de la Commune Est (☎ 514-866-0633; www.caroulemontreal.com)

By car

If there were no cars in the streets, Montréal would be an easy city to navigate. Unfortunately, the driving culture here is somewhat distinct from the rest of Canada. Drivers don't ask; they take. For example, in other cities, drivers request a lane change by using their turn signals. Montréalers don't really wait for an answer, they just signal and squeeze right in, often simultaneously — that is, if they bother to signal at all.

There's more. You can't turn right on a red light in Montréal (a fine rule when you consider that many drivers here are still learning to associate red lights with full stops). A green arrow means you can turn only in that direction; a solid green means you can go in any direction. Advanced (flashing) green lights can occur either at the beginning or at the end of a green light's phase. On a flashing green, the oncoming traffic has a red light, pedestrians are supposed to stay put, and drivers with the light can turn right and left at will.

And then there are the turning signs. Rather than say where you can't go at an intersection, Québec's traffic signs tell drivers where they *can* go. Most intersections have a white sign with a green circle around a set of black arrows. These black arrows indicate the directions a car can legally turn at that intersection. A sign with an arrow pointing straight ahead and an arrow pointing to the right means you *can't* turn left. Go figure. If you don't see a sign with green arrows, you can turn in any direction.

Filling up

In Canada, car owners buy their gasoline or diesel fuel by the liter, which is roughly equivalent to a quart. Canadian gas prices are somewhat more expensive than in the United States but are still considerably cheaper than European fuel. Multiply the per-liter price by four for an approximate gallon comparison.

Parking tips for the brazen

Like any big city, parking in Montréal is a hassle. Deciphering the parking signs is probably the most difficult part. You need not only a keen eye but a firm grasp of the days of the week in French. (Beginning with Monday, they are: *lundi, mardi, mercredi, jeudi, vendredi, samedi,* and *dimanche.*) Most of the time, these words appear in their abbreviated form on the signs, which is just the first three letters of each. You also need to familiarize yourself with 24-hour (military) clock times.

One plus to driving is that Montréal has lots of metered parking downtown and in the commercial areas of the city. You can also find free parking in the residential neighborhoods just north of rue Sherbrooke; though, to be honest, you may spend half the evening looking for a spot.

Montréal residents with parking permits add to the confusion, hogging much of the residential curbsides. Arrows delineate the extent of their permit parking zones. If you see two empty spots in a row, chances are, you're staring at a restricted zone.

The downtown area has plenty of parking lots. They hit you up for C$12 to C$15 per day (US$10.25–US$12.75) — not bad compared to other large cities, but it still hurts.

By taxi

Montréal taxis don't sport bold color schemes or patterns like cabs in other cities. A white light mounted on its roof is the only indication that a vehicle is a taxicab. When the light is on, the cab is available. Getting around in one of them is a reasonable proposition as long as you don't get snarled in traffic. At that point, your ride can begin to get expensive. The meter starts at C$3.15 (US$2.75) and climbs at a rate of roughly C$3.00 (US$2.50) per mile of driving or C55¢ (US50¢) per minute of waiting in traffic. Trips across the downtown core usually range between C$5 and C$15 (US$4.25–US$13). The city's chauffeurs are a mixed bag, from career cabbies, who can tell you that boulevard René-Levesque used to be called rue Dorchester, to recently arrived immigrants, sometimes sitting on their PhDs in chemistry. Hailing a cab is easy. Just stick out your hand, and cabs swarm you like gadflies. Late at night, the more enterprising chauffeurs sometimes honk gently at pedestrians to remind you of their presence.

If you aren't near a main artery or don't feel like waiting for a taxi to pass, you can call for one. These are the two big local cab companies:

- ✓ **Taxi Co-op, ☎ 514-725-9885**
- ✓ **Taxi Diamond, ☎ 514-273-6331**

Chapter 9

Checking In at Montréal's Best Hotels

In This Chapter
▶ Checking into Montréal's best hotels
▶ Choosing small inns as alternatives

*W*ith more than 25,000 rooms, Montréal has the highest proportion of hotel rooms per capita in North America. Options run the full gamut, giving you loads of choices for your stay. You can opt for the cinder block austerity of a college dorm room, the opulent luxury of a penthouse suite, and anything in between. However, booking a room on short notice can be a problem, especially during weekends or any time during the high tourist season (May–Sept). To get the room you want, plan ahead. Making your reservations well in advance can save you money, too.

Getting to Know Your Options

Prices for double rooms at the most lavish hotels begin around C$250 (US$213) a night. That may sound steep, but compared to elsewhere in the world, it's a steal. The weak Canadian dollar sweetens the deal, so Montréal may be the place to splurge on lap-of-luxury accommodations if that's what you're into. If that's not what you want, Montréal offers loads of affordable options, too.

Boutique hotels

Step into a world of design-forward surroundings and attentive care. Because boutique hotels usually offer fewer than 100 rooms, you receive the conscientious hospitality that has long since disappeared from the hustle and bustle of larger hotel operations. The good feng shui and the Zen-like service make you feel like you've stumbled into a futuristic utopia.

Luxury hotels

The classic elegance and grandeur of these hotels make them the pinnacle of luxury accommodations. The committed staff in dapper uniforms buzz about seeing to the guests' every desire (well, almost). The rooms are top-notch, and the amenities usually include a pool, a spa, and a gym.

Chain hotels

A familiar name can be comforting when you're away from home. International hotel chains, such as Hilton, Holiday Inn, Marriott, Novotel, and Sheraton, offer guests a similar product the world over, so you know more or less what to expect. Most of these large, somewhat anonymous hotels are downtown and cater to business travelers and convention-goers. The rooms are well kept, and the décor is usually subdued and inoffensive.

Independent hotels

The rooms and services can vary greatly among independently owned and operated establishments. They tend to be smaller, offer more personalized service, and exude greater amounts of local character and flair than large chain hotels.

Bed-and-breakfasts

Bed-and-breakfasts (B&Bs) can be anything from one to half a dozen rooms in a private house. The home usually has a separate bathroom for guests, but you may have to share it if other guests are at the B&B. In-room bathrooms are available at some B&Bs but usually at a premium. As the name indicates, the deal includes breakfast — either continental or full. The proprietors are usually welcoming, helpful types, brimming with interesting perspectives and insider recommendations. Although they don't offer the amenities of a large hotel, these places can sometimes be a surprisingly inexpensive way to travel.

In Montréal, several agencies broker the available rooms at the bed-and-breakfasts in the city:

- ✓ **B&B Downtown Network (☎ 800-267-5180)**
- ✓ **Bienvenue B&B (☎ 800-363-9635** or 514-844-5897)
- ✓ **Montréal Oasis (☎ 514-935-2312)**

Finding the Best Room at the Best Rate

The timing of your trip dictates how much you end up spending on accommodations. Hotel room prices are higher during the tourist season, which is from early May through September. During the summer, Montréal hosts a variety of festivals and special events, and rooms can be scarce during the festival season. Check what's going on during your stay, and then book well in advance if you plan to arrive during a major event. (See Chapter 3 for Montréal's festival and events schedule.) During the rest of the year, expect to pay between 10 and 15 percent less than during the summer peak.

Finding the best rate

The *rack rate* is the maximum rate that a hotel charges for a room. It's the rate you get if you walk in off the street and ask for a room for the night. Hotels are happy to charge you the rack rate, but you almost always can do better. Perhaps the best way to avoid paying the rack rate is surprisingly simple: Just ask for a cheaper or discounted rate. You may be pleasantly surprised.

In all but the smallest accommodations, the rate you pay for a room depends on many factors — chief among them is how you make your reservation. A travel agent may be able to negotiate a better price with certain hotels than you can get by yourself. (That's because the hotel often gives the agent a discount in exchange for steering his or her business toward the hotel.)

Reserving a room through the hotel's toll-free number may also result in a lower rate than by calling the hotel directly. On the other hand, the central reservations number may not know about discount rates at specific locations. For example, local franchises may offer a special group rate for a wedding or family reunion, but they may neglect to tell their central booking line. Your best bet is to call both the local number and the toll-free number and see which one gives you a better deal. If the telephone operator tries to steer you to the reservations call center, trump her move by asking to speak with the front desk.

If you're staying only for a couple days in the middle of the week, be sure to ask for the mid-week rate.

Room rates (even rack rates) change with the season, as occupancy rates rise and fall. But even within a given season, room prices are subject to change without notice, so the rates quoted in this book may be different from the actual rate you receive when you make your reservation. Be sure to mention memberships (AAA, AARP, unions, professional associations, and so on).

In order to make a meaningful price comparison between room rates, always ask whether the quoted price includes sales tax. If it doesn't, count on paying 15 percent more at checkout. Ask about any other hidden charges that you may encounter during your stay, like parking.

Surfing the Web for hotel deals

Gleaning impressions from the Internet can be helpful when you're choosing accommodations. Through the pictures on a hotel's Web site, you can get a feel for its lobby, facilities, rooms, and neighborhood location — invaluable information.

Remember that unless you see an advertised discount for booking online, the prices on the Web are the rack rates. So much for trying the back door. At best, you get a ballpark figure that you can use to haggle for a better price.

However, you can use the Web in other ways to hunt for discounted rooms. Of the "big three" travel booking sites, **Expedia** (www.expedia.com) offers a long list of special deals and "virtual tours" or photos of available rooms so you can see what you're paying for (a feature that helps counter claims that the best rooms are often held back from bargain booking Web sites). **Travelocity** (www.travelocity.com) posts unvarnished customer reviews and ranks its properties according to the AAA rating system. Also reliable are **Hotels.com** and **Quikbook.com**. An excellent free program, **TravelAxe** (www.travelaxe.net), can help you search multiple hotel sites at once — even ones you may never have heard of — and conveniently lists the total price of the room, including taxes and service charges. Another booking site, **Travelweb** (www.travelweb.com), is partly owned by the hotels it represents (including the Hilton, Hyatt, and Starwood chains) and is, therefore, plugged directly into the hotels' reservations systems — unlike independent online agencies, which have to fax or E-mail reservation requests to the hotel, a good portion of which get misplaced in the shuffle. More than once, travelers have arrived at the hotel, only to be told that they have no reservation. To be fair, many of the major sites are undergoing improvements in service and ease of use, and Expedia, for example, will soon be able to plug directly into the reservations systems of many hotel chains — none of which can be bad news for consumers. In the meantime it's a good idea to **get a confirmation number** and **make a printout** of any online booking transaction.

In the opaque Web site category, **Priceline** and **Hotwire** are even better for hotels than for airfares. With both, you're allowed to pick the neighborhood and quality level of your hotel before offering up your money. Priceline seems much better at getting 5-star accommodations for 3-star prices, rather than anything at the bottom of the scale. Be sure to go to the **BiddingForTravel** Web site (www.biddingfortravel.com) before bidding on a hotel room on Priceline; it features a fairly up-to-date list of hotels that Priceline uses in major cities. For both Priceline and Hotwire, you pay up front and the fee is nonrefundable. *Note:* Some hotels don't provide loyalty-program credits or points or other frequent-stay amenities when you book a room through opaque online services.

Reserving the best room

To ensure you get peace and quiet in your room, request one on an upper floor, away from the hotel's meeting areas, dining rooms, and other noisy amenities like the pool. Also ask that your room be away from any scheduled renovations. In addition, more and more hotels distinguish between smoking and nonsmoking rooms. If you feel adamant about getting one room or the other, be sure to tell every person handling your reservation about your preference.

Corner rooms are often big and bright, and sometimes one is available at the same rate as a standard room. If you're traveling as a family or small group, consider asking about a suite, which may sleep as many people but usually costs less than two separate rooms. If you're not happy with your room, tell the front-desk staff immediately. Most hotels will exchange your room if another is unoccupied.

Arriving without a Reservation

If you're trundling around at dusk with no place to stay, call one of Tourism Québec's **Infotouriste Centres** (☎ 877-266-5687) or stop in. The centers are open from 8 a.m. to 7:30 p.m. Monday through Friday and from 9 a.m. to 5 p.m. on weekends. In Montréal, the office is located downtown at 1001 Square Dorchester, near the corner of rue Peel and rue Ste-Catherine. Look for the blue-and-white question-mark sign. The staff there can get you situated for one night or for the duration of your stay.

Tourism Québec's member hotels set aside rooms for a proprietary database spanning every price range and star rating. Friendly bilingual representatives tell you whether any are available in places that may otherwise claim to be sold out. They can also book B&Bs, condos, chalets, and university dormitories. The latter are available only during the summer season.

Montréal's Best Hotels from A to Z

Each hotel listing includes $ symbols, indicating the price range of the hotel's rack rates (based on double occupancy) for one night. Table 9-1 shows what to expect in each price category.

Table 9-1	Key to Hotel Dollar Signs	
Dollar Sign(s)	*Price Range*	*What to Expect*
$	Less than C$100 (US$85)	Simple and inexpensive, these accommodations should offer all the basics: a room with a lock, a firm bed, and clean towels and sheets. A light continental breakfast may be included. Hotels offering rooms at these prices probably don't have an extensive catalog of services to cater to your every whim, but the front-desk clerks are usually delighted to point you in the right direction for whatever you want.

(continued)

Table 9-1 *(continued)*

Dollar Sign(s)	Price Range	What to Expect
$$	C$100–C$199 (US$85–US$169)	Many of the rates offered by the chain hotels fall into this price range, as do the rates of the fancier independents. You can already expect the amenities to be better, like bathrooms with hair dryers, coffeemakers with complimentary coffee, and Internet access. Some hotels in this category may have kitchens that provide late-night room service or a breakfast cart. Some even have swimming pools.
$$$	C$200–C$299 (US$170–US$254)	Along with the upper-end of the chain hotels, boutique hotels and luxury hotels begin competing in this price bracket, with fine bed linens, feathery pillows, fluffy towels, and bathtubs built for two. The first-class hotels seem to differentiate themselves by striving for regal scale and elegance, while boutique hotels are strikingly modern. Expect high-speed Internet access in your room.
$$$$	C$300 (US$255) or above	At this price, you should want for nothing in terms of your stay. Expect a great view, an in-room hot tub, a CD player, thick terry-cloth bathrobes, and even flowers. Highly deferential, personalized service is included, as well.

Rack rates merely provide a rough guideline, so don't be afraid to investigate an interesting choice even if it seems pricey. Most of the time, a better rate is available, so make sure to ask.

Auberge Bonaparte
$$–$$$ **Vieux-Montréal**

Located in Vieux-Montréal, this gem of a hotel has 30 rooms on 5 floors decked out in early-19th-century antiques, while the bathrooms are modern and shaped out of marble slabs. Hardwood floors, exposed brick walls, large windows, and views of the Basilique Notre-Dame (ask for a room at the back) are some of the charming features that visitors can look forward to when they step inside this centuries-old building. The rooms here are neither fancy nor modern, like the bigger hotels. No, the brand power at work here is the simplicity and elegance of old-world refinement.

Vieux-Montréal Accommodations

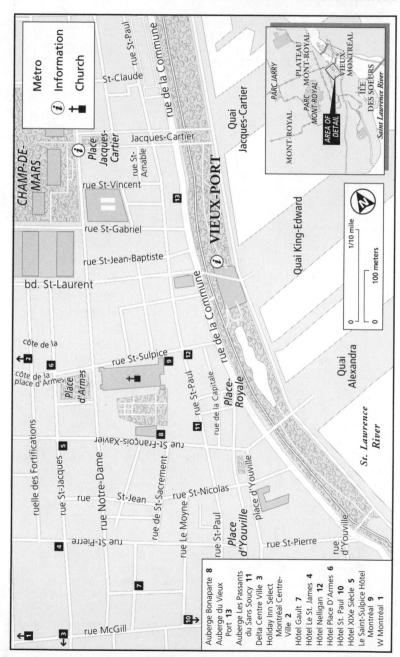

Métro *i* Information *✝■* Church

CHAMP-DE-MARS

Place Jacques-Cartier

rue St-Paul
St-Claude
rue de la Commune
Jacques-Cartier
rue St-Amable
rue St-Vincent
rue St-Gabriel
rue St-Jean-Baptiste
bd. St-Laurent

VIEUX-PORT

Quai Jacques-Cartier
Quai King-Edward

côte de la
rue St-Sulpice
côte de la place d'Armes
Place d'Armes
rue St-Paul
rue de la Capitale
Place-Royale
rue de la Commune

Quai Alexandra

St. Lawrence River

ruelle des Fortifications
rue St-Jacques
rue St-François-Xavier
rue Notre-Dame
rue de St-Sacrement
St-Jean
rue St-Nicolas
rue Le Moyne
place d'Youville
Place d'Youville
rue St-Pierre
rue d'Youville
rue St-Pierre

rue McGill

PARC JARRY
PLATEAU MONT-ROYAL
PARC MONT-ROYAL
VIEUX-MONTRÉAL
ÎLE DES SŒURS
MONT-ROYAL
AREA OF DETAIL
Saint Lawrence River

1/10 mile
100 meters
0

Auberge Bonaparte **8**
Auberge du Vieux Port **13**
Auberge Les Passants du Sans Soucy **11**
Delta Centre Ville **3**
Holiday Inn Select Montréal Centre-Ville **2**
Hôtel Gault **7**
Hôtel Le St. James **4**
Hôtel Nelligan **12**
Hôtel Place D'Armes **6**
Hôtel St. Paul **10**
Hôtel XIXe Siècle **5**
Le Saint-Sulpice Hôtel Montréal **9**
W Montréal **1**

Downtown Montréal Accommodations

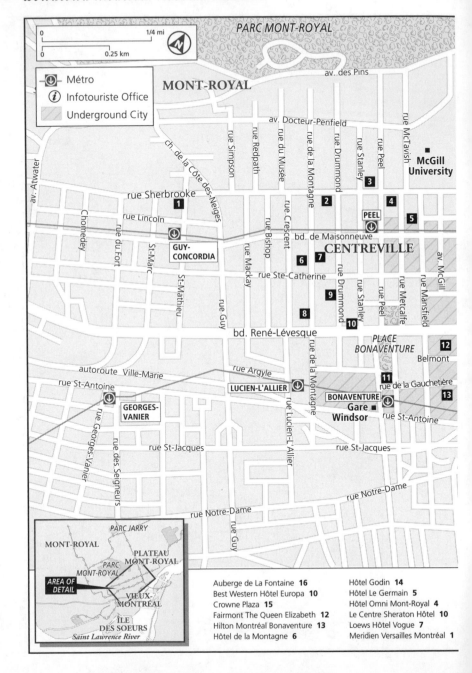

Auberge de La Fontaine **16**
Best Western Hôtel Europa **10**
Crowne Plaza **15**
Fairmont The Queen Elizabeth **12**
Hilton Montréal Bonaventure **13**
Hôtel de la Montagne **6**

Hôtel Godin **14**
Hôtel Le Germain **5**
Hôtel Omni Mont-Royal **4**
Le Centre Sheraton Hôtel **10**
Loews Hôtel Vogue **7**
Meridien Versailles Montréal **1**

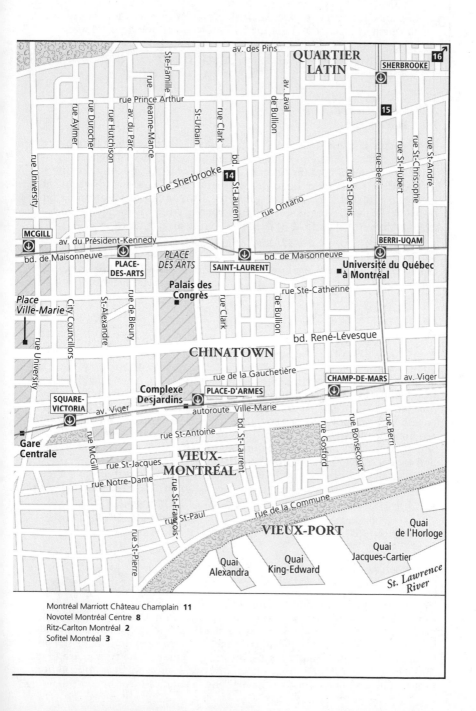

Montréal Marriott Château Champlain **11**
Novotel Montréal Centre **8**
Ritz-Carlton Montréal **2**
Sofitel Montréal **3**

For breakfast they serve delicious, fresh croissants in the main-floor dining room, which is also a popular spot for lunch and dinner among locals.

447 rue St-François-Xavier. ☎ *514-844-1448. Fax: 514-844-0272.* www.bonaparte. ca. *Parking: C$12 (US$10.25). Rack rates: C$140–C$210 (US$119–US$179). AE, DC, MC, V. Métro: Place-d'Armes.*

Auberge de La Fontaine
$$$ The Plateau

Staying at this inn on Montréal's third-largest park lets you be a temporary resident of the uber-trendy Plateau neighborhood. Two attached, renovated town houses contain 21 rooms. An elaborate and healthy continental breakfast is served in the lobby, which has large windows for gazing at lovely La Fontaine Park, across the street. Two suites with hot tubs that overlook the park are extremely popular among guests. Stroll along nearby avenue Mont-Royal and rue St-Denis to your heart's content.

1301 rue Rachel Est. ☎ *800-597-0597 or 514-597-0166. Fax: 514-597-0496.* www. aubergedelafontaine.com. *Parking: Three free spaces behind the hotel and on the surrounding streets. Rack rates: C$193–C$253 (US$164–US$215). Rates include continental breakfast. AE, DC, DISC, MC, V. Métro: Sherbrooke, Mont-Royal.*

Auberge du Vieux Port
$$$ Vieux-Montréal

This 27-room hotel in a late-19th-century building in Vieux-Montréal was once a warehouse and general store. Consequently, the rooms have a decidedly period-loft feel: stone and brick walls; high ceilings with huge, wooden pillars and beams; hardwood floors; and wrought-iron beds. The rate includes a breakfast and evening cocktail, the latter allowing hotel guests a rare opportunity to socialize. The streets surrounding the hotel are continually streaming with daytime tourists or nighttime revelers, which can be noisy for light sleepers. Many of the rooms look out over the St. Lawrence River and Old Port area. If yours doesn't, the rooftop terrace provides an eye-popping panorama. The pricey in-house restaurant serves market cuisine featuring *terroir* ingredients and an extensive wine list.

97 rue de la Commune Ouest. ☎ *888-660-7678 or 514-876-0081. Fax: 514-876-8923.* www.aubergeduvieuxport.com. *Parking: C$19 (US$16.25). Rack rates: C$200–C$290 (US$170–US$247). AE, DC, DISC, MC, V. Métro: Champ-de-Mars.*

Auberge Les Passants du Sans Soucy
$$ Vieux-Montréal

An extremely personable and engaging staff, wonderful breakfasts, and a unique setting will make your stay at this small inn a memorable part of your visit to Montréal. Book early, particularly during high season. Just nine rooms makes landing one on short notice nearly impossible. The would-be lobby is actually a street-front art gallery. The rooms are in a 19th-century warehouse building, so they're somewhat raw and rustic: stone walls and bare wooden beams. The fireplaces have been updated from logs to gas-burning hearths. The breakfasts feature fluffy omelets, French toast, croissants, and other baked goods. Copious quantities of fresh fruit and a variety of juices accompany these morning feasts.

171 rue St-Paul Ouest. ☎ *514-842-2634. Fax: 514-842-2912.* www.lesanssoucy. com. *Parking: C$12.75 (US$10.75). Rack rates: C$155–C$195 (US$132–US$166). AE, DC, MC, V. Métro: Champ-de-Mars.*

Best Western Hotel Europa
$$ Downtown

Although the lobby resembles the far-off land of Atlantis, the Europa provides the familiar comforts of the Best Western hotel brand. Located just south of rue Ste-Catherine, the Europa has 180 rooms, on 6 floors. Each room contains a king-size, queen-size, or two double beds; contemporary, European wood furnishings finish the room. The white bathrooms have no frills but seem particularly clean. You find plenty of English-language service in this part of the city.

1240 rue Drummond. ☎ *800-361-3000 or 514-866-6492. Fax: 514-908-2879.* www. europahotelmtl.com. *Parking: C$15 (US$12.75). Rack rates: C$139–C$159 (US$118–US$135). AE, MC, DC, V. Métro: Peel.*

Crowne Plaza
$$–$$$ The Plateau

Well located near the Plateau, Quartier Latin, and the Gay Village, this 24-story converted apartment building has spacious rooms and excellent views and is a good foothold for exploring the trendy neighborhoods east of boulevard St-Laurent. It is also adjacent to the Sherbrooke Métro station. Painted vines climb along the low archways of the marble-floored lobby. Stark landscape murals, plants, and flower arrangements give it a winter garden feel. The rooms are quite large and include a sitting area and a large desk but come with a standard-size bathroom.

505 rue Sherbrooke Est. ☎ *800-477-3365 or 514-842-8581. Fax: 514-842-8910.* www. cpmontreal.com. *Parking: C$19 (US$16.25). Rack rates: C$160–C$210 (US$136–US$179). AE, DC, DISC, MC, V. Métro: Sherbrooke.*

Delta Centre-Ville
$$–$$$ Downtown

This 28-story glass tower is part of a Canadian chain of corporate hotels and is of no relation to the airline. Its spacious rooms offer great skyline and river views and all the amenities that today's weary business travelers demand. When it opened in 1977, this hotel was state-of-the-art. Today, the Delta still has the city's only revolving restaurant on its top floor, amusingly named, *Tour de Ville.*

777 rue Université. ☎ *800-268-1133 or 514-879-1370. Fax: 514-879-1761.* www.delta hotels.com. *Parking: C$18 (US$15.25). Rack rates: C$189–C$239 (US$161–US$203). AE, DC, DISC, MC, V. Métro: Square-Victoria, Bonaventure.*

Fairmont The Queen Elizabeth
$$$–$$$$ **Downtown**

Built atop the Gare Centrale, the Queen E is the grande dame of Montréal's hotels. It's also where John and Yoko did their nude rendition of "Give Peace a Chance" in 1969, while they were on their honeymoon. Now a Fairmont property, the Queen was cited on *Condé Nast Traveler*'s 2002 Gold List. The hotel's Beaver Club restaurant is one of the best places for fine Continental cuisine in Montréal. You'll find several grades of accommodation, but even the so-called moderate rooms are pretty lavish. The downtown location is convenient, but there's lots of traffic.

900 bd. René-Levesque Ouest. ☎ *800-441-1212 or 514-861-3511. Fax: 514-954-2256.* www.fairmont.com. *Parking: Valet C$24 (US$20.50). Rack rates: C$280–C$378 (US$238–US$321). AE, DC, DISC, MC, V. Métro: Bonaventure.*

Hilton Montréal Bonaventure
$$$ **Downtown**

A serene penthouse perched above Place Bonaventure — 17 floors up — this two-story Hilton comprises a perimeter of modular, concrete-walled rooms that surround an immense, landscaped parkland inspired by the Canadian wilderness. The emphasis here is on quiet. All the hotel's services are in a central hub, away from the rooms, which are spacious and come with bathrooms finished in marble. The hotel makes children feel at home by giving them a welcoming gift and stocking the concierge desk with games to loan.

900 rue de la Gauchetière Ouest. ☎ *800-267-2575 or 514-878-2332. Fax: 514-878-1442.* www.hilton.com. *Parking: C$17 (US$14.50) or valet C$24 (US$20.50). Rack rates: C$200–C$300 (US$170–US$255). AE, DC, DISC, MC, V. Métro: Bonaventure.*

Holiday Inn Select Montréal Centre-Ville
$$ **Downtown**

From the Chinese pagoda-like exterior to the central atrium lobby, feng shui principles influence the design of this 235-room hotel. For example, the hotel has no fourth floor because the Chinese consider the number bad luck. Conveniently located in Chinatown, the hotel's décor is Asian throughout, from the framed Chinese prints to the emerald bedspreads. On the whole, it's refreshing and unusual. The décor and the large rooms make this a select-level Holiday Inn, a notch above the brand's usual level of hospitality.

99 av. Viger. ☎ *888-878-9888 or 514-878-9888. Fax: 514-878-6341.* www.yul-downtown.hiselect.com. *Parking: C$16 (US$13.50). Rack rates: C$169–C$200 (US$144–US$170). AE, DC, DISC, MC, V. Métro: Place-d'Armes.*

Hotel de la Montagne
$$–$$$ **Downtown**

Elegance, location, and particularly large rooms are what recommend this hotel, a former 20-story apartment building. With 135 rooms in all, each floor offers a choice of nine different units, all of which have modern bathrooms with separate tub and shower. All rooms have balconies facing east or west and provide great views of downtown. The back of the hotel fronts rue Crescent, a vibrant nightlife strip. If you're a particularly light sleeper, you may want to request a room on the other side, away from the action.

1430 rue de la Montagne. ☎ *800-361-6262 or 514-288-5656. Fax: 514-288-9558.* www. hoteldelamontagne.com. *Parking: Valet C$15 (US$12.75). Rack rates: C$185–C$225 (US$157–US$191). Rates include breakfast on weekends. AE, DC, DISC, MC, V. Métro: Peel.*

Hôtel Gault
$$$–$$$$ **Vieux-Montréal**

The immense rooms of this 30-room boutique hotel feel like loft apartments. The floors are of polished concrete, and the rooms are furnished with mobile, custom cabinetry made from white oak. Rooms include a wooden trellis at the door for increased privacy. Some rooms have secret terraces and ornate 19th-century wrought-iron detailing in the windows. Most impressive are the bathrooms, with large tubs and heated floors. The furniture in the lobby, with a bar, seating area, and reading room, are all reproductions of design classics, like Harry Bertoia chairs and Artemide lamps.

449 rue Ste-Hélène. ☎ *866-904-1616 or 514-904-1616. Fax: 514-904-1717.* www. hotelgault.com. *Parking: Valet C$20 (US$17). Rack rates: C$200–C$580 (US$170–US$493). Rates include breakfast. AE, DC, MC, V. Métro: Square-Victoria.*

Hôtel Godin
$$$–$$$$ **The Plateau**

At the foot of all the action on boulevard St-Laurent, just steps away from avenue St. Denis, and not far from the festivals, this 146-room boutique hotel is an ideal *pied-à-terre* for a fabulous weekend on the town. The calm atmosphere at the Godin seems just right for rejuvenating a hung-over rock star. The lighting is soft, almost moody, and the interior's textures are rich and its lines dramatic. The rooms are a thrilling example of how less can be more, with sparse, yet functional, custom furnishings and ledges. A luxurious, well appointed, white bed is the centerpiece. The imposing ceilings are of exposed concrete and set the tone for the rest of the color scheme: dark browns and charcoal grays. Despite the muted tones, the rooms are warm and inviting. The concrete, see, is a theme. The hotel occupies a heritage building, the first ever in North America to be made out of poured concrete.

10 rue Sherbrooke Ouest. ☎ *866-744-6346 or 514-843-6000. Fax: 514-843-6810.* www. hotelgodin.com. *Parking: Valet C$24 (US$20.50). Rack rates: C$275–C$375 (US$234–US$319). AE, DC, MC, V. Métro: Sherbrooke, Saint-Laurent.*

Hôtel Le Germain
$$$–$$$$ Downtown

According to the concierge, "Art Deco minimalism with a touch of Zen" is what awaits you at this 99-room boutique hotel. Outside, the color scheme is dark and earthy, but inside it's clean and contemporary. The smaller scale of this hotel operation allows the staff to be meticulous in its service and upkeep. Fresh flowers, a sumptuous seating area, and a wood-burning fireplace greet guests in the subdued lobby. Perhaps the most intriguing detail is that each bathroom has a glass wall. The architects envisioned it as a way of allowing natural light into the bathroom.

2050 rue Mansfield. ☎ *877-333-2050 or 514-849-2050. Fax: 514-849-1437.* www.hotel boutique.com. *Parking: Valet C$23 (US$19.50). Rack rates: C$210–C$400 (US$179–US$340). Rates include breakfast. AE, DC, MC, V. Métro: McGill.*

Hôtel Le St-James
$$$$ Vieux-Montréal

The last time the Rolling Stones were on tour in Montréal, they booked this entire hotel. The 61 units, many of them suites, are among the most deluxe and expensive accommodations in Montréal, with huge marble bathrooms and working fireplaces. The lobby and guest rooms are ornate and decorated with art and antiques. At night, the building's Second Empire facade lights up and looks spectacular. Its Vieux-Montréal location is away from much of the tourist melee and slightly closer to downtown than other hotels in this neighborhood.

355 rue St-James. ☎ *866-841-3111 or 514-841-3111. Fax: 514-841-1232.* www. hotellestjames.com. *Parking: Valet C$30 (US$25.50). Rack rates: C$400–C$475 (US$340–US$404). AE, DC, DISC, MC, V. Métro: Place-d'Armes.*

Hôtel Nelligan
$$$–$$$$ Vieux-Montréal

This 63-room boutique hotel was named after Québec poet Emile Nelligan, whose verses are sprinkled on its interior walls. Located in two historic buildings on rue St-Paul, one of Vieux-Montréal's main strips, Hôtel Nelligan is filled with galleries, cafes, and boutiques. Originally built in 1850, the premises have exposed stone and brick walls that create a warm and welcoming aura. Guest rooms feature dark woods and leather furnishings along with high ceilings, fireplaces, and hot tubs. Nightly wine-and-cheese gatherings welcome hotel guests in the lobby's central atrium, which is also a popular restaurant and bar.

106 rue St-Paul Ouest. ☎ *877-788-2040 or 514-788-2040. Fax: 514-788-2041.* www. hotelnelligan.com. *Parking: Valet C$17 (US$14.50). Rack rates: C$215–C$625 (US$183–US$531). Rates include breakfast and evening cocktail. AE, DC, DISC, MC, V. Métro: Place-d'Armes.*

Hotel Omni Mont-Royal
$$$–$$$$ Downtown

For a central downtown location, the Omni can't be beat. You can walk just about anywhere, and the Peel Métro station is close at hand. Be sure to ask for a room facing Mont-Royal for an excellent view. Plus, the rooftop pool is heated year-round. However, for the money, some guests feel that Montréal's Omni leaves something to be desired, with standard-size rooms that have a somewhat tired feeling, particularly in the '80s vintage bathrooms.

1050 rue Sherbrooke Ouest. ☎ *800-843-6664 or 514-284-1110. Fax: 514-845-3025.* www.omnihotels.com. *Parking: Valet C$26 (US$22). Rack rates: C$200–C$330 (US$170–US$281). AE, DC, DISC, MC, V. Métro: Peel.*

Hotel Place d'Armes
$$$–$$$$ Vieux-Montréal

This 44-room boutique hotel, located near the Basilique Notre-Dame and the Montréal Convention Center, has a rooftop terrace overlooking the many patina copper rooftops of Vieux-Montréal. The architects harnessed the beauty of the facade and carried it over into the design of the interior. The result is a welcoming environment that's cozy, contemporary, and comfortable. Brick walls and wood furnishings add to the warmth. Many of the black-and-white marble tiled bathrooms have a hot tub built for two.

701 côte de la place d'Armes. ☎ *888-450-1887 or 514-842-1887. Fax: 514-842-6469.* www.hotelplacedarmes.com. *Parking: Valet C$17 (US$14.50). Rack rates: C$275–C$375 (US$234–US$319). Rates include breakfast and an evening cocktail. AE, DC, DISC, MC, V. Métro: Place-d'Armes.*

Hôtel St-Paul
$$$ Vieux-Montréal

Despite an imposing exterior, the inside of this 120-room boutique hotel is ephemeral and ultra-modern, making a good case for the less-is-more argument. The lighting is almost theatrical — definitely moody — from the mysterious hearth hovering in alabaster in the lobby to the knee-level, colored floodlights in the halls. The dark, 100-year-old wooden floors of the rooms are warm and welcoming. The rooms are sparsely furnished — intentionally, of course. Along with other custom pieces, a television screen in each room displays the room-service menu, which changes on a daily basis.

355 rue McGill. ☎ *514-380-2222 or 866-380-2202. Fax: 514-380-2200.* www.hotelstpaul.com. *Parking: Valet C$18 (US$15.25). Rack rates: C$250–C$300 (US$213–US$255). Rates include breakfast. AE, DC, MC, V. Métro: Square-Victoria.*

Hotel XIXe Siècle
$$$ Vieux-Montréal

A Victorian reading room — resembling a set on *Masterpiece Theatre* — with extremely high ceilings, sets a tone of intimate grandeur in this

Vieux-Montréal boutique hotel in a renovated, 19th-century, neoclassical bank building. The 59 rooms are of the same scale and thoughtfully decorated in French Second Empire style. The large and luxurious bathrooms have black-and-white tiled floors, large marble countertops, and deep tubs. Rates include a lavish continental breakfast, featuring a selection of breads, jams, juices, yogurts, and so on, served in the main floor dining room.

262 rue St-Jacques Ouest. ☎ *877-553-0019 or 514-985-0019. Fax: 514-985-0059.* www. hotelxixsiecle.com. *Parking: Valet C$20 (US$17). Rack rates: C$230–C$290 (US$196–US$247). AE, DC, MC, V. Métro: Place-d'Armes.*

Le Centre Sheraton Hotel
$$$ **Downtown**

Montréal's Sheraton is in an excellent downtown location: across the street from the Bell Centre, a block from rue Ste-Catherine, and a quick amble from the nightlife and restaurants on rue Crescent. All the rooms have all the latest amenities, including the Sheraton's own Sweet Sleeper bed (also for sale), minibars with infrared sensors, and automated billing systems. Built in 1982, the marble bathrooms lack nothing — except hot tubs.

1201 bd. René-Levesque Ouest. ☎ *888-627-7102 or 514-878-2000. Fax: 514-878-3958.* www.sheraton.com/lecentre. *Parking: C$18 (US$15.25) or valet C$22 (US$18.75). Rack rates: C$235–C$305 (US$200–US$259). AE, DC, DISC, MC, V. Métro: Peel.*

Le Saint-Sulpice Hôtel Montréal
$$$–$$$$ **Vieux-Montréal**

Near Basilique Notre-Dame in the heart of Vieux-Montréal, this spacious and classy 108-suite hotel is splendid and lavish without being gaudy. Each condo-style suite, between 51 and 139 sq. m (550 and 1,500 sq. ft.), has a full kitchen, a living room with leather seating, and French doors that open to a courtyard or the streets of Vieux-Montréal. Many have their own fireplaces. The bathrooms are well lit, stocked with high-end toiletries, and have large showers. The staff is helpful, energetic, and well trained in the art of pampering.

414 rue St-Sulpice. ☎ *877-785-7423 or 514-288-1000. Fax: 514-288-0077.* www.le saintsulpice.com. *Parking: Valet C$24 (US$20.50). Rack rates: C$239–C$499 (US$203–US$424). Rates include American buffet breakfast. AE, DC, DISC, MC, V. Métro: Place-d'Armes.*

Loews Hotel Vogue
$$$–$$$$ **Downtown**

Loews, a luxury hotel brand, owns distinct properties in cities across North America. In Montréal, it's the 142-room Hotel Vogue, right downtown and a block away from rue Crescent. For some guests, the large marble bathrooms, featuring a two-person hot tub and a television, are absolutely to die for. However, you may be disappointed if you're expecting a room with a view. The black-and-white marble lobby is elegant, though.

1425 rue de la Montagne. ☎ *800-465-6654 or 514-285-5555. Fax: 514-849-8903.* www. loewshotels.com/vogue. *Parking: Valet C$30 (US$25.50). Rack rates: C$239–C$389 (US$203–US$331). AE, DC, DISC, MC, V. Métro: Peel.*

Meridien Versailles Montréal
$$–$$$ Downtown

A fancy name for a fancy hotel, the Versailles walks the walk with its understated elegance. Located in the western part of the downtown core, this 106-room hotel is at the end of a long stretch of antiques shops, art galleries, and designer boutiques on rue Sherbrooke. The lobby is small and cozy, just a front desk and a seating area. The rooms are large and tastefully finished in neutral tones and lush textures.

1808 rue Sherbrooke Ouest. ☎ *800-543-4300 or 514-933-8111. Fax: 514-933-7102.* www.versailleshotels.com. *Parking: Valet C$21 (US$17.75). Rack rates: C$189–C$230 (US$161–US$196). AE, DC, DISC, MC, V. Métro: Guy-Concordia.*

Montréal Marriott Château Champlain
$$$ Downtown

This 36-floor high-rise, halfway down the hill between downtown and Vieux-Montréal, offers standard-size rooms, but with all the amenities and services of a first-class hotel. The north-facing view is the best, with a close-up of the other buildings in the downtown core. Inspired by glorious Windsor Station next door, the Moorish-style, semicircular, floor-to-ceiling windows are particularly remarkable. Otherwise, the look and level of comfort are what you expect from a Marriott property.

1 place du Canada. ☎ *800-200-5909 or 514-878-9000. Fax: 514-878-6761.* www. mariotthotels.com/yulcc. *Parking: C$16 (US$13.50). Rack rates: C$260–C$300 (US$221–US$255). Rates include breakfast on weekends. AE, DC, DISC, MC, V. Métro: Bonaventure.*

Novotel Montréal Centre
$$ Downtown

You detect subtle differences in this hotel's approach to hospitality from the minute you enter the lobby until you depart. For example, rather than a long front counter, guests check in at individual islands. The service is considerate but expedient. The rooms have a modern feel with clean lines, warm tones, and accents of primary colors. It is just steps away from shopping on rue Ste-Catherine and the restaurants and bars of rue Crescent.

1180 rue de la Montagne. ☎ *800-668-6835 or 514-861-6000. Fax: 514-861-2295.* www. novotel.com. *Parking: C$13.50 (US$11.50). Rack rates: C$159–C$185 (US$135–US$157). AE, DC, DISC, MC, V. Métro: Lucien-L'Allier or Peel.*

Ritz-Carlton Montréal
$$$–$$$$ Downtown

Opened in 1912 and recently refurbished, Montréal's Ritz-Carlton, the only Ritz in Canada, remains a bastion of elegance — the crown jewel of downtown's Golden Square Mile that's filled with art galleries, swank boutiques, and antiques shops. The quality of service is high; the staff seems to remember each guest's name. Surprisingly, it is not the most expensive hotel in town — although it is definitely the grandest. High tea is served daily, and in the summer you can sit in the garden. The rooms and suites are spacious with large closets, chandeliers, and marble bathrooms. Some have working fireplaces. Liz Taylor married Richard Burton here, many moons, and perhaps even more husbands, ago.

1228 rue Sherbrooke Ouest. ☎ *800-363-0366 or 514-842-4212. Fax: 514-842-3383.* www.ritzcarlton.com/hotels/montreal. *Parking: Valet C$30 (US$25.50). Rack rates: C$200–C$325 (US$170–US$276). AE, DC, DISC, MC, V. Métro: Peel.*

Sofitel Montréal
$$$–$$$$ Downtown

This 258-room hotel offers its guests modern European elegance and refinement on a grand scale in a part of downtown known as the Golden Square Mile. Owned by a French hotel group, the Sofitel is a well-known brand throughout Europe. The hotel is allegedly designed on the principals of the *art de vivre* — something like a French version of feng shui. Despite its minimalist and understated décor, the luminous lobby's 18-foot ceilings make it an imposing space. The floor-to-ceiling windows in the rooms are only half as high and offer spectacular views of the downtown core. The rooms, with soft tones of taupe and rust, have original artwork on the walls and teak furniture. Large bathrooms of ocher marble and black granite countertops feature a glass-walled shower and a deep tub.

1155 rue Sherbrooke Ouest. ☎ *877-285-9001 or 514-285-9000. Fax: 514-289-1155.* www.sofitel.com. *Parking: Valet C$26 (US$22). Rack rates: C$285–C$345 (US$242–US$293). AE, DC, DISC, MC, V. Métro: Peel.*

W Montréal
$$$ Vieux-Montréal

After much anticipation, in November 2004 the W finally opened in the converted Bank of Canada Building on Victoria Square on the western fringe of Vieux-Montréal. Overnight, the building went from a drab financial institution to an institution of cool. A W, to some extent, sanctifies a city as being a world capital of global culture. You have to want the W experience, because it is somewhat over the top by regular hotel standards — from the gargantuan front doors to no less than three 12-foot waterfalls in the lobby area. You never escape the feeling of being in a nightclub, be it the futuristic lounge areas, house music in the elevators with green lighting, or the actual throb of bass from the wildly popular bar below. Ask for a park-facing, upper-floor room for the most peace and quiet. There's so much eye candy and mood lighting here that it's hard to imagine ever shutting your eyes. The rooms are predominantly in black and white and have electric blue accents throughout, from the glowing night tables to a sheet of blue-tinted glass, which is all that separates the bathroom and shower from the rest.

901 Victoria Square. ☎ *514-395-3100. Fax: 514-395-3150.* www.whotels.com. *Parking: Valet C$30 (US$25.50). Rack rates: C$210–C$279 (US$179–US$237). AE, DC, DISC, MC, V. Métro: Square-Victoria.*

Chapter 10

Dining and Snacking in Montréal

· ·

In This Chapter
▶ Understanding the ins and outs of dining in Montréal
▶ Finding Montréal's top dining spots
▶ Locating the best snacks and light meals

· ·

*Y*our options are staggering when dining in Montréal, one of the world's great restaurant cities and a food-lover's paradise. Montréalers eat out often, so the city is brimming with contenders hoping to be the next "it" restaurant with the "in" crowd. But don't be intimidated. Eating in Montréal doesn't have to be an ordeal. Many restaurants offer tasty and diverse options at a good price, and the city has an endless variety of ethnic eats. In fact, Montréalers looking to score a quick bite are likely to choose a *shish-taouk* (Lebanese souvlaki), a *samosa* (meat or veggie Indian pastry), or sushi over a burger and fries. Don't fret: You can find burgers and fries, too.

In this chapter, I attempt to simplify your choices by offering a representative selection of Montréal's best places to eat, including fine dining, trendy spots, and some neighborhood gems. After that, I tell you where to find the best picnic food, coffee, BYOB restaurants, and more.

Getting the Dish on the Local Scene

Montréal's real specialty, of course, is French food. Although the better French restaurants tend to be a little on the expensive side, I think they're worth every penny. If you leave Montréal without eating at least one great French meal, you'll miss out on one of the best things about the city.

Your terroir is my local ingredient
Many of Montréal's best restaurants offer some variation of French or contemporary continental cuisine. What's particularly new and exciting is the trend toward *terroir,* the French word describing high-quality,

locally produced, seasonal ingredients. (Actually, the trend started in France about ten years ago.) Menus of finer restaurants are cluttered with names of specialty ingredients from Québec's bountiful rural regions. Thankfully, most of the best kitchens go beyond obvious Canadian staples like salmon and maple syrup and some offer items you've probably never heard of before.

The brunch bunch

Does anyone in Montréal have the makings of a sensible breakfast in their fridge anymore? Not if you judge by the action in the Plateau neighborhood. On weekends, Montréalers flock here looking for somewhere to land a late-morning or midday brunch. Lines are common at the better places, and new spots specializing in all-day breakfasts are popping up at an amazing rate. Brunch patrons are a mixed bag, a potentially volatile combination of chipper morning people and groups of extremely hung-over friends. Everyone's happy, though, as waiters arrive with elaborate breakfasts on oversized plates accompanied by fresh juice and hot coffee. See "The big breakfast bonanza" section later in this chapter for locations.

Tasty tapas for fast friends

Tapas refers to the small plates Spaniards use to cover the carafes of wine so that flies don't get into the drink. Bars there serve them topped with bite-sized appetizers to accompany the alcohol, rounding out the experience some and allowing patrons to linger longer. They're ideal for sharing between busy friends with competing schedules, who can just manage to meet for drinks. They provide sustenance without having to sit down for a formal meal. In Spain, it's a specific culinary tradition with dishes like garlic shrimp, chorizo and dates, seared scallops, frittata, and ham Serrano. Several places in Montréal carry on in this vein, while other *tapas* joints cast a wider net, offering starters from around the globe. So the term has been diluted some. Basically, if you see a *tapas* menu, it means there's food available to go with your drinks and you can expect, hopefully, something above and beyond the traditional pub grub of nachos, chicken wings, pies, and so on.

Super-fun supper clubs

This recent restaurant category blurs the line between dinner, party, and celebrity. You sit down at a table for dinner and when you get up the restaurant has transformed into a full-on nightclub, with a picky door man and an expensive cover — which helps keep the riff-raff out. When the second part of the night has begun, the only way to secure a table is to buy a bottle of liquor. Then, out comes a tray with cranberry and orange juice as mixers, a bucket of ice and a stack of glasses. You get to play Mr. Magnanimity and host your own little party making drinks as strong as you'd like and giving them to whomever you'd like. Much mingling ensues. You don't have to buy a bottle to go to these raucous dens, but if you don't, you have to line up at the busy bars. The food portion of the evening usually features contemporary and daring dishes served by leggy waitresses culled from local modeling agencies.

Trimming the Fat from Your Budget

Eating is not particularly expensive in Montréal, especially when you consider how good the food generally is. Still, you can find a few ways to cut corners on your food budget without sacrificing too much:

- ✔ **Pack a picnic.** This obviously isn't an option in mid-winter, but during the summer months, it makes sense. With plenty of parks across the city where you can find a shady corner to have a light meal, even if you splurge on some fancy cheese or pâté, you'll still save.

- ✔ **Enjoy a French breakfast.** An economical breakfast, which is typically French and easy enough to reconstruct in Montréal, is a croissant or two and a bowl of café au lait. Jam and dipping are optional. See my picks for the best croissants in the "Coffee and pastries" section later in this chapter.

- ✔ **Eat your big meal at lunch.** Lunch menus are considerably cheaper than their equivalent at dinner. Check the lunch *table d'hôte*, a fixed menu including a starter and dessert, which is often a very good deal.

- ✔ **Check your memberships.** You may be eligible for discounts of 10 to 15 percent off your restaurant bill if you're a member of clubs like AAA. Always ask.

- ✔ **Eat in your own kitchen.** If your hotel room has a kitchenette, you can store some milk, bread, and a few staples. Eat in for breakfast, pack a picnic lunch, and save your dining dollars for the evening.

- ✔ **Bring your own wine.** Montréal has many BYOB restaurants. Taste-wise, you may have difficulty deciding on a wine when you have yet to look at the menu. But budget-wise, you'll come out ahead.

Homing In on Dining Etiquette

Here are a few do's and don'ts for dining out:

- ✔ **Dressing:** In Montréal, people look together when they go out to eat, but they don't really dress up. For both men and women, a nice pair of pants or even jeans (*nice* jeans) and a decent top make you feel comfortable almost anywhere.

- ✔ **Deciphering the menu:** Don't worry about language barriers between you and your plate. In most restaurants, the menu is available in English. When it's not, waiters are used to translating. Just take note of one common trap to spare you from some confusion: an *entrée* in French actually means a starter. A main course, therefore, is not an entree but a *plat principal*.

✓ **Dining hours:** Montréalers typically eat later than other North Americans. Many restaurants don't fill up until 10 p.m., especially on weekends. That's good news if you're an early eater and want a table at a popular restaurant: You can almost always find something available around 6:30 p.m. or so. The restaurant may be dead, but the food will taste the same as it does at 10 p.m.

✓ **Cigarettes:** Smoking in restaurants and bars became illegal in Québec, as of May 31, 2006. Now people craving a cigarette have to go outside.

✓ **Cellphones:** As a matter of common courtesy, annoying ring tones, no matter how soft, should be off during dinner at a restaurant. If you absolutely need to be reached, put your phone on vibrate. When the time comes, excuse yourself from the table and scout out an appropriate location to have your conversation. Outside with the smokers is a safe bet. Otherwise, afford yourself the time to enjoy the food and company — uninterrupted.

✓ **Reservations:** Reservations guarantee you a table at a particular time. If your schedule's tight or you're dead set on a meal at a certain spot, by all means, call in advance so they'll have a table waiting for you. Reserving is also a good practice when it's a large group, a special occasion, or on Thursday through Saturday, the busiest nights of the week. However, except for in the poshest of places, you usually don't need to reserve in advance to get a table. So, just walk in. Actually, this is an excellent tactic for getting a table at a restaurant where you couldn't get a reservation over the phone. If you're no more than two people, you can usually snag something by just showing up. If you do try this, have a Plan B in case things don't work out.

✓ **Tipping:** The standard is 15 percent, and you can give more or less depending on your appreciation of the service. A good way to come up with this amount is to add up the two sales taxes (the TVQ and TPS). They also equal 15 percent of what you ordered.

Montréal's Best Restaurants from A to Z

To simplify your choices, I give you two ways to evaluate how expensive each place is. The first way is a dollar-sign rating. This represents the price of one complete meal (appetizer, main course, and dessert) including tip; the dollar signs correspond with the price ranges in Table 10-1.

Downtown and Vieux-Montréal Dining and Snacking

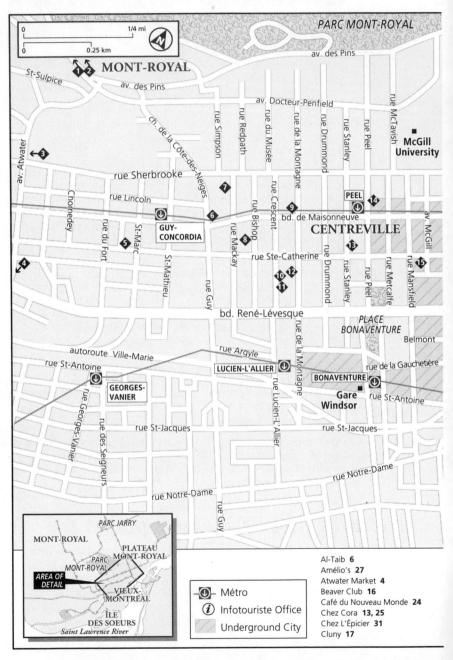

Al-Taib **6**
Amélio's **27**
Atwater Market **4**
Beaver Club **16**
Café du Nouveau Monde **24**
Chez Cora **13, 25**
Chez L'Épicier **31**
Cluny **17**

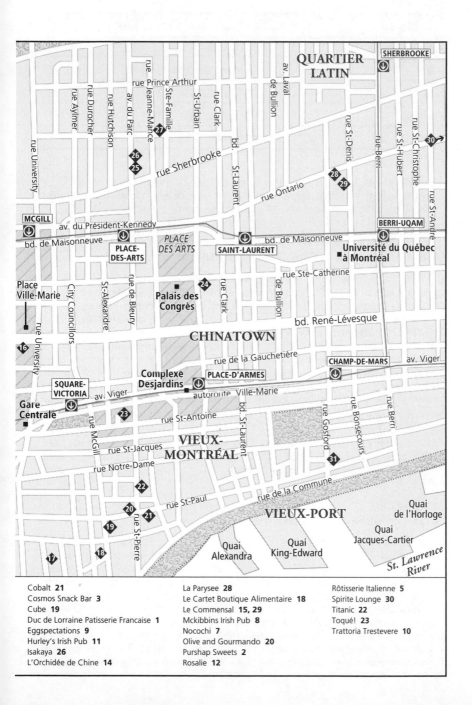

Cobalt **21**
Cosmos Snack Bar **3**
Cube **19**
Duc de Lorraine Patisserie Francaise **1**
Eggspectations **9**
Hurley's Irish Pub **11**
Isakaya **26**
L'Orchidée de Chine **14**

La Parysee **28**
Le Cartet Boutique Alimentaire **18**
Le Commensal **15, 29**
Mckibbins Irish Pub **8**
Nocochi **7**
Olive and Gourmando **20**
Purshap Sweets **2**
Rosalie **12**

Rôtisserie Italienne **5**
Spirite Lounge **30**
Titanic **22**
Toqué! **23**
Trattoria Trestevere **10**

Table 10-1	Key to Restaurant Dollar Signs
Dollar Sign(s)	*Price Range*
$	Less than C$20 (US$17)
$$	C$20–C$39 (US$17–US$33)
$$$	C$40–C$59 (US$34–US$50)
$$$$	C$60 (US$51) or above

In my reviews, I also include the price range of a main course, from lowest to highest. That price does not include drinks, taxes, or tip. It just gives you an idea of what the prices on the menu will actually be.

Au Pied de Cochon
$$$–$$$$ Plateau   FRENCH CONTEMPORARY

In 2002, *En Route,* Air Canada's in-flight magazine, named Au Pied de Cochon one of the ten best new restaurants in Canada. Chef-owner Martin Picard is the man behind the inspired and upscale French cooking. But a word to the wise: Delicate and decorative nouvelle cuisine this is not. Instead, the kitchen's forte is hearty, almost peasantlike comfort food, prepared with the finest ingredients and the greatest of care. Come hungry. As the name suggests, the restaurant specializes in pork and even serves pigs' feet. You also find a choice of excellent venison, lamb, and duck plates. Foie gras (goose liver) is a bit of a fetish item on the menu, appearing in several new and unusual places, like in a foie gras burger and foie gras *poutine.* (See the "Eating like a local" section, later in this chapter, for more info about this local delicacy.) The restaurant is nonsmoking.

536 av. Duluth Est (near rue St-Hubert). ☎ *514-281-1114. Reservations recommended. Main course: C$13–C$45 (US$11–US$38.25). AE, MC, V. Open: Dinner Tues–Sun. Wheelchair accessible. Métro: Sherbrooke.*

Beaver Club
$$$$ Downtown   FRENCH

Don't be put off by the dated, old-money feel of the Fairmont The Queen Elizabeth's restaurant, which actually was an exclusive men's club dating back to the 18th century. Beaver Club, a restaurant since 1959, ranks among the top ten hotel restaurants in the world. Star chef Alain Pignard, hired to rework the menu in 1999, offers an absolutely delectable range of classic French dishes, many made with Canadian ingredients, including Québec veal, lobster, caviar, foie gras, and more. The French sommelier is a great fan of Canadian wines and will gladly find a way for you to taste as many as possible. Service is warm, congenial, and beyond reproach. Prices are surprisingly reasonable, considering the level of artistry you experience.

Plateau and Mile End Dining

Au Pied de
 Cochon **33**
Boucherie Jos &
 Basile **1**
Buona Notte **29**
Café Italia **2**
Café Olympico **9**
Cafe Santropol **18**
Casse-Croûte La
 Banquise **42**
Chez Clo **46**
Eggspectations **14**
Épicerie Latina **8**
Euro Deli **27**
Fairmont Bagels **15**
Fondumentale **37**
Golden Curry House
 Restaurant **16**
Il Piatto Della
 Nonna **17**
Jean Talon Market **3**
L'Avenue **41**
L'Express **32**
La Binerie
 Mont-Royal **39**
La Cabane **24**
La Colombe **34**
La Croissanterie **10**
La Veille Europe **26**
Le Continentale **36**
Le P'tit Plateau **38**
Le Reservoir **22**
Le Roi du Plateau **19**
Le Vaudeville **6**
Marché des
 Saveurs **4**
Moishe's Steak
 House **23**
Mount Royal
 Hot Dog **43**
Ouzeri **40**
PA Supermarché **13**
Patati Patata **21**
Philinos **12**
Piton de la
 Fournaise **35**
Pizzedélic **30, 44**
Pizzeria Napolitana **5**
Restaurant
 Lafleurs **31**
Rumi **11**
Schwartz's **25**
Shed Café **28**
St-Viateur Bagels **7**
Taquéria
 Mexicaine **22**
Yoyo's **45**

In Fairmont The Queen Elizabeth, 900 bd. René-Levesque Ouest. ☎ *514-861-3511.*
Reservations strongly recommended. Main course: C$39–C$42 (US$33–US$35.75).
AE, DC, MC, V. Open: Lunch Mon–Fri, dinner Tues–Sat. Wheelchair accessible.
Métro: Bonaventure.

Buona Notte
$$$–$$$$ **Plateau** **SUPPER CLUB**

This snazzy, contemporary Italian restaurant is a fixture on boulevard St-Laurent and a popular destination for A-list celebrities like Bono, Jim Carrey, and Jacques Villeneuve. Check out the wall of signed plates at the back of the restaurant for proof of their passing through. Buona Notte has been one of the city's trendiest spots practically since it opened in 1992, thanks at least in part to the exceptionally statuesque and leggy waitresses that saunter about the quasi-industrial space. But the place doesn't get by on good looks alone: The kitchen is meticulous about its cuisine, serving fresh takes on classic Italian ingredients. Along with delicate starters and fresh pasta dishes, the menu offers main courses of meats and fish. For three consecutive years, the restaurant's wine cellar, stocked exclusively with Italian wines, has won coveted awards from *Wine Spectator* magazine.

3518 bd. St-Laurent (north of rue Milton). ☎ *514-848-0644. Reservations recommended. Main course: C$16–C$48 (US$13.50–US$40.75). AE, DC, MC, V. Open: Lunch Mon–Sat, dinner daily. Métro: Saint-Laurent or Sherbrooke.*

Chez L'Épicier
$$$$ **Vieux-Montréal** **FRENCH CONTEMPORARY**

At first sight it's hard to figure out exactly what this establishment is. The first thing you see when you walk in are rows of jams and preserves on shelves. However, if the name — which means "grocery store" — suggests the everyday and banal, wait until you taste. Plates are inventive and fun, like the oh-so-French foie gras glazed with tandoori sauce or the dessert club sandwiches. Whimsical as it sounds, the food is top notch.

311 rue St-Paul Est (near rue St-Claude). ☎ *514-878-2232. Reservations recommended. Main course: C$21–C$33 (US$17.75–US$28). AE, DC, MC, V. Open: Lunch Mon–Fri, dinner daily. Métro: Champ-de-Mars.*

Café du Nouveau Monde
$$$ **Quartier Latin** **FRENCH BISTRO**

Mingle among Québec's cultural elite in a restaurant reminiscent of a Parisian *grand café*. It's attached to the province's premier French-language theater and the main-floor dining room bleeds into the lobby. There can be a crush of people at the bar before and after a show, so the traffic keeps things lively. Busy waiters bustle about attending to the clientele's various demands, yet stopping long enough to provide considerate advice about the menu. Upstairs is a more sedate and intimate dining room with a heavier menu. The same kitchen cooks for both, and the menus have several items in common; however, the downstairs one includes paninis, club sandwiches, and the like, whereas upstairs the selections tend toward braised meats and duck. Both have an excellent wine list with several selections by the glass. The eye-catching, undulating, green roof housing the downstairs cafe, on the corner of rues Ste-Catherine and St-Urbain, has large, floor-to-ceiling windows that open onto the street. During the warmer months, when the festival season is in full swing, it's an ideal perch for people-watching. Closed, the windows' yellow stain adds warmth to the interior.

84 rue Sainte-Catherine Ouest (Corner rue St-Urbain). ☎ *514-866-8669. Reservations recommended. Main course: C$11.50–C$20 (US$9.75–US$17). AE, MC, V. Open: Lunch and dinner daily. Métro: Place des Arts.*

Cube
$$$$ Vieux-Montréal   FRENCH CONTEMPORARY

In the mood for a truly slick dining experience? The minimalist décor and rich-artist clients that linger about the tables at this hotel restaurant in Vieux-Montréal make you feel as though you're eating among the gods of cool. Young as it feels, though, you have to be old enough to pay for it — this place is pricey. But like many fine-eating destinations in Montréal, it's worth it. Cube offers a (need I say?) minimalist menu of modernized French classics, items such as oysters, foie gras, and warm goat salad for appetizers followed by fish, seafood, venison, and veal main dishes. Try some endives cooked in grapefruit juice, sample some fine Québec cheeses on raisin bread and hazelnut toasts, or nibble on scallops dressed in a mousse of Jerusalem artichoke. Everything is imaginatively conceived, exquisitely prepared, and immaculately presented.

355 rue McGill (in the Hotel St-Paul). ☎ *514-876-2823. Reservations recommended. Main course: C$28–C$42 (US$23.75–US$35.75). AE, DC, MC, V. Open: Lunch Mon–Fri, dinner daily. Métro: Square-Victoria.*

Euro Deli
$ Plateau   ITALIAN AMERICAN

The campy approach of this cafeteria-style pizza and pasta spot attracts boulevard St-Laurent hipsters at all hours of the day. No one seems to mind the bright-red plastic trays, paper plates, and disposable cutlery, probably because the fresh pasta is so amazing. In terms of being seen on boulevard St-Laurent in the summer, there is nothing quite cooler than sipping an espresso on Euro Deli's marble stoop. Open later on weekends, there's often a mad rush of revelers chowing down late-night until it closes. During the day, it's perfect for a quick lunch. The pesto tortellini, the Caesar salad, and the plain cheese pizza are all good choices. Otherwise, you can select a type of pasta and sauce from a list or get a slice of pizza or *panzerotti* (pizza pockets) on display.

3619 bd. St-Laurent (north of rue Prince-Arthur). ☎ *514-843-7853. Reservations not accepted. Main course: C$5.75–C$10 (US$5–US$8.50). Cash only. Open: Mon–Wed 8 a.m. to midnight, Thurs 8 a.m.–1 a.m., Fri 8 a.m.–2 a.m., Sat 9 a.m.–2 a.m., Sun 9 a.m. to midnight. Métro: Saint-Laurent or Sherbrooke.*

Fondumentale
$$–$$$ **Plateau FONDUE**

What better way to kick back with a friend than by dunking morsels of bread, meat, or veggies into a pot of fondue? If you crave fondue and a fun time, this is where it's at, right in the thick of the action on stylish rue St-Denis. Fondumentale's laid-back, slightly rumpled atmosphere makes it a perfect place to let your hair down. Fondue is not fine dining, but Fondumentale's cheese, broth, and oil fondues have kept locals coming back for years. Make an evening of it.

4325 rue St-Denis. ☎ *514-499-1446. Reservations essential. Main course: C$16–C$27 (US$13.50–US$22.95). AE, MC, V. Open: Dinner daily. Métro: Mont-Royal.*

Golden Curry House Restaurant
$–$$ **Plateau INDIAN**

Locals call this place the Golden Closet, but that's exaggerating a little. It's actually a narrow hallway packed with tables. In spite of the severe space restrictions — one table is even squished behind the front door, where you would normally expect to see a plant — this place is almost always packed. I can't say with absolute certainty that this is the best Indian food you'll find in Montréal, but popular opinion ranks it highly; the locale is great, and the prices are very reasonable, so it's hard to knock. The menu is classic Indian fare: nan bread; samosas; beef, lamb, and chicken curry; tandoori chicken; agaloo peas; and more. Wash it down with a pint of Guinness. Waiters are polite and do their job well with, literally, very little breathing room, so don't complain if service is on the perfunctory side.

5210 bd. St-Laurent. ☎ *514-270-2561. Reservations recommended on weekends. Main course: C$6–C$15 (US$5–US$12.75). AE, DC, MC, V. Open: Lunch Mon–Sat, dinner daily. Métro: Laurier.*

Il Piatto Della Nonna
$$–$$$ **Mile End ITALIAN**

It sure is fun to find truly traditional Italian cooking in the Mile End, a neighborhood where most traditions are giving way to the yuppie tastes that are taking over the neighborhood. Il Piatto Della Nonna is a family-run establishment that offers fresh, homemade pasta and hearty dishes like grilled Italian sausage, chicken legs stuffed with cheese and bread crumbs, and veal shank. This is a good place to fill up if you're on a budget. The menu, which changes regularly, is a *table d'hôte* (appetizer, main course, dessert, and coffee) posted on a chalkboard. Service is warm and informal (the owner's little girl lends a hand to the wait staff every now and again). The coffee and biscotti are excellent.

5171 bd. St-Laurent. ☎ *514-843-6069. Reservations recommended on weekends. Table d'hôte: C$15–C$27 (US$12.75–US$23). MC, V. Open: Lunch Mon–Fri, dinner daily. Métro: Laurier.*

Isakaya
$$$ Downtown   JAPANESE (SUSHI)

First things first: Isakaya has the best sushi in town. That said, *isakaya* is the generic word for Japan's informal eateries, so, true to form, this restaurant features a wide variety of what amounts to Japanese pub-fare favorites. Of course, these popular Japanese dishes are much more delicate than their Western counterparts, and they're healthier, too. Start with an order of *edamame*, steamed and salted pods of baby soybeans, which go well with beer. *Gyoza* (browned dumplings of pork and cabbage) and *yakitori* (barbecued skewers of chicken) are also good starters. If you really want to wow your date with your sushi savoir faire, ask for a spot at the bar. Gently lean into the sushi chef and ask for, "a selection of what he thinks is best," some sashimi, some nigiri, and some maki rolls. A delightful parade of sushi will follow.

3469 av. du Parc (south of rue Milton). ☎ *514-845-8226. Reservations recommended. Main course: C$14–C$23 (US$12–US$19.50). AE, DC, MC, V. Open: Dinner daily. Wheelchair accessible. Métro: Place des Arts.*

La Croissanterie
$–$$$ Outremont   FRENCH

There's always a bit of action at La Croissanterie. People flow in and out as they please — for a late-morning coffee and croissant, a light midday meal, a late-night snack of French onion soup, or a glass of wine any time of the day. That's probably what makes it so charming — that, and the breezy, quiet, expansive outdoor terrace, which is a jewel in the hot summer months. If you're not feeling up to a full-force French feast, but you still have a hankering for something Gallic, not too pricey, and a place you can rest your hind quarters for a while without remorse, La Croissanterie is your destination. Soups and sandwiches are served all day long, and dishes like filet mignon, chicken breast, and fish are available in the evening.

5200 rue Hutchison. ☎ *514-278-6567. Reservations not accepted. Main course: C$4–C$16 (US$3.50–US$13.50). AE, MC, V. Open: Lunch and dinner daily. Métro: Laurier.*

Le Continentale
$$$–$$$$ Plateau   FRENCH CONTEMPORARY

This rue St-Denis restaurant is a long-time favorite among Montréalers in the know, because it's consistently good. The menu offers bistro classics, contemporary dishes with unique twists, and a good wine list. The kitchen excels at steak frites, duck confit, pasta carbonara, and seared tuna steak, served on a bed of exotic fruits. The chatty crowd creates a lively atmosphere, which becomes almost electric on a busy night, as everyone clamors over the colorful and attractively presented plates. The ever-changing nightly specials, such as salmon filet wrapped in nori and flash-fried in tempura batter, tend to get the most "oohs" and "aahs." The décor is based

on early-20th-century air-travel motifs, like black-and-white photos of pro-
peller planes.

4169 rue St-Denis (at rue Rachel). ☎ *514-845-6842. Reservations recommended.
Main course: C$14–C$27 (US$12–US$23). AE, DC, MC, V. Open: Dinner daily.
Wheelchair accessible. Métro: Mont-Royal.*

Le Roi du Plateau
$$ Plateau   PORTUGUESE GRILL

Le Roi du Plateau has a reputation for the best chicken, among the
Portuguese grills that dot the several blocks on either side of "The Main"
(boulevard St-Laurent) between avenue Duluth and rue Marianne. They'll
baste your half chicken with a spicy sauce that adds zest but no real heat.
The house specialty is grilled meat, all forms of it, braised over the embers
of a charcoal fire, from squid and sardines to steak and lamb. On a busy
evening, families and boisterous groups of friends who flock there create
a loud din over carafes of red wine. Snapshots adorn the wood-paneled
walls and ledges are adorned with trinkets and souvenirs from Portugal.

51 rue Rachel Ouest (at the corner of rue Clark). ☎ *514-844-8393. Reservations
required. Main course: C$9–C$25 (US$7.75–US$21.25). V. Open: Dinner daily, except
Sun. Métro: Sherbrooke or Mont-Royal.*

Le Vaudeville
$$–$$$ Mile End   FRENCH BISTRO

Looking for a good authentic French meal at a decent price? In Montréal,
it takes a Greek to deliver this perfect formula: George Paradisis, a cook-
entrepreneur who opened this place 15 years ago. Vaudeville is a super-
quaint bistro on the northern tip of the Plateau neighborhood. A
quasi-diner revamped with white cotton lampshades and walls speckled
with the work of local artists (for sale), you feel like you're hiding out in
some obscure town in France. On the small menu, there are hearty serv-
ings of variations on classics such as duck confit, warm goat cheese salad,
and steak frites.

361 rue Bernard Ouest. ☎ *514-495-8258. Reservations recommended. Main course:
C$12–C$24 (US$10.25–US$20.50). AE, MC, V. Open: Dinner Tues–Sat, brunch Sat–Sun.
Métro: Laurier.*

L'Express
$$–$$$$ Plateau   FRENCH BISTRO

You may have heard the term *brasserie* floating around to describe a category of French cuisine and wondered whether it's a food or a place. The
answer: It's both. L'Express, a Montréal landmark since 1979, is brasserie
in the purest form — or at least in the purest North American form. A
bustling restaurant-bar complete with black-and-white tiled floors and a
zinc bar, L'Express serves steak frites, duck confit, and other French comfort food with a jar of pickles and basket of baguettes on the table. The

white tablecloths and bow-tied waiters may trick you into thinking that formality is de rigueur here, but don't be fooled. Brasseries are high-quality but casual eating. Whether you want to linger over a leisurely meal or wolf down a swift lunch, the waiters will figure it out and cater to you accordingly. Just don't expect them to spend hours talking to you. They're busy!

3927 rue St-Denis. ☎ *514-845-5333. Reservations recommended. Main course: C$12–C$22 (US$10.25–US$18.75). AE, DC, MC, V. Open: Lunch and dinner daily. Wheelchair accessible. Métro: Sherbrooke.*

L'Orchidée de Chine
$$$–$$$$ Downtown   CHINESE

Located in central downtown, this four-floor restaurant with a pared-down décor may feel a bit cold at first, but the food will definitely warm you up. Don't come here looking for inexpensive, buffet-style Chinese food. L'Orchidée de Chine has been one of Montréal's most popular Chinese restaurants for years because of the sophistication and refinement of its fare. The uniform sea of soy sauce that plagues so much Chinese food is not to be seen here. Sauces are light and subtle. Don't miss the juicy five-flavored spare ribs and perfectly crispy fried spinach.

2017 rue Peel. ☎ *514-287-1878. Reservations essential. Main course: C$14–C$22 (US$12–US$18.75). AE, MC, V. Open: Lunch Mon–Fri, dinner Mon–Sat. Métro: Peel.*

Moishe's Steak House
$$$–$$$$ Plateau   STEAK

A revered restaurant that has been in business for 65 years, Moishe's is Montréal's steak mecca, hands-down. A recent face-lift has given the establishment a modern allure, but it is still very much a remnant of the days when "The Main" (boulevard St-Laurent) was the heart of Montréal's Jewish community. The Lighter brothers, who inherited this place from their father, consider the quest for quality meat a high art. Their steaks come exclusively from corn-fed beasts raised on a hand-picked ranch in Colorado, and the best cuts will melt in your mouth. Accompanying potatoes and vegetables are also top notch, and the walls are stocked with bottles of fine wine. Career waiters are knowledgeable and friendly, glad to entertain even the most obscure questions. Come with an appetite. English speakers feel very comfortable here.

3961 bd. St-Laurent. ☎ *514-845-3509. Reservations recommended. Main course: C$26–C$52 (US$22–US$44.25). AE, MC, V. Open: Lunch Mon–Fri, dinner daily. Métro: Sherbrooke.*

Ouzeri
$$ Plateau   CONTEMPORARY GREEK

Exposed brick walls and storeroom shelves stocked with bottles of wine and vats of olive oil give Ouzeri a warm, yet stripped-down feel with a designer edge. A bit of a scene for Montréal's work-hard, play-hard crowd, this is where urbanites in their late 20s and 30s stop in for a late dinner. It's a great place for Greek tapas, the restaurant's specialty. Service is friendly and expedient as the waiters rush about the main dinning room. Two other spaces, one upstairs, the other down, are more intimate and less noisy.

4690 rue St-Denis (at the corner of rue Gilford). ☎ 514-845-1336. Reservations recommended. Main course: C$9.50–C$16 (US$8–US$13.50). AE, MC, V. Open: Lunch and dinner daily. Wheelchair accessible. Métro: Laurier.

Patati Patata
$-$$ Plateau   DINER

Quirky is the word for this little fish andchips and burger joint on boulevard St-Laurent. The 20-something owners converted a minuscule old 12-chair diner into a miniscule new 12-chair diner. They whip up tasty, fresh fast food behind the counter while you watch — breading the fish, tossing the salad, and frying the burgers before your eyes. The entertainment value is great, but the food is even better. Don't scrimp on the skinny fries, even if you're on a diet. Homemade brownies also hit the spot.

4177 bd. St-Laurent (at corner of rue Rachel). ☎ 514-844-0216. Reservations not accepted. Main course: C$1.50–C$6 (US$1.25–US$5). Cash only. Open: Breakfast, lunch, and dinner daily. Métro: Mont-Royal or Sherbrooke.

Philinos
$$-$$$ Plateau   GREEK

Avenue du Parc, just north of Parc Mont-Royal, is Montréal's traditional Greek neighborhood, and oodles of souvlaki joints and fish restaurants line this busy avenue and the smaller side streets nearby. Philinos stands out for its solid, satisfying food and inviting atmosphere. It's usually full of Greek customers, which is always a good sign. You can order from a selection of tapas-style appetizers, like *szatiki,* or go for generous plates of kebabs. Don't miss the divine dessert of thick yogurt drizzled with honey.

4806 av. du Parc. ☎ 514-271-9099. Reservations recommended. Main course: C$15–C$40 (US$12.75–US$34). AE, DC, MC, V. Open: Lunch and dinner daily. Wheelchair accessible. Métro: Laurier.

Rosalie
$$$$ Downtown   SUPPER CLUB

During the summer, the long narrow terrace with immense, black, canvas parasols in the front is a major draw for the suits from downtown office buildings. They arrive for after-work drinks, and then linger for a big-ticket dinner. It's usually money well spent as Dave McMillan, the restaurant's executive chef, devises contemporary yet refined dishes. Appetizers include a foie gras (goose liver) sundae and salmon tartare with mixed greens. The main courses feature a variety of meats, such as pork, fish, duck, sweetbreads, and rabbit, and come in robust and flavorful sauces. The restaurant's contemporary yet serene interior can best be summed up as retro-Scandinavian, with lots of wood, chrome, and black leather seats and banquettes. The pleasant sommelier can help you choose from the extensive wine list.

1232 rue de la Montagne (south of rue Ste-Catherine). ☎ 514-392-1970. Reservations recommended. Main course: C$20–C$30 (US$17–US$25.50). AE, DC, MC, V. Open: Lunch Mon–Fri, dinner daily. Wheelchair accessible. Métro: Peel.

Rôtisserie Italienne
$–$$ Downtown   ITALIAN

Don't let the counter service, bright lighting, plastified check tablecloths, and lackluster dinning room faze you — the pasta dishes are irreproachable. Excellent Italian fare at a great value is the trade-off for the odd setting. There's a disproportionate amount of oblivious, lovey-dovey couples doing their own version of the scene from Disney's *The Lady And The Tramp*. Perhaps the fresh pasta and house wine here have a quickening effect on the evening. A wall of signed hockey sticks is testament that it's also a mecca of sorts for out-of-town hockey players. They flock to this eatery looking to load up on carbs and protein before the big game. The pizzas have thin, crunchy crusts and come in individual-sized pans. The convivial cooks dressed in white behind the counter beckon you to approach. The menu is at the front, above the refrigerated display. Don't forget to consider the daily special, scrawled on a whiteboard, it's often what everyone's eating. They'll call your name when your order's ready. In the meantime find a seat or engage the willing staff in pleasantries.

1933 rue Ste-Catherine Ouest (corner of rue Towers). ☎ 514-935-4436. Reservations not accepted. Main course: C$6–C$13.25 (US$5–US$11.25). Cash only. Open: Lunch and dinner Mon–Fri. Métro: Guy Concordia.

Rumi
$$–$$$ Outremont   MIDDLE EASTERN

For atmosphere, this Middle Eastern cafe–style restaurant is hard to beat. The interior is warm, spacious, and comfortable, decorated with oriental trimmings. The sidewalk terrace, spanning half a block on the corner of two quiet streets, is one of the most relaxing in the city. A haven of peace, Rumi is a good place to put an end to a busy day. Tapas-style portions of Middle Eastern standards include hummus and marinated red peppers, as well as more substantial plates like veal kebabs and seasonal fish. In the summer, arrive before 7 p.m. if you want a spot on the terrace, or you can call to reserve a table.

5198 rue Hutchinson (at the corner of rue Fairmont). ☎ 514-490-1999. Reservations recommend. Main course: C$12–C$24 (US$10.25–US$20.50). AE, DC, MC, V. Open: Lunch and dinner Tues–Sun. Métro: Laurier.

Schwartz's
$–$$ Plateau   SMOKED MEAT

This cramped deli, staffed mainly by surly seniors, is a fixture on boulevard St-Laurent and positively the best place to sample Montréal's famous
smoked meat. While you'll find little else on the menu, order these juicy
slices of beef brisket, cured, smoked, spiced, then heaped on rye bread
and served with mustard. The sandwiches or plates come in lean, medium,
or fatty varieties. The medium-fatty is my favorite. French fries, pickles,
roasted red peppers, and coleslaw sides are available separately. Tradition
dictates a black cherry soda to wash it all down. Most days bring a long
line outside, but it's definitely worth the wait.

3895 bd. St-Laurent. ☎ *514-842-4813. Reservations not accepted. Main course:
C$8–C$18 (US$6.75–US$15.25). Cash only. Open: Lunch and dinner daily. Métro:
Sherbrooke.*

Taquéria Mexicaine
$ Plateau   MEXICAN

Taquéria Mex offers the usual selection of tacos, burritos, quesadillas, and
more — all in beef, chicken, and vegetarian versions, with a choice of
salad, rice, or chips. The ingredients are fresh. The salad is never wilted
and is always accompanied by perfectly ripe avocados. The fresh tomatoes even taste good year-round. We're not sure how they do it, actually,
but we've never been disappointed. Kids will find familiar fare here, like
tacos and tortilla chips. This place is hard to beat if you want a satisfying
meal for under C$10 (US$8.50) a head.

4306 bd. St-Laurent. ☎ *514-982-9462. Reservations not accepted. Main course:
C$4.25–C$12.25 (US$3.50–US$10.50). MC, V. Open: Lunch and dinner daily. Métro:
Mont-Royal or Sherbrooke.*

Toqué!
$$$$ Downtown   FRENCH CONTEMPORARY

If you're willing to lay down some big money for a serious gastronomic
experience, don't miss this high-end French restaurant, considered one of
the best in the province. Québec celebrity chef Normand Laprise uses as
many fresh local ingredients as possible to make dishes like veal, scallops,
red snapper, risotto, guinea hen, and delectable French desserts. The food
is wildly imaginative, but it's dished out in small portions. The atmosphere
is chic and intimate, and the same can be said about the crowd. Don't
worry about dressing up, but most of all, don't be intimidated by the
snobby-looking waiters. Many are chefs-in-training, along with decent
types who know a lot about their vocation. They magically lose their attitude if you ask a straightforward question. Reserve a week ahead to get a
table on the weekend and don't plan anything else for the evening.

900 place Jean-Paul Riopelle. ☎ *514-499-2084.* www.restaurant-toque.com.
*Reservations recommended. Main course: C$28–C$42 (US$23.75–US$35.75). AE, DC,
MC, V. Open: Lunch Tues–Fri, dinner Tues–Sat. Métro: Place-d'Armes.*

Use these handy Post-It® Flags to mark your favorite pages.

Trattoria Trestevere
$$–$$$ Downtown ITALIAN

This inconspicuous locale, on southern Crescent, below rue Ste-Catherine, serves some of the city's best Italian food. It has a strong base of regular clientele, happy to be back for another authentic meal. Middle-aged, career waiters welcome guests and make them feel at home with warm and knowing smiles. The service is discreet and reassuring — the wait staff feels like a band of Italian uncles you never had. The semi-basement has stucco walls and Roman arches, the whole scene is vaguely reminiscent of a wine cellar or grotto. If you've never felt strongly about gnocchi, a pasta dumpling made from potatoes, you can make up your mind after trying it here. It's mind-boggling. You can have it with any of the sauces on the menu. In fact, you can also mix and match the sauces with any of the fresh, homemade pastas. Ask your waiter what's best, if you can't make up your mind. The pastas are velvety and melt-in-your-mouth — al dente, not over cooked. However, pasta and sauces aren't the only thing on the menu. As you gaze over the other choices of old-world, Italian classics, rest assured that you'll get a true rendition of whatever you're craving.

1237 rue Crescent (south of rue Ste-Catherine). ☎ *514-866-3226. Reservations recommended. Main course: C$14–C$35 (US$12–US$30). AE, DC, MC, V. Open: Lunch and dinner daily, except Mon. Métro: Peel, Guy-Concordia, Lucien L'Allier.*

Dining and Snacking on the Go

In Montréal, fast food doesn't equal tasteless — not even close. If you don't want to go out for fine dining every night, don't despair. Montréal's food festival carries on in every corner of the city's dining experience, from pizza and picnicking to *poutine.*

Pizza and burgers

Almost everything you eat in Montréal has a distinct local twist, including these fast-food staples. Like the French, many Montréalers prefer pizzas with very thin crusts. If you want to try one, hit a **Pizzadélic,** with various locations around town: 1250 av. Mont-Royal Est (☎ **514-522-2286**) and 1641 rue St-Denis (☎ **514-499-1444**). An Italian butcher cum gourmet shop cum pizza parlor a block away from the Marché Jean Talon is one this town's best kept pizza secrets: **Boucherie Jos & Basile,** 6995 av. Casgrain (☎ **514-274-6358**).

If you like the thicker-crust variety of pizza, try **Pizzeria Napolitana,** 189 rue Dante (☎ **514-276-8226**), in Little Italy; or **Amélio's,** 201 rue Milton (☎ **514-845-8396**), right downtown. The tastiest delivery pizza in the city comes from **Tasty Food Pizza,** 6660 bd. Décarie (☎ **514-739-9333**), as its name suggests. An Arab bakery, **Al-Taib,** 2125 rue Guy (☎ **514-931-1999**), holds the title of best pizza in the west end of downtown. It's open 24 hours and broadcasts a live satellite feed of Al-Jazeera.

Montréal isn't a big burger town, but if you get a craving, a few places seem to have perfected the genre. Downtown, try **La Paryse,** 302 rue Ontario Est (☎ 514-842-2040). On boulevard St-Laurent, there's **Shed Café,** 3515 bd. St-Laurent (☎ 514-842-0220), and **La Cabane,** 3872 bd. St-Laurent (☎ 514-843-7283). **Hurley's Irish Pub,** 1225 rue Crescent (☎ 514-861-4111), has garnered quite a reputation for its fine burgers. Feel like bison? Try a bison burger at **Mckibbins Irish Pub,** 1426 rue Bishop (☎ 514-288-1580).

The best bagels

A war rages on over who bakes the best bagels: New York or Montréal. (I don't have to tell you whose side I'm on.) But even inside Montréal, there's a civil war of sorts between bagel lovers who love one of two major bagel bakeries in Montréal. Don't show your colors to locals until you know which side they're on.

St-Viateur Bagels, 102 rue St-Viateur Ouest (☎ 514-272-6548), is my favorite. Bagels come piping hot out of a wood-burning oven, drawing a faithful following from all corners of the city. From the fridges beside the counter, you can buy cream cheese, smoked salmon, and other toppings.

Fairmont Bagels, technically the Bagel Factory, 74 rue Fairmount Ouest (☎ 514-272-0667), offers several variations on its famous sesame-seed bagel. Here, you can try bagels with raisins and cinnamon or even olives and sun-dried tomatoes, plus a variety of toppings.

Sandwich, anyone?

Montréalers love good bread — in particular, long, thin, crusty baguettes, and that's good news for anyone looking for a sandwich. Whether you grab one on the run or settle into a cafe for a bite, this section gives you some options.

Le Cartet Boutique Alimentaire, 106 rue McGill (☎ 514-871-8887) is a mega-mall for your stomach, disguised as a hip gourmet shop and bustling lunch counter, the walls are chock-full of upmarket, gourmet grocery items, like spring water from Japan. It's a foodie's delight. The sandwiches are made fresh and go quickly with all the Vieux-Montréal office workers cramming in a quick bite. The kitchen also makes rather elaborate main courses. The choices are scrawled on a blackboard above the kitchen. There's always a pasta, a meat, a fish — but what they are changes on a regular basis.

Cluny, 257 rue Prince (☎ 514-866-1213), tucked away in an up-and-coming warehouse district adjacent to Vieux-Montréal, this daytime cafe shares its locale with an artists' cooperative in a former foundry. Sandwiches, antipasto, and a more substantial daily special are what the "in" crowd of new media professionals comes for.

Olive and Gourmando, 351 rue St-Paul Ouest (☎ 514-285-1000), has some of the best sandwiches in town. Choose from the sausages and cheese or more-exotic ingredients, like portobello mushrooms. The bread is always fresh.

Titanic, 445 rue St-Pierre (☎ 514-849-0894), in Vieux-Montréal, is also considered one of the city's best lunch spots. Sandwich-wise, it serves rather exotic combinations of ingredients on delicious crusty bread. Homemade soups, daily specials, and heaping antipasto plates are all delicious.

Au Pain Doré, one of Montréal's major bakery chains, has locations throughout the city. Each sells very respectable prewrapped sandwiches — classics like ham and cheese or smoked salmon. This is a good place to stop, if you need to grab something on the run. Popular downtown locations include 556 rue Ste-Catherine Est (☎ 514-282-2220) and 1415 rue Peel (☎ 514-843-3151). In the Plateau, head to 1145 av. Laurier Ouest (☎ 514-276-0947).

Ditto **Première Moisson,** which also has several outlets throughout the city. Some stores have cafes with many choices of sandwiches and salads and other market-inspired, ready-to-eat lunchables. One is in the promenade of the Gare Centrale, the downtown train station, at 895 rue de la Gauchetière Ouest (☎ 514-393-6540). Another is at 1490 rue Sherbrooke Ouest (☎ 514-931-6540), near the Montréal Museum of Fine Art.

The big breakfast bonanza

Montréalers are extremely fond of working off their morning blues (or hangover) over a plate of eggs and bacon. Join a citywide ritual and load up at one of the following renowned breakfast joints. You can have it fancy, surrounding yourself with stylish locals and fruit smoothies, or go in for classic, greasy-spoon formula.

Le Cartet (see the preceding section) and **Le Reservoir,** 9 rue Duluth Est (☎ 514-849-7779), deserve special mention here. These are the Johnnys-come-lately to the city's brunch scene yet they've upped the ante in terms of what to expect. Although the brunch places first distinguished themselves by serving copious quantities of fresh fruit — and have largely stuck to that formula — Reservoir and Cartet turned this weekend ritual into a gastronomic adventure of carefully matched flavors and breathtaking presentations. **Cobalt,** 312 rue St-Paul (☎ 514-842-2960), is another popular brunch destination that's made a recent splash. Here, live jazz accompanies your meal.

L'Avenue, 922 av. Mont-Royal Est (☎ 514-523-8780), located in the heart of the hip Plateau neighborhood, has been extremely popular for years. Trendy denizens line up for the breakfasts; to beat them, aim to arrive before 11 a.m.

Mont-Royal Hot Dog, 1001 av. Mont-Royal Est (☎ 514-523-3670), is one of the few remnants of this neighborhood's working-class past. Breakfasts are generous and cheap, the gum-smacking waitresses give you exactly what you want, and you don't have to listen to any jazz while you're eating.

Eggspectations, 98 av. Laurier Ouest (☎ 514-278-6411) and 1313 bd. de Maisonneuve Ouest (☎ 514-842-3447), as well as other locations around the city, is a chain that serves eggs any which way, all day long. It's on the fancier side of the greasy-spoon scale, and so are the prices.

Chez Cora, another chain of breakfast spots, has restaurants all over the city. For the basic variations on eggs, bacon, baked beans, and potatoes, you can't go wrong here. Downtown locations include 3465 av. du Parc (☎ 514-849-4932) and 1425 rue Stanley (☎ 514-286-6171).

Cosmos Snack Bar, 5843 rue Sherbrooke Ouest (☎ 514-486-3814), is a tiny, family-owned, Greek restaurant that serves only breakfast. Sit at the counter and listen to the family at work. It's My Big Fat Greek Breakfast: a kind of comic-tragedy set in a greasy spoon. Breakfast here gets you through a lumberjack's day.

Chez Clo, 3199 rue Ontario Est (☎ 514-522-5348), is a Montréal landmark. Authentic, Québec-style breakfast and lunch at absurdly low prices.

Picnicking and markets

The best place to picnic in Montréal, by far, is **Parc Mont-Royal** (see Chapter 11 for details). Prime spots are the slope in front of **Beaver Lake,** or the slope facing avenue du Parc. To pick up some bread, cheese, pâté, or cold cuts, visit nearby **PA Supermarché,** 5029 av. du Parc; **La Veille Europe,** 3855 bd. St-Laurent; or **Épicerie Latina,** 185 rue St-Viateur Ouest.

Montréal's two major outdoor markets are also great places to pick up some light fare and explore among the locals. Both are conveniently located next to Métro stops. To get to the **Atwater Market** in the west end of downtown, get off either the orange or green line at Lionel-Groulx station. To get to the **Jean Talon Market** in Little Italy, go to Jean Talon station, at the intersection of the blue and orange lines.

These are great places to taste locally grown Québec *terroir* products. Both markets begin carrying local produce by mid-June and are usually going strong well into October. At the Jean Talon Market, don't miss the **Marché des Saveurs,** 280 place du Marché-du-Nord, one of the best specialty food stores in the city, which carries Québec wines, cheese, maple syrup products, and more.

As an added bonus, municipal authorities remain convinced that drinking wine in a park with a meal poses no greater danger to public morality than drinking wine at a sidewalk restaurant. As long as you're eating a meal, drinking wine and beer in parks is legal.

Eating like a local

Like the French, Québeckers love fine cuisine. But in the dietary staples here — notably *steamies* (steamed hot dogs), *bines* (baked beans), and *poutine* (fries served with gravy and cheese curds) — Québeckers distinguish themselves as a totally separate gastronomic race. These regional favorites are true fuel. Loaded with fat and dripping with grease, this is the kind of food that sticks to your stomach and keeps you warm on winter nights, although, come to think of it, people eat it all year round.

Give local delicacies a try, ideally on a very empty stomach. The legendary **La Binerie Mont-Royal,** 367 av. du Mont-Royal Est (☎ 514-285-9078), is Québec's spiritual home of baked beans. **Casse-Croûte La Banquise,** 994 rue Rachel Est (☎ 514-525-2415), is reputed to make the best *poutine* in Montréal, and has more varieties than you can shake a stick at. **Restaurant Lafleurs,** 3620 rue St-Denis (☎ 514-848-1804), also makes a noteworthy *poutine*. At **Chez Clo,** 3199 rue Ontario Est (☎ 514-522-5348), you can move up the *habitant* (Québec native) food chain a little and eat Québec specialties like pea soup, meat ball *ragoût* (stew), or *toutière* (meat pie).

The vegetarian scene

Most Montréal restaurants are enlightened enough to offer at least one vegetarian option on their menus. But most of the time, the vegetarian choice seems like an afterthought. Luckily, some restaurants around town cater exclusively to Montréal's vegetarians, who are no longer considered just patchouli-scented, placard-bearing, long-haired social activists.

Right in the heart of the Quartier Latin, **Le Commensal,** 1720 rue St-Denis (☎ 514-845-2627), was the first venue of what's now a vegetarian chain with several restaurants around the city. Its downtown location, 1204 av. McGill-College (☎ 514-871-1480), is extremely popular at lunch with the business crowd. Food is sold by weight, and both spots offer three different buffets at three different rates: hot, cold, and dessert. An average meal costs about C$20 (US$17).

Cafe Santropol, 3990 rue St-Urbain (☎ 514-842-3110), occupies the first floor of a house at the corner of avenue Duluth. The restaurant has a wonderful back garden with rocks, trees, and a babbling fountain, making it an urban oasis on a hot summer day. Inside, it's a cozy place to warm up over a bowl of vegetarian chili after walking up the mountain on a blustery fall day. Sandwiches of thick sliced bread, stuffed with fresh and original flavor combinations (cream cheese is a staple) are the main attraction. A couple of sandwiches include meat, so you can bring your carnivore friends, but the rest of the menu is all vegetarian.

Pushap Sweets, 5195 rue Paré (☎ 514-737-4527), is nirvana for vegetarians and Indian-food lovers, and it's not a bad deal either. Excellent samosas make good starters. Delicious and affordable *thalis* are what everyone's eating. These are combo platters that vary from day to day, usually featuring two different curries and served with a choice of flatbreads. Pushap also makes traditional Indian baked goods, which are very sweet.

Spirite Lounge, 1205 rue Ontario Est (☎ 514-522-5353), is an outlandish dining experience by any standard. Located in a sort of no-man's-land between the Quartier Latin and the Gay Village, its walls are covered with crumpled aluminum foil. This is deep-vegetarianism with a fascist bent. At the beginning, a waiter brandishing a riding crop lays down the exact rules. There is no menu, but a meal is three courses, each consisting of a dizzying list of ingredients, organic whenever possible. Choose your portion-size wisely, because if you don't finish your main course or starter, you don't get dessert . . . plus you have to pay a fine of C$2 (US$1.70). The restaurant matches the fine and gives it to charity. If you don't finish your dessert, you're banned from the restaurant for life. If you use your cellphone, you're thrown out on your other ear.

BYOB

One thing that makes Montréal's dining landscape unique in Canada is the availability — abundance, even — of restaurants that don't serve alcohol but allow you to Bring Your Own Bottle (BYOB) of wine to accompany your meals. This arrangement is ideal. It allows you to save substantially on alcohol or afford a better bottle of wine than you would normally order. I recommend striving to do both.

Unfortunately, in an attempt to compensate for its nonexistent liquor sales, the majority of Montréal's BYOB restaurants, particularly those concentrated along the pedestrian part of rue Prince-Arthur, try to turn tables quickly. Quality and care can suffer, and the wham-bam approach to service can ruin your appetite as you begin to feel you're part of a giant, feeding herd. L'Academie, spanning three floors on the corner of rue St-Denis and avenue Duluth, packed most nights, is the worst offender in this regard.

However, a select few BYOBs are owned by artful restaurateurs, rather than proprietors blinded by their bottom lines. These are the hidden gems of Montréal's restaurant scene. Because they are usually small and extremely popular, you may need to reserve a couple of days in advance in order to get a table. Walking in on a weekend night is a gamble, but you may get lucky if you're looking only for a table for two. At these places, you can expect to pay between C$20 and C$30 (US$17–US$25.50) per person, before tip and taxes, for a three-course meal.

Somewhat far-flung, **Yoyo's,** 4720 rue Marquette (☎ 514-524-4187), is located in the northeastern reaches of the Plateau, on an otherwise mainly residential street. It is considered one of the best BYOBs in town. The most serious gastronomes among the clientele bring magnums of cherished vintages from their own cellars for decanting, because they are confident that the kitchen will come through with food to match.

Named after an active volcano, **Piton de la Fournaise,** 835 av. Duluth Est (☎ 514-526-3936), is the only restaurant in town that serves Creole cuisine from Reunion Island, a former French colony in the Indian Ocean. The flavorful dishes are a combination of French, African, and Indian influences. They are heavily seasoned, but not necessarily spicy. Bring a light red, slightly chilled wine.

La Colombe, 554 av. Duluth Est (☎ 514-849-8844), is a French BYOB that incorporates North African influences. Fish first, and then meat are the specialties here. Of the four main courses, two are usually fish, although the menu items change daily based on what the chef finds on his morning shop at the market.

Reserve a table for the second of the two seatings (at 7 p.m.) at **Le P'tit Plateau,** 330 rue Marie-Anne Est (☎ 514-282-6342). The first seating, at 5:30 p.m., can feel a tad rushed. But no matter — when you dine here, the classic French is first rate. The chalkboard menu changes regularly but usually features beef, pork, fish, and game.

Coffee and pastries

Montréalers who are serious about their coffee regularly trek to the northeastern reaches of the city to get their fix. In Mile End, **Café Olympico,** at the corner of rue Waverly and rue St-Viateur, is a neighborhood hangout for young couples, artsy types, grad students, and a supporting cast of colorful characters. A fair number of regulars hang out here, and everyone acts as though they're nonchalantly in the know.

Further up boulevard St-Laurent, in Little Italy, **Café Italia,** 6840 bd. St-Laurent (☎ 514-495-0059), is also reputed for its coffee. Here, too, the café au lait comes in a glass. You can also order a cappuccino or an espresso. The remnant 1950s décor and the elderly Italian men give the place an old-world feel.

Downtown, near rue Crescent, the Montréal Museum of Fine Art, and Concordia University's downtown campus, **Nocochi,** 2156 rue Mackay (☎ 514-989-7514), makes a curious selection of delicate Middle Eastern pastries, cookies, and treats.

If you're trippin' about how French everything is, you may have a hankering for a croissant to top it off. The best in the city are baked at the **Duc de Lorraine Patisserie Francaise,** 5002 Cote-des-Neiges (☎ 514-731-4128). They're good enough to give a Frenchman pause.

Chapter 11

Discovering Montréal's Best Attractions

- -

In This Chapter

▶ Checking out Montréal's best sights and activities

▶ Finding sights and activities for families, museumgoers, sports enthusiasts, and more

▶ Choosing a guided tour

- -

*I*n this chapter, I give you Montréal's top sights and activities and tell you how to see them yourself or with the help of a guided tour. I also fill you in on some attractions that are perfect for families, sports fans, and others.

Montréal's Top Sights from A to Z

Wondering what to do while in Montréal? Read through my suggestions in this section and choose the attractions that interest you most. You probably won't have enough time to see them all, so don't run yourself ragged trying.

Basilique Notre-Dame (Notre-Dame Basilica)
Vieux-Montréal

Basilique Notre-Dame is a new-world version of Paris's Notre Dame Cathedral, a grandiose church overlooking a broad *place,* or square, in the heart of the historic city. Okay, so the style is Gothic Revival, not Gothic, and it was built in the 19th century, not the 12th. But still, this Catholic church is a feast for the eyes, from the intricately carved altar to the gilded ornamentation throughout. The effect is so moving that the basilica's Protestant architect, James O'Donnell, actually converted to Catholicism when it was completed. You can explore on your own or take a guided tour (available in English) at various times, starting at 9 a.m. Sound and light shows were recently introduced, with two performances nightly Tuesday through Saturday.

110 rue Notre-Dame Ouest (on Place-d'Armes). ☎ *514-842-2925. Admission: Free for praying; otherwise, adults C$4 (US$3.50), students C$2 (US$1.75). Light show: Adults C$10 (US$8.50), seniors C$9 (US$7.75), children 7–17 C$5 (US$4.25), children 6 and under free. Light show open Tues–Fri 6:30 p.m. and 8:30 p.m., Sat 7 p.m. and 8:30 p.m. Métro: Place-d'Armes or Square-Victoria.*

Biodôme de Montréal (Montréal Biodome)
East Montréal

Built to fill the velodrome from the 1976 Olympics, Montréal's Biodôme is like a zoo and an indoor nature walk combined. You start at the penguin pool, a universal favorite among kids and grownups. Then you follow the trail through four different ecosystems: a Laurentian forest, the St. Lawrence marine system, a tropical rain forest, and a polar environment, each complete with its own plants and animals. You spend your visit largely in temperate surroundings, but you may want to bring a pullover for the Polar World segment. Kids go nuts here. Allow one hour.

4777 av. Pierre-de-Coubertin (next to Stade Olympique). ☎ *514-868-3000.* www. biodome.qc.ca. *Admission: Adults C$11.75 (US$10), seniors and students $9 (US$7.75), children 5–17 C$6 (US$5), children under 5, free. Open: Daily 9 a.m.–5 p.m. (until 6 p.m. in summer). Métro: Viau.*

Boulevard St-Laurent
Plateau

"The Main," as it is known to English Montréalers, is the city's oldest north-south artery. It extends up from Vieux-Montréal through Chinatown and beyond Little Italy and the Jean Talon Market to the farthest reaches of the island. It also divides the city's street addresses between Est and Ouest. There are many interesting parts to boulevard St-Laurent. The most colorful and liveliest stretch runs between rue Sherbrooke and avenue Mont-Royal, where the foot traffic is heavy all day and well into the night; a multitude of cafes, boutiques, delis, restaurants, and shops are frequented by a cosmopolitan clientele. By night, boulevard St-Laurent is one of the city's booming nightlife strips. It's a major destination and quite a scene for debonair dons and flesh-bearing divas who cram behind velvet ropes and crowd burly bouncers looking to get into *the* spot. The eternal big question is, "Are you on the list?" Just say that you are.

☎ *514-286-0334.* www.boulevardsaintlaurent.com.

Casino de Montréal (Montréal Casino)
Vieux-Montréal

The Casino de Montréal opened in 1993, occupying the French and Québec pavilions built for Expo '67 on the banks of Île Notre-Dame. Lit up at night, it looks like a remnant building from Superman's home planet of Krypton. Minutes from downtown, past Habitat '67, another architectural gem from the World's Fair, and over *Pont de la Concorde,* the casino's chiming

Downtown Montréal Attractions

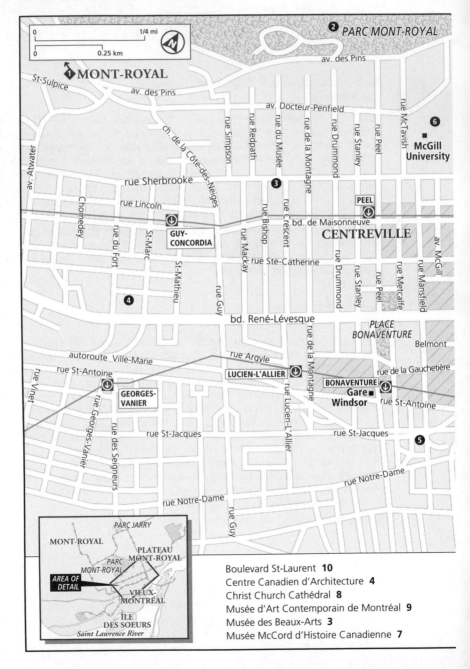

Boulevard St-Laurent **10**
Centre Canadien d'Architecture **4**
Christ Church Cathédral **8**
Musée d'Art Contemporain de Montréal **9**
Musée des Beaux-Arts **3**
Musée McCord d'Histoire Canadienne **7**

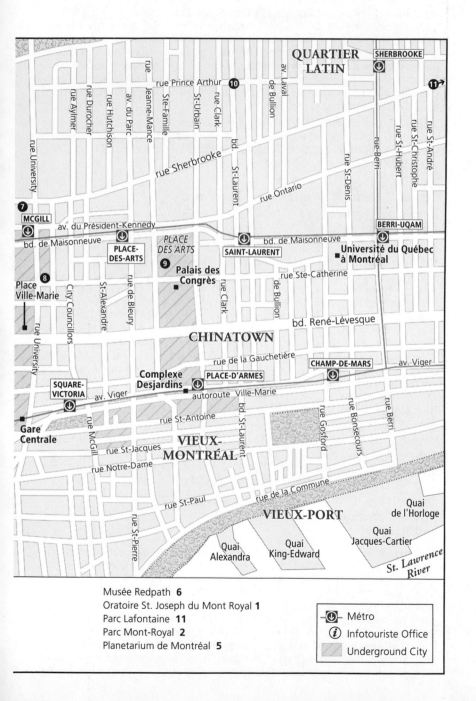

Musée Redpath **6**
Oratoire St. Joseph du Mont Royal **1**
Parc Lafontaine **11**
Parc Mont-Royal **2**
Planetarium de Montréal **5**

— Métro
(i) Infotouriste Office
Underground City

machines and velvety gaming tables span five floors. Every year, six million guests pass through its doors to gamble, to catch a show at the cabaret theater, or to dine at one of the four restaurants. One of them, Nuances, nestled away on the fifth floor and offering spectacular views of the St. Lawrence and the downtown skyline, is one of two five-star restaurants in Montréal. You can also join the all-night cronies and early-morning gamblers — who must be quite a sight to behold — for brunch on Saturdays and Sundays starting at 9:30 a.m.

1 av. du Casino. ☎ *800-665-2274 or 514-392-2746.* www.casino-de-montreal. com. *Admission: Free; tickets to matinee and evening shows at Le Cabaret are C$45–C$65 (US$38.25–US$55.25). Open: 24 hours, 365 days per year. Métro: Jean-Drapeau; take the shuttle from there.*

Centre Canadien d'Architecture (Canadian Center for Architecture)
East Montréal

Tucked away on the southwestern edge of the downtown neighborhood, the impressive grounds of the CCA occupy a whole city block. The two buildings — one austere and contemporary, the other a grandiose late-19th-century home — combine to make up the 12,077 sq. m (130,000 sq. ft.) of exhibition galleries, a library and study center, a theater, and a bookstore, all devoted to the understanding, appreciation, and betterment of architecture. As museum-going goes, the photography, blueprints, and three-dimensional models can be a refreshing change from the paintings and sculptures of most art museums. The CCA's exhibits focus on architecture, urban planning, and landscape design. While CCA attracts architecture enthusiasts from around the globe, it is usually interesting and accessible enough for regular folk, too. Across boulevard René-Levesque, to the south, the CCA Garden is a unique sculpture garden — ideal at sunset.

1920 rue Baile (between rue du Fort and rue St-Marc). ☎ *514-939-7026.* www.cca. qc.ca. *Admission: Adults C$10 (US$8.50), seniors C$7 (US$6), students C$5 (US$4.25), children aged 6–12 C$3 (US$2.50). Open: June–Sept Tues–Sun 10 a.m.–5 p.m. (until 9 p.m. on Thurs); Oct–May Wed–Fri 11 a.m.–6 p.m. (until 8 p.m. on Thurs), Sat–Sun 11 a.m.–5 p.m. Métro: Atwater, Georges-Vanier, or Guy-Concordia.*

Jardins Botanique (Botanical Garden)
East Montréal

Montréal's Jardins Botanique offers a respite from the concrete jungle within the city's limits. By combining a visit here with the nearby Biodôme and Insectarium (see the "Finding More Cool Things to See and Do" section), you can make nature the theme of this daylong urban excursion. Spread over 72 hectares (178 acres) just north of the Stade Olympique, the gardens contain more than 22,000 plant species and offer a different treat for every season. In May, expect acres of fragrant lilac trees. Roses bloom from mid-June until fall. In winter, ten greenhouses shelter bonsai and tropical plants. In the fall, don't miss the Magic of Lanterns, a cooperative effort

Vieux-Montréal Attractions

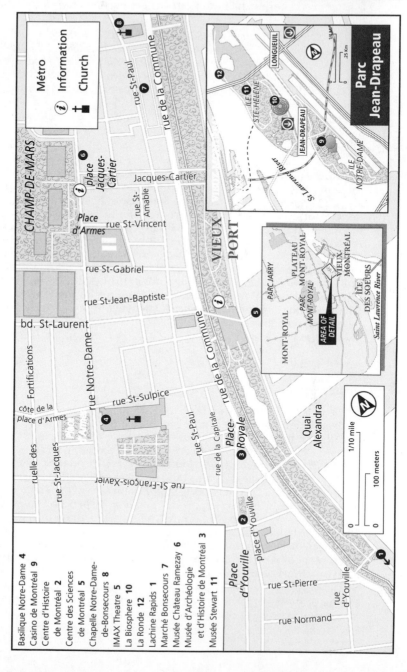

Map legend:
- (i) Métro
- (i) Information
- ✝■ Church

Parc Jean-Drapeau

LONGUEUIL

¼ mi
.25 Km

ÎLE STE-HÉLÈNE
JEAN-DRAPEAU
ÎLE NOTRE-DAME
St Laurent River

rue St-Paul
rue de la Commune
CHAMP-DE-MARS
place Jacques-Cartier
Jacques-Cartier
rue St-Amable
Place d'Armes
rue St-Vincent
rue St-Gabriel
rue St-Jean-Baptiste
bd. St-Laurent
rue Notre-Dame
Fortifications
côte de la place d'Armes
ruelle des
rue St-Jacques
rue St-François-Xavier
rue St-Sulpice
rue St-Paul
rue de la Capitale
rue de la Commune
Place-Royale
VIEUX PORT
Quai Alexandra
Place d'Youville
place d'Youville
rue St-Pierre
rue d'Youville
rue Normand

PARC JARRY
PLATEAU MONT-ROYAL
PARC MONT-ROYAL
MONT-ROYAL
VIEUX MONTRÉAL
ÎLE DES SŒURS
Saint Laurence River
AREA OF DETAIL

1/10 mile
100 meters

Legend:
- Basilique Notre-Dame **4**
- Casino de Montréal **9**
- Centre d'Histoire de Montréal **2**
- Centre des Sciences de Montréal **5**
- Chapelle Notre-Dame-de-Bonsecours **8**
- IMAX Theatre **5**
- La Biosphere **10**
- La Ronde **12**
- Lachine Rapids **1**
- Marché Bonsecours **7**
- Musée Château Ramezay **6**
- Musée d'Archéologie et d'Histoire de Montréal **3**
- Musée Stewart **11**

between Montréal and Shanghai, and the biggest of its type outside China. During this lantern exhibit, the gardens are particularly pretty at sunset. Picnics permitted.

4101 rue Sherbrooke Est (opposite Stade Olympique). ☎ *514-872-1400.* www.ville. montreal.qc.ca/jardin. *Admission: May–Oct adults C$11.75 (US$10), seniors and students C$9 (US$7.75), children 5–17 C$6 (US$5), free for children under 5; Nov–Apr adults C$8.75 (US$7.50), seniors and students C$6.75 (US$5.75), children 5–17 C$4.50 (US$3.75), free for children under 5. Open: From 9 a.m. year-round; closing hours vary. Métro: Pie-IX.*

Lachine Rapids
Vieux-Montréal

La chine is French for China, which is where early French explorers thought they were when first thwarted in navigating this impressive stretch of rapids in the St. Lawrence River south of Montréal. Montréal has done a lot of work on its waterfront areas in recent years, and more improvements are planned. It's still hard to believe that Montréal is surrounded by so much moving water, but you'll see for yourself strolling, cycling, or inline skating down the riverside path along the rapids. The rapids look tame from a distance, but watch for the odd, brave kayaker bobbing at breakneck speed and you'll get the gist. Several companies offer rafting trips through the rapids. **Lachine Rapids Tours** (☎ **514-284-9607**) has 90-minute jet boat trips leaving from Vieux-Montréal. Call for prices, schedules, and locations.

Métro: De l'Église station and walk south several blocks south to boulevard LaSalle.

La Ronde
Vieux-Montréal

Located on the former grounds of Expo '67, this amusement park is the pinnacle of a Montréal kid's summer fun. Six Flags recently bought La Ronde, and then renovated the grounds to the tune of C$90 million (US$76.5 million) — and it shows. It's clean, slick, and packed with 35 rides. If you have a sturdy stomach, give Le Monstre, a classic wooden roller coaster, a try. Or venture onto Le Cobra, a stand-up roller coaster that reaches speeds of 60 mph and will definitely bring your last meal to mind. There's only one catch: La Ronde is packed in the summer, especially on weekends. According to my ten-year-old source, who waited an hour to get onto Le Monstre, the lines can almost take the fun out of the whole experience. Luckily, though, waits are short for kiddy rides like the Tchou Tchou Train. If you need to take a break between rides, try the rock-climbing wall or carnival booths galore.

22 MacDonald Way (on Île Ste-Hélène). ☎ *514-397-2000.* www.laronde.com. *Admission: Grounds C$28 (US$23.75); rides ages 12 and over C$35 (US$29.75), ages 3–11 C$24 (US$20.50); parking C$12 (US$10.25). Open: Last week in May, Sat–Sun only; June–Aug and Labor Day weekend 10 a.m.–9 p.m. Métro: Papineau, then bus 169.*

East Montréal Attractions

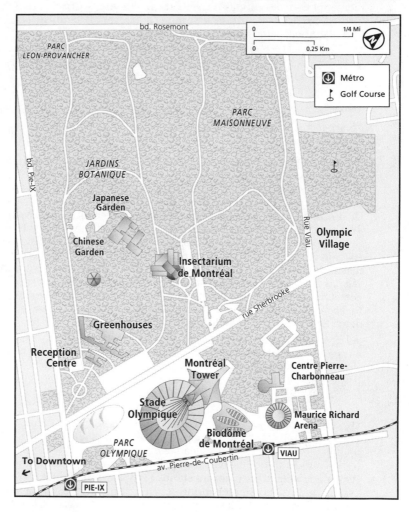

Marché Bonsecours (Bonsecours Market)
Vieux-Montréal

You'll be sorely disappointed if you come expecting the vibrant market that closed in 1963. Today, the inside of the market building is a slick mall selling up-market tourist trinkets, mainly Québec jewelry, native crafts, and contemporary shelf furnishings. Yet, the Marché Bonsecours is an impressive neoclassical building in its own right, with many columns and a silver dome. It remains an important Vieux-Montréal landmark and one of the top ten heritage buildings in Canada. Since its completion in 1847, it also served (alternately) as a meeting place of Montréal's hob-nobbing, men-only Beaver Club; as a theater where a young Charles Dickens performed as part of a touring troupe; as City Hall; and, briefly, as the Parliament of United Canada.

350 rue St-Paul Est (at the bottom of rue Gosford). ☎ *514-872-7730.* www.marche bonsecours.qc.ca. *Open: Daily 10 a.m.–6 p.m., until 9 p.m. on some nights. Métro: Champs-de-Mars.*

Musée d'Archéologie et d'Histoire de Montréal (Montréal Museum of Archeology and History)
Vieux-Montréal

If you visit just one museum while in Montréal, this is my choice. And because it's a great introduction to Montréal's history, for the benefit of the rest of your stay, visit this superb and unusual museum first. Officially opened on the city's 350th anniversary in 1992, this museum is located in the **Point à Callière building,** an uber-modern construction by Montréal architect Dan Hanganu. It was built on the site of the original French settlement of 1642 — what would become today's Montréal. After a brief multimedia presentation, a self-guided tour takes visitors underground to discover, literally, layers of artifacts from the centuries of civilization and the partially excavated ruins of the city's first buildings, canal system, and cemetery. Along the way, five historical figures engage the willing in a virtual conversation. A cafe on the third floor is popular for lunch among the office workers in Vieux-Montréal.

350 place Royale (at rue de la Commune). ☎ *514-872-9150.* www.pacmusee.qc.ca. *Admission: Families C$23 (US$19.50), adults C$11 (US$9.35), seniors C$8 (US$6.75), students C$6.50 (US$5.50), children ages 6–12 C$4 (US$3.50). Open: Sept–June Tues–Fri 10 a.m.–5 p.m., Sat–Sun 11 a.m.–6 p.m.; July–Aug Mon–Fri 10 a.m.–6 p.m., Sat–Sun 11 a.m.–6 p.m. Métro: Square-Victoria or Place-d'Armes.*

Musée d'Art Contemporain de Montréal (Montréal Museum of Contemporary Art)
Downtown

Everything about this new museum is light and airy, as if it were custom-designed for daydreamers and escapists. Situated just off the sprawling plaza of **Place des Arts,** it's a great place to take a breather from the bustle of downtown. About 60 percent of the museum's permanent collection comprises works by contemporary Québec painters. There are also works from international painters such as Jean Dubuffet, Max Ernst, Jean Arp, Larry Poons, and Antoni Tàpies, as well as photographers Robert Mapplethorpe and Ansel Adams. The museum is a little light on explanations, but it does offer a few of the guiding principles of the major schools of modern art.

185 rue Ste-Catherine Ouest. ☎ *514-847-6226.* www.macm.org. *Admission: Families C$16 (US$13.50), adults C$8 (US$6.75), seniors C$6 (US$5), students C$4 (US$3.50), children under 12 free; free on Wed 6–9 p.m. Open: Tues–Sun 11 a.m.–6 p.m., until 9 p.m. Wed. Métro: Place des Arts.*

Musée des Beaux-Arts de Montréal (Montréal Museum of Fine Arts)
Downtown

Since Toronto took over as Canada's business center 20 years ago, Montréal has been repositioning itself as the nation's cultural and artistic capital. Hence, the role and profile of the Montréal Museum of Fine Arts (MMFA) continues to grow. The permanent exhibit features an excellent survey of modern and contemporary Canadian art, including works by the Group of Seven and Emily Carr. It also displays paintings and sculptures by a number of the art world's international heavyweights, like El Greco, Renoir, Monet, Picasso, and Cézanne. In 1991, the completion of a modern-looking wing, directly across the street from the original neoclassical building, tripled the exhibition floor space. Throughout the year, the MMFA hosts temporary exhibits of an international caliber.

1380 rue Sherbrooke Ouest (at rue Crescent). ☎ *800-899-6873 or 514-285-2000.* www.mmfa.qc.ca. *Admission: Entrance to the permanent collection is by donation; tickets for temporary exhibits vary but are half-price Wed 5:30–9 p.m. Open: Tues–Sun 11 a.m.–5 p.m., Wed until 9 p.m. Métro: Guy-Concordia.*

Musée McCord d'Histoire Canadienne (McCord Museum of Canadian History)
Downtown

In the mood for some local history? This is the place to discover the past of Canada, Québec, and Montréal. The displays of clothing and artifacts may feel a little hokey by today's slick museum standards, but the collections are intelligently planned and well presented. Moderate history buffs will leave the museum with a concrete idea of how Québec's native population lived and how early settlers survived in hostile conditions with few comforts. Actually, you may leave wondering what kind of crazed, ice- and snow-loving souls decided to come here in the first place. Texts are in English and French. There's a cafe by the entrance and a great gift shop with books and work from local artisans, including jewelry, scarves, and other souvenir-friendly items.

690 Sherbrooke Ouest (at rue Victoria). ☎ *514-398-7100.* www.mccord-museum. qc.ca. *Admission: Adults C$10 (US$8.50), seniors C$7.50 (US$6.50), children ages 6–12 C$3 (US$2.50), free for children 5 and under. Open: Tues–Fri 10 a.m.–6 p.m., Sat–Sun 10 a.m.–5 p.m.; during the summer, open daily starting at 9 a.m. Métro: McGill.*

Parc Jean-Drapeau
Vieux-Montréal

Let the expansive green spaces and varied leisure activities offered by these two islands in the St. Lawrence River take you away from the stop and go of the downtown. Directly south of Vieux-Montréal and minutes away by ferry, Métro, or bridge, **Île Notre-Dame** and **Île Ste-Hélène** make up the park, recently renamed after the mayor who built them. Mayor Drapeau's city workers constructed Île Notre-Dame entirely out of the land-fill excavated from the tunnels for the Métro. They also enlarged Île Ste-Hélène. The two islands were the site for the '67 Expo, widely considered the best World's Fair of the last century. Now, the parklands of the islands have some of the city's main attractions, like Casino de Montréal, the Biosphère, and La Ronde, but they are also a haven for swimming, canoe-ing, sailing, cycling, inline skating, picnicking, and strolling through the landscaped gardens. In the winter, for three successive weekends in February, Île Ste-Hélène is the site for Montréal's winter carnival, the *Fête des Neiges*.

Île Ste-Hélène and Île Notre-Dame. ☎ *514-872-6120.* www.parcjeandrapeau. com. *Métro: Jean-Drapeau.*

Parc Mont-Royal
Plateau

Montréalers from all walks of life agree that Parc Mont-Royal is a gem. Built 125 years ago, the park is the brainchild of Frederick Law Olmsted, who also designed New York's Central Park. If you follow the wide trail that starts at the monument, you circle around the mountain all the way to the top. It's an easy walk, and you won't feel like you're climbing; although there's not much to see except trees and other walkers until you get to the top. From there, the lookout onto the city and the river is spectacular. There's a chalet where you can rest and buy refreshments. Keep following the trail until you reach Montréal's famous cross, a huge, lit cross on the top of the mountain that's visible from the east side of the city. The whole walk takes about two hours. Although not particularly dangerous, the park is not lit, so plan to be out before sunset. Watch out for the odd mountain biker who springs out of the woods onto the trail.

Access from avenue du Parc. ☎ *514-843-8240.* www.lemontroyal.qc.ca. *Métro: Place-des-Arts, then take bus 80 and get off at the Monument Sir George-Étienne Cartier.*

Stade Olympique (Olympic Stadium)
East Montréal

Known locally as the Big O, the facilities of the 1976 Olympics are consid-ered either a feat of architectural prowess, an enormous concrete debt, or perhaps both, depending on which local you ask. Built by French architect Roger Taillibert, the gigantic, 60,000-to-80,000-capacity, white dome-shaped stadium topped by a sloping Eiffel-like tower is an impressive structure. And no matter what your tastes, it's worth seeing up close. Okay, so the retracting roof has never worked and parts of the sloping tower ceded to the combined forces of time and gravity. The grounds of the complex still give you a distinct back-to-the-future experience, and the view of the city from the tower is incredible. The tour gives some highlights of the '76 Games and explains the municipal drama of preparing for the Montréal Olympics.

4141 rue Pierre-de-Coubertin. ☎ *514-252-8687. Admission: Tower adults C$13 (US$11), seniors and students over 18 C$10 (US$8.50), students 5–17 C$6.50 (US$5.50); stadium tours adults C$7.50 (US$6.50), seniors and students over 18 C$6.75 (US$5.75), students 5–17 C$5.75 (US$4.75). Open: Daily; English tours depart at 12:40 and 3:40 p.m.; the hours of the observation deck vary throughout the year. Métro: Pie-IX or Viau.*

The Underground City
Downtown

Eighteen miles of underground corridors, passageways, galleries, and atria full of shops, boutiques, food courts, an indoor ice rink, Métro stations, and movie theaters comprise Montréal's *ville souterraine,* the largest network of its kind in the world. It all began innocently enough in 1962, with the completion of the Ville-Marie skyscraper, which boasted as much retail space underground as the total square footage of its 47 stories of office space above. Other downtown buildings soon followed suit, converting their lower levels into retail malls. Over time, they began to connect haphazardly. **The Infotouriste Centre** has a good map of what's not much more than a maze of stores. It's handy as a scenic alternate route or as a hideout from any harsh weather, because it's always warm in the winter and cool in the summer. Ideal conditions = a shopper's paradise.

Vieux-Montréal

Settled in the 17th century, much of Vieux-Montréal's magic is due to its European flair, unique in North America. You feel eons away from the rest of the city's 21st-century hubbub. Today, Vieux-Montréal is at once a port, a waterfront park, and a financial district, chock-full of cafes, boutiques, art galleries, and hotels. After you've explored **rue St-Paul, Place Jacques-Cartier,** and **rue des Artistes,** head down to the waterfront. This narrow parkland stretches down several peers, along the St. Lawrence River, and eventually gives way to a network of bike paths. One leads to the Formula One track on nearby **Île Ste-Hélène.** Inline skates and bikes are available for rent from several shops along rue de la Commune and the boardwalk.

www.tourism-montreal.org, www.oldportofmontreal.com, www.old.montreal.qc.ca. *Métro: Champs-de-Mars, Place-d'Armes, or Square-Victoria.*

Finding More Cool Things to See and Do

If the preceding section of top sights isn't enough to keep you busy, don't fret. There's plenty more to see and do in Montréal. The following sections give you some ideas for how to entertain kids and ways to get outside, plus museums, churches, and sports teams.

Kid-pleasers

In this section, you find some all-time favorite Montréal kids' attractions guaranteed to amuse.

Centre des Sciences de Montréal (Montréal Science Center)
Vieux-Montréal

Who said learning isn't fun? Not the kids who go to the Montréal Science Centre. First of all, a trip to a museum where you can actually touch everything is way far-out. Room after room of interactive displays will keep them engaged and running between exhibits. Each zone contains experiments and games about a particular theme or is geared to a particular age group.

2 rue de la Commune Ouest (in the Old Port). ☎ *877-496-4724 or 514-496-4724.* www.centredessciencesdemontreal.com. *Admission: Adults C$10–C$22 (US$8.50–US$18.75), seniors and students 13–17 C$9–C$20 (US$7.75–US$17), children C$5–C$18 (US$4.25–US$15.25). Open: Mon–Fri 9 a.m.–3:30 p.m., Sat–Sun 10 a.m.–5 p.m. Métro: Champ-de-Mars.*

IMAX Theatre
Vieux-Montréal

Kids get giddy watching hikers scale Mount Everest, divers explore coral reefs in Mexico, or cameras swoop through the Grand Canyon on a seven-story screen.

2 rue de la Commune Ouest (behind the Science Centre). ☎ *877-496-4724 or 514-496-4724.* www.centredessciencesdemontreal.com. *Admission: Adults C$10–C$22 (US$8.50–US$18.75), seniors and students 13–17 C$9–C$20 (US$7.75–US$17), children C$5–C$18 (US$4.25–US$15.25). Open: Mon–Fri 9 a.m.–3:30 p.m., Sat–Sun 10 a.m.–5 p.m. Métro: Champ-de-Mars.*

Insectarium de Montréal (Montréal Insectarium)
East Montréal

If you go to the Jardins Botanique, the Insectarium is included in the admission. See over 3,000 varieties of bugs, from butterflies to beetles and maggots. In November and December — delight of delights — you can even indulge in an insect tasting!

4581 rue Sherbrooke Est (at Jardins Botanique). ☎ *514-872-1400. Admission: May–Oct adults C$12.75 (US$11), seniors and students C$9.50 (US$8), children 5–17 C$6.50 (US$5.50), free for children under 5; Nov–Apr adults C$9.75 (US$8.25), seniors and students C$7.25 (US$6), children 5–17 C$4.75 (US$4), free for children under 5. Open: Summer daily 9 a.m.–7 p.m.; rest of year daily 9 a.m.–5 p.m. Métro: Pie-IX or Viau.*

La Biosphère (The Biosphere)
Parc Jean-Drapeau

Located in the former American pavilion of Expo '67, this interactive nature museum is much more focused on ecology than the Biodôme. With exhibits on the Great Lakes and St. Lawrence River ecosystem, this museum explains the effects of pollution and other environmental issues.

160 Chemin Tour-de-l'Île (on Île Ste-Hélène). ☎ *514-283-5000. Admission: Families C$19 (US$16.25), adults C$8.50 (US$ 7.25), seniors and students C$6.50 (US$5.50),* *children 5–17 C$5 (US$4.25). Open: Late June–Labor Day daily 10 a.m.–6 p.m.; Labor Day–late June Tues–Sat 10 a.m.–4 p.m. Métro: Jean-Drapeau.*

Planetarium de Montréal (Montréal Planetarium)
Downtown

For junior astronomers or any stargazers, this domed center explains it all: how the stars change with the seasons, space travel, the collisions of stars, and more. Shows alternate between English and French.

1000 rue St-Jacques (corner of rue Peel). ☎ *514-872-4530.* www.planetarium. montreal.qc.ca. *Admission: Adults C$7.75 (US$6.50), seniors and students C$6 (US$5), children under 18 C$4 (US$3.50). Open: The English programming varies, call for the current schedule. Métro: Bonaventure.*

Best city parks

If people-watching or just plain hanging out is on your agenda, don't miss these green spaces.

Parc Lafontaine
Plateau

Lovers loll about the shaded, grassy slopes of this park, while ducks and paddle-boaters swirl about its large kidney-shaped pond. Parc Lafontaine is a very European-style park, as idyllic as it sounds. A great spot for a picnic or even a nap. Throughout the summer, the open-air theater, **Théâtre de Verdure,** presents many free music concerts and modern-dance performances in the evenings from the end of June through August.

Between rue Sherbrooke and rue Rachel, on avenue Parc-Lafontaine. Métro: Sherbrooke.

Parc Maisonneuve
East Montréal

Near the Stade Olympique, this former golf course is now one of the most popular and vibrant parks in Montréal, so score a point for the good guys. It's always buzzing with action, from inline skating, cycling, and Ultimate Frisbee to cultural festivals and the annual celebrations of Québec's national holiday, June 24 — St-Jean-Baptiste Day. The remains of the golf course's 19th hole now serve as the park's restaurant and facilities.

4601 rue Sherbrooke Est. Métro: Pie-XI or Viau.

Museums

Museum-wise, Montréal has much more than just art. Get your fill of natural history, local history, or even some humorous history while you're at it. (**Note:** Many of the museums and galleries are closed on Mondays.)

Look into scoring a Montréal Museum Pass, which works in 25 of the city's gated attractions. It's valid for two days, over a three-day span. Meaning you can skip a day and do something else. The pass costs C$39 (US$33.25) and includes a pass for the subway and buses. You can buy them at the participating museums, the Infotouriste office on Dorchester Square, or at many hotels.

Centre d'Histoire de Montréal (Montréal History Center)
Vieux-Montréal

Find out about Montréal's First Nations residents and the early European settlers, who started arriving in the 17th century. The museum tells about famous historical figures and gives you a pretty good idea of what every-day life was like over the past four centuries.

335 place d'Youville (at rue St-Pierre). ☎ *514-872-3207. Admission: Adults C$4.50 (US$3.75), seniors, students, and children $3 (US$2.50). Open: Tues–Sun 10 a.m.–5 p.m. Métro: Square-Victoria.*

Musée Château Ramezay (Château Ramezay Museum)
Vieux-Montréal

Built in 1703, this medium-sized flagstone house with gated grounds is an anomaly smack in the middle of the otherwise chock-a-block historic dis-trict. Back then it was the palatial residence of Québec's governor, the king's representative in the New World. In 1775, Benjamin Franklin crossed the threshold of this building, but he was unsuccessful in convincing locals to fight the British in the American Revolution. (During his visit, he helped found the *Montréal Gazette,* which is still Montréal's oldest paper and the only English daily.) The château's exhibits reveal the early days of colo-nial life, through art, costumes, popular artifacts, and coins. During the summer months, don't miss the French garden at the back; it is one of only three in Montréal, and the only one accessible to the public.

280 rue Notre-Dame Est (across the street from City Hall, at the top of Place Jacques-Cartier). ☎ *514-861-3708.* www.chateauramezay.qc.ca. *Admission: Adults C$7 (US$6), seniors C$6 (US$5), students C$5 (US$4.25), children C$4 (US$3.50). Open: June–Oct 10 a.m.–6 p.m.; Nov–May 10 a.m.–4:30 p.m., closed Mon during the winter season. Métro: Champ-de-Mars.*

Musée Redpath (Redpath Museum)
Downtown

This small natural-science museum may seem quirky by today's slick stan-dards, with its old-school museology style, but it happens to have Canada's second largest collection of artifacts from ancient Egypt. If fossils and geological fragments are your cup of tea, check it out.

859 rue Sherbrooke Ouest (on the campus of McGill University). ☎ *514-398-4086.* www.mcgill.ca/redpath. *Admission: Free. Open: July–Aug Mon–Thurs 9 a.m.–5 p.m., Sun 1–5 p.m.; Sept–June Mon–Fri 9 a.m.–5 p.m., Sun 1–5 p.m. Métro: McGill.*

Musée Stewart (Stewart Museum)
Vieux-Montréal

The year is 1758, and costumed interpreters go about the daily chores of the era at this military and maritime museum in Montréal's last standing fort, including making bread, repairing weapons, telling stories, and recruiting. Built after the War of 1812 between the Americans and the British, this fortification even has a moat. The permanent collection features artifacts from the colonial period, including soldiers' uniforms, rifles, cannons, early navigation instruments, portraits of historic figures, and household fineries brought over in cross-Atlantic trade. It's a fascinating look at 300 years of North American and European history. During the summer months (June–Aug), a garrison of soldiers parade around the grounds and reenact various military drills at various times throughout the day.

Vieux Fort, Chemin Tour de l'Île (Île Ste-Hélène). ☎ *514-861-6701.* www.stewart-museum.org. *Admission: Families C$16 (US$13.50), adults C$8 (US$6.75), seniors and students C$6 (US$5),, free for children under 7. Open: May–Sept 10 a.m.–6 p.m.; Oct–Apr 10 a.m.–5 p.m. Métro: Île Ste-Hélène.*

Churches
Montréal's religious heyday is long gone, but, luckily, many of the city's glorious church buildings remain. Here are a few of the best.

Chapelle Notre-Dame-de-Bonsecours
Vieux-Montréal

Originally built in the 17th century, this church is known as the Sailor's Church, thanks to its proximity to Montréal's port. Enjoy excellent views of the harbor and the Old City from the church's tower.

400 rue St-Paul Est (near the Bonsecours Market). ☎ *514-282-8670.* www.marguerite-bourgeoys.com/index_new_en.html. *Admission: Free for praying and attending mass; otherwise, adults C$6 (US$4.50), seniors and students C$4 (US$3), children 6–12 C$3 (US$2.25), children 5 and under are free. Open: May–Oct Tues–Sun 10 a.m.–5:30 p.m.; Nov to mid-Jan and Mar–Apr Tues–Sun 11 a.m.–3:30 p.m.; mid-Jan to Feb closed. Sunday mass in English Mar to mid-Jan 10:30 a.m. Métro: Champ-de-Mars.*

Christ Church Cathedral
Downtown

Located on one of the busiest, most commercial streets in the city, this graceful, 19th-century, Gothic-style cathedral has an elegant interior that's worth exploring. Local musicians give concerts here year-round.

635 rue Ste-Catherine Est. ☎ *514-843-6577.* www.montreal.anglican.org/cathedral. *Open: Daily 8 a.m.–6 p.m. Sunday services 8 a.m., 10 a.m., and 4 p.m. Métro: McGill.*

Oratoire St. Joseph du Mont Royal (St. Joseph's Oratory)
Outremont

Located on the far side of the Mountain, dividing the neighborhoods of Outremont and Westmount, the green, copper dome of this oratory and basilica pierces the Montréal skyline. It's worth the trip for the devout — the late Pope John Paul II thought so in 1982, as do many pilgrims who climb the hundreds of steps on their knees. What lies inside is the crypt of Brother André, a local monk said to have healing powers. The pope's blessing elevated him to a status just under sainthood in the Catholic realm.

3800 Chemin Queen Mary (corner of avenue Côte des Neiges). ☎ *514-733-8211.* www.saint-joseph.org. *Open: Daily 6 a.m.–9 p.m. Métro: Côte des Neiges.*

Spectator sports

Hey, sports fans! Montréal is a great sports town and currently home to professional hockey, football, and soccer teams. Montréal is, first and foremost, a hockey town, and the Montréal Canadiens are the most storied team in the history of the game. Since 1929, the Canadiens have won a record 24 Stanley Cup Championships while playing in the National Hockey League.

Canadiens (hockey)

The relationship between the team and its city runs deep and is infinitely complex. The red, white, and blue jerseys are part of Montréal's cultural fiber.

Every season, from mid-September to the beginning of April, the Canadiens play about half of their 82-game schedule downtown at the **Bell Centre,** also called the New Forum or the Phone Booth. The original Montréal Forum, at the corner of rue Atwater and rue Ste-Catherine, is now a movie megaplex.

If you're in town for a Canadiens home game, definitely check it out. Buying a ticket on game day isn't easy, though; try buying them in person at the **Bell Centre Ticket Office,** 1260 rue de la Gauchetière Ouest, or phone the **Admission Ticket Line** at ☎ **800-361-4595** or 514-790-1245. You can get also your seats on the Web at either www.admission.com or www.canadiens.com. If the game is sold out, on most nights you'll find people outside the Bell Centre with extra tickets, and some may be willing to negotiate a price.

Alouettes (football)

Canadian football is like the football played in the United States, but the field is longer and wider. Also, on offense, teams only have three tries to advance ten yards for a first down. The season, including exhibition games and playoffs, runs from early June to mid-November.

The Canadian Football League's Montréal Alouettes returned in 1996 to roost in Montréal. The previous flock folded because of financial troubles about a decade earlier. The Alouettes weren't much of a draw for some time. Their recent move to McGill University's Percival Molson Stadium downtown revitalized the franchise, and they now sell out games on a regular basis. In 2002, the Montréal Alouettes won the Grey Cup Championship, so they're enjoying an all-time high in popularity and their tickets are hot. The Alouettes' home field is at the top of avenue University, halfway up Mont-Royal.

Watching the Als and their *gentille* cheerleaders can be a pleasant outing on a Saturday afternoon in the late summer or fall. The **Alouettes' Ticket Office** (☎ **514-871-2255**) is downtown at 646 rue Ste-Catherine Ouest. You can also purchase tickets by phone (☎ **800-361-4595** or 514-790-1245) or on the Web at www.admission.com.

Impact (soccer)

The new kids on the sports block, the Montréal Impact (☎ **514-328-3668;** www.montrealimpact.com), started in 1992 by a local cheese company, are already perennial contenders in the American Professional Soccer League (APSL). Soccer, not hockey, is currently Canada's fastest-growing sport in the amateur ranks, which translates into capacity crowds packed into the 7,500-seat Claude Robillard Stadium, 1000 av. Émile-Journault (Métro: Crémazie), for the Impact season, from late April to early September.

Buy tickets by phone (☎ **800-361-4595** or 514-790-1245) or on the Web at www.admission.com.

Seeing Montréal by Guided Tour

Will a guided tour give you a better excursion than going it alone? It depends on what you want. If you want specialized explanations of neighborhoods or themes, or you want to see sights that are difficult to access on your own, a guided tour is hard to beat. Someone else takes care of the planning and answers your questions, to boot. If meeting and talking to locals is your thing, you can take a pass on the guided tours.

No matter how good it sounds on paper, call ahead to find out if the tour is right for you. Ask how long the tour lasts, what you'll see, how much it costs, what's included (and not), how many people will be on it, whether the tour is in English, and whether there is anything you should bring along. Call a day ahead to reserve a spot.

Walking it

Montréal is a great city for walking because it's full of interesting neighborhoods with their own architecture, history, and flavor. Most of the walking tours available in Montréal focus on particular neighborhoods. These are the most popular ones.

✔ **Guidatour** (☎ **514-844-4012;** www.guidatour.qc.ca) offers
daily tours of Vieux-Montréal in the summer. Tours depart from
Basilique Notre-Dame at 11 a.m. and 1:30 p.m. Tickets are adults
C$15 (US$12.75), seniors and students C$12 (US$10.25), and children ages 6 to 12 C$7 (US$6). Tickets are available 15 minutes
before departure, but try to buy them earlier. The two-and-a-half-
hour tour is available in English.

✔ **Visites de Montréal** (☎ **514-933-6674;** www.visitesdemontreal.
com) offers walking tours of Vieux-Montréal, including the Basilique
Notre-Dame, for groups of up to 20 people. Reserve one week ahead
of time. Prices vary for the two-hour tour.

✔ **Heritage Montréal** (☎ **514-286-2662;** www.heritagemontreal.
qc.ca) offers architectural tours of various Montréal neighborhoods on foot or bicycle from June to September. Popular tours
include the Plateau neighborhood, downtown churches, the Mile
End neighborhood, and a tour of Montréal's Métro system. Tickets
are adults C$12 (US$10.25), seniors and students C$10 (US$8.50).

Riding it

Feel like a break from the walking? Want to sit back and let someone else
run the show for a while? Because Montréal is such a great walking city,
I don't recommend bus tours. However, bus tours do have their merits,
especially if you have trouble walking long distances. Here are your
options:

✔ **Gray Line** (☎ **514-934-1222;** www.grayline.com) operates 11
different sightseeing tours, departing from the tourism office on
Square Dorchester. The basic city tour lasts about an hour and a
half and costs C$35 (US$29.75) for adults and children; children
under 5 are free. Call for information on more specialized trips.

✔ **Impérial Autocar** (☎ **514-871-4733;** www.autocarimperial.com)
offers narrated trips on open-top double-decker buses. Tours last
six hours. Tickets are adults C$35 (US$29.75), students C$32
(US$27.25), and children ages 5 to 12 C$28 (US$23.75). Buses depart
from Square Dorchester. On some tours, you can get on and off the
buses as you please.

✔ **Amphi-Bus** (☎ **514-849-5181**) offers tours of Vieux-Montréal with
a twist: At the end of the tour, the bus waddles into the harbor.
Reservations required. The basic one-hour tour costs adults C$16
(US$13.50), seniors and children under 12 C$15 (US$12.75).

Boating it

Nothing beats the view of the city from the waters of the St. Lawrence.
These companies offer short tours and longer dinner cruises:

↙ **Le Bateau-Mouche** (☎ 800-361-9952; www.bateau-mouche.com) offers 90-minute excursions in air-conditioned, glass-enclosed barges (like the ones on the Seine in Paris) leaving the Jacques Cartier Pier mid-May through mid-October daily at 10 a.m., noon, 2 p.m., and 4 p.m. Tours cost adults C$22.50 (US$19), seniors and students C$20.50 (US$17.50), children 6 to 17 C$9.50 (US$8); free for children under 5. Call for information on dinner cruises.

↙ **Croisières du Port de Montréal/AML Cruises** (☎ 800-667-3131 or 514-842-3871; www.croisieresaml.com) offers Montréal harbor cruises from May to October daily, departing from the Clock Tower Pier (at the foot of rue Berri). This company also cruises from Montréal to Québec City. Call for departures times and rates. Fares are adults C$25 to $40 (US$21.25–US$34), seniors and students C$22 to C$35 (US$18.75–US$29.75), children 12 and under C$22 to C$38 (US$18.75–US$32.25), families of two adults and two children C$10 to C$20 (US$8.50–US$17). The higher prices are for dinner cruises.

Hoofing it

You can also tour around Vieux-Montréal or Parc Mont-Royal in a horse-drawn carriage, known as a *calèche*. No need to reserve. You see them along **rue de la Commune** in the Old Port, and they line up at **Place-d'Armes** (corner rue Notre-Dame and rue St-Sulpice). Count on spending C$35 (US$29.75) per half hour or $60 (US$51) per hour. Carriages take four or five people, and drivers usually explain historic and architectural sights along the way. In winter, horse-drawn sled-carriages are also available.

Chapter 12

Shopping the Montréal Stores

In This Chapter

▶ Getting to know Montréal's shopping scene

▶ Checking out the best neighborhoods

▶ Locating the big names and big centers

C all it the French connection. If you're looking to adorn yourself, unearth unique treasures, or bring home something special for friends and family, Montréal is something of a shopper's horn of plenty. From the thriving fashion industry, vibrant gallery scene, and numerous shopping malls to the underground city, Montréal has your shopping needs covered.

Surveying the Scene

Shopping hours in Montréal are similar to those in the rest of Canada. Stores generally open at 9:30 or 10 a.m. and close at 5 or 6 p.m., Monday through Wednesday. On Thursdays and Fridays, most stores stay open until 9 p.m. On Saturdays, the hours swing back to 9 or 10 a.m. to 5 or 6 p.m. Most stores are also open on Sundays: Hours vary, but you can usually count on finding stores open from noon to 5 p.m.

These are the standard hours for stores in commercial areas. In neighborhoods like Westmount along rue Sherbrooke Ouest, which have many small boutiques, the hours can vary from one store to another, and owners of small shops sometimes close without warning to take a coffee break.

In Montréal, you can find pretty much any major brand-name item available anywhere else in North America. But you can also find a lot of items you probably can't find elsewhere. If you're looking for something unique, the following are Montréal's areas of strength:

✔ **Clothes:** The city's fashion industry gets better practically every season, and you can often buy clothing directly from the designers themselves. **Rue St-Denis** (between rue Sherbrooke and avenue Mont-Royal) are full of boutiques of local designers, with unique, quality fashion at reasonable prices. **Boulevard St-Laurent** specializes in extremely cool clothes for a youthful clientele, while **downtown** has a great mix of homegrown clothing chains for both men and women, plus big-name shops of major designers. More and more new designers are also setting up shop in Vieux-Montréal.

✔ **Antiques:** French-speaking Québeckers don't actually care much for the old, rustic look, which means that tons of antiques and vintage pieces are available to you at good prices. (Antiques dealers from New York flock to the city to skim off the best of them.) **Rue Notre-Dame,** way west, is Montréal's Antiques Alley, with dozens of shops to pick through, whether you're looking for furniture, home accessories, or memorabilia.

✔ **Art:** Several high-quality fine arts schools supply Montréal with what seems like a never-ending source of new talent. In addition, established painters sell their work in the city's traditional gallery strip on **rue Sherbrooke** around **rue Crescent.** The **Plateau** neighborhood has many smaller galleries featuring younger, more affordable artists. **Vieux-Montréal** has several galleries, as well as an artists' cooperative featuring drawings, lithographs, etchings, and more.

✔ **Home décor:** If you like knickknacks and cool home accessories, you'll be in heaven. Boutiques specializing in household decorations can be found all over the city, including downtown, but especially on **rue St-Denis** and **avenue Laurier.**

✔ **Specialty foods and liquor:** The last decade in Québec has seen a surge of interest in local culinary specialties — from maple syrup and blueberry liqueurs to fine chocolates and Québec cheeses. The **Jean-Talon** and **Atwater markets** are good places to pick up local delicacies, as is **avenue Laurier.** Look to get your hands on some local unpasteurized cheese. Although wine and spirits are sold by a provincial liquor board, their offerings are anything but standard issue. The **Société des alcools du Québec (SAQ)** (look for the maroon and blue signage) offers an impressive selection of wines from France and other wine-producing nations. Québec's climate doesn't grow good grapes, but there's an increasing amount of producers of iced ciders, Québec's knee-jerk reaction to the neighboring province of Ontario's recent success with ice wine.

✔ **Books:** Not one other place in North America comes close to offering the quantity and variety of books in French that Montréal does. And the selection in English is good, too. Montréal has even managed to hold on to several independent English-language booksellers. Most of the English scene is downtown, while French bookstores are practically everywhere.

✔ **Music:** What I say about books is also true of music in Montréal. Compared to New York or even Toronto, Montréal can hardly be called CD city, but after Paris, this is probably one of the best places in the world to sample French-language music. Several large chains, mostly **downtown,** pretty much dominate the market.

Sounds great, but how much stuff can you bring home?

If you spend more than two days in Canada, you're entitled to bring back US$800 worth of goods duty-free. Included in that price, you're allowed to take home 33.8 fluid ounces of alcohol and 200 cigarettes. You may bring back tinned goods, but no fresh foods. For more info on what you can and cannot take back to the United States, visit the Customs and Border Protection Web site at www.customs.ustreas.gov.

If you're a citizen of Australia, the United Kingdom, or New Zealand, check out the regulations on what you can bring back by contacting the following agencies:

✔ **Australian Customs Services:** ☎ 02-9213-2000, www.customs. gov.au

✔ **HM Customs and Excise (UK):** ☎ 0181-910-3744, www.hmce. gov.uk

✔ **New Zealand Custom Services:** ☎ 09-4-359-6655, www.customs. govt.nz

Hold on to your receipts in case you have to prove your case at the border. Actually, hold on to your receipts so you can keep track of your spending and count up the cost of your loot *before* you get to the border. Customs agents aren't known to provide calculators to frenzied travelers.

If you bring more than US$800 in goods back to the United States with you, don't worry — no one is going to throw you in jail. You just have to pay a small tax on your purchases. And if you stay less than 48 hours in Canada, your duty-free limit drops to US$200 per person.

 Taxes, taxes. They're rather steep in the Great White North. Don't forget that almost 15 percent will be tacked on to your purchases. For more information on taxes and how to get a refund, see Chapter 4.

Checking Out the Big Names

Department stores have taken a beating over the last decade, but downtown Montréal still has several venerable old stores that sell goods the old-fashioned way:

✔ **Holt Renfrew,** 1300 rue Sherbrooke Ouest (☎ 514-842-5111), is a luxury clothing store for the well-heeled and label-conscious.

✔ **La Baie,** 585 rue Ste-Catherine Ouest (☎ 514-281-4422), also known as the Hudson's Bay Company, is a three-centuries-old Canadian institution. The Montréal store sells everything from cosmetics to clothing to kitchen appliances, and it's a great place to pick up crystal, china, and bedding.

✔ **La Maison Simons,** 977 rue Ste-Catherine Ouest (☎ 514-282-1840), originally a Québec City chain, is the new kid in town. Great for clothes, coats, and accessories.

✔ **Ogilvy,** 1307 rue Ste-Catherine Ouest (☎ 514-842-7711), is an upscale department store that feels like a collection of rather fancy boutiques.

Discovering the Best Shopping Neighborhoods

Montréal is a great shopping city, but like all cities of plenty, you need to know where to go to get the goods. The following sections show you the prime stomping grounds of the city's consumer culture.

Downtown

You can always go — downtown. The noise and the hurry can help your worries. And so can a little retail therapy at the shops, boutiques, and department stores along Montréal's main shopping drags. You'll feel better and look great in no time at all.

Rue Ste-Catherine

Montréal's downtown area is definitely not the most charming or quaint part of the city; parts of rue Ste-Catherine are actually pretty crass. Still, although it's not really a neighborhood for strolling among unique boutiques, it's *the* place to find the city's big department stores (see the "Checking Out the Big Names" section earlier in this chapter). It's where you find most of the shopping centers, movie theaters, and large bookstores. You also get a great concentration of chain stores of all sorts, although most are Canadian.

The downtown core is also home to Montréal's famous **underground city,** with over 1,500 boutiques. The 18-mile underground complex links up many of the major hotels, major shopping complexes, and most of the downtown Métro stations. You're likely to happen upon underground city shops as you pop in and out of it via a shopping center, Métro station, or hotel. The underground city is full of chain stores and cheap outlets for everything from shoes to electronics. Very few Montréalers actually shop in the underground city, because better stores exist above ground.

Unless the weather is particularly vicious (making the underground city particularly attractive), your best bet for downtown is shopping on **rue Ste-Catherine,** between rue Guy on the west and avenue du Parc on the east. Here are the shopping complexes you'll find there:

✔ **Centre Eaton,** 705 rue Ste-Catherine Ouest (☎ 514-288-3708; Métro: McGill): Eaton's used to be Canada's main mid- to high-end department store. It went out of business several years ago, but this five-floor shopping complex with 175 shops, cinemas, and eateries has retained the name.

✔ **Cours Mont-Royal,** 1455 rue Peel (☎ 514-842-7777; Métro: Peel): The shops in this center are a little more chic, and the whole effect is slightly more elegant than at the Centre Eaton. It's the place to go if you're looking for items from upmarket fashion labels.

✔ **Les Ailes de la Mode,** 677 rue Ste-Catherine Ouest (☎ 514-282-4537; Métro: McGill): Montréal's newest shopping complex is also the sleekest and the priciest. When it opened in 2002, it was hyped as a "new concept in shopping." Unfortunately, most shoppers report that they just can't find their way around the place.

✔ **Les Promenades de la Cathédrale,** at the corner of avenue University and rue Ste-Catherine (☎ 514-849-9925; Métro: McGill). Located right next to the Centre Eaton, this shopping center is virtually indistinguishable from it.

Also of note are some Montréal shops worth mentioning on their own. For contemporary Canadiana — leather, shoes, bags, clothes, and accessories — check out the sporty classic **Roots,** 1035 rue Ste-Catherine Ouest (☎ 514-845-7995). For home décor and stylish modern kitchenware, try the new lifestyle store, **Caban,** 777 rue Ste-Catherine Ouest (☎ 514-844-9300), a spin-off of the clothing chain Club Monaco.

Chapters Bookstore, 1171 rue Ste-Catherine Ouest (☎ 514-849-8825), is Canada's largest chain bookstore. The Montréal store is four floors high and includes an Internet cafe. A few blocks west, **Indigo,** 1500 av. McGill-College (☎ 514-281-5549), is part of the same chain and has a huge selection of books and a comfortable cafe. If you prefer a more intimate environment, check out the independent bookseller **Paragraphe Bookstore,** 2220 av. McGill-College (☎ 514-845-5811). For the best selection of French books, check out one of the **Renault Bray** stores, either at 4380 rue St-Denis (☎ 514-844-1781) or at 5117 av. du Parc (☎ 514-276-7651).

For CDs, visit **HMV,** 1020 rue Ste-Catherine Ouest (☎ 514-875-0765). For a better selection of French CDs, try the big **Archambault** store near Place des Arts at 500 rue Ste-Catherine Est (☎ 514-849-6201).

Rue Crescent

If you head west along rue Ste-Catherine, away from the department stores and malls, you soon hit **rue Crescent,** which has a handful of chic shops and upscale stores, including art galleries, antiques stores, and clothes stores, **Shan Boutique,** 2150 rue Crescent (☎ 514-787-7426), is where to go for designer bathing suits. **Aqua Skye,** 2035 rue Crescent (☎ 514-985-9950), is fun for fashionable jewelry. And **Formes Femme**

Underground City

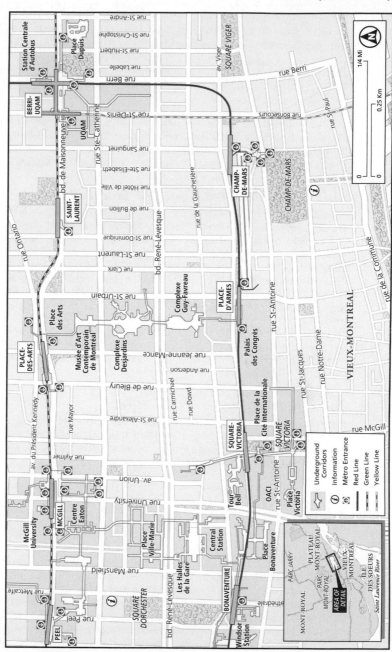

Enceinte, 2185 rue Crescent (☎ 514-843-6996), is a locally designed line of maternity wear that will flatter forms of expectant mothers. **Olam,** 1374 rue Ste-Catherine Ouest (☎ 514-875-9696), is every pretty girl's favorite shop, with the latest designs of locals, such as Myco Anna, as well as international names like Miss Sixty, Killah, and Muchacha.

This neighborhood is a nice one in which to stroll about after visiting the Montréal Museum of Fine Art, and you can also find plenty of cafes and bars to choose from.

Continuing west along rue Ste-Catherine, look for more fun stores on both sides. **Fly Boutique,** 1970 rue Ste-Catherine Ouest (☎ 514-846-3324), is the strip's last outpost of cool, just before rue du Fort. Hipsters will find that it's worth the trek west for the store's many urban styles.

Mile End/Outremont (avenue Laurier)

This upscale shopping street, the playground of Montréal's well-heeled Outremont residents, was hit hard by the recession that gripped the city in the early 1990s, but it's making a remarkable comeback at the moment. West of avenue Parc, you find great gourmet food stores like **Gourmet Laurier,** 1042 av. Laurier Ouest (☎ 514-274-5601), and **Anjou Québec,** 1025 av. Laurier Ouest (☎ 514-272-4065). The boutiques between avenue du Parc and boulevard St-Laurent sell upscale goods ranging from clothing for an older, more conservative shopper to kitchenware and home furnishings.

For a wide choice of travel supplies, like bags, suitcases, sun hats, money pouches, electricity converters, and more, visit **Jet-Setter,** 66 av. Laurier Ouest (☎ 514-271-5058).

The Plateau

If you've noticed that Montréalers are a particularly fashionable bunch, this is where they come to perfect their look. Although you find more familiar offerings at the big stores downtown, the Plateau is the best place to go native.

Boulevard St-Laurent

South of rue Sherbrooke, boulevard St-Laurent is home to Montréal's small, slightly run-down Chinatown. Walk north on boulevard St-Laurent, cross rue Sherbrooke, and St-Laurent turns into one of the hippest streets in the city — chock-full of trendy hair studios; even trendier clothes stores; and fashionable lounges, bars, and restaurants that recruit their wait staffs from local modeling agencies. For cosmetics, check out the St-Laurent store of the Canadian blockbuster makeup company **MAC Cosmetics,** 3487 bd. St-Laurent (☎ 514-287-9297). **Fidel,** 3525 bd. St. Laurent (☎ 514-296-5151), is a small shop featuring clothes by a local designer. Fidel's T-shirts have reached cult status, especially among Montréal men, who seem to deem them fit for all occasions. **Boutique**

Scandale, 3639 bd. St. Laurent (☎ 514-842-4707), always has eye-catching outfits in its windows; if you step inside, you'll see that this boutique keeps its promise with an eclectic yet irresistible selection of clothes.

Head north on St-Laurent, and your shopping opportunities diversify, and food options abound until just before avenue Mont-Royal. There, you find yourself smack in the middle of Montréal's up-and-coming furniture and interior-design neighborhood, including popular stores like **Montauk,** 4404 bd. St-Laurent (☎ 514-845-8285), and **Biltmore,** 5685 bd. St-Laurent (☎ 514-844-3000). Farther north, you find antiques, frame stores, clothing stores, galleries, and more.

For used CDs, vintage clothes, and more clothes designers, head east on **avenue Mont-Royal** from boulevard St-Laurent. This former working-class neighborhood is reaching the peak of a decade-long colonization process led by students and young professionals. The result is tons of interesting little boutiques and shops.

Rue St-Denis

The stretch between rue Sherbrooke and avenue Mont-Royal is the spiritual home of Montréal's bourgeoisie and the location of several higher-end, more established Montréal fashion designers. Rue St-Denis is a great shopping street featuring elegant clothing and unique home accessories. Alas, the last few years have been a little hard on the area, with stores coming and going a little faster than normal. It remains a lovely street to stroll, with many inviting cafes.

 Check out the big **Mexx** store at the corner of rue Rachel, 4190 rue St-Denis (☎ 514-843-6399). Farther north, don't miss the increasingly popular **Boutique Do,** 4439 rue St-Denis (☎ 514-844-0041), with reasonably priced, local designs for women. **Révenge,** 3852 rue St-Denis (☎ 514-843-4379), is another great store with local designs. **Artéfact,** 4117 rue St-Denis (☎ 514-842-2780), has lovely and unusual suits and dresses by Québec designers.

For home décor and gourmet kitchenware, check out **Arthur Quentin,** 3960 rue St-Denis (☎ 514-843-7513).

St-Henri (rue Notre-Dame)

Although it looks a little downtrodden at first sight, the western strip of **rue Notre-Dame,** between rue Guy and avenue Atwater, is Montréal's Antique Alley, with dozens of shops selling collectible furniture and memorabilia.

Check out **Lucie Favreau Antiques,** 1904 rue Notre-Dame Ouest (☎ 514-989-5117), for crazy collectibles; **Les Antiquités Grand Central,** 2448 rue Notre-Dame Ouest (☎ 514-935-1467), for more-elegant pieces; and **Lussier Antiques,** 3645 rue Notre-Dame Ouest (☎ 514-938-2224), for bargains on lamps, chests, and fixtures.

David S. Brown Antiques, 995 rue Wellington (☎ 514-844-9866), carries European and North American antiques from the 18th and 19th centuries. And **Obsession Antiques,** 1886 rue Notre-Dame Ouest (☎ 514-933-6375), is one of the more reputable dealers on the Antique Alley strip.

At avenue Atwater, just to the south, is the **Atwater Market,** with farmers, butchers, fishmongers, and gourmet shops.

Further north on av. Atwater, at the corner of rue St-Antoine, look into the showroom of **Harricana,** 3000 rue St-Antoine Ouest (☎ 877-894-9919), which makes warm things for winter out of secondhand fur. *Note:* As of a couple of seasons ago, to everyone's collective surprise, fur made a big comeback on the catwalks showing their winter collections.

Vieux-Montréal (rue St-Paul)

Until several years ago, Vieux-Montréal was not considered much of a shopping area, unless you were in the market for cheesy tourist souvenirs. Large cash injections over the last decade changed all that, and **rue St-Paul** in particular has profited from the renaissance. This is *the* street to scout for arts and crafts. Check out **La Guilde Graphique,** 9 rue St-Paul Ouest (☎ 514-844-3438), where more than 200 artists display their work, or visit a craftspeople's collective **L'Empreinte,** 272 rue St-Paul Ouest (☎ 514-861-4427).

For modern-art galleries, try **Gallery 2000,** 45 rue St-Paul Ouest (☎ 844-1812); **Galerie Parchemine,** across the street at 40 rue St-Paul Ouest (☎ 514-845-3368); or **Galerie St-Dizier,** 20 rue St-Paul Ouest (☎ 514-845-8411).

Westmount (rue Sherbrooke Ouest)

Rue Sherbrooke Ouest around avenue Greene is very much the traditional English area of the city. You can find the usual selection of upscale clothing, shoes, and home furnishings. Over the last few years, perhaps because more and more French-speakers are moving into the neighborhood, stores in this district have taken on a more European flavor. In particular, don't miss **L'Occitane,** a popular French cosmetics chain, full of luxurious soaps, moisturizers, and perfumes from Provence at 4972 rue Sherbrooke Ouest (☎ 514-482-8188).

Lululemon Athletica, 1394 av. Greene, on the corner of Sherbrooke (☎ 514-937-5151), sells Canadian-designed, uber-trendy yoga gear, made of high-tech fabrics that breathe and wick away sweat. **Scarpa,** 4901 rue Sherbrooke Ouest (☎ 514-484-0440), is the best place for shoes in the city; there's another location at 4257 rue St-Denis (☎ 514-282-6363). **James,** 4910 rue Sherbrooke Ouest (☎ 514-369-0700), is a boutique selling trendy looks by famous labels.

Chapter 13

Following an Itinerary: Five Great Options

● ●

In This Chapter

▶ Seeing the best of Montréal no matter how much time you have
▶ Discovering what makes Montréal a city like no other

● ●

*T*he Montréal experience is greater than the sum of its architecture, shopping, entertainment, dining, and attractions. There is something quintessentially Montréal happening in the city's streets all the time, whether you're on commercial strips, landscaped parks, outdoor terraces, or among the festival crowds. You feel the city's attitude and spend your whole holiday trying to put in words just what it is — and that's je ne sais quoi.

Residents and visitors alike spend many an hour contemplating that question. (Answer: It's many things.) If you're in a car, though, chances are, Montréal's ephemeral nature will pass you by. If you're on foot and still don't know what I mean, go for a drink on the back patio of **Bar St-Sulpice** on rue St-Denis on a busy summer night. Experience, wonder, discuss.

What follows are five suggested itineraries that will let you experience the city like a Montréaler. They're less about getting around among various attractions, and more about exploring neighborhoods and indulging in experiences and rituals that are favorites here.

Montréal in Three Days

Three days is an ideal block of time for an excellent introduction to Montréal, say, over a holiday long weekend. Sleep could become a real issue, depending on how late you're willing to stay up. Or, you can take it slow and have a relaxing time not doing anything in particular, wandering through Montréal's street scenes, which can be entertainment enough; there's always something to behold.

The following is a medium-paced itinerary with suggestions for stringing together several of the attractions and other worthwhile destinations mentioned in this guide.

Day 1

If you're just in for 24 hours, here's what to do. The idea is to get a quick taste of some quintessential experiences. It's **Vieux-Montréal** in the morning; start at Métro Square-Victoria (the exits open onto avenue McGill). Wind your way south and east, willy-nilly, through the streets, until you hit the rue de la Commune and the waterfront. Don't go too far east or you'll have to backtrack. As a more direct alternative, you can also walk straight down McGill and turn left when you hit the end. You're looking for the **Musée d'Archéologie et d'Histoire de Montréal** located on the same site as the first European settlement. If you arrive before the museum opens, find a coffee shop with fresh baked goods and café au lait. If you've already located the museum, nearby, **Olive and Gourmando,** at the corner of rues St-Paul and St-Pierre is just the spot.

You can sip your coffee over a copy of one of the local papers — *The Montréal Gazette* (English) or *La Presse* (French). It's not only a good way to catch up on local affairs but the "Arts" and "Life" sections (or equivalent sections) often have a calendar of events that lists what's going that same day. The free-press weeklies, the *Mirror* and the *Hour* in English and *Ici* and *Voir* in French, cover the city's cultural calendar from Thursday to Wednesday. Even in the French papers, it's pretty easy to decipher the what, when, and where of an event.

Or, you can head back out into the street with your coffee and croissant and watch the neighborhood waking up. Vieux-Montréal is filled with office spaces, so the streets will already be bustling with people rushing to work.

After visiting the museum, reward yourself with some shopping by taking a stroll along **rue St-Paul,** Vieux-Montréal's busiest street, jammed with galleries, restaurants, boutique hotels, and more. It runs just behind the **Old Customs House** on **Place Royale.** Walking north, from de la Commune, turn right on St-Paul and continue for about 5 blocks until you hit **Place Jacques-Cartier.** This sloped square, bearing the name of the explorer who first made landfall here, is the main gathering point for people in the neighborhood. Touristy restaurants with terraces and touts posted out front line both sides. Continue past Place Jacques-Cartier until you hit **Marché Bonsecours,** which has been everything from a market and a city hall, to Canada's legislature. In its current role, it is an upscale mall selling Québec-designed decorative arts, Native Canadian crafts, jewelry, and other potential souvenirs. Time permitting, after this shopping run you can head to the waterfront and witness the mighty currents of the St. Laurent, from the boardwalk or atop a clock tower at the end of a pier in the **Old-Port.**

Make your way back to Place Jacques-Cartier and head for the street at the top **(rue Notre-Dame).** In front and just to the right is Montréal's **Hôtel-de-Ville** or City Hall. In 1967, French president Charles de Gaulle fanned the flames of Québec separatism, by shouting "Vive le Québec libre!" from the balcony, which roughly translates into, "Long live a free Québec!" Across the street from city hall, on the same side as Place Jacques-Cartier is **Château Ramsey,** a museum about the colonial history of New France. During the summer and early fall, it's worth a stroll in their French garden at the back. If you don't feel like entering the museum, you can access the garden free from behind the museum, just off of Place Jacques-Cartier.

Back on rue Notre-Dame, turn left and walk several blocks until the Basilique Notre-Dame. This is where Céline Dion's wedding was. If you're enchanted with Vieux-Montréal and would like to come back, around sunset, take note of the horse-drawn carriages parked in front of the church, which you can hire to take an extended tour at a romantic pace.

Now it's time for lunch. See Chapter 10 for my recommendations: **Le Cartet** and **Cluny** are good choices at this point, but they're back near rue McGill where you started your day. You can continue along rue Nortre-Dame to get there, or wander willy-nilly once again. Or if you're feeling adventurous, from the basilica, head north into **Montréal's Chinatown,** boulevard St-Laurent between rue Viger and avenue Réne Lévesque.

After lunch, it's time for some shopping. Surface at the Mont-Royal Métro station. Turn left on avenue Mont-Royal and go to rue St-Denis. An ambitious but rewarding retail circuit would be a left turn down St-Denis; right when you hit Carré St-Louis, a small square with a fountain in the middle, cross the square; take rue Prince-Arthur, a pedestrian mall, and turn right on boulevard St-Laurent; carry on until avenue Mont-Royal, where you make a right. Soon you'll wind up back in front of the Métro station where you started. This lap will take you past some of the city's best boutiques and along several hot stretches of the Plateau neighborhood. Take a look at a map beforehand to gauge how far this really is. Of course, you can bail at any point, depending on what you see and how long you take in the stores. This is your afternoon activity.

Return to your accommodations, drop your loot, freshen up for dinner, and it's out the door for a pre-dinner glass of wine. If it's summer, find a terrace. The action will be liveliest there. See Chapter 15 for some of my recommendations. In terms of picking a neighborhood for a drink, check out the **Quartier Latin,** there are a multitude of choices and it will leave you in a good position for a variety of dinner destinations. Or perhaps you scouted something on your walk around town and would rather go there.

After dinner, it's time to step out into the night. If you're looking for some live music, check out the schedules at Montréal's larger venues, **Le Spectrum, Metropolis, Club Soda,** and **Le Cabaret.** See Chapter 15 for details and a slew of other nightlife recommendations.

Day 2

Start by following the "Brunch, Tam-tams, and Beyond" itinerary later in this chapter. Grab breakfast, or brunch, at **Café Souvenir** on rue Bernard or wait until rue St-Viateur and grab a coffee at **Café Olympico** and a bagel at **St-Viateur Bagels.** If it's not a Sunday or during warm weather, Tam-tams, a weekly drum circle and catch-all pagan gathering in Parc Mont-Royal won't be happening. So your last stop for this first segment is avenue Laurier and the several blocks of charming shops and boutiques on either side of avenue du Parc.

Jump in a cab or hop on a bus and head downtown; bus 80 runs along avenue du Parc. If you hailed a cab, tell the driver that you're off to the **Canadian Centre for Architecture.** By bus, grab a transfer and get off at the Place-des-Arts Métro. Duck underground. Take the subway (direction Angrinon to Métro Guy-Concordia); the CCA is a short walk from there.

By now it's lunch. You're downtown and starving. A great choice nearby is **Rotisserie Italienne.** Or there is a strip of pan-Asian, stir-fry places along rue Ste-Catherine just north of the CCA that are popular. One of the more notable choices is **59 Bangkok,** which has the best pad thai.

After lunch, stroll east along rue Ste-Catherine, in the same direction as the car traffic, until rue Crescent. Turn left and walk up this busy strip. Crescent above and below Ste-Catherine is a hopping nightlife district, but by day the boutiques and galleries, north of boulevard Maisonneuve, are of greater interest. At the top of the street, on your left, is **Musée des Beaux-Arts de Montréal.** The permanent collection is free, but the museum requests a donation. They charge admission to see the temporary exhibitions, which usually feature international-caliber artists.

When you emerge from the museum, take a walk east along rue Sherbrooke. In 2 blocks on the same side, there's an Art Deco building housing **Holt Renfrew,** Canada's answer to Bloomingdale's. You can either stop here for some chic shopping or continue along several more blocks and visit the gated campus of **McGill University.** The university bookstore is on rue McTavish, 1 block before the main gates to the campus.

Walk through the gates and the building you see in the middle; at the top of the road, is the Arts Building — the oldest of the bunch. This central quadrangle is usually filled with collegiate activity; sports or campus events on the playing field; and students going to class, sitting outside, or loitering in front of the library. The **Musée Redpath,** a natural history museum, is to the left, beyond the soccer field. If it's still before 5 p.m., it's a fun, free visit to round out this portion of the day.

When you're done on campus, exit by the Milton Gates, which are to the right of the Arts Building. Walk east along avenue Milton to boulevard St-Laurent, you're passing through the "McGill Ghetto" — don't worry, it's perfectly safe — it's named this way because so many McGill students live around here. It's several blocks through mainly residential streets. Halfway, you'll cross avenue du Park. Hungry, now? **Isakaya,** the best sushi in town, is a couple doors down from Milton. Otherwise, carry on just a little bit farther to the glitz and glamour of "The Main."

You can spend the rest of the evening on boulevard St-Laurent shopping for the remaining business hours, having dinner, and going out after. Don't worry: It will all become perfectly clear when you get there. The action is dense, the hip quotient off-the-chart, so you can freestyle your evening from here. If you're too tired and just want to sit down, or you're looking for something more sedate, catch a film at **Excentris,** a rep cinema with extra-comfy seats. If you're looking for more specific recommendations, see Chapter 10 for dining, Chapter 12 for shopping, and Chapter 15 for your nightlife options around here. Instead of reading through the entries, start by looking at the maps, seeing what's nearby, and then going from there.

Day 3

Start your day by hopping on the Métro's green line (direction Honoré Beaugrand) and get off at Pie IX. You'll spend the first part of today touring around the Olympic Village of the 1976 Summer Games. The **Stade Olympique,** once home to Major League Baseball's Montréal Expos, was built by French architect Roger Tallibert, at a cost of over C$1 billon, which Montréal taxpayers just finished paying off in 2006. The "Big O," as it is known among sports fans (or the "Big Owe" among its critics), has a tower that is the world's tallest leaning structure. (Take that, people in Pisa!) It was designed as a crane to retract the stadium's roof but the idea never really worked. There's an observatory with great views of the city's skyline at the top and you can tour the stadium, which remains a daring architectural feat.

The **Biodome de Montréal,** in an adjacent building, amounts to an indoor zoo. You can walk through different ecosystems. The penguins are everyone's favorite.

Depending on what you want to do for lunch you can either grab a snack from the concessions on-site or head downtown for something more meal-oriented. From Olympic Stadium in the east end you're not really close to anything, so find something in Chapter 10 that sounds appealing and head there.

A reason to stay in the vicinity of the Olympic Stadium would be a visit to the **Jardins Botanique,** which is a peaceful green space, with over 22,000 species of plants. On the grounds of the Botanical Gardens is the **Insectarium,** which can be "cool" or "gross" depending on which kid you ask. Every second year they have "insect tastings," which allows overly curious visitors to eat specially prepared insects. Dishes in the past years included Atta ants in a tortilla, roasted crickets served on a cucumber canapé and bruschetta with olive tapenade and bamboo worms (I'm not kidding).

After lunch, a choice: two more museums or a hike up "The Mountain" in **Parc Mont-Royal.** The hike is an alternate outdoor activity, say, if you didn't already go to the Botanical Gardens. The two museums to round out your three days of attractions are the **Musée McCord d'Historie Canadienne (Métro McGill)** and the **Musée d'Art Contemporain (Métro Place-des-Arts),** both downtown and within a short walk of each other.

To get to the top of "The Mountain," start at the **Monument Sir George-Étienne Cartier** (for its exact location see the directions and map in the "Brunch, Tam-tams, and Beyond" itinerary later in this chapter), and follow the gravel paths to the top. You'll eventually reach the summit with a lookout and a chalet.

Montréal in Five Days

So you've fallen in love and decided to postpone your return, at least for a couple of days. Or, for whatever reason, you just have more time, here's are another two days' worth of suggested ways to go about seeing the best of Montréal.

Remember, many of these activities are interchangeable on different days. Mix-and-match the mornings and afternoons that suit you best. Or, return to your favorite places several times.

Day 4

By now you should have your bearings, you can begin to explore further into the city or circle back for a double-take, looking for things you missed or want to see again. You may have certain morning rituals, a favorite place for coffee or a bakery where you like to start your day.

Today, when you're ready to go, head to **Marché Jean Talon** (Métro: Jean-Talon), for a morning stroll through the busy aisles lined by chatty merchants behind bountiful stalls of fruits and vegetables. Don't miss the cheese shops and gourmet boutiques in the surrounding buildings and streets. It's a hive of activity and a feast for the senses.

When you're done exploring the different corners of the market, take a walk, south, down boulevard St-Laurent. This is the main strip of the **Little Italy** neighborhood, between rues Jean Talon and Beaubien. There's a high concentration of cafes, gourmet shops, fashion boutiques, and stores selling imported shoes, all with an Italian flair.

Around lunch, some good options are **Boucherie Jos & Basile** and **Pizzeria Napolitana,** or stop in for an espresso at **Café Italia.**

This afternoon, perhaps consider one of the options you missed on Day 3: the McCord museum, the Montréal Museum of Contemporary Art, or a hike up "The Mountain". If you choose the latter, be sure to stock a backpack with goods from the Jean Talon market for a spontaneous, mid-afternoon picnic.

If you're looking for a kid-friendly activity, head to the **Vieux** for the **IMAX Theatre** and the **Centre des Sciences de Montréal.**

Any of these afternoon activities will leave you well placed to make your way to Chinatown for dinner. **Kung Kee** on rue de la Gauchetière is a great bet. Also look for the stall, on the south side, just east of rue Clark, selling "Dragon Beard" candy. "Bubble tea" is a neighborhood curiosity: It's tea, hot or cold, flavored and served with tapioca beads in the bottom, which are the "bubbles." **L2 Lounge,** 71A rue de la Gauchetière Est, is an Internet cafe and youth hangout, and it's where to go for this sweet delicacy.

After dinner, how about a night of big money and high stakes at the **Casino de Montréal?** It's on the Île Notre-Dame, so a cab is probably your best bet at this point in the evening. The casino is open 24 hours so you can also go after the bars close, depending on your habits. From Chinatown head north to the boulevard St-Laurent and rue Prince Arthur hub for frenzied nightlife action or south to Vieux-Montréal where the bars are more intimate and sedate, for a more tranquil evening.

If gambling's not your thing, but you're still a sporting type, you may want to catch a game with one of Montréal's professional sports teams. The **Montréal Canadiens** are by far the most popular, so tickets are the most difficult to come by (on short notice try the scalpers outside the Bell Center). The **Montréal Alouettes** (football) and **Impact** (soccer) also have legions of fans. Join in cheering on the home team or support the visiting team at your own risk.

Day 5

So it's your last day in town? It's time to get down to the essentials. What quintessential experiences are you missing: Have you been to **Schwartz's** for a smoked meat sandwich? **Café Olympico** for a café au lait? Have you tried the bagels from **St-Viateur Bakery?** Did you stroll the cobblestoned streets of **Vieux-Montréal?** The boardwalk of the **Vieux-Port?** If it's a Sunday, you must drop by **Tam-tams** in **Parc Mont Royal.** Whatever festival is going on during your stay, did you catch any of the free programming? Shopping on **rue St-Denis?** Have you sat on one of the crowded outdoor terraces for the always-busy *cinq à sept,* the after-work cocktail hours? **Jello Bar** or **Salon Daome** on a Thursday night? Did you splurge at a supper club, yet? If you're missing any of these, please add them to your to-do list.

If you feel your Montréal experience is complete, head for the hills on a day trip to the outlying regions, the **Laurentians** or **Eastern Townships.** In the winter, these are both popular destinations for skiers and snow-boarders alike; in the summer, mountain-bikers and hikers abound. Many of the ski hills are within an hour's drive of Montréal. There are also coach buses from the **Station Centrale** that offer round-trips to the most popular ones.

Nearby **Ottawa** and **Québec City** are also two good options for day trips. Both are significantly smaller than Montréal so you can cover a lot of ground, seeing the major attractions, in a single day. For art lovers, Ottawa's **National Gallery of Canada** is often worth the trip alone. Francophiles who want to get deeper into the French-speaking part of the province can opt for Québec City.

Connecting with Your French Roots

The term "two solitudes" describes coexisting universes of English and French in the province of Québec — and the abyss between them. Despite anyone's best efforts toward bilingualism in Montréal, two separate camps remain. They are not exclusive clubs, but they remain distinct for their differing senses of humor and ways of living the city life.

Assuming you're more comfortable in English than in French, you're going to experience the city as an *Anglophone* (English speaker). But keep in mind, there's a whole *Francophone* (French-speaking) world out there, with its own politicians, city officials, celebrities, rock stars, hockey players, biker gangs, talk radio, newspaper tabloids, sitcoms, music videos, and workplace humor.

You can visit Montréal and remain blissfully unaware of the French around you, partly because everyone in the service and tourism industries speaks very passable, if not impeccable, English. There's also plenty of English spoken around town, and most menus are bilingual. But, at any one time, the majority of the Montréalers surrounding you (over 60 percent) are French speaking and lead somewhat different lives from the English minority.

After Paris, Montréal is the second-largest French-speaking city in the world, so it stands to reason that there's plenty going on in French as well. This itinerary is a gentle introduction to Montréal's French side, guiding you on a stroll among the many shoppers and denizens on the Plateau's main commercial streets. There are no real destinations along the way, just suggested landmarks to guide your journey.

If you're a true *Francophile* (lover of all things French) and want to dabble further in this part of the city's cultural calendar, try to decipher the listings in either of the two free French weeklies, *Voir* and *Ici,* which come out on Thursdays. Their English counterparts, the *Mirror* and the

Connecting with Your French Roots

1 Le Quai des Brumes
2 Bily Kun
3 Restaurant Lafleurs
4 Bar St-Sulpice
5 Les Deux Pierrots

Hour, also list some of the Francophone community's events, but they are not as thorough.

Most of this itinerary runs along the orange line of the Métro, between Mont-Royal and Champs-de-Mars stations. You can use it at your discretion to get between the most interesting parts of the different segments I describe. You can walk this whole route quickly, in about two hours, or stretch it out into an afternoon and evening.

Starting at the Mont-Royal Métro station, turn right and walk along the central artery of the trendy Plateau neighborhood, once a hotbed for bohemian artists and now a hot real-estate market and shopping district.

Avenue Mont-Royal is packed with every kind of merchant imaginable. Small, locally owned businesses rule the blocks. Used-book and -CD stores, designer-clothing boutiques, small grocers, health-food shops, salons, outdoor-sports outfitters, bakeries, restaurants, cafes, and bars all cater to the locals, who justifiably feel that they are in the center of it all. Meander until you've had your fill and then return in the direction of the Métro.

Continue past the Mont-Royal Métro station and pause on the corner of rue St-Denis. If you're into vintage clothing, you may want to make a detour at this point by continuing straight on avenue Mont-Royal, past rue St-Denis. For several blocks up a slight grade, shops on both sides of the street sell retro clothing and some of their own designs.

Depending on the hour, this may also be time for refreshment. Both bars I recommend here are typically French Montréal but completely different. The first spot represents a somewhat dated mentality in Montréal, while the second is all about Montréal today. **Le Quai des Brumes,** located around the corner on the left at 4481 rue St-Denis (☎ 514-499-0467), is a smoky and dark place festering with anti-Federalist sentiment and known as a hangout for staunch, but graying, separatists. Do try to start a conversation, but I suggest not opening with a line about the late, former Canadian Prime Minister, Pierre Trudeau. **Bily Kun,** 354 av. Mont-Royal Est (☎ 514-845-5392), is a block to the west. It's populated with good-looking but casual 20- and 30-somethings, engaged in animated chatter over microbrewery beer and light snacks. Ostrich-head trophies high on the walls overlook the scene.

Back on rue St-Denis, you're faced with a similar scene to where this walk started on Mont-Royal, but the storefronts are glitzier, the foot traffic heavier, and the pace faster. It goes on at this rate for 4 long city blocks.

At the bottom of this strip, there's a break in the action, but soon, on your right, you see the illuminated yellow sign of **Restaurant Lafleurs,** 3620 rue St-Denis (☎ 514-848-1804) — *the* place to sample *poutine,* a local delicacy of French fries, cheese curds, and gravy. Lafleurs is the benchmark for all *poutines.*

Poutine, while delicious, is best consumed in small quantities. Finishing a small *poutine* at Lafleurs is a feat in itself. Sharing is probably a good idea. Do not order the *familiale* size — ever, under any circumstances.

If the weather is pleasant, you may as well ask for your *poutine* to go and enjoy it in nearby **Carré St-Louis,** where 19th-century town houses surround and enhance an already beautiful square with a multilayered, birdbath fountain as its core. Benign loafers of all kinds hang out on the benches and on the ledge of the fountain.

Continue south on rue St-Denis. After crossing rue Sherbrooke, you descend into the Quartier Latin. I suggest you plan your arrival for the early evening, after the shops close on upper St-Denis. That's when the night starts to get going in the streets below, surrounding the Université de Québec à Montréal (UQAM). The neighborhood's central location makes it a favorite destination for locals heading out for libations. It is jammed with choices, but the **Bar St-Sulpice,** 1680 rue St-Denis (☎ **514-844-9458**), is the most popular place to meet up for pitchers of beer or sangria, particularly in the summer, when the bar opens its immense back patio.

At this point, you may want to take the Métro at the Berri-UQAM station. The entrance is just a bit farther down rue St-Denis on the same side, just across boulevard Maisonneuve. You take it for only one stop, to Champs-de-Mars, but the walk isn't scenic — actually, it's a bit of a hike, and it goes through something of a no-man's land. Plus, you may be feeling a tad sluggish after all that *poutine.* If you still want to walk, keep going straight down St-Denis for several blocks until you come to rue Notre-Dame, and turn left.

Out of the Champs-de-Mars Métro station, follow the arrows to Vieux-Montréal, walk up the hill to rue Notre-Dame, and turn right.

On the right, you pass City Hall, and on the left is Place Jacques-Cartier, which bustles in the summer with street performers and bands of tourists. Cross the square diagonally and aim for 2 blocks down, at rue St-Paul. A couple of doors farther west, you hit your final destination. By now it should be late at night, and **Les Deux Pierrots,** 104 rue St-Paul Est (☎ **514-861-1270**), is in full swing. This is a traditional *boîte à chansons,* where legions of French Montréalers gather to sing and clap along to Québec folk favorites. The songs won't be familiar, but they're catchy nonetheless. You'll be tapping your feet in no time, but it may take you considerably longer to learn the lyrics.

The English Establishment

The historic conflict between the French and English in Québec was not only about two separate languages, religions, and identities, but also about two social classes. After 1759, when the English took over Montréal and the city began to industrialize, an increasing divide grew between the blue-collar French and the white-collar English. By the 1800s and early into the next century, much of Canada's wealth was concentrated in the **Golden Square Mile,** what's now the western part of Montréal's downtown.

Canada's post-industrial economy has gone a long way toward leveling the playing field, but the stately, 19th-century, gray stone town houses of the Golden Square Mile have thankfully stood the test of time and can be seen in and among the city's modern office buildings.

The English Establishment

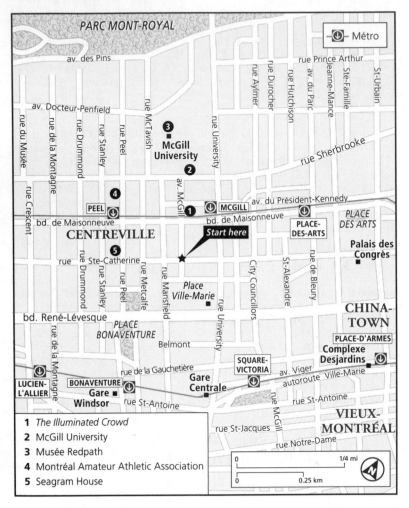

1 The Illuminated Crowd
2 McGill University
3 Musée Redpath
4 Montréal Amateur Athletic Association
5 Seagram House

Begin at the **corner of avenue McGill-College and rue Ste-Catherine** (Métro: McGill), one of the downtown's major intersections. McGill College is usually the recipient of the city's best landscaping efforts, including outdoor photo exhibits in the summer and millions of white Christmas lights during the winter.

Walk north up the slight grade on avenue McGill-College; at the top you see huge wrought-iron gates. Along the way, on the right-hand side of the street, you pass a sculpture that looks like it's made out of butter. The numerous near life-size figures stand together making up *The Illuminated Crowd*, a 1979 sculpture by Raymond Mason.

At the top of the street, you're at the main entrance to **McGill University,** a gated campus and a serene and scenic retreat, right in the downtown core. You're welcome to go in and walk around. Go up the central drive, which comes to a fork after the playing field. Hang a left. The building on your right is the **Musée Redpath.** Admission is free.

From the museum, continue traveling in the same direction (west) through a smaller set of gates. Turn left, down rue McTavish, and walk past the university's student union and bookstore.

At rue Sherbrooke, turn right. Then take a left at the first light, onto rue Peel. The red-brick building that dominates the right-hand side of the block is the **Montréal Amateur Athletic Association.** Now a posh sports club, it's a holdover of the era of English-speaking private men's clubs.

Almost at the end of the next block is the **Seagram House,** a 1929 castle-like structure and former headquarters of the Bronfman family, who built a liquor empire during Prohibition.

Brunch, Tam-tams, and Beyond

Summer Sundays are still sacred in Montréal but are no longer a strictly Catholic affair. The day's main events are **brunch** (whenever) and **Tam-tams,** an all-afternoon drum-circle with dancers and a hippie crafts market at the Monument Sir George-Étienne Cartier at the foot of Mont-Royal.

Weekend brunch spots do brisk business on Saturday and Sunday. Most places serve breakfast specials until late in the afternoon, so there's absolutely no rush to get out of bed. And no one does. You see plenty of mussy-haired, rosy-cheeked couples grinning sleepily at each other and their menus.

This itinerary begins on **rue Bernard** in Mile End. From downtown, hop on bus 80 at Place-des-Arts Métro, heading north up avenue du Parc. After brunching at one of the hidden spots I recommend, you crisscross avenue du Parc several times as you explore its cross streets, while working your way south. You end up amid the masses in Parc Mont-Royal. The city blocks in between are particularly long in this part of town, but the route is really not that far. At any point, you can catch bus 80 going south to get between the different stops I suggest.

Ideally, attempt this itinerary on a sunny Sunday, beginning by late morning or in the early afternoon, before scoring breakfast. You can even follow this route on a Saturday or on weekends during the winter, but no one will be beating drums at the last stop.

Start by taking bus 80 up avenue du Parc to rue Bernard. You'll be in front of the **Théâtre Rialto,** 5723 av. du Parc, with its striking Art Nouveau facade and marquee. Take your pick of excellent brunch

Brunch, Tam-tams, and Beyond

1 Théâtre Rialto
2 Restaurant Senzala
3 Café Souvenir
4 Le Petit Milos
5 St-Viateur Bagels
6 Epicerie Latina
7 Café Olympico
8 Pâtisserie De Gascogne
9 Toi Moi et Café
10 Monument Sir George Etienne Cartier

choices along rue Bernard: You can turn right and go a block to the east to the Brazilian **Restaurant Senzala,** 177 rue Bernard Ouest (☎ **514-274-1464**), for a tropical brunch. I like the Tropicana: poached eggs in avocado or mango halves topped with tomato sauce and melted cheese, served with fried plantains and grilled fruit. Or, from the starting point in front of the Rialto, turn left and go west to **Café Souvenir,** 1261 rue Bernard Ouest (☎ **514-948-5259**), which is several blocks down. Its menu is clever: Within each item are more choices, allowing you to customize, to a certain extent, what will appear on your breakfast plate. It's a small, neighborhood spot that also harks of faraway destinations, because dioramas of European capitals adorn the walls. During the summer, the seating spills out onto a sidewalk terrace.

After your *n*th refill of coffee, make your way back to the intersection of rue Bernard and avenue du Parc. Turn south on avenue du Parc and walk toward downtown.

At the next intersection, avenue St-Viateur, you find **Le Petit Milos,** 5551 av. du Parc (☎ 514-274-9991), a gourmet shop selling Greek specialty items, like fine olive oils. Around the corner, to the left, is **St-Viateur Bagels,** 263 av. St-Viateur Ouest (☎ 514-276-8044). Although food may be the farthest thing from your imagination after a big brunch, tasting one of this bakery's famous bagels, fresh out of the oven, is a must — at least, I strongly suggest it. If you can't do another bite, pick some up for a light picnic that you'll unveil at Tam-tams, the last stop along your route.

You can also find lots of small shops farther along avenue St-Viateur, on both sides of the street. At the next corner, **Epicerie Latina,** 185 av. St-Viateur Ouest (☎ 514-273-6561), is a gourmet grocery store, specializing in Italian ingredients. The market has produce as well as butcher and cheese counters. If you're even slightly curious about any of their cheeses, the grocer slices you off a sample taste.

At this point, you may already be saturated with coffee and seeking a bathroom, instead of looking for more. But if you can stand another cup, the coffee at **Café Olympico,** 185 av. St-Viateur Ouest (☎ 514-273-6561), is as good as it gets in Montréal. The scene there is worth taking in, if only for a moment.

Now, turn back and walk a block toward avenue du Parc. Turn left, going south along **avenue de l'Esplanade.** The town houses on this street are some of the prettiest and most typical in the neighborhood. When you reach the next street, **avenue Fairmount,** jog to your right, by turning first to the right, and then immediately to the left, continuing down rue Jeanne-Mance, until **avenue Laurier.**

This street, to the east and west of avenue du Parc is an upscale shopping district, with clothing boutiques, cafes, restaurants, and magazine and video stores, mainly at the service of the sedate and upscale clientele who putter in from the uber-affluent neighborhood of Outremont. It's where they go when they don't want to fight the traffic and riffraff downtown.

If you're coming all the way from rue Bernard, you can window-shop along avenue Laurier to your heart's content. You can also locate several brunch options around here, offering an abridged version of this itinerary. You'll be right beside **Pâtisserie De Gascogne,** 237 av. Laurier Ouest (☎ 514-490-0235), a French bakery with bread, pastries, a coffee bar, and seating. Across the street, **Toi Moi et Café,** 244 av. Laurier Ouest (☎ 514-369-1150), roasts its own coffees and serves a brunch menu that's consistently good.

When you're ready to leave avenue Laurier, head south along avenue du Parc, once again. After 3 blocks, you come to avenue Mont-Royal ("The Mountain") on your right. A bit farther, beyond the lights, you come to the Sunday ritual of **Tam-tams,** which has grown to such an extent that tour buses now stop to gawk.

Beginning at 2 p.m., drummers and percussionists from all over Montréal converge on the **Monument Sir George-Étienne Cartier,** on avenue du Parc at the foot of "The Mountain" — you're in Parc Mont-Royal. After they begin, their beats roll up "The Mountain's" slopes and drone on for the rest of the afternoon. A crowd of dancers forms in front of them, and the whole thing gathers momentum. People keep coming from every direction armed with blankets, Frisbees, dogs — the works — and they set up camp on the grassy hills surrounding the monument, which are all within earshot of the incessant drums. It is a veritable circus, and everyone gets in on the act, including children. Out on the fringes, there's even a group of Dungeons and Dragons kids whacking each other with foam and duct-tape swords.

Chapter 14

Going Beyond Montréal: Three Day-trips

. . . .

In This Chapter

▶ Stretching your legs beyond the city limits
▶ Visiting Ottawa, the nation's capital
▶ Day-tripping into rural Québec

. . . .

"***P***aris is Paris, but it's not France," goes the French expression. The same holds true for Montréal, which is not quite representative of the rest of the province of Québec. Montréal is Babylon by comparison. Beyond the bright lights of the big city, the province of Québec is a vast landscape, at times rural, at times rugged, dotted with many charming small towns, whose inhabitants are, by and large, French speaking, and where hockey and Catholicism are still the predominant religions.

Depending on how much time you have, you may want to escape Montréal and explore its surrounding regions. A jaunt into the hills of the countryside can be especially magical from late September to mid-October, when the leaves change colors. Ditto for anytime it snows, although the driving can be treacherous in heavy snowfall.

 Of course, the first place you want to check out after Montréal is Québec City (see Part IV of this book). And it's doable in a day. You may want to stay longer, though; Québec City is perfect for an overnight visit — very romantic. I strongly recommend fitting this historic capital into your travel itinerary, if at all possible. It's very different from Montréal.

In this chapter, I present three other trips you can do in a day. For each, I also provide lodging information, should you decide to stay overnight. All three trips are between an hour and two hours by highway from Montréal.

For the first day-trip to Ottawa, you can get there by bus, train, or airplane, but renting a car is probably the most practical route. You don't need a car, however, because taxis and an extensive bus system can get you around. For the other two more rural destinations, a car is also the best option — for mobility's sake.

Ottawa, the Nation's Capital

Ottawa is so Canadian. After all, it's the nation's capital. But Ottawa, which is in the province of Ontario, is completely different from Montréal and more like the rest of Canada. The difference is palpable.

Getting there

By car, Ottawa is about two hours, or 190km (118 miles), away from Montréal. Be sure to get an early start, especially if you're visiting only for the day. From Montréal, travel west on Autoroute 40, which runs along the top of the Island of Montréal. Stay on the 40 until the 417, which goes to Hull and Ottawa.

When you're in Ottawa proper, take exit 119, Metcalfe Street, and follow it as it twists and turns to the downtown area. After several blocks, the street ends smack in front of **Parliament Hill,** Ottawa's crown jewel and the seat of Canada's legislature.

Seeing the sights

Across from the Parliament Buildings is a tourist information center called the **Capital Infocentre,** 90 Wellington St. (☎ 800-465-1867; www.canadascapital.gc.ca). It's open daily 8:30 a.m. to 9 p.m. from May to September, and 9 a.m. to 5 p.m. the rest of the year. The people at the center can help you round out the recommendations I provide here.

Because you're in Ottawa only for a short visit, don't feel pressured to see everything. In this section, I include the best of the Canadian capital, which makes for a full day of sightseeing. Ottawa's downtown is small, compact, and ideal for walking around. And you may be surprised by how much of the city you can cover on foot.

Ottawa's main attraction is **Parliament Hill,** 1 Wellington St. (☎ 613-239-5000; www.parl.gc.ca), set on a bluff overlooking the Ottawa River. It is mecca for civic-minded Canadians and an interesting window into the nation's inner workings.

You can take a free, half-hour guided tour, which runs throughout the day. For a self-guided tour, pick up the "Discovering the Hill" booklet. Take the elevator to the top of the Peace Tower for a 360-degree view of the city and the Ottawa River.

On the grounds during the summer, you find plenty going on. At 10 a.m., a **Changing of the Guard ceremony** with dapper and unflappable soldiers in fur hats is just like the ones in England! By night, you can watch free sound and light shows. To the left of the central Parliament Building and behind the library is a peculiar cat sanctuary. And when parliament is in session (about 137 days per year), you can attend question-and-answer periods in the public galleries of either the Senate or the House of Commons.

Downtown Ottawa

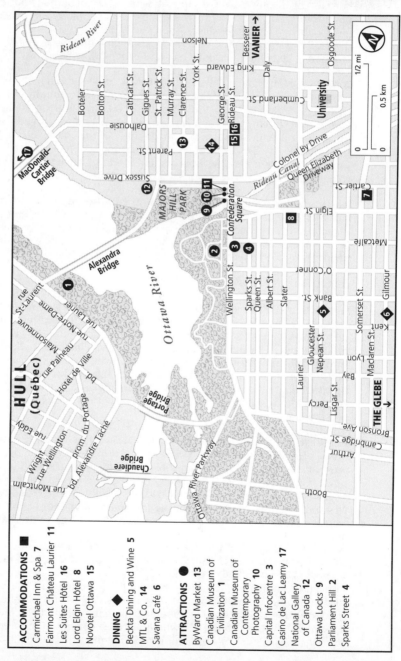

ACCOMMODATIONS ■
Carmichael Inn & Spa **7**
Fairmont Château Laurier **11**
Les Suites Hôtel **16**
Lord Elgin Hôtel **8**
Novotel Ottawa **15**

DINING ◆
Beckta Dining and Wine **5**
MTL & Co. **14**
Savana Café **6**

ATTRACTIONS ●
ByWard Market **13**
Canadian Museum of
Civilization **1**
Canadian Museum of
Contemporary
Photography **10**
Capital Infocentre **3**
Casino de Lac Leamy **17**
National Gallery
of Canada **12**
Ottawa Locks **9**
Parliament Hill **2**
Sparks Street **4**

Sparks Street runs parallel to Wellington Street and is a block south of Parliament Hill. It's a pedestrian mall with plenty of shops, boutiques, restaurants, and bars. During the summer, many Sparks Street establishments open sidewalk terraces. If you feel so inclined, a walking tour of the mall departs from the intersection of Elgin and Sparks every Saturday at 2 p.m. It lasts an hour and a half and costs C$5 (US$4.25).

Just east of Parliament Hill are the **Ottawa Locks,** which make up the north entrance of the **Rideau Canal.** The waterway, built in 1827, starts with eight flights of locks and runs all the way to Kingston on Lake Ontario. Originally built for strategic purposes and employed mainly as a trading route, the canal is now an 11km (6¾-mile) parkland that runs through the city like a ribbon. In the winter, it becomes the world's longest ice rink, and office workers and students alike use it to skate to work and class.

The **Canadian Museum of Contemporary Photography,** 1 Rideau Canal (☎ 613-990-8257; http://cmcp.gallery.ca), housed in a reconstructed railway tunnel, displays photos from its large permanent collection and also hosts traveling exhibitions. The museum's own collection spans from the 1960s to the present. Admission is free.

The striking **National Gallery of Canada,** 380 Sussex Dr. (☎ 613-990-1985; www.gallery.ca), opened in 1988. The glass and granite structure was designed by Moshe Safdie, the same architect behind Montréal's Habitat '67 and the Museum of Fine Arts. Light shafts and reflective panels make the most of natural light, which floods into the galleries, but in a way that's doesn't damage the art. The long, inclined walkway to the Grand Hall, an impressive landmark on its own, provides a dramatic view of the Parliament Buildings above the churning Ottawa River. The gallery has the country's most extensive collection of Canadian art, but it also features important works by artists from other countries and from periods throughout the ages.

Between Parliament Hill and the National Gallery and to the east of Sussex Drive is the **ByWard Market** (☎ 613-244-4410; www.byward-market.com) area. A two-story market building, formerly a farmers' market, is at the center of this neighborhood. The surrounding streets of 19th-century brick-and-stone buildings are filled with trendy shops, restaurants, pubs, and bars. During the summer, vendors at all kinds of outdoor stalls hawk their wares, while street performers do their thing.

Across the Alexandra Bridge — that is, over the Ottawa River and back in Québec province — is the **Canadian Museum of Civilization,** 100 rue Laurier (☎ 800-555-5621 or 819-776-7000; www.civilization.ca), housed in a futuristic, riverfront building. The permanent exhibits celebrate Canada's aboriginal people and the evolution of this young country. Extensive artifacts are on display from native Canadian cultures; of special note is the Grand Hall, which features 43 authentic totem poles from the West Coast. Other exhibits document various aspects of

Canada's history, culture, and development. Also on premise are an IMAX theater and a children's museum with "hands-on" displays.

For something completely different, you can try your luck at the **Casino du Lac Leamy,** 1 bd. du Casino (☎ 800-665-2274; www.casino-du-lac-leamy.com). Also in Québec province, it's open daily from 9 a.m. to 4 a.m. To get there from downtown Ottawa, take the Macdonald-Cartier Bridge, which becomes Highway 5, and get off at Exit 3.

Where to stay

You may decide to have dinner in Ottawa, and dinner may turn into drinks. Suddenly, staying the night seems like a clever idea. Here are my choices for accommodations. All are centrally located, close to the places you're touring.

The **Fairmont Château Laurier,** 1 Rideau St. (☎ 800-441-1414 or 613-241-1414; www.fairmont.com), adjacent to the Rideau Canal and steps away from Parliament Hill, is the city's grandest hotel, in the same tradition as the Château Frontenac in Québec City and the Queen Elizabeth in Montréal. The **Lord Elgin Hotel,** 100 Elgin St. (☎ 800-267-4298 or 613-235-3333; www.lordelginhotel.ca), overlooks Confederation Park in downtown Ottawa, which is home to many seasonal events like the Jazz Festival. **Les Suites Hotel,** 130 Besserer St. (☎ 800-267-1989 or 613-232-2000; www.les-suites.com), offers a few more amenities than the average hotel room and is adjacent to Rideau Centre's 180 shops as well as the restaurants of the ByWard Market area. The **Carmichael Inn & Spa,** 46 Cartier St. (☎ 613-236-4667; www.carmichaelinn.com), is a heritage home in a quiet neighborhood, but it's still close to the action and offers spa treatments. Lastly, **Novotel Ottawa,** 33 Nicholas St. (☎ 800-668-6835 or 613-230-3033; www.novotelottawa.com), is a sure bet. This outpost of the French hotel chain is centrally located. In the typical European tradition, the rooms are efficient and compact but appointed for its business-traveler clientele.

Where to dine

If you're looking for a place to eat, here's the insider track. In 2003, **Beckta Dining and Wine,** 226 Nepean St. (☎ 613-238-7063), ranked as the fourth-best new restaurant in Canada in a biannual survey by *EnRoute Magazine.* It's the first Ottawa restaurant to break the top ten. Beckta serves seasonal cuisine in a modern and intimate setting. **MTL & Co.,** 47/49 William St. (☎ 613-241-6314), seems like a fitting recommendation, given that MTL is short for Montréal, and true to its name, the restaurant becomes a lively club after dinner. On the menu are reasonably priced fusion dishes. **Savana Café,** 431 Gilmour St. (☎ 613-233-9159), serves dishes inspired by the traditional ingredients of the Caribbean and the Pacific Rim.

The Laurentian Mountains

For the quickest and easiest day-trip around Montréal, drive 45 minutes north to the Laurentian Mountains. These are rolling hills, not breathtaking peaks, but the Laurentians are impressive all the same.

Getting there

The Laurentian Highway, or Autoroute 15, takes you directly to the Laurentians and gives you the scenic route to boot. You can reach Autoroute 15 by driving north from downtown Montréal (along boulevard St-Laurent is fine) and catching Autoroute 40 West (you drive about ten minutes until the Autoroute 15 interchange). Then follow signs to St-Jérôme. Autoroute 15 takes you through some urban sprawl for about 15 minutes, but the scenery is pretty after that.

If you have a little extra time, exit at St-Jérôme and pick up old Route 117. St-Jérôme is a small town with a quaint main street, a couple of pubs, and some gifts and craft shops. It's remarkable more so for its charm than its substance. This takes you to the village of **Ste-Agathe des Monts** and through some typical older towns of the region along the way.

A good visitor information center covering the Laurentians area is in St-Jérôme: **La Maison du Tourisme des Laurentides,** 14142 rue de la Chapelle (☎ **800-561-6673** or 450-436-5309; www.laurentides.com). Take Exit 39 off Autoroute 15 and follow the signs. The tourist office is in a red-roofed stone cottage. It's open daily in the summer from 8:30 a.m. to 8:30 p.m.; from 9 a.m. to 5 p.m. during the rest of the year.

Orleans Express buses leave regularly from Montréal's **Central Bus Station,** 505 bd. de Maisonneuve (☎ **888-999-3977** or 514-842-2281), with stops at Ste-Agathe, Ste-Adèle, St-Jovite, and Mont-Tremblant. For schedules, call the bus station or visit www.orleansexpress.com. The express bus to Ste-Adèle takes about an hour and a half; the trip to St-Jovite and Mont-Tremblant takes about two hours.

Seeing the sights

The Laurentians boast a number of interesting villages; each one can be a day-trip in itself, depending on what you want to do and how much time you want to spend doing it. Driving from Montréal, your first stop is **Saint-Sauveur-des-Monts,** a popular ski resort town with lots of restaurants and street activity. In summer, the water park, **Parc Aquatique du Mont-St-Sauveur,** 350 rue St-Denis (☎ **800-363-2426** or 450-227-4671; www.parcaquatique.com), is a popular attraction because of its wave pool and mountain water slide.

Next stop is **Ste-Adèle** (Exit 67 off Route 117), a pretty village whose main street, **rue Valiquette,** is lined with cafes, galleries, and bakeries. The popular **Chantecler** ski resort here has 22 trails. For information, call the town's **Centre Municipal** at ☎ **450-229-2921.** For more downhill

The Laurentian Mountains

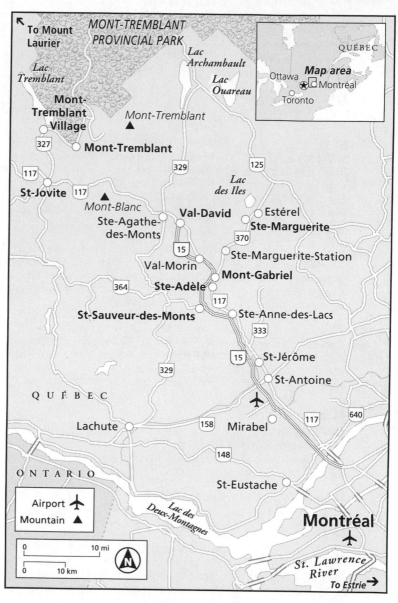

To Mount Laurier

Lac Tremblant

MONT-TREMBLANT PROVINCIAL PARK

Lac Archambault

Lac Ouareau

QUÉBEC

Ottawa   **Map area**

Montréal

Toronto

Mont-Tremblant Village

327

Mont-Tremblant ▲

Mont-Tremblant

117   329   125

St-Jovite   117

▲ Mont-Blanc

Lac des Iles

Val-David   Estérel

Ste-Agathe-des-Monts   **Ste-Marguerite**

370

15   Ste-Marguerite-Station

Val-Morin   **Mont-Gabriel**

364   **Ste-Adèle**

117

St-Sauveur-des-Monts   Ste-Anne-des-Lacs

333

15   St-Jérôme

329   St-Antoine

QUÉBEC

158   Mirabel   117   640

148

ONTARIO

St-Eustache

Lachute

Lac des Deux-Montagnes

Montréal

Airport ✈
Mountain ▲

0   10 mi
0   10 km

N

St. Lawrence River

To Estrie →

skiing, continue along Route 117, and then take Route 327 to **Mont-Tremblant,** the highest peak in the Laurentians and an hour-and-a-half drive from Montréal. The commercial center that serves the area is **St-Jovite,** whose main street, **rue Ouimet,** is lined with cafes and shops. For information on skiing and summer activities in this popular resort area, contact the **Bureau Touristique de Mont-Tremblant** on rue du Couvent in Mont-Tremblant (☎ 819-425-2434).

Where to stay

Most of the accommodations in the Laurentians are resorts.

In Saint-Sauveur-des-Monts, the **Relais St-Denis,** 61 rue St-Denis (☎ 888-997-4766 or 450-227-4766), offers quite luxurious rooms and suites with fireplaces in a country club atmosphere, complete with a heated outdoor pool and a nearby golf course. The **Manoir Saint-Sauveur,** 246 chemin du Lac-Millet (☎ 800-361-0505 or 450-227-1811), is a large resort hotel with year-round activities, including racquetball, squash, and in-house movies.

In Ste-Adèle, the **Hotel Alpine,** 1440 chemin Pierre Péladeau (☎ 877-257-4630 or 450-229-1545), offers different types of accommodations in rustic log structures with meals served at communal tables. The **Chantecler** resort, 1474 chemin Chantecler (☎ 800-363-2420), has rooms and suites, many with fireplaces and hot tubs.

Popular resorts in Mont-Tremblant include the deluxe motel **Auberge La Porte Rouge,** 1874 chemin Principale (☎ 800-665-3505 or 819-425-3505), with rooms to accommodate up to ten people, and **Gray Rocks,** 525 chemin Principale (☎ 800-567-6767 or 819-425-2771), a family-friendly resort that offers horseback riding, boating, tennis, and golf.

Where to dine

Rue Principale in Saint-Sauveur-des-Monts has many restaurants. One of the best known is **Les Oliviers,** 239 rue Principale (☎ 450-227-2110), which serves what you can probably call French country cuisine, including beef, duck, and salmon dishes.

In Ste-Adèle, **L'Eau à la Bouche,** 3003 bd. Ste-Adèle (Route 117) (☎ 450-229-2991), serves a changing menu with seasonal fish, meats, and vegetables, plus a selection of Québec cheeses.

In St-Jovite, try **Antipasto,** 855 rue Ouimet (☎ 819-425-7580), for Italian cuisine, including individual pizzas cooked in a brick oven. For carefully prepared traditional Québec cuisine, try **La Table Enchantée,** 600 Rte. 117 Nord (☎ 819-425-7113), considered one of the best dining spots in the Laurentians area.

In Mont-Tremblant, **Aux Truffes,** 3035 rue Principale (☎ 819-681-4544), serves upscale contemporary French cuisine.

The Eastern Townships

The **Eastern Townships** are one of Québec's best-kept tourism secrets. A beautiful landscape of rolling hills, mountains, farms, and small villages, the area has several quaint villages that are frequented mainly by Québec tourists. Much of the townships were originally settled by British loyalists who fled to the region during the Revolutionary War, and although 90 percent of the people speak French as their first language, you can see traces of English presence everywhere. Many towns and villages have English names or names that combine the original English name with that of a Catholic saint (given by the French-speakers who later moved into the region).

For tourist information about the Eastern Townships, contact **Tourism Cantons-de-l'Est,** 20 rue Don-Bosco Sud in Sherbrooke (☎ **800-355-5755;** www.cantonsdelest.com).

Getting there

To head to the townships, count on two hours of driving. I suggest visiting either the small city of **Magog** (Lac Memphrémagog) or the quaint village of **North Hatley** (Lac Massawippi), which is about half an hour from Magog. Leave Montréal on the Champlain Bridge, which becomes Autoroute 10. Then follow directions toward Sherbrooke. Autoroute 10 goes directly to Magog. If you want to get there along a more scenic country road, leave the Autoroute 10 at Exit 37 and follow Route 112 East. To get to North Hatley, take Autoroute 108 east from Magog for about 20 minutes.

Buses for Magog and Sherbrooke leave Montréal's **Central Bus Station,** 505 bd. de Maisonneuve (☎ **888-999-3977** or 514-842-2281), roughly every two hours during the week. Call for daily schedules.

Seeing the sights

Small and mainly industrial, the city of Magog is not where you want to spend a lot of time. Head straight to the waterfront area on **Lac Memphrémagog,** with its cafes and bars. You can take a **lake cruise** aboard the **Aventure** cruise ships. Call ☎ **819-843-8068** for information or contact the **Bureau d'Information Touristique Memphrémagog** at 55 rue Cabana in Magog (☎ **800-267-2744** or 819-843-2744). Near Magog, visit the popular provincial **Parc National du Mont Orford,** which offers a golf course and 48km (30 miles) of skiing and hiking trails. To get there, take Exit 115 north off the Autoroute 10. For information, call ☎ **819-843-9855.** Admission is C$8.75 (US$7.50) for adults, C$6.50 (US$5.50) for seniors, and C$4.25 (US$3.50) for children 6–17 years old.

North Hatley is a tiny, beautiful village on the shore of Lac Massawippi. A former resort town for rich Americans, it is now the place well-to-do Québeckers come to relax and buy paintings in the village's many art galleries. The village's main street, **rue Principale,** is also full of cute

The Eastern Townships

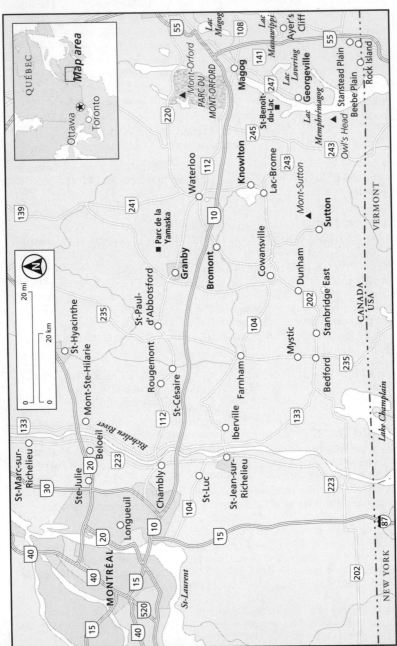

cafes, restaurants, and boutiques selling crafts and clothing. There aren't many tourist attractions here per se. Instead, people come here for the exceptional atmosphere, beautiful lakefront scenery, and all-'round New England feel. The **Gallerie Jeanine Blais,** 100 rue Principale (☎ 819-842-2784), has lovely, fanciful folk art, and **Au Grenier de Gife,** 330 chemin de la Rivière (☎ 819-842-4440), sells painted furniture and works by local artists.

Where to stay

Lodging in Magog is neither plentiful nor very nice. If you want to stay the night, I suggest the **Relais de l'Abbaye,** 2705 chemin Gendreau (☎ 450-847-3721), a luxurious mansion-style guesthouse with elegant rooms.

But you'll probably be happier staying in North Hatley. **Le Tricorne,** 50 chemin Gosselin (☎ 819-842-2692; www.manoirletricorne.com), is an impeccably decorated, 125-year-old guesthouse. Rooms start at about C$125 (US$106), and some include hot tubs. If you're interested in something more luxurious, the famous **Auberge Hatley,** 325 rue Virgin (☎ 819-842-2451), has rooms decorated with antiques and cre com-pleted with hot tubs and fireplaces; on-site is a gastronomic restaurant. **Serendipity,** 680 chemin de la Rivière (☎ 819-842-2970), is a reasonably priced B&B with nice views.

Where to dine

The upscale inns in North Hatley offer exceptional dining choices. The **Auberge Hatley** serves fine, gourmet meals based on local ingredients like duck, venison, and bison and has a wine cellar with more than 10,000 bottles. *Table d'hôte* (complete meal) menus start at C$60 (US$51). The **Auberge Ripplecove,** 700 chemin Ripplecove (☎ 800-668-4296), has a reputation for serving creative dishes based on local delicacies, like cari-bou. For less expensive but still tasty food, **Pilsen,** 55 rue Principale (☎ 819-842-2971), has a publike atmosphere and serves quick food like nachos, burgers, and pasta. This is a great place to indulge in a large selection of locally brewed beers. Another good choice is the **Café Massawippi,** 3050 chemin Capelton (☎ 819-842-4528), for inventive but reasonably priced meals.

Chapter 15

Living It Up after Dark: Montréal Nightlife

. . . .

In This Chapter

▶ Watching performing arts for a dose of culture

▶ Figuring out where the beautiful people go at night

▶ Dancing the night away

▶ Hitting the right bars and clubs in the right order

. . . .

*I*n this chapter, I open the curtains on Montréal's vibrant performing arts scene. Montréal's performing arts scene tends to be on the edgy and daring side. I also organize the nightlife scene by category, giving you my top choices for each type of nightlife pursuit, regardless of where they're located.

Applauding the Cultural Scene

Besides the many festivals, Montréal has a bevy of performing arts troupes that put on shows during their annual seasons, which usually run from the beginning of fall into the late spring. There's cirque, theater, symphony and opera, just to name a few of the most popular. Really, these are only the tip of Montreal's cultural iceberg.

Getting the inside scoop

The *Montréal Gazette,* the city's only English daily newspaper, as well as the *Hour* and the *Mirror,* two free English weeklies, cover the city's cultural calendar. These publications list films, art venues, events, music shows, and more. The weekly publications come out on Thursday mornings and preview the coming week. You can find them in the entrance-ways of many boutiques, cafes, restaurants, and bars and in Montréal's neighborhoods.

Attending the performing arts these days is a surprisingly casual affair. People seem to go in all sorts of dress — whatever makes them most comfortable. You should, too, although you won't be out of place if you dress up for the occasion.

Although much of Montréal's cultural scene is conducted in French, you can find plenty in English; besides, music and dance need little translation. Check the free weekly newspapers for listings.

Raising the curtain on the performing arts

Deserving special mention, partly because it defies quick and easy categorization, is Québec's own **Cirque du Soleil** (www.cirquedusoleil. com), a performance spectacle under a big top, but eons and galaxies beyond the corny entertainment that people sometimes associate with a circus. Founded in Québec, now an international entertainment empire, a Cirque du Soleil performance is a human zoo of acrobats, contortionists, singers, dancers, and musicians all taking part in an elaborate fantasy. Although the show tours the world, a troupe usually returns home to Montréal every year in the spring.

Theater

Most of Canada's English-language television and film productions, as well as the Broadway musical performances, happen in Toronto. This leaves Montréal's *Anglophone* (English-speaking) actors to fill the roles of the city's small-scale, short-run stage productions. But this situation can be a recipe for excellent theater. Before *Mambo Italiano* was a moderately successful movie, it was a hit play in Montréal, written by a local playwright.

Here are some of the best venues for Montréal theater today:

- ✔ **Centaur Theatre Company,** 453 rue St-François-Xavier, Vieux-Montréal (☎ 514-288-3161), occupies a 1903 building, once the city's first stock exchange. Over the course of a season (end of Sept–end of May), Montréal's premier English-language theater company presents several plays on its two stages, including productions of modern classics, works of contemporary Canadian playwrights, and foreign adaptations. Métro: Place-d'Armes.

- ✔ **Geordie Theatre Productions** (☎ 514-845-9810), a professional children's theater company, stages a season's worth of kids classics. Intended for grade- and high-school audiences, the company's main stage is the **D.B. Clarke Theatre,** 1455 bd. de Maisonneuve Ouest (☎ 514-848-4742), on Concordia University's downtown campus. Métro: Guy-Concordia.

- ✔ **Saidye Bronfman Centre for the Arts,** 5170 Côte Ste-Catherine, West Montréal (☎ 514-739-2301), has a full season of plays that runs from late fall to early summer. This multidisciplinary arts center, which includes a gallery and fine-arts school, presents dramatic works from around the world, both contemporary and modern. Métro: Côte-Ste-Catherine.

Dance

Following is a selection of Montréal's best dance offerings:

- ✔ **L'Agora de la Danse,** 840 rue Cherrier, Plateau (☎ 514-525-1500), is a part of the Department of Dance at the Université de Québec à Montréal (University of Québec at Montréal). **Le Studio,** its 256-seat venue, is the center of Canada's modern-dance community. Métro: Sherbrooke.

- ✔ **Les Ballets Jazz de Montréal,** 3450 rue St-Urbain, fourth floor, Plateau (☎ 514-982-6771), is a contemporary dance troupe that tours internationally. Its reputation is solidly established for translating the latest artistic trends into dance. Métro: Place-des-Arts.

- ✔ **Les Grands Ballets Canadiens de Montréal,** 4816 rue Rivard (☎ 514-849-8681), produces four shows throughout its season and welcomes several visiting companies. The company adds fresh choreography to this classic ballet. Métro: Laurier.

- ✔ **Tangante,** 840 rue Cherrier (☎ 514-525-5584), bills itself as intimate laboratory theater. Dedicated to contemporary dance and experimental performance art, Tangante attempts upward of 90 performance projects during its September-to-June season. Métro: Sherbrooke.

Classical music and opera

Classical music and opera are the pinnacle of highbrow cultural consumption. For some, the challenge is to stay awake; for the true connoisseurs, it's a waking dream. Consider the following options:

- ✔ **L'Opera de Montréal,** 260 bd. de Maisonneuve Ouest, Downtown (☎ 514-985-2258), marries music, singing, plot, costumes, and set design in six elaborate productions per season. Métro: Place-des-Arts.

- ✔ **L'Orchestre Symphonique de Montréal (OSM),** 260 bd. de Maisonneuve Ouest, Downtown (☎ 514-842-9951), one of Canada's major orchestras, performs in the Salle Wilfrid-Pelletier of the Place-des-Arts. The OSM performs regularly at New York's Carnegie Hall. Métro: Place-des-Arts.

Hitting the Clubs and Bars

Whether you prefer a quiet cocktail at a jazz club or a night on the town flitting from one hot spot to the next, Montréal delivers an awesome nightlife — you can paint the town whatever color you choose. Activities peak between Thursday and Sunday, but something's always going down.

It all begins at quitting time on Thursday with the *cinq à sept* (the hours from 5 to 7 p.m.), the unofficial opening ceremonies of the weekend, when Montréal's office workers flock to their favorite watering holes to drink and snack, commiserate and socialize, and, of course, see and be seen. The party then carries on in the bars, cafes, pubs, restaurants, live-music venues, and dance clubs well into the night. Saturday is definitely the pinnacle of Montréal's frenzied nightlife activities. If it's a long week-end (a Monday holiday), concerts and all-night dance parties continue on Sunday, too.

True to its Latin spirit, Montréal's nocturnal activities start later and end later than other cities in North America. Last call is at 3 a.m., so don't be surprised if the pace doesn't really pick up until after 11 p.m. — many people are just finishing dinner at that hour — and peak around 1 a.m. Québec's legal drinking age is 18.

So where are the city's hot spots? Great spots are everywhere, but many can be found on rue Crescent and boulevard St-Laurent, the city's two main nightlife strips. You don't need to be excessively concerned about safety in these neighborhoods. Montréal's streets are relatively safe at night, partly because so many people are out. Everyone's very friendly, as people tend to be after a drink or two.

The cost of a night out can vary greatly. Many bars and clubs charge a cover, which ranges from C$5 to C$25 (US$4.25–US$21.25). Drinks can cost anywhere from C$5 to C$8 (US$4.25–US$6.75), depending on how snazzy the bar deems itself to be.

With four university campuses scattered around the downtown core, students rule the night and set the tone. Everywhere you go, all night, you're bound to see packs of students staggering about. Don't worry, though. Few bars in Montréal cater exclusively to students, so you don't risk stumbling into a scene from *Animal House.*

In fact, stepping out in Montréal requires a touch of class. No one in Montréal really dresses up at night, but people are still pretty chic on the whole. You won't see any baseball caps, fraternity sweatshirts, or running shoes. Some places even enforce a dress code. If you're not sure what to wear, just don black.

In terms of music, rock is almost dead and DJs rule the city. But you can find great live music if you like funk, jazz, world beat, Latin, bluegrass, blues, or punk. A number of venues host big-name acts passing through on the northeastern legs of their North American tours. The free week-lies are the best place to find out about who's playing where and when. Heck, you can spend the night as a groupie.

NightLife, a free glossy magazine with articles in both English and French, is also a good source. Each issue includes an exhaustive nightlife directory for the whole city, with a series of icons describing each establishment.

Downtown Montréal Nightlife

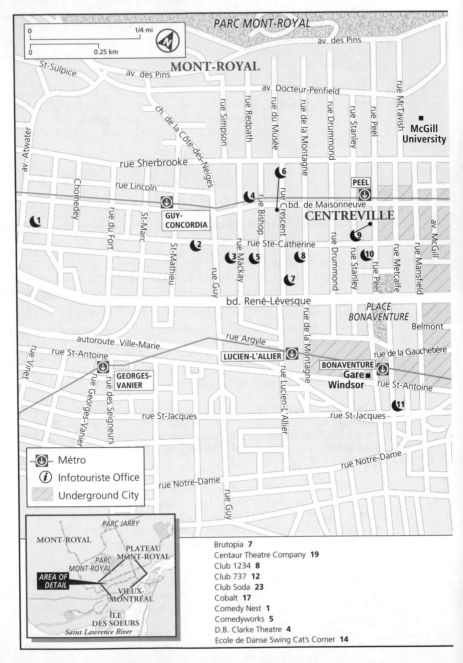

Brutopia **7**
Centaur Theatre Company **19**
Club 1234 **8**
Club 737 **12**
Club Soda **23**
Cobalt **17**
Comedy Nest **1**
Comedyworks **5**
D.B. Clarke Theatre **4**
Ecole de Danse Swing Cat's Corner **14**

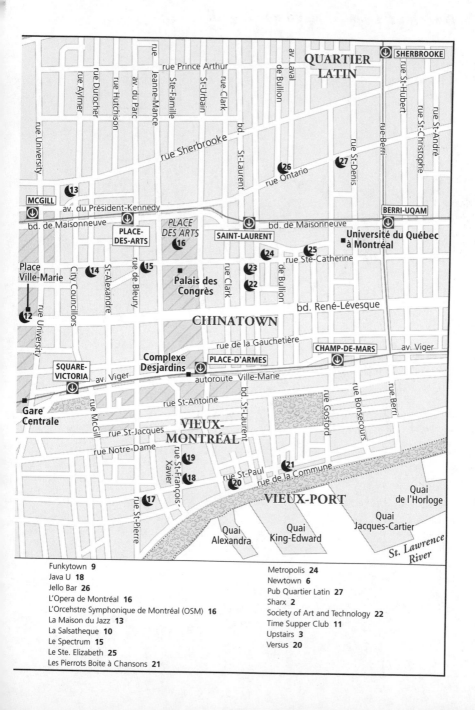

Funkytown **9**
Java U **18**
Jello Bar **26**
L'Opera de Montréal **16**
L'Orchestre Symphonique de Montréal (OSM) **16**
La Maison du Jazz **13**
La Salsatheque **10**
Le Spectrum **15**
Le Ste. Elizabeth **25**
Les Pierrots Boite à Chansons **21**

Metropolis **24**
Newtown **6**
Pub Quartier Latin **27**
Sharx **2**
Society of Art and Technology **22**
Time Supper Club **11**
Upstairs **3**
Versus **20**

Plateau, Mile End, and Gay Village Nightlife

Baldwin Barmacie **3**
Barfly **17**
Barraca Rhumerie & Tapas **12**
Bily Kun **9**
Blizzart **20**
Brasserie Dieu Du Ciel! **4**
Cabaret à Mado **28**
Cactus **11**
Cafe Saint Laurent Frappe **21**
Cafeteria **24**
Casa Del Popolo **5**
Edgar Hypertavern **13**
Else's **22**
Go Go Lounge **23**
Jello Bar **21**
L'Agora de la Danse **27**
Laika **18**
La Sala Rosa **6**
Le Cabaret **26**
Le Divan Orange **16**
Le Quai des Brumes **10**
Le Reservoir **19**
Les Ballets Jazz de Montréal **25**
Les Grands Ballets Canadiens de Montréal **7**
Mile End Bar **1**
Mocha Dance **2**
Salon Daome **8**
Sky Complex **30**
Sofa **15**
Tangante **27**
Tango Libre **14**
Unity II **29**

Also keep your eyes open for the events and acts advertised via guerilla marketing techniques: flyers and posters littering the downtown core, left on windshields, taped to poles, or pasted to the plywood barriers surrounding a construction site. For environmental reasons, I don't sanction them. But when you're looking for the latest nightlife happenings, they're hard to beat.

Shaking your groove thing: The best dance clubs

The following sections list venues where the dance floor is the main attraction.

The hottest clubs

DJs rule the night at these clubs, where the bold and beautiful clientele dance the night away. So go ahead: Strut your stuff and make the scene.

- ✔ **Blizzart,** 3956-A bd. St-Laurent, Plateau (☎ **514-843-4860**), is a long, narrow spot that feels like a cafe and oozes with street-cred. Each night of the week, local DJs play a different sound: dance hall, reggae, drum 'n' bass, and so on. Open: Daily 9 p.m.–3a.m. Cover: Wed–Sat C$3–C$5 (US$2.50–US$4.25). Métro: Sherbrooke.

- ✔ **Club 1234,** 1234 rue de la Montagne, Downtown (☎ **514-395-1111**), pronounced *twelve thirty-four,* located in a beautiful Victorian mansion, is something of a phenomenon as of late. The main-room dance floor is packed and sweaty. The drinks are expensive and the bouncers rude — yet no one seems to mind. In front, there's a lineup several people deep and it's impossible to make sense of the chaos after 11 p.m. Forget it! You're not getting in. To see the mayhem unfold on the inside, arrive before 10:30. The clientele seems to enjoy pitching stacks of napkins in the air like confetti — how festive. By the end of the night, everyone's wading through them, almost ankle-deep. Open: Thurs–Sat 10 p.m.–3 a.m. Cover: C$10–C$15 (US$8.50–US$12.75). Métro: Peel.

- ✔ At **Funkytown,** 1454 rue Peel, Downtown (☎ **514-282-8387**), an older clientele gathers to reminisce to a medley of remixed disco classics. When a '70s anthem plays, everyone rushes to the dance floor, where they sing along at the top of their lungs. Open: Fri–Sat 10 p.m.–3.a.m. Cover: C$6–C$8 (US$5–US$6.75). Métro: Peel.

- ✔ **Mile End Bar,** 5322 bd. St-Laurent, Mile End (☎ **514-279-0200**), north of the main St-Laurent strip, has become a fixture of Thursday's *cinq à sept* landscape. Droves of flirting office workers, fresh from a hard day on the job, jam the bar downstairs. The action later moves to the nightclub upstairs, where there's a lofted seating area and a suspended catwalk. Open: Thurs–Fri 5 p.m.–3 a.m., Sat 7 p.m.–3 a.m. Cover: Usually C$5 (US$4.25) Fri–Sat. Métro: Laurier.

- ✔ **Salon Daome,** 141 av. Mont Royal Ouest, Plateau (☎ **514-282-8777**), is an upstairs hideaway for lovers of funky and soulful music. The second-floor loft space feels more like an apartment than a nightclub, but it gets packed nonetheless. Tuesdays are a happening tech-house night, if you're looking for somewhere to go at the beginning of the week. Wednesdays are salsa. Thursdays through Saturdays a DJ spins funk, rare groove, and Afro-Latin-influenced sounds. Occasionally someone beats on a jembe as accompaniment. Open: Tues–Sat 8 p.m.–3 a.m. Cover: C$5–C$10 (US$4.25–US$8.50). Métro: Mont-Royal.

✔ **Society of Art and Technology (SAT),** 1195 bd. St-Laurent, Quartier Latin (☎ 514-844-2033), is the leader of the underground music scene. Its main room features video projections that play along with the music. The SAT often hosts parties in association with new-media, and also hosts music, festivals, and events, which makes nights here varied and eclectic, as is the clientele. The schedule is erratic, but there is usually something going on. Call or check its Web site (www.sat.qc.ca). Métro: St-Laurent.

✔ **Time Supper Club,** 997 rue St-Jacques, Downtown (☎ 514-392-9292), is wildly popular after dinner, when the chairs are cleared from the main floor and everybody gets up to dance. The party carries on at a feverish pace, as people crowd the bar, mingle in the walkways, and take turns dancing on the island in the middle of the dining room. Open: Thurs–Sat 7 p.m.–3 a.m. Cover: C$20 (US$17). Métro: Bonaventure.

✔ **Zoobizare,** 6388 St-Hubert, Rosemont (☎ 514-270-9331), is a recent addition to Montréal's nightlife map in the northern reaches of the city. If you're into a kitsch brand of cool, it's worth the trek for electro clash and synth punk sounds. On the second floor, above some stores, is a stone-walled room with arched ceilings. It feels like a wine cellar or a dungeon and makes for an offbeat setting. It's actually the reincarnation of a bar in Bordeaux, France. Open: Thurs–Sat 9 p.m.–3 a.m.; schedule varies during the rest of the week. Cover: C$5–C$10 (US$4.25–US$8.50). Métro: Jean Talon.

Salsa, swing, and tango

Ever since disco bottomed out in the '80s, there's been a growing nostalgia for couples dancing, in Montréal as everywhere else. These days, swing is not the only dance in town. Salsa and tango are also extremely popular. Whichever style you opt for, couples dancing makes for a great night out. You can dance, watch, or learn — I hope a bit of each.

Most of the following places give free lessons or crash courses earlier in the evening, before the real party starts. So you can walk in a complete beginner and tango home like a pro. Well, sort of. Call to find out when the sessions are on.

✔ **Cactus,** 4461 rue St-Denis, Plateau (☎ 514-849-0349), Montréal's other salsa hot spot, is on two floors of a town house just around the corner from the Mont-Royal Métro station. It's a little less intimidating than La Salsatheque, perhaps because the setting is more intimate. Beginners try out their moves on the upstairs dance floor, while the regulars tear it up front and center. Open: Thurs 9 p.m.– 3 a.m., Fri–Sat 10 p.m.–3 a.m., Sun 4–8 p.m. Cover: C$5 (US$4.25). Métro: Mont-Royal.

✔ **Ecole de Danse Swing Cat's Corner,** 486 rue Ste-Catherine Ouest, Suite 303, Downtown (☎ 514-874-9846), hosts the biggest swing night in Montréal on Fridays, with a crash course from 8:30 to 9:30 p.m., and then dancing until whatever hour. Open: Fridays 8:30 p.m.–1 a.m. Cover: C$7 (US$6). Métro: Place-des-Arts.

✔ **La Salsatheque,** 1220 rue Peel, Downtown (☎ 514-875-0016), is Montréal's oldest Latin club. The décor is somewhat dated, but no one seems to mind. The action's on the steel dance floor as couples shimmy and spin to a variety of Latin rhythms, predominantly salsa, merengue, and bachata. Open: Thurs–Sat 10 p.m.–3 a.m. Cover: Fri–Sat C$5 (US$4.25). Métro: Peel.

✔ **Mocha Dance,** 5175-A av. du Parc, Mile End (☎ 514-277-5575), is a dance studio with a bar and cafe, serving drinks and a light menu. Throughout the week, the space hosts evenings of tango (Tues, Fri, Sun) and salsa (Thurs, Sat). Sunday's Tango Brunch is from 1:30 to 7:30 p.m. Even if you have no intention of dancing, it's a romantic spot to spend a lazy Sunday afternoon. Open: Tues 9 p.m.–3 a.m., Thurs 9 p.m.–1 a.m., Fri 10 p.m–3 a.m., Sat 9 p.m.–3 a.m., Sun 1:30–7:30 p.m. Cover: C$5–C$8 (US$4.25–US$6.75). Métro: Laurier.

✔ **Tango Libre,** 1650 rue Marie-Anne Est, Plateau (☎ 514-527-5197), an intimate dance floor tucked away on a mainly residential street, has tango evenings beginning at 9:30 p.m. Friday and Saturday (Cover: C$7/US$6). Supervised practice sessions are Thursday and Sunday (Cover: C$6/US$5). In summertime, this tango studio organizes Sunday evening dances at parks around the city. Métro: Mont-Royal.

Grooving to live music

DJs may rule the city, but you can still find plenty of live, local music in the bars and clubs around town. And the summer festivals supercharge Montréal's concert schedule, drawing top talent and delighted crowds to city venues.

Intimate settings

Do you feel like live music for a change? This doesn't necessarily mean rocking out at a concert in a stadium. Instead, here are several spots around town where live music is the main draw — where you can hear up-and-coming talent or an offbeat sound.

✔ **Barfly,** 4062-A bd. St-Laurent, Plateau (☎ 514-284-6665), is a tiny spot on one of the city's main nightlife strips with a pool table and a stage. An eclectic mix of local talent plays lively and boisterous sets of folk music. Some nights are more brooding, when speakers and poets take the stage. Open: Daily 4 p.m.–3 a.m. Cover: Fri–Sat C$3–C$5 (US$2.50–US$4.25). Métro: Sherbrooke.

✔ **Casa Del Popolo,** 4873 bd. St-Laurent, Plateau (☎ 514-284 3804), bills itself as a vegetarian hot spot. During the day it's a cafe; by night, it's an intimate bar and live-music venue. Along with the musical acts, the owners book a variety of performances, which can be broadly categorized as urban folk and include DJ nights, traveling video road shows, and spoken word. Casa also runs La Sala Rosa, a space across the street at 4848 bd. St-Laurent, which is for larger happenings. Open: Daily noon–3 a.m. Cover: Occasional, C$5–C$10 (US$4.25–US$8.50). Métro: Laurier.

✔ **La Maison du Jazz,** 2060 rue Aylmer, Downtown (☎ 514-842-8656), formerly called Biddle's, was the haunt of late Montréal jazzman Charlie Biddle. Live jazz is played nightly on a small stage, with several tiers of seating in an Art Nouveau setting. Dinner is available and includes La Maison's famous ribs. The lounge and bar are just far enough removed to allow for quiet conversation. Open: Sun 6 p.m.–midnight, Mon–Wed noon–midnight, Thurs noon–1 a.m., Fri noon–2:30 a.m., Sat 6 p.m.–2:30 a.m. Cover: C$5 (US4.25) added to your bill. Métro: McGill.

✔ **Le Divan Orange,** 4234 bd. St-Laurent, Plateau (☎ 514-840-9090), is the latest bar to open on St-Laurent that features a vibrant live-music scene. It's a resto-cafe-showbar that has comfortable, cozy couches at the front; a long bar down the left-hand side; and a stage at the back. The vibe is laid back, deconstructed, and convivial. Open: Tues–Sun 11 a.m.–3a.m. Cover: Occasional, C$3–C$5 (US$2.50–US$4.25). Métro: Sherbrooke.

✔ **Le Quai des Brumes,** 4481 rue St-Denis, Plateau (☎ 514-499-0467), is a dark and smoky bar frequented by an older, mainly French-speaking clientele. The brick walls and wood paneling give it a warm ambience. Jazz, blues, or rock bands play on a small stage in the back every Wednesday and Saturday. Open: Daily noon–3 a.m. Cover: Depending on the talent, cover can vary from C$3–C$8 (US$2.50–US$6.75). Métro: Mont-Royal.

✔ **Les Pierrots Boite à Chansons,** 104 rue St-Paul Est, Vieux-Montréal (☎ 514-861-1270), is the premier spot to hear traditional Québec folk music, from Thursday through Saturday, when the place is usually rockin'. If you don't speak French, you won't be able to sing along, but you can still clap. For most of the crowd, the night is highly sentimental and emotionally charged as they sing along to the ballads they learned growing up. It's a memorable night out. Open: Daily 9 p.m.–3 a.m. Cover: C$5–C$6 (US$4.25–US$5). Métro: Champ-de-Mars.

✔ **Sofa,** 451 rue Rachel Est, Plateau (☎ 514-285-1011), a lounge with a cigar humidor and many bottles of port, has live acts, usually of the funk, soul, or R&B varieties, Thursday through Sunday. The bar is an island in the middle of the establishment. In front of it, a narrow space creates a sort of gauntlet for mingling 25- to 35-year-olds. Behind, groups of friends chill in the large alcoves with booths. Open: 4 p.m.–3 a.m. Cover: C$4–C$9 (US$3.50–US$7.75). Métro: Mont-Royal.

✔ **Upstairs,** 1254 rue Mackay, Downtown (☎ 514-931-6808), also offers jazz nightly, but in a more intimate setting. The stage seems no more than a windowsill, as ensembles of up to six musicians jam together in close quarters. Mondays and Tuesdays are "Fresh Jazz" nights, featuring the latest talent of McGill University's music students. Shows start at 9 p.m. Dining available. Open: Mon–Fri 12:30 p.m.–3 a.m., Sat–Sun 5 p.m.–3 a.m. Cover: Fri–Sat C$15–C$20 (US$12.75–US$17), Sun C$10 (US$8.50). Métro: Guy-Concordia.

Concert Venues

The clubs, or show bars, discussed in this section net a surprising amount of top talent on tour. They open only when there's a show, but that seems to be most nights. So, who's playing while you're in town? Find out by browsing Montréal's free weeklies, calling the box offices, or visiting the clubs' Web sites. You can also book your tickets in person, by phone, or on the Web. Be sure to check out the following:

✔ **Club Soda,** 1225 bd. St-Laurent, Quartier Latin (☎ 514-286-1010; www.clubsoda.ca; Métro: St-Laurent)

✔ **Le Cabaret,** 111 bd. St-Laurent, Quartier Latin (☎ 514-845-2014; Métro: St-Laurent)

✔ **Le Spectrum,** 318 rue Ste-Catherine Ouest, Downtown (☎ 514-861-5851; www.spectrumdemontreal.ca; Métro: Place-des-Arts)

✔ **Metropolis,** 59 rue Ste-Catherine Est, Quartier Latin (☎ 514-844-3500; www.metropolismontreal.ca; Métro: St-Laurent)

Hopping between hot spots: Montréal's cafes and bars

Montréal's nightlife begins early, carries on at a torrid pace, and ends late. Seasoned denizens look to hit at least two or three spots over the course of an evening. Choreographing the perfect night out is all about timing, variety, and keeping your options open.

Montréalers like to mix-and-match. The city's cafes and bars are perfect for this: meeting friends before a night of dancing or sharing impressions after a live show. Rather than clubs and concerts, where music is the main draw — and usually too loud for sustained conversation — the city's cafes and bars are definitely more social. This is also the best place to meet and mingle with the locals.

The expression in French is *M'as tu vu?* (pronounced *mah too voo,* and literally meaning "Have you seen me?"). The following places are very that:

✔ **Baldwin Barmacie,** 115 av. Laurier Ouest, Outremont (☎ 514-276-4282), serves up concoctions to a loud and flirtatious crowd seeking strong antidotes for its angst. The hallway entrance is like a catwalk due to its several large windows that open onto the bar. The long layout of the two rooms, one down a half-flight of stairs, is somewhat disconcerting. If you want to order a drink from the upper level, you must hail the bartenders who are several feet below where you are. Makes for an interesting conversation starter. Open: Mon–Fri 5 p.m.–3 a.m., Sat–Sun 8 p.m.–3 a.m. Cover: None. Métro: Laurier.

✔ **Cafeteria,** 3581 bd. St-Laurent, Plateau (☎ 514-849-3855), is really a restaurant. However, it is increasingly becoming a destination for drinks among the young and fashionable set. True to its name, the tables of the dining room are packed together, allowing for plenty of social mingling. Others mill around the bar. It's quite a scene that goes late into the night. Open: Daily 8 a.m.–3 a.m. Cover: None. Métro: Sherbrooke or St-Laurent.

✔ **Club 737,** 1 Place Ville-Marie, Downtown (☎ 514-397-0737), atop Montréal's tallest skyscraper, is easy to locate: Just find the source of the spotlights that stretch across the night's sky. On the ground floor, patrons line up for an elevator to shuttle them to the club on the 42nd and 43rd floors. Undeniably, the vistas of Montréal by night are spectacular! The experience is even better during the summer months, when the club allows patrons out onto one of the observation decks. I think the view is the main attraction here; otherwise, the two floors are dark, hot, and sweaty. Open: Fri–Sat 10 p.m.–3 a.m. Cover: C$10–C$15 (US$8.50–$12.75). Métro: Bonaventure.

✔ **Edgar Hypertavern,** 1562 av. Mont-Royal Est (☎ 514-521-4661), is several blocks east of St-Denis, in the heart of the Plateau. It's a popular destination for an attractive crowd of 20- and 30-somethings, dressed casually, yet at the height of fashion. The cramped quarters make the mingling rather intense. Large sculptures of sailfish trophies with hooks dangling from their bodies evoke thoughts of hunting and fishing, and perhaps set the tone of the evening. Open: Daily 3 p.m.–3 a.m. Cover: None. Métro: Mont-Royal.

✔ **Newtown,** 1476 rue Crescent, Downtown (☎ 514-284-6555), bears the nickname of its owner, former Formula One driver Jacques Villeneuve. It is a literal translation of his last name and what his pals called him on the F1 circuit. The three floors of his establishment include a restaurant and terrace upstairs and a club in the basement. The main-floor bar draws an older clientele than most other places on rue Crescent. The décor is sleek and sophisticated. Open: Daily noon–3 a.m. Cover: Fri–Sat C$10 (US$8.50). Métro: Guy-Concordia.

✔ **Versus,** 106 rue St-Paul Ouest, Vieux-Montréal (☎ 514-788-2040), is the bar of the Hotel Nelligan. It's particularly popular for after-work drinks among slick professionals working in the area. Plus, Hotel Nelligan seems to be the boutique hotel of choice among visiting A-list celebrities, which adds further mystique to the contemporary, yet warm, décor. Open: Daily 11 a.m.–1 a.m. Cover: None. Métro: Place-d'Armes.

Lounging like lizards

Sipping cosmopolitan martinis and other candy-colored concoctions — this has been "in" for a terribly long time. In the mid-1990s, even before the lounge scene became a widespread trend in North American urban centers, Montréal had already started opening places with comfy seating, retro décor, and long drink lists of elaborate cocktails with fancy names, all served in martini glasses.

- **Go Go Lounge,** 3682 bd. St-Laurent, Plateau (☎ 514-286-0882), is mayhem. It's, at times, so crowded that girls resort to dancing on the bar. Some of the staff are "in character" — with decked out wigs and disco fashions, their get-ups are inspired by Go Go's full-on retro décor. There's no cover, but the line out front is notoriously slow; so, get there early or prepare to be patient. Open: Mon–Fri 5 p.m.–3 a.m., Sat–Sun 7 p.m.–3 a.m. Cover: None. Métro: Sherbrooke.

- **Java U,** 191 rue St-Paul Ouest, Vieux-Montréal (☎ 514-849-8881), serves cafe snacks during the day and a dinner menu in the evening, but by 11 p.m. (Tues–Sat), it's just drinks and DJs. Yes, here you can get martinis — both the classic and newfangled versions. It's probably the most legit spot in Vieux-Montréal — sleek, but not necessarily packaged for tourists, unlike many of the other places in the city's historic district. Open: Tues–Sat 11 a.m.–3 a.m., Sun 11 a.m.–midnight. Cover: None. Métro: Place-d'Armes.

- **Jello Bar,** 151 rue Ontario Est, Quartier Latin (☎ 514-285-2621), was one of the forerunners of Montréal's martini movement. Its success in re-creating a '70s lounge environment coincided with the public's sudden and insatiable appetite for all things retro and a newfound and considerable thirst for sophisticated-looking drinks. DJs and live bands enhance the ambience in the form of jazz, Latin, funk, soul, R&B, and other lounge-friendly musical tangents. Open: Tues–Fri 5 p.m.–3 a.m., Sat 9 p.m–3 a.m. Cover: C$5–C$8 (US$4.25–US$6.75). Métro: St-Laurent.

- **Laika,** 4040 bd. St-Laurent, Plateau (☎ 514-842-8088), is centrally located, so it's an ideal place for friends to meet throughout the day, and particularly popular in the evening. A different local DJ of some repute spins sets throughout for the denizens bobbing their heads and chatting away, sitting at the cocktail tables in the front. At the back, the space narrows only leaving room for a long, wooden bar. Large windows open onto boulevard St-Laurent, poorly disguised rubbernecking from both sides of the pane is common practice. Open: Daily 9 a.m.–3 a.m. Cover: None. Métro: Sherbrooke.

✔ **Pub Quartier Latin,** 318 rue Ontario Est, Quartier Latin (☎ 514-845-3301), located just off of St-Denis. Its inconspicuous location makes it hard to just happen upon. They play funk and rare groove, supposedly the variety of stuff you'd find pressed on 45 rpm records. A central bar anchors the first room surrounded by intimate banquettes along the wall. The second room is somewhat larger. An elevated area at the back is a makeshift stage for the funk and world music bands that play there. Open: Daily 3 p.m.–3 a.m. Cover: None. Métro: Sherbrooke, Berri-UQAM.

Dropping into neighborhood bars

At the establishments in this section, you'll find plenty of locals and not many tourists. But don't be shy: Belly up to the bar, order a drink, and strike up a conversation with a regular.

✔ **Barraca Rhumerie & Tapas,** 1134 av. Mont-Royal Est, Plateau (☎ 514-525-7741), offers up a potentially volatile mix of booze and food, an extensive menu of aged rums, and a shorter list of tasty appetizers. Rich tones of stained wood, wrought-iron accents, and parchment lampshades, contribute to the boudoirlike atmosphere. The long and narrow space is often crowded, making it extremely difficult to reach the small terrace in the back. Open: Daily 3 p.m.–3 a.m. Cover: None. Métro: Mont-Royal.

✔ **Bily Kun,** 354 av. Mont-Royal Est, Plateau (☎ 514-845-5392), is a dimly lit and somewhat cavernous room, finished with bold lines, a beautiful tile floor, and ostrich-head trophies on the walls. It is a modern-day pub that attracts a hip but unpretentious clientele in their mid-20s and up. Order your drinks from the waiter; ask the busboy about the menu of light snacks. Open: Daily 3 p.m.–3 a.m. Cover: None. Métro: Mont-Royal.

✔ **Cobalt,** 312 rue St-Paul Ouest, Vieux-Montréal (☎ 514-842-2960), is a single room with stone walls; exposed, wooden beams running across the ceiling; and beautiful, period windows. The understated furniture and dim lighting accentuate these historic features — the room feels both ancient and timeless. Music from a jamming live jazz trio, a wide selection of beers and scotches, and a respectable menu served late draws a mixed crowd: young and old, couples eating dinner, friends out for drinks. It's laid back and comfortable — cozy, even. Open: Daily 11:30 a.m.–3 a.m. Cover: None. Métro: Square Victoria.

✔ **Else's,** 156 rue Roy Est, Plateau (☎ 514-286-6689), is a comfortable, intimate spot that seems like a well-kept secret, with its inconspicuous location, soft lighting, and the constant murmur of conversation. Actually, it is quite popular. The bar's liquor license is such that you have to buy a token snack with your alcohol. On tap is an interesting selection of beer from Québec's microbreweries, as well as cider. Open: Daily 8 a.m.–3 a.m. Cover: None. Métro: Sherbrooke.

✔ **Le Ste-Elisabeth,** 1412 rue Ste-Elizabeth, Quartier Latin (☎ 514-286-4302), is hidden away, just off a seedy stretch of rue Ste-Catherine. But, put any apprehension aside and persevere, and you will be rewarded. It's a real gem on a summer night: an intimate outdoor terrace with tables and chairs on two levels, surrounded by ivy-covered walls, several stories high. In addition, it is right between the downtown's two festival sites, Place des Arts and rue St-Denis. Monday, all year around, the bar has a special: C$3 (US$2.50) for pints of Boreal beer. Open: Daily 3 p.m.–3 a.m. Cover: None. Métro: Berri-UQAM.

What's brewing in Montréal?

If you take your obligations as a tourist seriously, you should try as many of the locally brewed beers as possible. Not only are there a wide variety of suds brewed by the provinces' microbreweries, but several brewpubs also craft their own beer, which is not available anywhere else. Here are my recommendations:

✔ **Brasserie Dieu Du Ciel!,** 9 av. Laurier Ouest, Mile End (☎ 514-490-9555), features over 30 house recipes brewed on-site. The bar is dark and cozy, ideal for a quiet time on a cold night. A window allows patrons to peer down into the basement to see where the beer's made. Open: Daily 3 p.m.–3 a.m. Cover: None. Métro: Laurier.

✔ **Brutopia,** 1219 rue Crescent, Downtown (☎ 514-868-9916), consists of three bars and several rooms spread over three floors. By the main bar, there's a small stage for the nightly, live music. Sundays are a popular open-mic. During the warmer months, the brewery offers seating outside, both in back and out front. Brutopia brews its house beers in large brass barrels in the room behind the bar; try Indian Pale Ale, Raspberry Blonde, or Apricot Wheat. Open: Daily 3 p.m.–3 a.m. Cover: None. Métro: Guy-Concordia.

✔ **Le Cheval Blanc,** 809 rue Ontario Est, Quartier Latin (☎ 514-522-0211), was the first brewpub in Montréal and is responsible for launching this segment of bars, which has now matured into all-the-rage. The unpretentious crowd is a mixed bag. Serious beer aficionados come for the ales on tap, neighborhood-types are drawn-in by the red glow of the Asian lanterns. Open: Daily 3 p.m.–3 a.m. Cover: None. Métro: Berri-UQUAM.

✔ **Le Reservoir,** 9 av. Duluth Est, Plateau (☎ 514-849-7779), has a window on its brewing operation to the right of the bar. Groups of friends and couples chat, seated at tables with votive candles. During the summer, the main-floor windows open onto the street, and the second-floor terrace is in full swing. Open: Mon–Fri noon–3 a.m., Sat–Sun 10:30 a.m.–3 a.m. Cover: None. Métro: Sherbrooke.

Racking up in a pool hall

You don't have to be a shark or a rounder to frequent a pool hall these days. In Montréal, they're practically chic. You can play for rounds of drinks, but be sure to size up your competition before making such a suggestion — lest you get fleeced. Here are two of the more popular places to play pool:

 ✔ **Cafe Saint Laurent Frappe,** 3900 bd. St-Laurent, Plateau (☎ 514-289-9462; Open: Daily noon–3 a.m.; Métro: Sherbrooke)

 ✔ **Sharx,** 1606 rue Ste-Catherine Ouest, Downtown (☎ 514-934-3105; Open: Daily 11 a.m.–3 a.m.; Métro: Guy-Concordia)

Yucking it up at comedy clubs

As the annual **Just For Laughs Festival** continues to grow, Montréal is increasingly a mecca for stand-up and improv comedians. They say it's the hardest profession in the world. Here are two places to try:

 ✔ **Comedy Nest,** 2313 rue Ste-Catherine Ouest, Downtown (☎ 514-932-6378; Open: Thurs–Sat, shows at 8:30 p.m. and 10:30 p.m.; Métro: Atwater)

 ✔ **Comedyworks,** 1238 rue Bishop, Downtown (☎ 514-398-9661; Open: Mon–Fri 4 p.m.–3 a.m., Sat–Sun 7 p.m.–3 a.m.; Métro: Guy-Concordia)

Being out and proud in Gay Village

Montréal is quickly becoming the hottest gay destination in North America, and the city's gay community has a thriving nightlife scene. Gay Pride and the Black and Blue weekends are annual highlights on the city's nightlife calendar. Rue Ste-Catherine, east of rue St-Hubert, is packed with innumerable restaurants, cafes, bars, and clubs that are always hopping throughout the year. Following are some of the hottest spots.

 ✔ **Cabaret à Mado,** 1115 rue Ste-Catherine Est, Gay Village (☎ 514-525-7566), has drag queens strutting in cabaret shows on some nights. The rest of the time they emcee for karaoke, stand-up comedy, and theme parties. Open: Daily 11 a.m.–3 a.m. Cover: C$3–C$6 (US$2.50–US$5). Métro: Beaudry.

 ✔ **Sky Complex,** 1474 rue Ste-Catherine Est, Gay Village (☎ 514-529-6969), is a pub, restaurant, cabaret, male strip club, mega-dance club, and rooftop terrace in one. For gay men, it's a sort of one-stop shop. Open: Mon–Tues 2 p.m.–1 a.m., Wed–Sun 2 p.m.–3 a.m. Cover: Fri–Sat C$3 (US$2.50). Métro: Papineau.

 ✔ **Unity II,** 1171 rue Ste-Catherine Est, Gay Village (☎ 514-523-2777), is a mega-club in the Village spread over three floors and topped by a terrace on the roof. Take advantage of the two-for-one specials every day from 4 to 8 p.m. Open: Wed, Fri, Sat 10 p.m.–3 a.m. Cover: C$3–C$5 (US$2.50–US$4.25). Métro: Beaudry.

Part IV

Settling Into and Exploring Québec City

The 5th Wave   By Rich Tennant

In this part . . .

A couple of hours downriver from Montréal is Québec City, a place that makes you feel as though you've stepped into another age. In this part, I explain where to go and what to do to get the most out of your visit. I tell you where to find the best hotels, restaurants, and attractions. I even give you a handy historical tour of Québec's Old City, so that you can see all the highlights in one afternoon.

Chapter 16

Arriving and Getting Oriented in Québec City

In This Chapter

▶ Getting to Québec City

▶ Figuring out the city's neighborhoods

▶ Traveling around the city

*Y*ou're likely to spend almost all your time in Québec City in the Old City, which is divided into a fortified **Haute-Ville** (Upper City), built behind walls on a cliff overlooking the St. Lawrence River, and a **Basse-Ville** (Lower City), at the foot of the cliff running along the riverfront, to the south and east. You can easily get lost in the winding cobblestone streets in either neighborhood, but don't worry if you do. The whole point of Québec City is strolling around and soaking up the unbelievable atmosphere. This chapter explains how to get to Québec City and how to get around after you arrive.

No matter how you get to Canada from abroad, you have to pass through Customs. See Chapter 8 for details on what to expect from the stern-faced Customs agents you encounter at the border.

Making Your Way to Your Hotel

Whatever you may have thought of your trip so far, get ready, Québec City will charm your pants off. Getting to your hotel will feel like traveling back in time: from the suburban outskirts littered with modern-looking malls to the historic, walled city. You'll feel the centuries peeling away. You may feel younger, too: The setting seems to appeal to the long-lost romantic in everyone.

If you arrive by plane

If you arrive in Québec City by air, you will land at the small **Jean Lesage International Airport,** 500 rue Principale Sainte-Foy (☎ **418-640-2700**). No shuttles are available to downtown Québec City. A taxi ride costs a fixed rate of C$25 (US$21.25). If you want to rent a car, the following major agencies have desks at the airport:

- ✔ **Avis:** ☎ **800-879-2847** or 418-872-2861

- ✔ **Budget:** ☎ **800-268-8900** or 418-872-9885

- ✔ **Hertz Canada:** ☎ **800-654-3131** or 418-871-1571

- ✔ **Thrifty:** ☎ **800-367-2277** or 418-877-2870

You may land at the province's main international airport, which is actually in Montréal: **Trudeau International Airport** (☎ **800-465-1213** or 514-394-7377). See Chapter 8 for more details about arriving here and traveling by land between Montréal and Québec City.

If you arrive by car

From **New York City,** follow I-87 to Highway 15 to Montréal, and then pick up Autoroute 20 to Québec City. To get into the city, take Autoroute 73 Nord (Highway 73 North) across the Pierre-Laporte Bridge (Pont Pierre-Laporte) and exit on boulevard Champlain. Turn left at rue Parc des Champs-de-Batailles and follow it to Grande-Allée. When you get to Grande-Allée, turn right, and head straight into the Old City.

From **Boston,** take I-89 to I-93 in Montpelier, Vermont, which connects with Highway 55 in Québec to link up with Autoroute 20. Follow the preceding directions.

From **Montréal,** you can take either Autoroute 20, which follows the south shore of the St. Lawrence River or the more scenic, less-trafficked Autoroute 40, which follows the north shore. Either way, the trip takes about two and a half hours.

If you arrive by train or bus

Trains pull into Québec City train station, **Gare du Palais,** 450 rue Gare-du-Palais (☎ **418-692-3940**). **Via Rail** handles all passenger train travel in Canada (☎ **888-842-7245;** www.viarail.ca).

Adjacent to the train station is the bus station, **Terminus Gare du Palais,** 320 rue Abraham-Martin (☎ **418-525-3000**). There are several different lines that serve the region but, for Québec City, they all stop here.

Figuring Out Québec City's Neighborhoods

Québec's Old City is really quite small, but it's so dense and packed with interesting sites, shops, museums, cafes, restaurants, and other attractions that you can spend a lot of time wandering its winding streets and still be surprised by new sites and curiosities. The only neighborhood that you'll likely want to visit outside the Old City is the Grande-Allée, a long, wide street running west of the St-Louis Gate that's lined with restaurants, boutiques, and bars. During the summer evenings, this street is hopping, and its terraces are packed with revelers.

Haute-Ville (Upper City)

This is the biggest part of the Old City, a neighborhood entirely surrounded by thick ramparts. Most of Québec City's main attractions can be found here, including the **Château Frontenac,** the **Place d'Armes,** the **Basilique Notre-Dame,** the **Québec seminary and museum,** and the **terrasse Dufferin** (a long promenade with a view of the St. Lawrence River below). Most of the buildings are at least 100 years old, some much older. The city was not built on a grid, so it can be disorienting, but don't worry — sooner or later, you'll arrive at a wall, a cliff, or a gate, and you'll be able to figure out where you are on a map.

Basse-Ville (Lower City)

Historically, this part of the city was reserved mainly for poor families that worked in the docks. Now, it's pretty much a continuation of the Haute-Ville. In the Basse-Ville, you find similar architecture, many restaurants, some small inns, and several major attractions, including the spectacular **Musée de la Civilisation (Museum of Civilization).** Rue St-Paul is a lovely strip with many art galleries and antiques stores and some very cute accommodations.

Take the elevator or the stairs down from the terrasse Dufferin or Place d'Armes, and you wind up on the delightful rue Petit Champlain, a pedestrian alley full of shops of varying quality. Don't forget to stroll along the port area. Recent development and an interest by the cruise industry have made the area more attractive and festive. You'll be in awe of the massive cruise ships from around the world that dock at the port.

Grande-Allée

If you exit the Haute-Ville at the St-Louis Gate and keep walking west past Québec's Parliament Buildings, you end up on Grande-Allée. Although this street offers a lot of hotels and accommodations, it is known mainly for its many restaurants and bars with sidewalk terraces. It's a meeting point for the city's young, and it's lively all summer long. Keep heading west for about 15 minutes on foot and you'll reach avenue Cartier on your right — another lively street with many B&Bs, restaurants, shops, and bars.

Finding Information after You Arrive

Québec City has two good tourist information centers in handy locations. The main office is **Centre Infotouriste,** 12 rue Ste-Anne, just opposite the Château Frontenac at Place d'Armes (☎ **800-363-7777** or 418-692-2608). The office is well stocked with tons of brochures and is well

Québec City Orientation

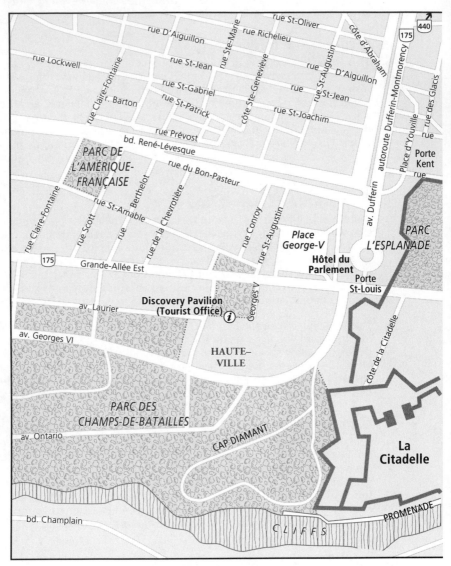

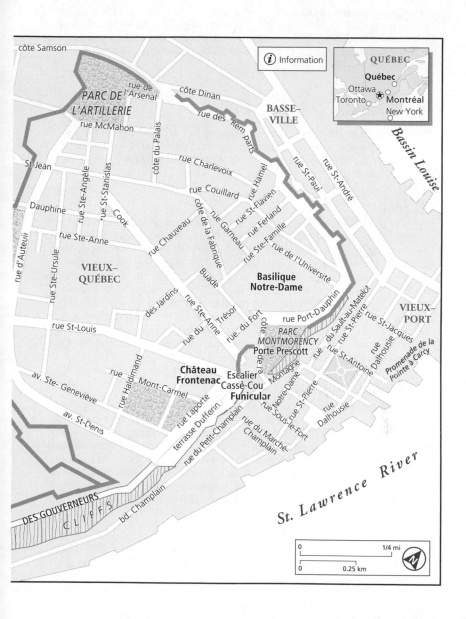

côte Samson

PARC DE
L'ARTILLERIE

rue de l'Arsenal

côte Dinan

rue des Remparts

BASSE-
VILLE

rue McMahon

côte du Palais

St-Jean

rue Charlevoix

rue Couillard

rue St-Paul

rue St-André

Dauphine

rue Ste-Angèle

rue St-Stanislas

Cook

rue Chauveau

côte de la Fabrique

rue Garneau

rue St-Flavien

rue Hamel

rue Ferland

rue Ste-Famille

rue de l'Université

rue d'Auteuil

rue Ste-Ursule

rue Ste-Anne

VIEUX–
QUÉBEC

Buade

Basilique
Notre-Dame

rue St-Louis

des Jardins

rue Ste-Anne

rue du Trésor

rue. du Fort

côte de la

rue Port-Dauphin

rue du Sault-au-Matelot

rue St-Pierre

rue St-Jacques

VIEUX–
PORT

rue St-Antoine

rue Dalhousie

Promenade de la
Pointe à Carcy

av. Ste- Geneviève

rue Haldimand

Mont-Carmel

Château
Frontenac

Escalier
Casse-Cou
Funicular

PARC
MONTMORENCY
Porte Prescott

Montagne

rue Notre-Dame

rue St-Pierre

rue
Dalhousie

av. St-Denis

rue Laporte

terrasse Dufferin

rue du Petit-Champlain

rue du Marché-
Champlain

rue Sous-le-Fort

DES GOUVERNEURS

CLIFFS

bd. Champlain

St. Lawrence River

Bassin Louise

Information

QUÉBEC

Québec

Ottawa

Toronto

Montréal

New York

0   1/4 mi
0   0.25 km

staffed with bilingual employees who help you find information or book hotel rooms and tours for you. The **Greater Québec Area Tourism and Convention Bureau,** 835 av. Laurier, near the Plains of Abraham and not too far from Grande-Allée (☎ 418-649-2608), offers the same services but tends to be a little less busy.

Getting Around Québec City

Québec City's small size makes it a snap to get around. By foot is best; however, at some point, you have to contend with the steep hill between the Haute-Ville and Basse-Ville. This is when the *funiculaire* (elevator) comes in handy.

By foot

If you're in reasonably good shape and have comfortable walking shoes, you can probably dispense with all motorized transport while in Québec City, especially if your hotel is in the Old City. Walking is definitely the best way to travel; the only challenge on foot is getting between the Upper and Lower cities. To do so, you have to climb the steep stairs that join Côte de la Montagne (near the Petit Champlain) to the Dufferin Terrace. If you want, you can take the *funiculaire* that leaves from the head of rue Petit-Champlain and also arrives on the Dufferin Terrace. In the north part of the Old City, near rue St-Jean, you can take advantage of a more gradual decline to get to the Basse-Ville by following rue Côte-du-Palais down a gentle slope to rue St-Paul.

By public transportation

I have only one exception to the rule of walking: if you're staying too far away from the Old City to make the trip in by foot. In that case, several buses run frequently into the Old City. Bus 7 runs up and down rue St-Jean; bus 11 runs along Grande-Allée and rue St-Louis. Both take you into the Old City, making stops all the way to Place d'Youville, just outside the walls on the north side of town. These buses pass about every ten minutes. Fares are C$2.25 (US$2) of exact change, or you can purchase tickets at a *dépanneur* (convenience store) for C$1.90 (US$1.50).

By taxi

Taxis are plentiful in Québec City, and they're pretty easy to flag down around the big hotels and outside the gates of the Old City. Inside the Old City, you can find taxi stands at Place d'Armes and in front of the Hôtel-de-Ville (City Hall). The fares are the same as in Montréal, which can be a little expensive for short distances. The starting rate is C$2.50 (US$2), and then C$1.20 (US$1) per kilometer. To call a taxi, try **Taxi Coop** (☎ 418-525-5191) or **Taxi Québec** (☎ 418-525-8123).

By car

Trying to get around Québec City by car really makes no sense. You'll have great difficulty parking on the street in the Old City, which is so compact that you can walk everywhere easily on foot. That said, if you arrive at your hotel by car, you can find plenty of places to leave it while you stroll about the city. Hotels either have parking lots or have worked out deals with parking lots nearby, and most will be able to direct you where to go to find a spot. For most parking lots, expect to pay around C$10 to C$12 (US$8.50–US$10.25) per day. Some lots even allow you to come and go during the day at no extra charge.

By bicycle

Given how hilly and dense the Old City is, cycling isn't a very attractive option. Still, you can rent bikes for the day at several locations. Try **Cyclo Service,** 160 rue St-André in the Basse-Ville (☎ 418-692-4052), or **Vélo Passe-Sport Plein Air,** 22 rue Côte-du-Palais, near rue St-Jean (☎ 418-692-3643). The cost is around C$20 (US$17) for 12 hours.

Chapter 17

Checking in at Québec City's Best Hotels

In This Chapter
▶ Finding the best accommodations in Québec City
▶ Knowing how much you'll pay

*B*ecause Québec City is so small, accommodations can book up quickly for the high season (roughly May–Oct), so I suggest calling well in advance. If you're shopping around for a room before your trip, or if you need to find something at the last minute, check out my tips in Chapter 9 on how to get the best deal.

Each hotel listing in this chapter includes a $ symbol indicating the price range of the rooms. Prices included are the rack rates, the standard rate for a double room for one night, before taxes. Table 17-1 fills you in on what the $ signs represent.

Table 17-1	Key to Hotel Dollar Signs	
Dollar Sign(s)	*Price Range*	*What to Expect*
$	Less than C$100 (US$85)	Simple and inexpensive, these accommodations should offer all the basics: a room with a lock, a firm bed, and clean towels and sheets. A light continental breakfast may be included. Hotels offering rooms at these prices probably don't have an extensive catalog of services to cater to your every whim, but the front-desk clerks are usually delighted to point you in the right direction for whatever you want.

Dollar Sign(s)	Price Range	What to Expect
$$	C$100–C$199 (US$85–US$169)	Many of the rates offered by the chain hotels fall into this price range, as do the rates of the fancier independents. You can already expect the amenities to be better, such as bathrooms with hair dryers, coffeemakers with complimentary coffee, and Internet access. Some hotels in this category may have kitchens that provide late-night room service or a breakfast cart. Some even have swimming pools.
$$$	C$200–C$299 (US$170–US$254)	Along with the upper-end of the chain hotels, boutique hotels and luxury hotels begin competing in this price bracket, with fine bed linens, feathery pillows, fluffy towels, and bathtubs built for two. The first-class hotels seem to differentiate themselves by striving for regal scale and elegance, while boutique hotels are strikingly modern. Expect high-speed Internet access in your room.
$$$$	C$300 (US$255) or above	At this price, you should want for nothing in terms of your stay. Expect a great view, an in-room hot tub, a CD player, thick terry cloth bathrobes, and even flowers. Highly deferential, personalized service is included, as well.

Québec City Hotels from A to Z

Auberge du Quartier
$$ Grande-Allée

If you want some peace and quiet, slightly off the beaten path, this charming inn is a good choice. A 15-minute walk from Vieux-Québec, the 15 rooms are colorful and compact — including several with exposed brick walls. Guest rooms are available with single, double, and queen beds, and are priced accordingly. The atmosphere is relaxing and friendly, complete with cozy armchairs in the living room/library. Rooms don't have TVs, but the living room has an available Internet connection, as well as piles of Québec literature to leaf through.

Québec City Accommodations

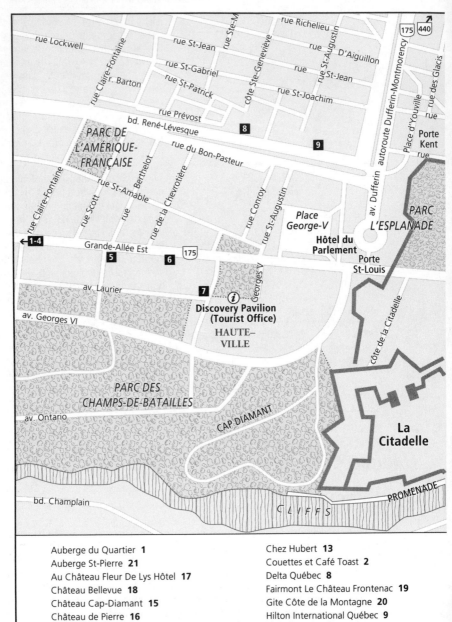

Auberge du Quartier **1**	Chez Hubert **13**
Auberge St-Pierre **21**	Couettes et Café Toast **2**
Au Château Fleur De Lys Hôtel **17**	Delta Québec **8**
Château Bellevue **18**	Fairmont Le Château Frontenac **19**
Château Cap-Diamant **15**	Gite Côte de la Montagne **20**
Château de Pierre **16**	Hilton International Québec **9**
Château Laurier **7**	Holiday Inn Select **26**

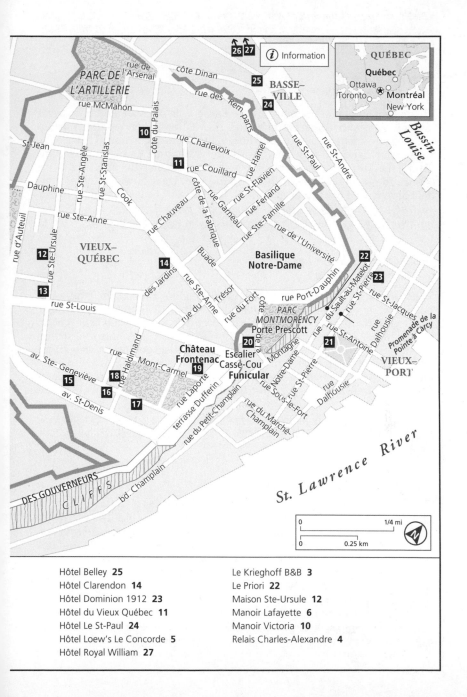

Hôtel Belley **25**
Hôtel Clarendon **14**
Hôtel Dominion 1912 **23**
Hôtel du Vieux Québec **11**
Hôtel Le St-Paul **24**
Hôtel Loew's Le Concorde **5**
Hôtel Royal William **27**

Le Krieghoff B&B **3**
Le Priori **22**
Maison Ste-Ursule **12**
Manoir Lafayette **6**
Manoir Victoria **10**
Relais Charles-Alexandre **4**

170 Grande-Allée Ouest. ☎ *800-782-9441 or 418-525-9726. Fax: 418-521-4891. www.quebecweb.com/ADQ. Parking: C$10 (US$8.50). Rack rates: C$100–C$149 (US$85–US$127). AE, DC, MC, V.*

Auberge St-Pierre
$$–$$$$ Basse-Ville

This new-ish hotel in the heart of the Basse-Ville does an almost magical job of looking and feeling antique, from the distressed painted furniture to deliberately scratched hardwood floors, high ceilings, exposed brick-and-stone walls, and old-fashioned hot-water radiators. But the rooms are utterly modern in term of amenities and convenience; the spacious bathrooms, for example, are generously equipped, right down to the built-in hair dryers. One luxurious suite has a hot tub and king-size bed.

79 rue St-Pierre. ☎ *888-268-1017 or 418-694-7981. Fax: 418-694-0406. Parking: Valet C$15 (US$12.75). Rack rates: C$110–C$335 (US$93.50–US$285). AE, DC, DISC, MC, V.*

Au Château Fleur De Lys Hôtel
$ Haute-Ville

The "Château" in the name may be a bit misleading; this quaint, family-run hotel occupies a stately, urban mansion built in 1876 on the uppermost part of the Haute-Ville. Perhaps it's most castlelike feature is a gorgeous spiral staircase with a wooden banister leading to 18 rooms over three floors. Otherwise it tends towards run-down, in a romantic sense, more reminiscent of a European inn. The rooms themselves are basic with comfortable beds and clean bathrooms. It's perhaps not the polish and pampering you were dreaming of, but the location and value of this Château are hard to beat.

15 av. Ste-Geneviève (corner of rue de la Porte). ☎ *877-691-1884 or 418-694-1884. Fax: 418-694-1666. Parking: C$11 (US$9.25). Rack rates: C$80–C$100 (US$68–US$85). AE, MC, V.*

Château Bellevue
$$–$$$ Haute-Ville

At first sight, you may mistake this small hotel for one of the oodles of B&Bs and guesthouses that surround it, all facing the peaceful Jardin des Gouverneurs park. Château Bellevue actually has 58 rooms, small (but not overly quaint), quiet, and equipped with basic amenities like phones and cable TV. Unlike many accommodations in the Old City, this place has an elevator, so you have no steep stairs to climb. The staff is very helpful. Some of the pricier rooms face the park, and in winter they have a view of the St. Lawrence River.

16 rue Laporte. ☎ *800-463-2617 or 418-692-2573. Fax: 418-692-4876. Parking: Free. Rack rates: C$120–C$219 (US$102–US$186). AE, DC, DISC, MC, V.*

Château Cap-Diamant
$$ Haute-Ville

The idyllic enclosed garden behind this Victorian guesthouse, with its crumbling rock walls, flower-filled porch, and fountain, is almost worth the price of a room itself. Each room in this quaint inn is different. All are decorated with antiques, and the place feels something like a work in progress. Bathrooms are tiny. Although most rooms are accessible by steep narrow stairs, there's a small elevator to lift luggage to the upper floors. Whew! Rooms have cable TV, and Internet access is available in the reception area. The owners are inviting and helpful. Ask for a room overlooking the rooftops of the Old City.

39 av. Ste-Geneviève. ☎ *418-694-0313. Parking: C$10 (US$8.50). Rack rates: C$125–C$185 (US$106–US$157). MC, V. No phones in rooms.*

Château de Pierre
$$ Haute-Ville

A European-style inn on a quiet, elegant street packed with small B&B-style hotels, the Château de Pierre distinguishes itself in the details: polished banisters, pretty wallpaper, a chandelier in the reception area, and a small patio for summer lounging. The owners want you to take your time here, relax, and stay in bed late. All 15 rooms are nonsmoking, and most have bathtubs. The only drawback of this place is very steep staircases that you have to climb to get to most of the rooms.

17 rue Ste-Geneviève. ☎ *418-694-0429. Fax: 418-694-0153. Parking: C$10 (US$8.50). Rack rates: C$115–C$135 (US$97.75–US$115). AE, DC, MC, V.*

Château Laurier
$$–$$$ Grande-Allée

Facing the elegant Place George V, this recently renovated, 154-room hotel keeps you in European-style comfort while putting you just a few minutes' walk from Vieux-Québec. The main reception area features a grand piano and sumptuous leather couches. Some rooms have working fireplaces, CD players, king beds, and Jacuzzis. Basic rooms are spacious and tastefully appointed. It's a family-owned establishment, but it feels like an upscale chain hotel. The hotel caters to tour groups, which yields a bustling atmosphere, but can also be a bit noisy. Ask for a room in the new wing (they're bigger) and facing the park.

1220 Place George V. ☎ *800-463-4453 or 418-522-8108. Fax: 418-524-8786. Parking: Valet C$10 (US$8.50). Rack rates: C$130–C$290 (US$111–US$247) double and suite. AE, DC, DISC, MC, V.*

Chez Hubert
$ Haute-Ville

This small B&B feels something like a nicely worn-in dollhouse, with its winding staircase and brightly painted, eclectic décor. It offers only three rooms, but each is large and handsomely renovated, with wood floors and lovely painted antique furniture. You'll find plenty of comfortable space for relaxing, but only one bathroom, and no TV or telephones in the rooms (both are available in the living room downstairs). Due to the presence of the family dog, no other animals are allowed. Call well ahead to reserve a room.

66 rue Ste-Ursule. ☎ 418-692-0958. Parking: Free. Rack rates: C$85 (US$72.25). Cash or traveler's checks only.

Couettes et Café Toast
$ **Avenue Cartier**

Located outside the walls of Vieux-Québec, this bed-and-breakfast is reputed as a linguistic guest home and encourages guests to immerse themselves in the French language and Québec's culture. Breakfast, over a large, communal table, is a group affair and mostly in French. There's a reading room with lots of Francophone magazines and other media to flip through to round out your experience. Otherwise the rooms are cozy and elegant. The neighborhood is a tucked-away commercial strip which has lots of charming boutiques and cafes — and it's really not that far away from the attractions in the historic district.

1020 av. Cartier (near boulevard Rene-Levesque). ☎ 418-523-9365. Fax: 418-523-6706. Parking: C$6 (US$5). Rack rates: C$75–C$85 (US$63.75–US$72.25). AE, MC, V.

Delta Québec
$$ **Boulevard Rene-Levesque**

This upscale, well-located hotel delivers comfortable rooms with all the trimmings — including a heated outdoor pool. Surprisingly easy to miss, it is actually connected to the Centre des Congrès, Québec City's convention center. The reception area is two floors up from the front entrance, and the maze of escalators and mezzanines are a little confusing, but you get the hang of it. Spacious, rustic-style rooms with pine furniture come with small desks equipped with ergonomic chairs and Internet connections. You're about a ten-minute walk from the Parliament Buildings and Vieux-Québec, making this a good choice for business or pleasure.

690 bd. Rene-Levesque Est. ☎ 888-884-7777 or 418-647-1717. Fax: 418-647-2146. www.deltaquebec.com. Parking: C$20 (US$17). Rack rates: C$150–C$170 (US$128–US$145) double and suite. AE, DC, DISC, MC, V. Wheelchair accessible.

Fairmont Le Château Frontenac
$$$$ **Haute-Ville**

A tourist attraction in itself, the 100-year-old Château Frontenac is definitely the place to stay if you want the full Vieux-Québec experience (and you pay for the privilege, of course). Perched on the terrasse Dufferin, it looks like a castle from the outside and feels like one on the inside — from the elaborate wood paneling of the reception area to the parking valets dressed in period costumes. The 618 rooms vary enormously, with every-thing from luxurious suites to standard, good-size rooms that are actually a decent value for the money. Prices vary a lot depending on season and availability, and you get the best rates, by far, in package deals. There's plenty to keep kids amused, from the pool to kids' programs and a video arcade.

1 rue des Carriéres. ☎ *800-828-7447 or 418-692-3861. Fax: 418-692-1751.* www. fairmont.com. *Parking: C$24 (US$20.50) or valet C$29 (US$24.75). Rack rates: C$399–C$450 (US$339–US$383). Rates include breakfast. AE, DC, DISC, MC, V.*

Gite Côte de la Montagne
$$ Basse-Ville

Just three large rooms, one more like a loft, make up this bed-and-break-fast with spectacular views of the river and the Château Frontenac from a rooftop terrace. This intimate hideaway would be well suited for a roman-tic weekend. Best of all, you get to set the time when they serve breakfast. The nearly 300-year-old freestone building is halfway up the hill and backs onto the "Breakneck stairs" for climbing up and down between the Haute- and Basse-Ville. The furnishings in the rooms are simple and rustic, but comfortable.

54 Côte de la Montagne (halfway up the hill). ☎ *888-794-4414 or 418-694-4414. Fax: 418-694-0889. Rack rates: C$120–C$180 (US$102–US$153). AE, DC, MC, V.*

Hilton International Québec
$$–$$$ Boulevard Rene-Levesque

In addition to all the comfort and pampering you expect from the name, Québec City's Hilton offers a simply amazing view of Vieux-Québec. In fact, you're probably better off staying here and looking at the stately Château Frontenac, than staying in the Frontenac itself. All the rooms are spacious and offer a view of the Old City. This Hilton is especially kid-friendly, with gifts, special kids' programs, and discount coupons for the hotel's restau-rant, where, among other things, you can indulge in an all-you-can-eat lob-ster dinner. Added amenities include a health center with trainers, a heated outdoor pool open year-round, and high-speed Internet connec-tions in every room. Plus, it's just a five-minute walk from the walls of Vieux-Québec and some 20 nearby gastronomic restaurants. Good rates are available off season.

1100 bd. René-Levesque Est. ☎ *800-445-8667 or 514-647-2411. Fax: 418-647-6488.* www.hilton.com. *Parking: C$17 (US$14.50). Rack rates: C$165–C$215 (US$140–US$183). AE, DC, MC, V. Some wheelchair-accessible rooms.*

Holiday Inn Select
$$–$$$ St-Roch

Up until recently, this hotel's location may have been a disadvantage. Suddenly, it's in the middle of the city's hottest action in terms of shop-ping, dining, and nightlife. St-Roch used to be roughneck, but now it is decidedly upmarket (the Hugo Boss boutique isn't far). An 18-story con-crete skyscraper, tall by Québec City standards, houses the 240 rooms. They tend to be large and outfitted with all the basics — no-frills but com-fortable — typical of the Holiday Inn brand. Perhaps atypically for a larger chain, the front-desk staff are keen and helpful, eager to point out the neighborhood's different destinations.

395 rue de la Courrone (corner of rue St-Joseph). ☎ *888-465-4329 or 418-647-2611. Fax: 418-640-0666.* www.holiday-inn.com. *Parking: C$12 (US$10.25). Rack rates: C$139–C$249 (US$118–US$212). AE, DC, MC, V.*

Hôtel Belley
$-$$ Basse-Ville

This is a fun and funky place to stay if you're looking for reasonably priced accommodations within walking distance of the art galleries and antiques stores along rue St-Paul. The Hôtel Belley has eight bright, if sparsely dec-orated, rooms; some with added touches such as exposed beams and brick walls and skylights. All rooms are nonsmoking. Bathrooms are extremely compact. Several rooms have extra pullout beds for kids, and one family-size room has a queen and two single beds. Light meals are available at all hours in the small tavern on the first floor of the hotel.

249 rue St-Paul. ☎ *418-692-1694. Fax: 418-692-1696.* www.oricom.ca/belley. *Parking: Available nearby for C$8–C$11/day (US$6.75–US$9.25/day). Rack rates: C$90–C$140 (US$76.50–US$119). AE, DC, MC, V.*

Hôtel Clarendon
$$-$$$ Haute-Ville

This elegant, well-maintained Art Deco–style hotel is one of the oldest hotels in Vieux-Québec and has even maintained its original, wicket-style reception desk. Located in the heart of the Haute-Ville, it couldn't be better situated, and you'll definitely feel as though you've been transported back in time. Rooms are rather dark and claustrophobic, but bathrooms are modern. There's a lively pub, known for its jazz evenings, right off the reception area. The hotel's restaurant, Le Charles Baillargé, offers excel-lent French food. Facials, body scrubs, and massages are available on loca-tion. Nonsmoking rooms are available.

57 rue Ste-Anne. ☎ *888-554-6001 or 418-692-4652. Fax: 418-692-4652. Parking: C$14 (US$12) in public parking lot. Rack rates: C$164–C$289 (US$139–US$246). AE, DC, DISC, MC, V.*

Hôtel Dominion 1912
$$-$$$ Basse-Ville

In 2005, *Condé Nast Traveler*'s readers rated this hotel tops in all of Canada. It also landed a spot in *Travel + Leisure*'s Top 500. It's located in Québec City's first skyscraper. The nine-story, 1912 structure now houses an ele-gant, 60-room, boutique hotel. Inside, the lobby's centerpiece is a black, marble fireplace surrounded by plush, shabby-chic couches for guests to lounge in and sip complimentary coffees and hot chocolate. The décor throughout is decidedly modern with a muted palette of black and grays. The high ceilings and large windows give many rooms on the upper floors spectacular views of the St. Lawrence River. The assured and competent staff are attentive and considerate and provide an elevated level of service. As is the case with boutique hotels, you can buy many of the items in the rooms.

126 rue St-Pierre (near rue St-Paul). ☎ *888-833-5253 or 418-692-2224. Fax: 418-692-4403.* www.hoteldominion.com. *Parking: $14 (US$12). Rack rates: C$169–C$209 (US$144–US$178). AE, DC, MC, V.*

Hôtel du Vieux-Québec
$$–$$$ Haute-Ville

Housed in a century-old brick manor, the Hôtel du Vieux-Québec offers a cool, comfortable ambience, including spacious rooms and a cozy living room, where you can rest after a busy day of sightseeing. This place is popular with families because many of the doubles have extra sofas. Extra guests stay for C$15 (US$12.75) per day. Kids stay for free in the winter, and significant rate reductions are available off season. The staff is friendly and helpful. The hotel is close to shopping, nightspots, and restaurants. Ask for one of the 24 recently renovated rooms.

1190 rue St-Jean. ☎ *800-361-7787 or 418-692-1850. Fax: 418-692-5637.* www.hvq. com. *Parking: C$11 (US$9.25) at the Hôtel-de-Ville (City Hall). Rack rates: C$139–C$239 (US$118–US$203). AE, DC, MC, V.*

Hôtel Le St. Paul
$$ Basse-Ville

This 26-room hotel occupies a three-story, 19th-century town house in the Basse-Ville, along a street dotted with antiques shops and cafes. It may feel out of the way, but rue St-Paul, the hotel's namesake, is *the* place to be in this part of town. The rooms tend to be on the large side with elegant Art Deco–inspired furnishings. The bathrooms are modern and some have large hot tubs. Throughout, the features of the old building add charm, but the amenities are completely up-to-date in the well-appointed rooms.

229 rue St-Paul (near rue St-Vallier). ☎ *877-778-8977 or 418-694-4414. Fax: 418-694-0889. Parking: C$18.25 (US15.50). Rack rates: C$150–C$200 (US$128–US$170). AE, DC, MC, V.*

Hôtel Loew's Le Concorde
$$$–$$$$ Grande-Allée

A large, upscale hotel, Loew's is smack in the middle of the action on Grande-Allée and a ten-minute stroll through a lively neighborhood to the gates of Vieux-Québec. Rooms on the side of the hotel facing the Old City have a remarkable view. The lobby is a little worn, with threadbare furniture, but the rooms are spacious and classic feeling and include good-size bathrooms with marble counters. The hotel has a gym and a pool. A revolving restaurant at the top, L'Astral, serves excellent French food while offering a panoramic view of the city. Meanwhile, you're only an elevator ride away from cafes and restaurants galore down below on Grande-Allée. Special rates for kids.

1225 Place Montcalm. ☎ *800-463-5256 or 418-647-2222. Fax: 418-647-4710.* www. loewshotels.com. *Parking: $19 (US$16.25) or valet C$21 (US$17.75). Rack rates: C$235–C$375 (US$200–US$319). AE, DC, DISC, MC, V.*

Hôtel Royal William
$$ St-Roch

Just a block away from the now bustling rue St-Joseph, the Royal William is in the up-and-coming district of St-Roch — somewhat removed from Old Québec and the concentration of the tourist attractions. However, when you discover this new commercial strip, you'll be glad your hotel is only a few steps away. The Royal William, named after the first steamship to cross the Atlantic Ocean, is a business-class hotel of 44 rooms with many amenities to satisfy this travel set.

360 bd. Charest Est (between rues de la Courrone et Dorchester). ☎ *888-541-0405 or 418-521-4488. Fax: 418-521-6868.* www.royalwilliam.com. *Parking: Valet C$12 (US$10.25). Rack rates: C$149–C$189 (US$127–US$161). AE, DC, MC, V.*

Le Krieghoff B&B
$ Avenue Cartier

This clean and convenient B&B is perched above the boutiques, restaurants, and bars on lively avenue Cartier. The five rooms are surprisingly big and airy, although basic, and not all have bathrooms attached. A living area on the first floor has a microwave, a fridge for guests' use, telephone and TV, a big comfy couch, and a small balcony that looks over avenue Cartier. The only drawbacks include two flights of stairs to climb to the rooms and slightly indifferent service. Breakfast is served in the cafe downstairs, where decent food and coffee are served at reasonable prices all day.

1091 av. Cartier. ☎ *418-522-3711. Fax: 418-647-1429.* www.cafekrieghoff. qc.ca. *Parking:C$10 (US$8.50). Rack rates: C$100–C$110 (US$85–US$93.50). MC, V.*

Le Priori
$$ Basse-Ville

Sleek and modern, this 26-room hotel, built inside an old building in the Basse-Ville, is a design buff's dream come true. It's reasonably priced and very conveniently located near the rue St-Paul strip of art galleries. Rooms are a little dark and on the small side, but the minimalist décor makes them seem spacious enough. All the comforts are there, including queen-size beds with down comforters. Suites have nice extras, including wood-burning fireplaces, kitchens, and Jacuzzis. The view is, unfortunately, restricted to neighboring rooftops. All rooms have Internet connection. Le Priori welcomes a mix of straight and gay guests.

15 rue Sault-au-Matelot (corner rue St-Antoine). ☎ *800-351-3992 or 418-692-3992. Fax: 418-692-0883.* www.hotellepriori.com. *Parking: Public lot nearby for C$15 (US$12.75). Rack rates: C$160–C$180 (US$136–US$153). AE, DC, DISC, MC, V.*

Maison Ste-Ursule
$ Haute-Ville

This popular guesthouse has a distinct youth hostel feel to it, with its peeling wallpaper and slightly bohemian clientele, but it offers good accommodations at an excellent price in an even better location on a quiet street in Vieux-Québec. The second oldest house on the street, built in 1739, it boasts stone walls and a lovely, leafy sitting garden out back. Breakfast is not available in the hotel but is easy to find nearby. Several smoking rooms are available. Parking is not included but is available nearby.

40 rue Ste-Ursule. ☎ *418-694-9794. Fax: 418-694-0875.* www.quebecweb.com/maisonste-ursule/introang.html. *Rack rates: C$80–C$100 (US$68–US$85). AE, MC, V.*

Manoir Lafayette
$$ Grande-Allée

The small, somewhat luxurious Manoir Lafayette puts you very close to Vieux-Québec while affording you some room to breathe. You get more of a big hotel feeling here than in the many small inns along the Grande-Allée. The elegant reception area is decorated with nice antiques, while rooms are of a decent size, modern, and offer queen or double beds.

661 Grande-Allée Est. ☎ *800-363-8203 or 418-522-2652. Fax: 418-522-4400. Parking: Valet C$10 (US$8.50). Rack rates: C$110–C$170 (US$93.50–US$145). AE, DC, DISC, MC, V.*

Manoir Victoria
$$–$$$$ Haute-Ville

The formal lobby of this small hotel, with its fireplaces, antique armchairs, and elegant dining room done up in dark burgundy and blue, projects an old-world feel. The 145 rooms are classic in style, but modern and spacious, with two double beds. The hotel offers all the perks and services you'd expect in a larger hotel, including valet parking, an indoor pool, sauna and fitness center, Internet lounge, and even babysitting. This end of the Haute-Ville is convenient, with restaurants of all types for all budgets, and lots of shopping on nearby rue St-Jean. In the low season, it's popular among the corporate crowd.

44 Côte-du-Palais. ☎ *418-692-1030. Fax: 418-692-3822.* www.manoir-victoria.com. *Parking: Valet C$17 (US$14.50). Rack rates: C$140–C$315 (US$119–US$268). AE, DC, DISC, MC, V.*

Relais Charles-Alexandre
$$ Grande-Allée

A cool, peaceful, and meticulously kept inn close to the Plains of Abraham, this is one of the best deals along the Grand-Allée and a regular hangout for vacationing New Englanders — and it's just a ten-minute walk to the Old City. The 24 guest rooms are bright, spacious, and recently renovated, with polished wood floors and flowery, matching curtains and bedspreads. Rooms are equipped with small desks and TVs and have queen or twin beds; bathrooms have showers or baths. The staff is helpful and friendly.

91 Grand-Allée Est. ☎ *418-523-1220. Fax: 418-523-9556. Parking: C$8 (US$6.75). Rack rates: C$120–C$130 (US$102–US$110). AE, MC, V.*

Chapter 18

Dining and Snacking in Québec City

. . . .

In This Chapter

▶ Getting to know the local dining scene

▶ Discovering Québec City's best restaurants

▶ Finding great snacks and light meals

. . . .

*F*rench, French, and more French. That's what you can expect to eat in the heart of historic New France — and, fortunately, Québec City has plenty of great French restaurants. But if you're not a fan of frogs' legs, don't worry: Québeckers are enthusiastic about all categories of culinary delights. You can find everything to satisfy your palate, from sushi to pizza and pasta.

You can find great places to eat all over the city, but in this chapter, I give you the best choices in and around the Old City and Grande-Allée. I just figure that's where you'll probably be when you get hungry.

Getting the Dish on the Local Scene

If you think locals avoid Québec City's touristy areas, think again. Many of the city's finest restaurants are in the Old City and on the Grande-Allée, and locals come here to indulge in a good meal.

The Old City

Both the Upper and Lower cities are full of quaint and charming eating spots that serve some variation of French food, from cafe fare to bistro meals and formal dining. Most of these serve quite traditional cuisine — you know, French onion soup; crêpes (in crêpe places); mussels and fries; steak frites; and lamb, pork, and fish dishes.

Prices at restaurants in the Old City aren't astronomically high, as you may have suspected, but you can save money by shopping around a little. Almost all restaurants in the Old City display menus in the window with prices. Check them out before you enter. Many offer a complete

Québec City Dining and Snacking

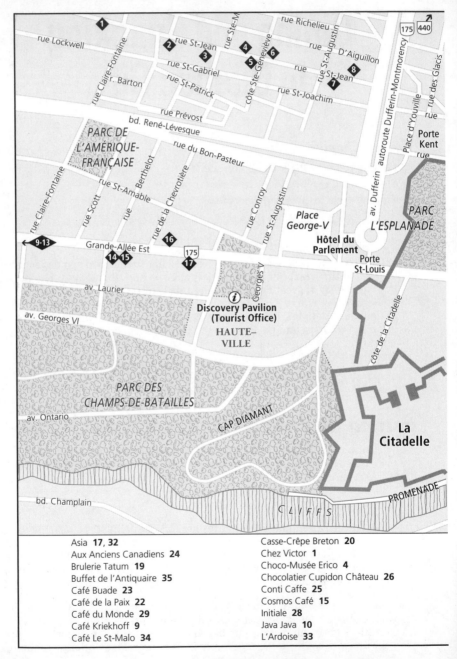

Asia **17, 32**
Aux Anciens Canadiens **24**
Brulerie Tatum **19**
Buffet de l'Antiquaire **35**
Café Buade **23**
Café de la Paix **22**
Café du Monde **29**
Café Kriekhoff **9**
Café Le St-Malo **34**

Casse-Crêpe Breton **20**
Chez Victor **1**
Choco-Musée Erico **4**
Chocolatier Cupidon Château **26**
Conti Caffe **25**
Cosmos Café **15**
Initiale **28**
Java Java **10**
L'Ardoise **33**

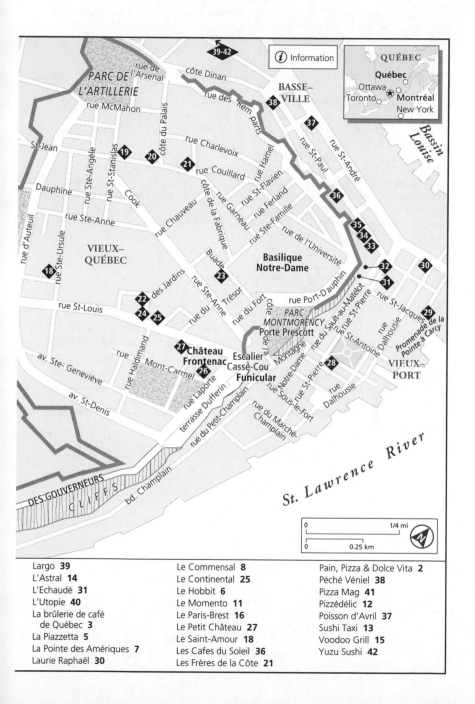

(i) Information

QUÉBEC

Québec

Ottawa
Toronto ★ Montréal
New York

Bassin Louise

PARC DE L'ARTILLERIE

rue de l'Arsenal
côte Dinan
BASSE–VILLE

rue des Remparts

rue McMahon

St-Jean

Dauphine

rue Ste-Anne

VIEUX–QUÉBEC

rue St-Louis

av. Ste-Geneviève

av. St-Denis

DES GOUVERNEURS

CLIFFS

bd. Champlain

rue Charlevoix

rue Couillard

côte du Palais

rue Ste-Angèle
rue St-Stanislas

Cook

rue Chauveau

côte de la Fabrique

des Jardins

rue Ste-Anne

Buade

Trésor

rue du Fort

PARC MONTMORENCY
Porte Prescott

Château Frontenac

Escalier Cassé-Cou
Funicular

rue Haldimand

rue Mont-Carmel

rue Laporte

terrasse Dufferin

rue du Petit-Champlain

rue Garneau

rue St-Flavien

rue Ferland

rue Ste-Famille

rue de l'Université

rue Hamel

rue St-Paul

rue St-André

côte Port-Dauphin

rue Port-Dauphin

côte de la Montagne

rue Notre-Dame

rue du Sault-au-Matelot

rue St-Pierre

rue St-Antoine

rue St-Pierre

rue Sous-le-Fort

rue Dalhousie

rue Dalhousie

rue St-Jacques

Promenade de la Pointe à Carcy

VIEUX–PORT

rue du Marché-Champlain

Basilique Notre-Dame

St. Lawrence River

0   1/4 mi
0   0.25 km

Largo **39**
L'Astral **14**
L'Echaudé **31**
L'Utopie **40**
La brûlerie de café de Québec **3**
La Piazzetta **5**
La Pointe des Amériques **7**
Laurie Raphaël **30**

Le Commensal **8**
Le Continental **25**
Le Hobbit **6**
Le Momento **11**
Le Paris-Brest **16**
Le Petit Château **27**
Le Saint-Amour **18**
Les Cafes du Soleil **36**
Les Frères de la Côte **21**

Pain, Pizza & Dolce Vita **2**
Péché Véniel **38**
Pizza Mag **41**
Pizzédélic **12**
Poisson d'Avril **37**
Sushi Taxi **13**
Voodoo Grill **15**
Yuzu Sushi **42**

meal menu *(table d'hôte)*, and they're usually a good deal. Many also offer a special lunch menu, and these are usually a *very* good deal.

Grande-Allée

As you step outside the Porte St-Louis and head down Grande-Allée, the restaurants get a little more modern. In the summer, after just a five-minute walk outside the gate, you see a broad boulevard lined with rows of tables on each side. It looks like one huge terrace, but it's actually the combined effect of patios of dozens of different restaurants, crammed together for blocks.

You can find just about every type of food here, from fine French dining to traditional Québec cooking, plus Italian restaurants, burger joints, bagel and sandwich spots, sushi restaurants, pizzerias, and seafood and steak places. Stroll along and read the menus, which are usually displayed near the sidewalk. Or just cut to the chase and head to the places I recommend in this chapter.

Québec City's Best Restaurants

In this section, you find my top choices for dining in Québec City.

The dollar sign ratings represent the price of one dinner (appetizer, entree, and dessert), including drinks and tip, and correspond with the price ranges in Table 18-1.

Table 18-1	Key to Restaurant Dollar Signs
Dollar Sign(s)	*Price Range*
$	Less than C$20 (US$17)
$$	C$20–C$39 (US$17–US$33)
$$$	C$40–C$59 (US$34–US$50)
$$$$	C$60 (US$51) or above

You can cut your dining costs in a variety of ways. I explain these techniques in Chapter 10, and a lot of them apply to Québec City, as well.

In the heady tourist atmosphere of Québec City at high season, the best restaurants fill up quickly. Make your dinner reservations at least in the afternoon of the same day, and preferably the night before. In the off season (Oct–Apr) — when the tourist frenzy in Québec City cedes to an atmosphere of barely discernible activity in the streets — you can get a table in most establishments on the spot. And they'll be happy to see you.

Asia
$$–$$$ Grande-Allée   ASIAN

This extremely popular restaurant is a great place to turn if you're getting tired of French food (not likely, but it happens). Asia offers a wide variety of dishes with Thai, Vietnamese, and Indochinese influences. Its specialty is grilled meats, but the restaurant also offers seafood plates, an excellent red curry chicken, and marinated shrimp and sautéed pork, plus Thai soup and pad thai. Asia has a second location in the Basse-Ville.

585 Grande-Allée Est. ☎ *418-522-0818. Basse-Ville location: 89 rue Sault-au-Matelot (*☎ *418-692-3799). Reservations recommended. Table d'hôte: C$24–C$26 (US$20.50–US$22). AE, MC, V. Open: Lunch Mon–Fri, dinner daily.*

Aux Anciens Canadiens
$$$ Haute-Ville   QUÉBEC

This restaurant brings historic Québec all together. It's housed in the oldest private dwelling in the Haute-Ville, the Maison Jacquet, built in 1690. Aux Anciens Canadiens is named after one of its early owners' novels. It translates into Canadians of Old. The food is authentic Québec cuisine, from old standards like pork and beans, ham, *tourtière* (meat pie), caribou, and blueberry pie to more recently discovered delicacies, such as duck, from the Eastern Townships (see Chapter 14). The servers are dressed in period costumes to complete the effect. If the price makes you hesitate, try it out at lunch, when the price of the *table d'hôte* is quite reasonable.

34 rue St-Louis (corner of rue Haldimand). ☎ *418-692-1627. Reservations recommended. Main courses: C$27–C$40 (US$23–US$34). AE, DC, MC, V. Open: Lunch and dinner daily.*

Buffet de l'Antiquaire
$–$$ Basse-Ville   QUÉBEC

Strolling by the antiques shops along rue St-Paul, you may not even notice this closet-sized restaurant at first. It's worth a stop, though. This is where locals go to eat authentic Québec specialties like *poutine* (fries with gravy and cheese curd) and *fèves au lard* (Québec's version of pork and beans: all lard, no meat). Meat dishes, like steak frites, or lighter meals, such as soup, sandwiches, and salads, are also on the menu. This place is definitely off the tourist track — yet right in the middle of the action — plus it's cheap.

95 rue St-Paul (near rue Sault-au-Matelot). ☎ *418-692-2661. Main courses: Under C$8–C$14 (US$6.75–US$12). AE, DC, DISC, MC, V. Open: Lunch and dinner daily.*

Café de la Paix
$$$$ Haute-Ville   FRENCH

It looks small and unpresuming from the street, but if you want high-quality, classic French cooking in a totally classic setting, this is the place.

You'll find frogs' legs, as well as beef sirloin, chateaubriand, rabbit, scallops, steak tartare, lobster, duck, and (need I say it?) French onion soup. The atmosphere is dark and cozy. Service is not genteel, but the career waiters — mostly surly older men — do know their stuff. You feel like you're in France.

44 rue des Jardins (between Donnacona and rue St-Louis). ☎ *418-692-1430. Reservations recommended. Main courses: C$15–C$50 (US$12.75–US$42.50). AE, DC, DISC, MC, V. Open: Lunch Mon–Sat, dinner daily.*

Café du Monde
$$–$$$$ Basse-Ville   FRENCH BISTRO

This legendary Québec City bistro recently moved from its small, Parisian-style digs on rue Dalhousie to a big, new, glamorous location in the *términal des croisières* (cruise liner terminal) facing the port. The two walls facing the river are made entirely of glass, so the river view is exceptional. And, I'm happy to say, the food is as good as ever. Famous for brasserie fare like mussels, steak frites, sausage, and duck confit, Café du Monde also serves up sandwiches, salads, and seafood selections. Service is friendly, but waiters don't have time to linger at your table. Reservations are not taken for the terrace (with river views), so get there early if you want to eat outside.

84 rue Dalhousie (near the cruise liner terminal on the Old Port). ☎ *418-692-4455. Reservations required; not accepted for the terrace. Main courses: C$12–C$32 (US$10.25–US$27.25). AE, DC, MC, V. Open: Lunch and dinner daily, brunch Sat–Sun 9:30 a.m.–2 p.m.*

Casse-Crêpe Breton
$–$$ Haute-Ville   CRÊPES

This little place on rue St-Jean is extremely popular — both with locals and tourists — and you almost always encounter a line at lunchtime. It's worth the short wait. The crêpes are perfect and very filling, and you can have them as a main course, dessert, or both. A long list of potential main course fillings includes ham, cheese, mushrooms, asparagus, eggs, and more, and dessert options range from chocolate to fruit to plain sugar. You can watch them being prepared in the open kitchen. Service is friendly, but don't dawdle: Other people are waiting for your seat!

1136 rue St-Jean (near rue Garneau). ☎ *418-692-0438. Reservations not accepted. Main courses: C$5–C$9 (US$4.25–US$7.75). MC, V. Open: Daily 7 a.m.–1 a.m.*

Conti Caffe
$$–$$$ Haute-Ville   ITALIAN

With its stone walls and fashionable modern décor, this new Italian bistro definitely stands out among the more traditional eateries on rue St-Louis. It's a great spot for lunch — you can have a three-course meal here with coffee for C$10 (US$8.50). At night, the menu gets a little more sophisticated, with additions like veal medallions, beef sirloin, and even escargot to the pasta and pizza selections. Pizza is of the thin-crust variety, with imaginative toppings.

26 rue St-Louis (next to its owner, Le Continental Restaurant, which has the same address). ☎ *418-692-4191. Main courses: C$17–C$26 (US$14.50–US$22). AE, MC, V. Open: Lunch and dinner daily.*

Initiale
$$$$ Basse-Ville   FRENCH

This is *the* place to go in Québec City for fine French cuisine in an elegant, rather formal setting. Located in a former bank building, its décor is classical and modern, with high ceilings and decorative moldings. Like most skilled, up-to-the-minute chefs these days, Yvan Lebrun focuses on local, seasonal ingredients. Plates range from French classics, such as grilled salmon, lamb, lobster, and filet mignon, to slightly more adventuresome dishes such as foie gras and pigeon. Give the Québec cheeses a try between your main course and dessert. Expect service to be attentive and none too quick. And the point here is savoring, not saving.

54 rue St-Pierre (corner of Côte de la Montagne). ☎ *418-694-1818. Reservations recommended. Main courses: C$36–C$45 (US$30.50–US$38.25). AE, DC, MC, V. Open: Lunch Mon–Fri, dinner daily.*

L'Ardoise
$$–$$$ Basse-Ville   FRENCH BISTRO

The dishes served in French bistros are what the French consider comfort food. That's what you'll get at L'Ardoise, which caters equally to locals and tourists with its welcoming casual atmosphere and hearty dishes. Specialties include mussels and fries — with seconds of mussels for free — grilled blood sausage, veal liver, rib steak, and fish selections. Fish lovers with an appetite should try the Royale de la mer (Royal Sea) dish of salmon, shrimp, mussels, and scallops in a rich sauce. This is a nice place to hang out and sip an after-dinner espresso.

71 rue St-Paul (near rue des Navigateurs). ☎ *418-694-0213. Reservations recommended for dinner. Main courses: C$24–C$30 (US$20.50–US$25.50). AE, DC, MC, V. Open: Lunch Mon–Sat, dinner daily, brunch Sun.*

Largo
$$$–$$$$ St-Roch   MEDITERRANEAN

If Québec City on the whole feels somewhat sedate, this hidden-away restaurant and jazz bar brims with brio. Jazz ensembles Wednesday through Saturday and a Mediterranean menu make it a hopping destination for dinner among a smartly dressed, middle-aged clientele. Despite the hushed tones and refined textures of the dining room's décor, the din of conversation indicates that everyone is delighted to be a part of the urbane atmosphere. A crush of patrons mingle at the bar, often having to wait for a table. "In the zone," waiters ferry large plates with inventive presentations of favorites from Provence and beyond: bowls of bouillabaisse and dishes of lamb, veal, fish, and pasta.

643 rue St-Joseph Est (between rues De la Chapelle and Du Pont). ☎ *418-529-3111. Main courses: C$18–C$39 (US$15.25–US$33.25). AE, MC, V. Open: Lunch and dinner daily.*

L'Astral
$$$–$$$$ Grande-Allée   FRENCH

With a capacity for a thousand guests, this rotating restaurant on top of the Loew's hotel on the Grande-Allée is obviously not the place to come for intimacy. But the view is as good as it gets, stretching dozens of miles across the Plains of Abraham and the Old City all the way to the Laurentian Mountains. For such a huge place, the food is, surprisingly, very good — a mix of mainly French-based plates with Asian and Cajun touches. Prices are reasonable and if you calculate the view, the whole experience is pretty easy on your wallet. Sunday brunches here are quite lavish. Just make sure the weather is clear before you go.

1225 cours du Général-de-Montcalm (corner Grande-Allée). ☎ *418-647-2222. Reservations recommended. Main courses: C$20–C$48 (US$17–US$40.75). AE, DC, DISC, MC, V. Open: Lunch Mon–Sat, dinner daily, brunch Sun.*

Laurie Raphaël
$$$$ Basse-Ville   CONTEMPORARY FRENCH

Daniel Vézina is Québec City's premier chef who hosts one of the province's TV cooking shows. His restaurant is one of the city's *grand tables*, a category of restaurant meaning *the* best. A native of the Île d'Orleans, a fertile island of farming communities just downriver, his market cuisine reflects his intimate knowledge of the region's seasonal *terroir* ingredients. Jean-Pierre Viau, a renowned Montréal designer, was behind the sharp lines, muted tones, and rich materials of the establishment's C$1 million makeover, including a large "peek-a-boo" window looking right into the kitchen. You can also sign up for a cooking course or visit the boutique showcasing the work of local producers and artisans.

117 rue Dalhousie (near rue St-André). ☎ *418-692-4555. Reservations required. Main courses: C$30–C$45 (US$25.50–US$38.25). AE, DC, MC, V. Open: Dinner Tues–Sat.*

L'Echaudé
$$–$$$ Basse-Ville   FRENCH BISTRO

This is one of the slicker French bistros in the Basse-Ville, with its checker-tiled floor, zinc bar, and Art Deco décor. The food, however, is very good and reasonably priced. Specialties include grilled meats, bouillabaisse seafood stew, fish selections, steak and salmon tartare, steak frites, and ravioli. Drinkwise, L'Echaudé distinguishes itself by carrying 24 brands of beer and 125 different wines, including ten wines by the glass.

73 rue du Sault-au-Matelot (near rue St-Paul). ☎ *418-692-1229. Reservations recommended. Main courses: C$20–C$40 (US$17–US$34). AE, DC, MC, V. Open: Lunch Mon–Fri and Sun, dinner daily.*

Le Continental
$$$$ Haute-Ville   CONTINENTAL

One of the oldest restaurants in Québec City, Le Continental has been a hangout for Québec's political class for the last five decades. Don't expect any great surprises, and you won't be disappointed — you get a classic menu with an atmosphere to match. Plates range from crab in hollandaise sauce to steak tartare and duck à l'orange. Waiters are attentive, courteous, and discreet — as they should be when they spend their days inadvertently listening in on gossip among Québec's political elite.

26 rue St-Louis. ☎ *418-694-9995. Reservations recommended. Main courses: C$24–C$37 (US$20.50–US$31.50). AE, DC, MC, V. Open: Lunch Mon–Fri, dinner daily.*

Le Momento
$$–$$$$ Grande-Allée   CONTEMPORARY ITALIAN

This modern-feeling restaurant has a trattoria feel and offers sophisticated Italian cooking with an emphasis on fresh ingredients — definitely not one of those places serving huge portions of pasta with stick-to-your-ribs meat sauce. Instead, you choose from eight California-style thin-crust pizzas with dressing like marinated chicken and sun-dried tomatoes; pasta selections with savory and interesting sauces; and heartier plates like *osso buco* and lamb dishes.

1144 av. Cartier (corner rue Aberdeen). ☎ *418-647-1313. Reservations recommended for dinner. Main courses: C$9–C$23 (US$7.75–US$19.50). AE, DC, MC, V. Open: Lunch Mon–Fri, dinner daily. Wheelchair accessible.*

Le Paris-Brest
$$$–$$$$ Grande-Allée   CONTEMPORARY FRENCH

Considered one of the best tables in Québec City, this fashionable restaurant offers French food with modern flair. The menu includes fancy items such as Dijon rib of beef and milk veal with Brie cheese, but it also includes higher-brow French classics, like lamb cutlets, scallops, steak tartare, and sweetbreads. Lighter selections include pasta dishes with seafood. Atmosphere is fairly informal, but neat.

590 Grande-Allée Est (corner of rue de la Chevrotière). ☎ *418-529-2243. Reservations recommended. Main courses: C$26–C$36 (US$22–US$30.50). AE, MC, V. Open: Lunch Mon–Fri, dinner daily.*

Le Saint-Amour
$$$$ Haute-Ville CONTEMPORARY FRENCH

Tucked in among the many B&Bs along rue Ste-Ursule, Le Saint-Amour offers a truly gastronomic experience. The décor is elegant and romantic, with lace curtains, flickering candles, and a glass roof for star-gazing lovers. Award-winning chef Jean-Luc Boulay presents delicacies with a regional flavor, like lobster from Québec's Gaspé area, caribou steak, and duck from the Eastern Townships (discussed in Chapter 14), and tops it off with selections like foie gras, served with fig compote and caviar. Expect the meal to move slowly — the waiters assume you want to take your time. If you're in a hurry, let them know.

48 rue Ste-Ursule. ☎ *418-694-0667. Reservations recommended. Main courses: C$34–C$48 (US$29–US$40.75). AE, DC, MC, V. Open: Lunch Mon–Fri, dinner daily.*

Les Frères de la Côte
$$–$$$ Haute-Ville ITALIAN

This lively pizzeria-cafe on rue St-Jean is a favorite of locals and a great place to bring kids. With 17 kinds of pizza — cooked in wood-burning ovens — plus pasta dishes and platters of meat and fish brochettes, you're sure to find something for even the pickiest pint-sized eater. The music is loud practically all the time, but the high spirits that reign here are infectious. Also open for Sunday brunch.

1190 rue St-Jean. ☎ *418-692-5445. Reservations recommended. Main courses: C$10–C$23 (US$8.50–US$19.50). AE, DC, MC, V. Open: Lunch and dinner daily, brunch Sun.*

L'Utopie
$$$$ St-Roch FUSION

When many guests leave here, their heads are slightly woozy thinking of superlatives to describe their experience. Smack in the middle of the rue St-Joseph renaissance, this is one of the destinations that's driving the action to this long overlooked and recently remodeled section of town. Monthly, the kitchen devises a special four-course menu around a particular ingredient, which appears in each dish. There's also another set menu of five-courses, each paired with a different glass of wine. All of the dishes are contemporary and ambitious, with a main course including selections of beef, duck, game, and several kinds of fish. Their wine list has several exclusive importations and an alarming number of choices by the glass.

226½ rue St-Joseph (near rue Carron). ☎ *418-523-7878. Reservations recommended. Main courses: C$25–C$32 (US$21.25–US$27.25). AE, MC, V. Open: Lunch Tues–Fri, dinner Tues–Sat.*

Péché Véniel
$$–$$$ Basse-Ville FRENCH BISTRO

For good food in a warm and inviting atmosphere, this informal little corner bistro off rue St-Paul is hard to beat. The menu consists of classic

French brasserie food, such as steak frites and mussels, and some traditional Québec cuisine, including smoked meat sandwiches and a very filling and satisfying version of Québec's famous Lac St-Jean meat pie. Lunch specials (around C$10/US$8.50) include soup, a main course, dessert, and coffee and are an excellent deal. Service is just what it should be. A nice place for a leisurely lunch that won't break the bank.

233 rue St-Paul. ☎ *418-692-5642. Main courses: C$14–C$36 (US$12–US$30.50). Reservations recommended. AE, DC, MC, V. Open: Lunch and dinner daily.*

Poisson d'Avril
$$–$$$ Basse-Ville   SEAFOOD

One of the few seafood restaurants in Québec City, the décor is straight out of Cape Cod: nautical motifs, hanging model ships, and marine prints. The expansive menu includes starters of mussels, crab, and smoked salmon, escargot, oysters, and fish soup. Main courses include combo plates with scallops and seasonal fish. The restaurant also serves mussels and shrimp; straightforward salmon, cod, and tuna plates; southern French bouillabaisse; and, of course, lobster. Prices are probably comparable to what you'd pay in Cape Cod, too: not cheap, but not outrageous.

115 quai Saint-André (in the Old Port, near rue St-Thomas). ☎ *418-692-1010. Reservations recommended. Main courses: C$12–C$40 (US$10.25–US$34). AE, DC, MC. V. Open: Lunch and dinner daily.*

Sushi Taxi
$$–$$$ Grande-Allée   SUSHI

Québec City is not exactly a sushi town, but this small chain has garnered a loyal following of locals for its good, reasonably priced offerings. The avenue Cartier restaurant recently expanded to add some atmosphere to the menu with 30 tables (30 more on the terrace in the summer) in a Zen-like décor. If you're unfamiliar with the art of eating raw fish, Sushi Taxi has a Discovery Plate with a bit of maki, nigiri, temaki, and sashimi.

813 av. Cartier. ☎ *418-529-0068. Table d'hôte: Lunch C$17 (US$14.50), dinner C$26 (US$22). AE, MC, V. Open: Lunch Mon–Fri, dinner daily.*

Voodoo Grill
$$$–$$$$ Grande-Allée   ASIAN/FRENCH

Quite a hot spot on Grande-Allée, this restaurant adds a bar atmosphere to its lounge look, which results in a restaurant with a post-modern Middle Eastern décor with African and designer influences. The menu is as variously inspired, with everything from Singapore chicken and Bangkok soup to volcano steak, with plenty of grilled fish selections and some sushi tossed in for good measure. Although the concept may sound a little unfocused, the food is surprisingly good, well prepared, and beautifully presented. Just be ready for some entertainment of dubious quality and mysterious origin — like belly dancers — and count on loud music. Servers were evidently hired more for looks than skill, but they do the job.

575 Grande-Allée Est. ☎ *418-647-2000. Reservations recommended. Main courses: C$15–C$45 (US$12.75–US$38.25). AE, DC, MC, V. Open: Dinner daily.*

Yuzu Sushi
$$$–$$$$ St-Roch   FUSION

If you've grown tired of the traditional Japanese restaurant experience, Yuzu is the place to refresh your palate. Modern, daring, and unusual, the dishes on the menu are in the same vein as the dining room's décor. The name refers to a Japanese citrus flavor — a widely used, secret ingredient of sorts in a variety of Japanese sauces. Besides the standard sashimi (raw fish), nigiri (raw fish on a rice ball), and maki (raw fish and rice rolled in seaweed paper) sushi, the menu boasts a section of Yuzu maki, original combinations devised by the chef. The main courses are fusion and combine ingredients from East and West. There are several other options as well: oyster shooters, dishes for sharing, or a five- or seven-course "discovery menu."

438 rue de l'Église (near rue St-Joseph). ☎ *418-521-7253. Reservations recommended. Main courses: C$11–C$36 (US$9.25–US$30.50). AE, DC, MC, V. Open: Lunch Mon–Fri, dinner daily.*

Québec City's Best Snacks

As a tourist town, Québec City is loaded with eating opportunities of all types and qualities. You're more likely to feel the anxiety over the abundance — rather than a lack — of eating options packed into this small area. The following sections list snacks and light food and should help you narrow the field when you want to grab a coffee, a sweet, or a bite to eat.

Cafes for coffee and more

Cafes aren't just for coffee, although you can usually get an excellent cup of joe at the following recommended places. You can often get light meals at these cafes, too, including soups, salads, and sandwiches.

- ✔ **Brulerie Tatum,** 1084 rue St-Jean (☎ **418-692-3900**), specializes in its own roasts of coffee and serves tasty snacks like *croque monsieurs* (a toasted roll with ham, tomato, and cheese).

- ✔ **Café Buade,** 31 rue de Buade (☎ **418-692-3909**), serves coffee and lighter meals, such as pizza and pasta, in a classic French cafe atmosphere.

- ✔ **Café Krieghoff,** 1091 av. Cartier (☎ **418-521-3711**), serves light tasty meals including salads, quiche, and soup in a down-to-earth, French-style cafe. In summer, a covered terrace offers pleasant street views.

✔ **Café Le St-Malo,** 75 rue St-Paul (☎ **418-692-2004**), with its charming sidewalk terrace and nautical décor, is a great place for a drink and a light bite.

✔ **La brûlerie de café de Québec,** 75 rue St-Jean (☎ **418-529-4769**), promises a good cup of joe from the moment you step inside. Wafts of roasting coffee greet customers at the door.

✔ **Le Hobbit,** 700 rue St-Jean (☎ **418-647-2677**), has a cafe on the first floor that serves coffee, while meals are served on the second floor.

✔ **Les Cafes du Soleil,** 143 rue St-Paul (☎ **418-692-1147**), is another roaster, but in Basse-Ville. This tucked-away place will feel like a find. There's a light menu and a strong base of regulars dropping in and out.

✔ **Java Java,** 1112 av. Cartier (☎ **418-522-5282**), is a fun place for coffee or snacks, such as panini sandwiches or burgers and fries.

Pizza and burgers

Québec is even less of a burger town than Montréal, so I have only two good burger joints to recommend, but they really are great, despite being members of a rare species. If you're looking for a quick meal, you'll find more choices in the pizza category.

✔ **Chez Victor,** 143 rue St-Jean (☎ **418-529-7702**), comes up with new and imaginative types of burgers every day.

✔ **Cosmos Café,** 575 Grande-Allée Est (☎ **418-640-0606**), right in the thick of the Grande-Allée action, serves respectable burgers and very good breakfasts.

✔ **La Piazzetta,** 707 rue St-Jean (☎ **418-529-7489**), a Québec chain, was one of the forerunners in the local trend toward European-style pizza. Pizzas have interesting toppings and very thin crusts.

✔ **Pain, Pizza & Dolce Vita,** 519 rue St-Jean (☎ **418-653-2741**), has a wide variety of fresh-baked goods in the Italian tradition: pizza, panini, and foccacia to name but a few. Nothing too fancy — square slices, delicious foccacia, and panini on homemade bread.

✔ **Pizzédélic,** 1145 av. Cartier (☎ **418-523-7171**), puts a psychedelic spin on the thin-pizza concept, offering one-serving pizzas with original toppings. Salads are great.

✔ **Pizza Mag,** 363 rue St-Paul (☎ **418-692-1910**), offers 20 different types of more traditional, thick-crust pizza, some with unusual toppings, such as leeks, escargots, and smoked fish.

✔ **La Pointe des Amériques,** 964 rue St-Jean (☎ **418-694-1199**), serves gourmet pizza, with all the combinations of toppings you can imagine.

For chocolate lovers

If you have a hankering for something tastier than the convenience-store quality of your favorite brown substance, you have two excellent places to go for chocolate in the Old City. You can find French, Belgian, and Swiss varieties at **Chocolatier Cupidon Château,** 1 rue des Carrières, behind the Château Frontenac (☎ 418-692-3340). At **Choco-Musée Erico,** 634 rue St-Jean (☎ 418-524-2122), high-quality chocolate comes in some very interesting forms.

All crêpes, all the time

It's hard to imagine visiting Québec City without eating crêpes at least once. They're a great option for lunch, because they're cheap and relatively quick. And no worries — you can really fill up on them, especially if you order them for your main course and dessert. I give you my top choices in this section, but honestly, crêpes are pretty hard to screw up (unless you order them in a place that doesn't specialize in them). They're just stuffed pancakes, after all.

My first choice is the **Casse-Crêpe Breton,** 1136 rue St-Jean (☎ 418-692-0438), both for its bustling atmosphere and delicious fresh dishes. In the shadows of the Château Frontenac, sits **Le Petit Château,** 5 rue St-Louis (☎ 418-694-1616), yet another good bet with a wide selection of sweet and savory crêpes.

A vegetarian outpost

Vegetarians are not exactly in the promised land in this town of blood sausage and veal scallops. There is really only one restaurant in the Old City that caters exclusively to vegetarians. **Le Commensal,** 860 rue St-Jean (☎ 418-647-3733), serves excellent buffet-style vegetarian food that is sold by weight.

Chapter 19

Exploring Québec City

● ●

In This Chapter

▶ Exploring Québec City's best attractions

▶ Seeing the city by guided tour

▶ Discovering Québec City's historical highlights

● ●

*Q*uébec City's most interesting attractions are conveniently packed together in an area that you could probably cross by foot in half an hour if you walked straight without stopping. Of course, you have many, many reasons to stop, so you're likely to linger a bit longer than 30 minutes. Half a day will give you a good overall impression, but several days still won't be enough to see absolutely everything. In this chapter, you find the top sights you want to try to hit.

Exploring Québec City's Top Sights from A to Z

There's plenty to do in Québec City. The past comes alive here because many of the attractions recount the history of this fortified city — the only one in North America.

Basilique Notre-Dame-de-Québec (Notre-Dame-de-Québec Basilica)
Haute-Ville

The site of the oldest Christian parish north of Mexico, Québec City's founder Samuel de Champlain originally chose this spot for a chapel back in 1633. Over the centuries, the Basilique Notre-Dame was built, torn down, burned, and expanded into roughly its present, neo-baroque style in the 1920s. The light inside is quite inspiring, combining the effects of candle-light and two floors of stained-glass windows depicting scenes of evangelists, arch angels, saints, and the Virgin Mary. Opinions are mixed about *Feux Sacrés (Sacred Fire)*, a 30-minute light and sound show on five centuries of Québec history that plays outside the basilica during the summer. Some say it's impressive; others say it's tacky. You be the judge.

20 rue Buade (at corner of Côte de la Fabrique). ☎ *418-694-0665. Admission: Free; guided tours C$2 (US$1.70) adults, C$1 (US85¢) children. Open: Daily 7:30 a.m.–5 p.m., until 4 p.m. Oct–Apr.*

Québec City Attractions

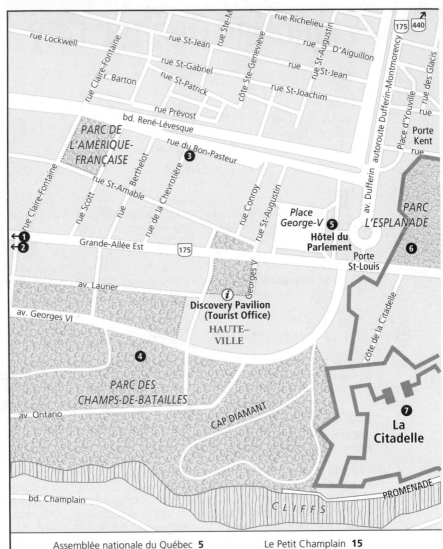

Assemblée nationale du Québec **5**
Basilique Nôtre-Dame-de-Québec **10**
Chapelle/Musée des Ursulines **9**
Château Frontenac **14**
Ferry Ride **16**
Fortifications de Québec **6**
La Citadelle **7**

Le Petit Champlain **15**
Musée de Cire (Wax Museum) **12**
Musée de l'Amérique Française **11**
Musée de la Civilisation **18**
Musée du Fort **13**
Musée national des beaux-arts
  du Québec **1**

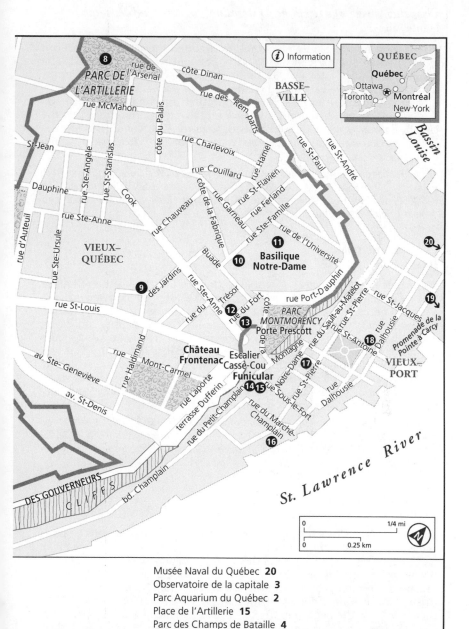

Musée Naval du Québec **20**
Observatoire de la capitale **3**
Parc Aquarium du Québec **2**
Place de l'Artillerie **15**
Parc des Champs de Bataille **4**
Place Royale **17**
Promenade de la Pointe à Carcy **19**

Chapelle/Musée des Ursulines (Ursuline Convent and Museum)
Haute-Ville

The French nun Marie de l'Incarnation founded the Ursulines order in Québec when she arrived in 1630; the convent was built in 1642. The chapel came much later, in 1902, but much of what you see in the interior dates to 1732. The museum and chapel interior are packed with artifacts, including Louis XIII furniture, a painting that was removed from Paris during the French Revolution, and altar cloths and church robes that the Ursuline nuns wove with gold thread. General Montcalm, who led the French troops when they lost Québec to the English in 1759, was originally buried here.

12 rue Donnacona (corner rue des Jardins). ☎ *418-694-0694. Admission: Chapel free; museum C$6 (US$5) adults, C$5 (US$4.25) seniors, C$4 (US$3.50) students, C$3 (US$2.50) children 12–16, children under 12 free. Open: Tues–Sat 10 a.m.–noon and 1–5 p.m., Sun 1–5 p.m., but hours vary seasonally.*

Château Frontenac
Haute-Ville

If one piece of architecture symbolizes Québec City, this is it. In Chapter 17, I recommend that you stay at this castlelike hotel, but in case you can't afford to actually spend the night, take a few minutes to wander inside. You really can't miss it. Just look for the pointy, green, copper roof rising above the cliff overlooking the St. Lawrence River. The château was built by the Canadian Pacific Railway in the early 1890s, and although it was inspired by the châteaux of the Loire Valley in France, it was designed by an American architect, Bruce Price. The inside is truly regal, with wood paneling, imposing antiques, and dainty boutiques surrounding the reception area. Guided 50-minute tours are given from May to October.

1 rue des Carrières (facing the terrasse Dufferin). ☎ *418-692-3861; for reservations 418-691-2166. Admission: Free for a peek; tours (reservations required) C$8 (US$6.75) adults, C$7.25 (US$6.25) seniors, C$5.50 (US$4.75) children 6–16, free for children 5 and under. Tours daily on the hour 10 a.m.–6 p.m.*

La Citadelle
Grande-Allée

Much of Québec City's history is dominated by the battles various empires waged to get control of this prime trading port on the St. Lawrence River. La Citadelle gives you a taste of the stormy military past — even though it was never actually used during a war. Still, you get an idea of the stakes of a possible enemy attack when you visit this star-shaped fortress comprising 25 separate buildings. First built by the French in the late 1700s, then rebuilt by the English in the 1830s, La Citadelle now houses a French Canadian regiment of the Canadian army. Notable features include a powder house and a prison. The guided tour is a little dry and perhaps better suited to military-history buffs, but the changing of the guards, usually once a day, is pretty cool.

1 Côte de la Citadelle (enter off rue St-Louis, leaving the St-Louis Gate in the direction of Grande-Allée). ☎ *418-694-2815.* www.lacitadelle.qc.ca. *Admission: C$8 (US$6.75) adults, C$7 (US$6) seniors, C$4.50 (US$3.75) children 7–17, free for persons with disabilities and children 6 and under. Open: July 1–Labor Day daily 9 a.m.–6 p.m.; off-season hours vary. Guided tours leave on the hour.*

Musée de la Civilisation (Museum of Civilization)
Basse-Ville

If you have time for only one major museum outing, this is the place. It won't teach you the most about the specific history of Québec City, but the permanent exhibits on daily life in the history of the province of Québec (called *Memoires,* or Memories) and on Canada's First Nations (called *Nous, les Premiéres Nations*) are totally captivating. Though light on written explanations, the exhibits have objects displayed beautifully and sensibly. They draw in visitors and satisfy all their senses (except maybe smell), while doing a good job of illustrating two distinct cultures. Plan on spending about two hours here. An added bonus: On the second floor, there's a lovely, bright, and modern visitors lounge with computers where you can check your E-mail for free.

85 rue Dalhousie (corner of rue St-Antoine). ☎ *418-643-2158. Admission C$8 (US$6.75) adults, C$7 (US$6) seniors, C$5 (US$4.25) students 18 and over, C$3 (US$2.50) children 12–17, free for children 11 and under. Open: Late June–Labour Day daily 9:30 a.m.–6:30 p.m.; Sept–June Tues–Sun 10 a.m.–5 p.m.*

Musée de l'Amérique Française (Museum of French America)
Haute-Ville

Housed in a former seminary built in 1663, this museum is an excellent place to get a French perspective on history. The museum is dedicated to showing the evolution of French culture and civilization in North America through the history of all seven French communities in the New World. The five floors of the museum contain 450,000 artifacts in all — everything from silverware and scientific instruments to paintings, engravings, parchments, old and rare books, and even the first Egyptian mummy to be brought to North America. Descriptions are in both English and French.

2 Côte de la Fabrique. ☎ *418-692-2843. Admission: C$5 (US$4.25) adults, C$4 (US$3.50) seniors, C$3 (US$2.50) students 16 and over, C$2 (US$1.70) children 12–16, free for children 11 and under. Open: Late June–Labour Day daily 9:30 a.m.–5 p.m.; Sept to mid-June Tues–Sun 10 a.m.–5 p.m. Guided tours available; call for information.*

Musée national des beaux-arts du Québec (Québec National Museum of Fine Art)
Grande-Allée

Not too far from the Parc Champs-de-Bataille, this museum houses the largest collection of Québec art in North America, including over 23,000 pieces dating from the 18th century to the present. Eight galleries are spread over three buildings. The Great Hall has a reception area and attached auditorium. The Gérard Morrisset Pavilion houses permanent exhibits, including works from the early colonial period, African masks and carvings, and musical instruments. The Baillargé Pavilion, a former prison built in 1867, holds temporary exhibits.

1 av. Wolfe-Montcalm (near Place George V). ☎ *418-643-2150.* www.mnba.qc.ca. *Admission: Permanent collection free; special exhibitions C$10 (US$8.50) adults, C$9 (US$7.75) seniors, C$5 (US$4.25) students, C$3 (US$2.50) children 12–16, children 11 and under free. Open: June 1–Labor Day daily 10 a.m.–6 p.m., Wed till 9 p.m.; Sept–May Tues–Sun 10 a.m.–5 p.m., Wed till 9 p.m.*

Parc des Champs-de-Bataille (Battlefield Park)
Grande-Allée

If the Château Frontenac stands as a symbol of Québec City, this park is the symbol of tension between Canada's English and French populations. Québec's Battlefield Park is where General Montcalm led the French against General Wolfe and the English in the famous battle of the Plains of Abraham in 1759 (the English won; both generals died). Although it's famous for a battle, the 108-hectare (267-acre) park is actually a rather idyllic place to stroll (with some 5,000 trees), not too far from the Grande-Allée. Locals like to cross-country ski here in the winter and Rollerblade and bike in the summer. Summer also brings theater and musical performances. The park's **Maison de la Découverte (Discovery Pavilion)** explains the significance of the Plains of Abraham to Québec.

Discovery Pavilion, 835 av. Laurier. ☎ *418-648-4071.* www.ccbn-nbc.gc.ca. *Admission: Free. Open: Park 24 hours; Discovery Pavilion daily 9 a.m.–5 p.m.*

Place-Royale
Basse-Ville

This quaint cobblestone square, located on the spot where Champlain founded Québec in 1608, feels like a microcosm of Vieux-Québec. Right at the bottom of the Breakneck stairs, Place-Royale is dominated by the Notre-Dame-des-Victoires church, the oldest church in Canada built in 1688, which is small and rather plain but contains some lovely paintings and a large model boat suspended from the ceiling. This was a town marketplace during the 17th and 18th centuries. Now you can see a bust of French King Louis XIV, a copy of the original bust erected in 1686. All the buildings around the square have been restored, and you can souvenir shop to your heart's content in this part of the Basse-Ville. The **Centre d'Interpretation de Place-Royale (Interpretation Center)** explains the history of the square.

Centre d'Interpretation de Place-Royale, 27 rue Notre-Dame (walk down the Breakneck stairs and take Côte de la Montagne to rue Notre-Dame). ☎ *418-646-3167. Admission: C$4 (US$3.50) adults, C$3.50 (US$3) seniors, C$3 (US$2.50) students 17 and over, C$2 (US$1.70) children 12–16, children 11 and under free. Open: Late June–Sept daily 9:30 a.m.–5 p.m.; Sept–June Tues–Sat 10 a.m.–5 p.m.*

Finding More Cool Things to See and Do

In this section, you find suggestions for following a specific interest, whether you want to keep the kids entertained; get your fill of wars, battles, and armory; make your teenagers happy; stroll some lovely streets; or take a tour.

Kid-pleasing places

Kids are sure to be enchanted by Québec City, whether it's the fairy-tale-castle effect of the Château Frontenac or the real (but not in use!) cannons and armory scattered around the city. The best museum for kids is the **Musée de la Civilisation,** which has great exhibits plus loads of room to run around. Following are a few other suggestions for entertaining children.

Centre d'Interprétation de la Côte-de-Beaupré (Côte-de-Beaupré Interpretation Center)
Outside Québec City

Set in an entirely restored convent — about 40 minutes out of town — kids get to peek at a period classroom and some of the other hardships of life in New France. The staff is in costume and "in-character," which is also a hoot. An animated diorama tells the history of the region — the site of Québec's earliest rural communities. Popular archaeological and religious artifacts exhibited throughout the convent make up the permanent collection, shown off by one of the guides.

7976 av. Royale (in the town of Château-Richer). ☎ *418-824-3677.* http://pages. globetrotter.net/cicb. *Admission: C$5 (US$4.25) adults, C$4 (US$3.50) seniors and students, free for children 16 and under. Open: May–Oct daily 10 a.m.–5 p.m.; Nov–Apr Mon–Fri 10 a.m.–6:30 p.m.*

Ferry Ride
Old Port

Not very expensive, but usually a thrill for the little ones, you can cross the river from Québec City over to Lévis in about ten minutes. The view of Québec City from the river is quite spectacular, especially at night. There's not much to do in Lévis, but take a stroll around anyway. The ferry leaves close to Place-Royale. Buy tickets at the Société des Traversiers du Québec building, right on the port.

Société des Traversiers du Québec, 10 rue des Traversiers. ☎ *418-644-3704. Tickets: C$2.50 (US$2.25) adults, C$2.25 (US$2) seniors, C$1.75 (US$1.50) children 5–11, free for children 4 and under. Departs from Québec three or four times per hour.*

Musée de Cire (Wax Museum)
Haute-Ville

Pop in to this 17th-century house to see wax renditions of major personal-
ities in Québec history. There are 60 individuals in all, in 16 settings. From
pop stars to military heroes, you get your fill of tackiness, and then some.

22 rue Ste-Anne. ☎ *418-692-2289. Admission: C$4 (US$3.50) adults, C$3 (US$2.50)
seniors and students, children 11 and under free with adult. Open: May–Oct daily
9 a.m.–9 p.m.; rest of year daily 10 a.m.–5 p.m.*

Observatoire de la capitale (Observation Deck)
Grande Allée

Kids go dizzy with vertigo on this observation deck, which is Québec City's
highest point. By modern-day, skyscraper standards this government
building is an unimpressive 31 floors, but the views of this historic city
and the St. Lawrence River are really worthwhile. The otherwise large-
looming Château Frontenac doesn't seem that big from here. It's the river
that's so impressive.

1037 rue de la Chevrotière. ☎ *888-497-4322 or 418-644-9841.* www.observatoire
capitale.org. *Admission: C$5 (US$4.25) adults, C$4 (US$3.50) seniors and students, free for children 11 and under. Open: Mid-June to mid-Oct daily 10 a.m.–5 p.m.;
mid-Oct to mid-June Tues–Sat 10 a.m.–5 p.m.*

Parc Aquarium du Québec (Québec Aquarium)
Ste. Foy

All kids leave this place wanting to be marine biologists, which is probably a good thing. Various-windowed tanks and glassed-tunnels lead visitors through several underwater ecosystems. Polar bears, penguins, and
seals cavort as a scuba diver in the deep-sea tank show visitors, up close,
some examples of the over 650 different species.

1675 av. des Hôtels (15 minutes from Vieux Québec; bus 13). ☎ *418-659-5264.* www.
spsnq.qc.ca. *Admission: C$15.50 (US$13.25) adults, C$14.50 (US$12.25) seniors,
C$12.75 (US$10.75) students 13–17, C$10.50 (US$9) children 6–12, C$5.50 (US$4.75)
children 3–5, free for children 2 and under. Open: Daily 10 a.m.–5 p.m.; Oct–Apr until
4 p.m.*

Parc de la Chute-Montmorency
Outside Québec City

A labyrinth of paths and wooden staircases leads to a suspended bridge
for daredevils to cross the frothy mouth of this 272-foot waterfall —
significantly higher than Niagara Falls. Summer or winter it's a dramatic
outdoor adventure. At the top are spectacular views of the river and surrounding area. The Manoir Montmorency, an enormous English country
house with a reputed kitchen serves regional cuisine with local, or *terroir*,
ingredients. It's a touch of civilization in an otherwise rugged place. Those
who don't feel like making the climb can take a cable car to the top.

2490 ave. Royale. ☎ *800-665-6527 or 418-663-3330. Admission: Round-trip on the cable car C$8 (US$6.75) adults, C$4 (US$3.50) children 6–16, free for children 5 and under. Parking: $8 (US$6.75). Open: Hours vary seasonally; call ahead.*

Terrasse Dufferin
Haute-Ville

Head straight to this square looking out onto the St. Lawrence River for a kind of one-stop children's entertainment package. Within a short walking distance (even shorter running distance), you have **coin-operated telescopes** for a look across the river. In the summer, **street entertainers** abound, from living "statues" to mimes to musicians playing wine glasses. If you want to burn off some serious steam, try tackling the Breakneck stairs, leading down to the Basse-Ville. For a real thrill, take the kids to nearby Place d'Armes and pick up a **horse-drawn carriage ride** (C$60/US$51 for a 35-minute ride).

For military and history buffs
Kids aren't the only ones fascinated by epic battles. If you like stories about warfare, this section gives you few places to find them.

Assemblée nationale du Québec (Québec Legislature)
Grande Allée

Heckle the ministers of Parliament from the gallery in Québec's legislature. Just kidding — don't. Instead, watch democracy in action and brush up on your knowledge of parliamentary procedure. Most of the law-making is done in French so it can be rather opaque, but not understanding somehow adds to the spectacle. You can take a free guided tour in English of this imposing 18th-century building inspired by the Louvre in Paris or eat breakfast or lunch in the restaurant among Québec's political elite. Access can vary depending on the official events of the day.

45 rue des Parlemaentaires (just outside the walls of the Haute-Ville). ☎ *418-643-7239.* www.assnat.qc.ca. *Admission: Free. Open: Year-round Mon–Fri 9 a.m.–4:30 p.m.; June–Sept Sat–Sun 10 a.m.–4:30 p.m.*

Musée du Fort
Haute-Ville

For explanations of sieges and battles fought in Québec City, this small museum just off Place d'Armes is hard to beat. Battles are retold using sound and light, in both English and French.

10 rue Ste-Anne. ☎ *418-692-1759. Admission: C$7.50 (US$6.50) adults, C$5.50 (US$4.75) seniors, C$4.50 (US$3.75) students. Open: Apr–Oct daily 10 a.m.–5 p.m.; Oct–April Thurs–Sun 11 a.m.–4 p.m.*

Musée Naval de Québec (Naval Museum of Québec)
Basse-Ville

The flow of the mighty St. Lawrence River is a constant reminder of Québec's naval history — both military and merchant. Did you know that there were German U-boats in the St. Lawrence River during World War II? This new museum's unique collection of over 1,000 objects reveals the different boating eras over the last century, but it focuses on the Battle of the St. Lawrence during WWII. It features several recovered items from torpedoed boats that sank nearby. The museum looks at the historical, social, and even environmental consequences that were at stake.

170 rue Dalhousie (near Promenade de la Pointe-à-Carcy). ☎ *418-694-5387.* www. mnq-nmq.org. *Admission: Free. Open: May–Sept daily 10 a.m.–5 p.m.; Oct–Apr Tues–Fri 1–4 p.m.*

Parc de l'Artillerie (Artillery Park)
Haute-Ville

Near the Porte St-Jean, this enormous military installation was the French military headquarters starting in 1747. Later, it housed the British garrison, and then became a munitions factory, which was in use until 1964. Now it serves as an interpretative center. Don't miss the scale model of Québec City, showing what the city looked like in the 1800s.

2 rue d'Auteuil (near St-Jean Gate). ☎ *418-648-4205. Admission: C$4 (US$3.50) adults, C$3.50 (US$3) seniors, C$2 (US$1.70) children 6–16, free for children 5 and under. Open: May–Sept daily 10 a.m.–5 p.m; Oct–Apr by reservation.*

Fortifications de Québec (Fortifications of Québec)
Haute-Ville

If the wall around Québec City — built to protect the city from marauding invaders — is still standing, it's because it was restored and remains a protected site. You can walk the complete 3-mile circuit starting at the kiosk of terrasse Dufferin or take a 90-minute tour and discover the wall's history.

Tour tickets available at kiosk at terrasse Dufferin. ☎ *418-648-7016. Tour: C$10 (US$8.50) adults, C$7.50 (US$6.50) seniors, C$5 (US$4.25) kids 6–16, free for children 5 and under. Open: June–Sept daily.*

Teen-tempting areas

Québec City is a popular destination for school trips, especially for the early teen demographic. If you happen to find yourself accompanied by members of that select group, this section tells you where you can take them.

Rue St-Jean

This street has shops galore. The busy commercial street on the north end of the Haute-Ville has souvenir boutiques, clothes stores, inexpensive cafes, bookstores and CD shops, and plenty of action to keep your teenagers engrossed for hours.

Place-Royale

Perhaps your teenagers aren't that interested in the history of early French colonialism. Not a problem. This little area has plenty of distractions for them, including cute boutiques and even cuter cafes. They'll go nuts. Just make sure each kid has a map.

The best strolling streets

There's really no such thing as just "strolling around" Québec City. Vieux-Québec is so packed with things to see and do, you're sure to get sidetracked. But whether you have some specific purchases in mind or you just want to stretch your legs, the walking suggestions in this section should do the trick.

Le Petit Champlain
Basse-Ville

This narrow pedestrian alley tucked into the base of the cliffs right below the Château Frontenac gets A's for atmosphere. One of the oldest streets in Québec City, opened in 1685, Le Petit Champlain originally housed artists, and then became the home of poor Irish immigrants in the 1800s. These days, it's packed with quaint, mostly high-quality souvenir shops, cafes, and restaurants. It's a good place to pick up items such as jewelry made by Québec designers, unique toys, clothing, and French kitchen implements. Take the Breakneck stairs, and then keep following Côte de la Montagne down the hill. You hit another set of stairs, and Le Petit Champlain starts at the bottom of them.

Rue St-Paul
Basse-Ville

Slightly off the beaten track — off the beaten *tourist* track, anyway — this street running parallel to the Bassin Louise has an authentic port feel to it. It's also packed with antiques shops, has a number of good art galleries, and boasts quiet little eateries where you can have a leisurely drink or coffee. Take Côte du Palais (just off rue St-Jean) and walk down past the city wall and down rue des Vaisseaux-du-Roi and you'll hit rue St-Paul. Turn right.

Rue St-Joseph
St. Roch

This is by far the most happening part of Québec City, and, unlike the rest, this strip is only a couple of years old. It already features several destination boutiques, some of the city's hottest restaurants, and a handful of nightlife options. The street was always there but recently it became the target of an urban renewal scheme. It feels trendy but not touristy, which could be a welcomed relief after a day of seeing the sights.

Promenade de la Pointe à Carcy
Old Port

The cruise-ship business in Québec City's port has really taken off over the last decade, and the port area has benefited from the increased activity. Unlike in Montréal, though, there is no commercial street running along Québec City's port (rue Dalhousie is the closest one). Instead, city authorities have transformed this area into a kind of urban park, with a bike trail, fountains, and scrupulous security guards who make sure tourists don't get too close to the edge. It's a great place to park on a bench and read or just wander around gazing at the river traffic.

Rue du Trésor
Haute-Ville

This little street runs between rue St-Louis and rue de Buade and is a veritable outdoor art market, with artists lined up the whole length of the street selling paintings, sketches, and engravings of various styles and qualities. More for shopping than walking, it's still worth checking out, just for the atmosphere. Head here if you want your caricature drawn.

Seeing Québec City by guided tour

If you're short on time, a guided tour is a good option for seeing a lot of Québec City with minimum effort. Walking is my first choice and should be yours (as long as you're able), but you can also get around by bus tours, horse-drawn carriages, or even river cruises. This section gives you my recommendations.

Walking tours

Walking is the best way to see the nooks and crannies of Québec City — and there are many of them. With a walking tour, you get history, hear insider info, and have areas of interest pointed out to you that you probably wouldn't normally notice on your own. Most walking tours leave from the terrasse Dufferin. The best idea is to see what's being offered at the nearby **Centre Infotouriste** at 12 rue Ste-Anne just opposite the Château Frontenac at Place d'Armes (☎ 800-363-7777). Or call the **Association des guides touristiques de Québec** (☎ 800-208-1463 or 418-683-1591), which provides guides for any length of time, on foot, or in your car or theirs.

Here are two other good tour companies:

- ✔ **La Compagnie des Six Associés** (☎ 418-802-6665) also offers thematic tours. "Vice and Drunkeness," explaining the underbelly of the history of Québec, is a popular one. Book your tour at the main tourist office opposite Place d'Armes. Tours cost C\$12 to C\$15 (US\$10.25–US\$12.75) per person.

- ✔ A new initiative, **Québec Trail,** is a series of over 40 stops on an audio tour. For around C\$10 (US\$8.50) travelers can buy a set of headphones at tourist offices as well as some stores, hotels, and restaurants around town. They come with a special adapter that allows you to plug in to the recording at each stop. It gives you the ultimate flexibility in seeing the sites — you can pick up on another day or just at random whenever you happen upon a listening post. Best of all, you get to keep the earphones when you're done.

Bus tours

If you're not up to walking, or if it's extremely hot (or cold) and you want to escape the elements (while not missing the sites), bus tours are a good solution. Two good companies offer tours year-round:

- ✔ **Les Tours du Vieux-Québec** (☎ **800-267-8687** or 418-664-0460) offers guided tours in small comfortable buses, both inside the city and in surrounding areas like Île d'Orléans. Québec City tours last about two hours and cost C$30 (US$25.50) per person.

- ✔ **Les Tours Dupont** (☎ **888-558-7668** or 418-694-9226; www. tourdupont.com) offers more-luxurious tours in bigger buses, both of the city and the surrounding area. Tours last about two hours and cost C$27 (US$23) per person.

Horse-drawn carriage tours

Get a tour of Québec City the old-fashioned way and experience not only the sights and sounds but also the smells of yesteryear. You can visit Vieux-Québec by *calèche* all year round. Rides cost C$75 (US$63.75) for 40 minutes. You can pick one up on the fly at **Place d'Armes** or call **Calèches du Vieux-Québec** (☎ **418-683-9222**) or **Balade en Caleche et Diligance** (☎ **418-624-3062**).

River cruises

You won't get the most out of seeing Québec City by boat, but if you like cruises, **Croisières AML** (☎ **800-563-4643** or 418-692-1159) offers 90-minute cruises aboard a renovated 1930s ferry, departing three times daily from Quai Chouinard, 10 rue Dalhousie, near Place-Royale in the Lower Town. The show comes with bilingual guides, and full dining facilities and a bar are right on the boat. Evening cruises last two and a half hours with dining and dancing included. Prices for day cruises start at C$30 (US$25.50) for adults, C$28 (US$23.75) for seniors, and C$13 (US$11) for kids, and go up in the evening. You can buy tickets at the kiosk on terrasse Dufferin.

Hitting the Historical Highlights of Vieux-Québec

Québec City *is* history. Step through any gate leading in to the Old City, and you see that for yourself. The walking tour in this section stops at some of the top historical sites and shows you some other nice things to

Historical Highlights of Vieux-Québec

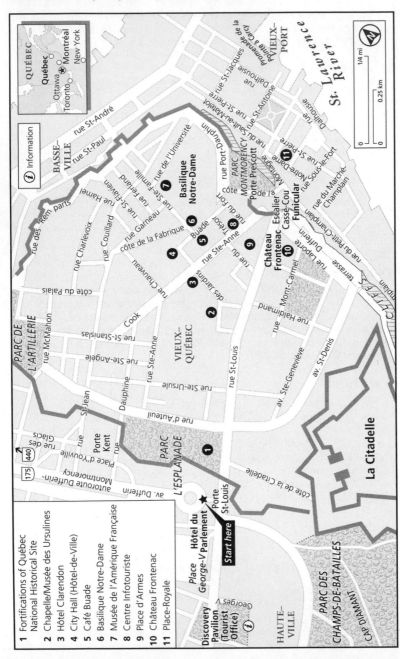

1 Fortifications of Québec
  National Historical Site
2 Chapelle/Musée des Ursulines
3 Hôtel Clarendon
4 City Hall (Hôtel-de-Ville)
5 Café Buade
6 Basilique Notre-Dame
7 Musée de l'Amérique Française
8 Centre Infotouriste
9 Place d'Armes
10 Château Frontenac
11 Place-Royale

see (and eat) along the way. You can wander along the itinerary at your own leisure or do the whole thing backward, if you like. Some sights are bound to interest you more than others, so pick and choose as you go along.

Start by entering Vieux-Québec at the **Porte St-Louis,** which you reach either by walking along the Grande-Allée or by turning left onto rue St-Louis from avenue Honoré-Mercier. The gate was designed to bring to mind medieval castles and horsemen, but it's actually Victorian — the work of an Irish architect that was completed in 1878.

A few steps inside the gate, on your left, is the **Fortifications of Québec National Historical Site,** where you can learn about the history of the wall that surrounds the Old City. The wall, originally wooden, was first erected by the French in 1693. The same French started working on the stone wall in 1745, but they had to hand the job over to the English when the Brits conquered the city in 1759.

Continue along rue St-Louis until your reach rue du Parloir, turn left and you'll see the **museum and the monastery of the Ursulines,** the first order of French nuns to set up shop in Québec, around 1630.

At the end of rue du Parloir, turn right on rue Donnacona, and then left on rue des Jardins. Follow this street to rue Ste-Anne. On your left, you'll see the **Hotel Clarendon,** the oldest hotel still operating in Québec City, built in 1870. Wander in and check out the Art Deco entrance. If all this history is exhausting you, the **L'Emprise** cafe/bar inside the hotel is a great place to stop for a coffee or beer.

Continue along rue des Jardins, and you'll see Québec City's old **Hôtel-de-Ville (City Hall),** built in 1895. If you're interested in knowing more about the history of urban planning in Québec, the **Centre d'Interprétation de la Vie Urbaine de la Ville de Québec (City Hall Interpretation Center)** is in the basement.

Continue along rue des Jardins to the end of the Place de l'Hôtel-de-Ville, turn right on Côte de la Fabrique and you'll see the **Basilique Notre-Dame,** first built in 1647, and then destroyed and built again about five times over until it took its final form around the end of the 1700s. (Well, actually, they were still putting finishing touches on it in 1959.) On the same street, you'll see the **Musée de l'Amérique Française (Museum of French America),** where you can get a thorough history of French colonization in the New World, in Québec, and beyond.

Time for another coffee break? Or maybe some lunch or a light snack? You're not too far from rue de Buade where the **Café Buade,** 31 rue Buade (☎ **418-692-3909**) offers pizzas, sandwiches, coffee, and the like at a reasonable price.

Keep going along rue de Buade until you reach **rue du Trésor.** The name (which means "treasury") dates from the French regime, when colonists used to pass along this street on their way to pay their taxes. Now it's a great little walkway where artists hang their paintings, sketching, etchings, and more.

Rue du Trésor takes you to rue Ste-Anne right in front of Place d'Armes. Turn left, and you'll see the **Infotouriste Center.** Cross Place d'Armes, and you'll be standing in front of the majestic, castlelike **Château Frontenac,** built in 1893 by the Canadian Pacific Railway Company.

If want to see the Basse-Ville from here, walk to the lookout area in front on the Château Frontenac. On your left are the **Breakneck stairs,** there since 1682. Take the stairs down to Côte de la Montagne, and then keep going down on this street until you reach the next set of stairs. These take you to **Le Petit Champlain,** one of the oldest streets in the city, where the houses date to the 17th and 18th centuries — a shopper's delight, to boot.

Your last stop should be the **Place-Royale,** down the hill from Le Petit Champlain (toward the river). This is where it all started. It's the spot where the French explorer Samuel de Champlain founded New France in 1608.

Chapter 20

Shopping the Québec City Stores

. . . .

In This Chapter

▶ Checking out shopping opportunities in Québec City

▶ Finding the big-name stores

▶ Discovering Québec City's best malls and shopping neighborhoods

. . . .

*O*n the whole, people in Québec City like things a little classy. Of course, given that tourism is a mainstay industry here, not-so-classy trinket boutiques abound, especially in the Old City. But don't be fooled by the trashy souvenir shops. Unique, high-quality items are available throughout Québec City, from Inuit art to antiques and clothing. Just don't go looking for bargains — you're likely to be disappointed.

Surveying the Scene

Souvenir stores aside, Québec City is probably best known as a place to buy antiques, art, and crafts. The antiques stores keep their tourist clientele in mind and tend to specialize in smaller, more portable items like lamps, china, and bedside tables and stools. Prices for antiques are reasonable, partly because Québeckers on the whole are not especially drawn to antiques (leaving plenty left over for you).

For a small city, Québec has a lot of art galleries. They run the full gamut of price and style, offering both traditional and abstract works done by new and established artists at both steep and affordable prices. Most — but not all — of the works for sale are from Québec artists. If you don't feel up to investing in art, the city has plenty of stores featuring less expensive crafts and creations from local artisans.

If shopping for clothes, books, or CDs is more your style, you'll find plenty of ways to spend your cash — believe me. Québec City residents are known for stylish dressing, and while you won't find the quantity of local designers available in Montréal, the clothing selection here reflects Québeckers' flair. Most books for sale in the city are French, but plenty of English books are available, as well. The city has a decent selection of music, but if you're looking in particular for French music, the selection is excellent.

Outside of the Old City, stores' hours in Québec City are similar to those throughout Canada. Most stores open at 9 or 10 a.m. and close at 5 or 6 p.m., Mondays through Wednesdays, and Saturdays. Thursdays and Fridays, stores usually stay open until 9 p.m. Many stores open Sunday from around noon until 5 p.m. In the Old City, however, hours are very seasonal. During the high season, you're likely to find shops open long hours, pretty much every day.

Remember to keep track of your purchases. You have to come clean at the border and fork over the details of your purchases to Customs agents before you leave. If you stay in Canada more than two days, you can bring back US$800 in goods without paying duty. This includes 200 cigarettes, 100 cigars, and 1 liter of an alcoholic beverage. If you stay less than two days, your limit drops to US$200. If you buy more than this, no one will throw you in jail — you'll just have to pay a tax that's a small percentage of the amount that surpasses your limit. Check out Chapter 12 for more details.

Before you commence your Québec City shopping frenzy, don't forget the Canadian tax man (or tax woman; these are modern times). You must pay taxes adding up to roughly 15 percent of your purchases. For information on how to get a refund on the Goods and Services Tax (which is about half the 15 percent), see Chapter 4.

Checking Out the Big Names

Downtown Québec City has only one big-name store, and that's **Simons** at 20 Côte de la Fabrique (☎ 418-692-3630). This slightly upscale department store, which opened in 1840, offers a good selection of clothing and accessories for men, women, and children, plus fine bed linens. This is the place to come if you unexpectedly find yourself in the middle of a cold spell and need a hat, scarf, and gloves — not a likely event until at least mid-October, but you never know.

The other big department store you find in Québec City is **La Baie** (The Bay, short for the Hudson's Bay Company), but you have to leave the confines of the downtown area and head out to the shopping malls in the 'burbs. You can find La Baie stores at **Galeries de la Capitale, Place Fleur de Lys,** and **Place Laurier.**

Going to Shopping Malls

People really like to shop here, and for a small city, Québec has an impressive roster of shopping malls. Maybe the winter weather drives Québeckers into these indoor havens of consumption.

You have two shopping mall options within walking distance of the Old City:

✔ **Les Promenades du Vieux-Québec,** 43 rue de Buade (☎ 418-692-6000): This small complex is just a few steps away from the Château Frontenac and has 12 upscale boutiques, where you can find jewelry, furs, perfumes, gifts, candies, fine art, arts and crafts, and more.

✔ **Place Québec,** 880 av. Honoré-Mercier (☎ 418-529-0551): A multi-level shopping complex attached to the Delta Hotel, this mall has 30 boutiques and is a ten-minute walk from the Old City.

Trouble is (for visitors, anyway), the biggest and best of the malls are a fair distance from the Old City. But if mall crawling is what you want (not a bad alternative when the weather works against you), catch a cab and take off to one of the following:

✔ **Galeries de la Capitale,** 5401 bd. des Galeries (☎ 418-627-5800): A 20-minute drive from the Old City, this mall has 250 shops and a small amusement park with games, rides, an IMAX theater, 12 movie theaters, and assorted restaurants.

✔ **Place Fleur de Lys,** 552 bd. Wilfrid-Hamel (☎ 418-529-8128): Winner of the Canadian Maple Leaf Award for the most beautiful shopping interior design, Place Fleur de Lys is a five-minute drive from downtown Québec City and has 250 boutiques plus major chains.

✔ **Place Laurier,** 2700 bd. Laurier (☎ 800-322-1828): A good 20-minute drive from the Old City, this is the mother of all shopping centers. It's the largest shopping center in Eastern Canada with some 350 stores.

✔ **Place Sainte-Foy,** 2450 bd. Laurier (☎ 418-653-4184): This is a fashionable mall, featuring 130 stores and boutiques; a 20-minute drive from the Old City.

Discovering the Best Shopping Neighborhoods

You can find loads of great shopping in Québec. I assume you want to spend most of your time in the Old City, or not too far from it, maybe venturing out, at most, to Grande-Allée for a change of scenery. So, for your shopping ease and pleasure, I break the city down into six shopping areas, discussed in the six following sections. Like almost everything else I recommend in the Québec City part of this book, all these areas are within walking distance of each other.

For antiques and art, you can't beat the **rue St-Paul** area in the Basse-Ville. For souvenirs, arts and crafts, and even clothes, I recommend the area around **Le Petit-Champlain** in the Basse-Ville, including Place-Royale and the area around the **Château Frontenac** in the Haute-Ville.

For less touristy types of shops, **rue St-Jean** is the place to go, with its books, CD, and clothes stores (and plenty of cafes and restaurants to rest between your shopping sprints). Finally, if you really want a break from the Vieux-Québec experience, I recommend strolling down Grande-Allée to **avenue Cartier,** where you find a small concentration of shops with items like clothes, outdoor items, and home décor. Yet, **rue St-Joseph** is perhaps the most exciting shopping street of them all. It is away from Vieux-Québec, somewhat, but here's where you'll see a more authentic version of the city.

Rue St-Paul

You can get to rue St-Paul in the Basse-Ville by following rue St-Pierre from Place-Royale. Or, you can start at the other end of the street. On rue St-Jean, take Côte du Palais. You pass through the city walls, and then walk down the slope to the Basse-Ville via rue des Vaisseaux-du-Roi.

This is where you find the biggest concentration of antiques stores in the city. But these aren't the kind of dusty, cluttered antiques stores you find on rue Notre-Dame in Montréal (see Chapter 12). Instead, most are neat places that specialize in a certain type of antiques. There's definitely something for everyone. This section lists a few places to visit on your stroll down rue St-Paul.

For old and rare books, check out **Argus Livres Anciens,** 160 rue St-Paul (☎ 418-694-2122). If Victorian and Edwardian furniture, silver, porcelain, and paintings are your thing, stop by **Boutique aux Memoires Antiquités,** 105 rue St-Paul (☎ 418-692-2180). For authentic Québec pine furniture, I recommend **Gérard Bourguet Antiquaire,** 97 rue St-Paul (☎ 418-694-0896). The store offers many 18th- and 19th-century pieces, but you can expect to pay a fair penny for them. **L'Héritage Antiquité,** 110 rue St-Paul (☎ 418-692-1681), also specializes in Québec furniture and sells clocks, oil lamps, and ceramics. For engravings, prints, and maps, the best place is **Les Antiquités du Matelot,** 137 rue St-Paul (☎ 418-694-9585). And if you're more interested in curiosities from the 1960s and 1970s, don't miss **Décennie,** 117 rue St-Paul (☎ 418-694-0403), for retro chairs, lamps, and décor.

Rue St-Paul's other specialty is art galleries, although you'd be wise to wander off along some of the neighboring streets like rue Sault-au-Matelot or rue St-Pierre to get the full experience. **Galerie Madeleine Lacerte,** 1 Côte Dinan (☎ 418-692-1566), is one of the best-known galleries of the neighborhood. It sells contemporary paintings and sculpture. **Galerie d'art Alain Lacaze,** 131 rue St-Paul (☎ 418-692-4381), sells oils and watercolors.

Other noteworthy boutiques along rue St-Paul fall outside of the art and antiques category. **Vitrine,** 329 rue St-Paul (☎ 418-694-7384), specializes in furniture and other objects made by local designers. For one of the best selections of fur coats in the Old City, visit **Les Fourrures du Vieux-Port,** 55 rue St-Pierre (☎ 418-692-6686).

Rue St-Jean

Rue St-Jean is probably the least quaint, yet most practical, of the shopping areas in the Old City. A busy commercial street, here you find a number of Québec chain stores. It's also a good place to head if you want specialty food items, books, CDs, clothes, or a comfortable pair of walking shoes. I include rue de la Fabrique in this area, which is a continuation of rue St-Jean uphill toward the Hôtel-de-Ville. The same bustling commercial spirit reigns on both streets.

This is the destination for clothes. For comfortable but elegant men's and women's fashions, Québec chain **America,** 1147 rue St-Jean (☎ 418-692-5254), is a good place to start. **Bedo,** 1161 rue St-Jean (☎ 418-692-0623), another chain, carries edgier, urban women's and men's fashions. Another good option for sportswear is **NRJ,** 1121 rue St-Jean (☎ 418-694-0086). **Louis Laflamme,** 1192 rue St-Jean (☎ 418-692-3774), carries stylish menswear. If you're looking for something to keep your feet comfortable (or warm), the Canadian chain **Roots,** 1150 rue St-Jean (☎ 418-692-2000), sells high-quality leather shoes at decent, although not bargain, prices. A little more into the "interesting" category of clothes, **Artisans du Bas-Canada,** 30 Côte de la Fabrique (☎ 888-339-2109 or 418-692-2109), offers a wide selection of outdoor garments, gifts, and collectibles.

Food-wise, if you're a chocolate fanatic, you'll love **Choco-Musée Érico,** 634 rue St-Jean (☎ 418-524-2122), where, with two days' notice, *chocolatier* Éric Normand sculpts whatever you like out of chocolate. You can get good ice cream here, too. For maple products and Québec wines and beers, visit the **Marché Je-An-Dré,** 1097 rue St-Jean (☎ 418-692-3647).

You can find plenty of bookstores along rue St-Jean. Although many are principally *Francophone* (French-speaking), you can find English books and magazines at **Archambault,** 1095 rue St-Jean (☎ 418-694-2088), and at the **Maison de la Presse Internationale,** 1050 rue St-Jean (☎ 418-694-1511).

For gifts, souvenirs, and jewelry, check out **Abaca,** 54 Côte de la Fabrique (☎ 418-694-9761), and **Collection Lazuli,** 774 rue St-Jean (☎ 418-525-6528).

Le Petit-Champlain/Place-Royale

Although extremely touristy, Place-Royale and Le Petit-Champlain are still your best bets for souvenirs. Although cheap trinkets abound, most stores offer high-quality items, and many specialize in handmade and Québec-made clothing and jewelry. Plus, a number of reputable art galleries are located here.

If you're in the market for one of those striped French nautical shirts, you can find it at the nautical store **Le Capitaine d'à Bord,** 63 Petit-Champlain (☎ 418-694-0624). Into leather? **Peau sur Peau,** 85 Petit-Champlain (☎ 418-692-5132), offers leather clothing, shoes, luggage, and accessories from Québec and international designers. **Ibiza,** 57 Petit-Champlain (☎ 418-692-2103), also carries leather goods by Québec designers. **Zazou,** 31 Petit-Champlain (☎ 418-694-9990), sells clothes made by Québec designers.

For wines and spirits, stop at the **Maison des Vins,** 1 Place-Royale (☎ 418-643-1214). Maple products, a true Québec specialty, abound at the **Petit Cabane à Sucre,** 94 Petit-Champlain (☎ 418-692-5875). **Le Jardin de l'argile,** 51 Petit-Champlain (☎ 418-692-4870), carries Québec-made porcelain, pottery, bronze works, and more.

Château Frontenac

Most of the nicer boutiques in and around the Château Frontenac in the Haute-Ville carry objects best qualified as "upscale souvenir."

Among these, don't miss the boutiques that sell Inuit art. **Aux Multiples Collections,** 69 rue Ste-Anne (☎ 418-692-1230), offers a wide selection of Native Canadian carvings in stone, bone, and tusk. You can also find a great choice of Inuit carving at **Brousseau et Brousseau,** 35 rue St-Louis (☎ 418-694-1828). **Kulik Art Inuit,** just inside the Château Frontenac at 1 rue des Carrières (☎ 418-692-6174), has a wide range of Inuit prints and sculptures.

Two other boutiques worth checking out in this area include the highly specialized **Boutique de Noël de Québec** (Québec Christmas Boutique), 47 rue de Buade (☎ 418-692-2457), which is open all year long. It's definitely a good spot to pick up a souvenir for that somebody who has everything. **La Maison Darlington,** 7 rue de Buade (☎ 418-692-2268), specializes in imported woolen garments including merino and cashmere sweaters, caps, ties, scarves, and gloves for children and adults.

If you want to bring back some locally made beer or Québec liqueurs made out of blueberry or maple syrup, the **SAQ Signature** spirits boutique has them. It's located just inside the Château Frontenac at 1 rue des Carrières (☎ 418-692-1182).

Avenue Cartier

As nice as the Old City is, its intensely touristy and cramped shops can make you feel claustrophobic. Avenue Cartier is a great place to go for a little breathing space. Leave the Old City from the St-Louis Gate and walk along rue St-Louis until it turns into Grande-Allée. Continue walking west for ten minutes and until you reach avenue Cartier on your right.

Avenue Cartier, with its many boutiques, feels like a pedestrian promenade even though cars are allowed to drive through. It's a nice place to stroll about and has plenty of interesting cafes and restaurants where you can take a break. For practical (but stylish) clothes, **Chez Boomer,** 970 av. Cartier (☎ 418-523-7047), carries items for children and adults; **Paris Cartier,** 1180 av. Cartier (☎ 418-529-6083), has elegant clothes for women. For home décor items, check out **Zone,** 999 av. Cartier (☎ 418-522-7373), a great store that's loaded with extremely tempting stuff for the kitchen, bathroom, or living room. **Azimut,** 1194 av. Cartier (☎ 418-688-7788), is an excellent outdoors store that sells tents, sleeping bags, and hiking boots. A good spot for CDs is **Sillons le Disquaire,** 1149 av. Cartier (☎ 418-524-8352).

Rue St-Joseph

Rue St-Joseph is a brand new Main Street for Québec City's residents. It's somewhat removed from the tourist sites. You'd never cross it just wandering around unless a local steers you straight. It's not far at all, just hidden away to some extent.

Rue St-Joseph may seem like an odd place for an upscale shopping district filled with "destination boutiques." This is mainly due to the fact that, as a visitor, your perception of the city, with the Château Frontenac in the middle, is somewhat skewed.

At the end of the 20th century, Québec City was a doughnut, meaning that most of the population lived in the surrounding areas, leaving the middle empty. And admittedly, Vieux-Québec can feel deserted at times.

In recent years, municipal authorities have taken it upon themselves to reverse this demographic trend and the once dingy rue St-Joseph is now at the heart of a major urban renewal project. It's rapidly becoming a glitzy strip filled with shops, restaurants, cafes, and bars attractive to both tourists and residents alike.

The buildings are larger in scale than in Vieux-Québec, the town-house architecture more recent; still, most of it dates from the late 19th century. Yet, rue St-Joseph feels light years away from the colonial smarminess of the historic district. It's a more day-to-day reflection of contemporary Québec City, hip and tuned into global culture.

Rue St-Joseph's recent makeover is far from complete. Yet already there's plenty of buzz and momentum. It's definitely the most exciting place to go in Québec City outside the traditional tourist agenda.

So, what do large European fashion houses think about the potential of this street? Well in November 2005, **Hugo Boss,** 505 rue St-Joseph Est (☎ 418-522-4444), opened its first "all-brand" store in North America. Unlike other Hugo Boss outlets on the continent, this one promises to carry every line made by the German designer. Swedish athletic outfitters, **Peak Performance,** 565 rue St-Joseph Est (☎ 418-525-5003), chose to open its first North American store just down the street.

Other stylish boutiques include **Flirt,** 525 rue St-Joseph Est (☎ 418-529-5241), for lingerie, sexy undergarments, and boudoir apparel. Québec City is such a romantic place that you'll want to get into the act. They carry different lines imported from Europe, some on an exclusive basis.

Don't be shy: The store prides itself on offering a selection that flatters many different silhouettes.

Next door, **Mademoiselle B,** 541 rue St-Joseph Est (☎ 418-522-0455), has unique jewelry designs from New York and Paris. **De Nîmes,** 557 rue St-Joseph Est (☎ 418-523-4848), carries a tight selection of European fashion lines for both men and women, like Nolita and Rare.

The hills surrounding Québec City are alive with all sorts of outdoor possibilities. Gear up at **Mountain Co-Op Equipment,** 405 rue St-Joseph Est (☎ 418-522-1200), a one-stop-shop for stuff like hiking boots and rock climbing harnesses to kayaks and bicycles, and almost everything in between.

If you're looking for more-refined pleasures, try **Plaisirs de Provence,** 529 rue St-Joseph Est (☎ 418-524-4114), a store packed with imports from France, fine tableware, and small decorative items. Or, **Villa,** 600 rue St-Joseph Est (☎ 418-524-2666), sells larger imports, luxury furniture for your chalet or vacation home — supposedly. **Baltazar,** 461 rue St-Joseph Est (☎ 418-524-1991), has an inventory of more contemporary and urban *objets.*

Benjo, 543 St-Joseph Est (☎ 418-640-0001), must be the largest toy store closest to the North Pole. And everyone knows what that means! Yes, this is where Santa shops. Kids get preferential treatment at the glassed entrance with small central doors covered by an elegant awning. Big people, please use the regular doors on the sides. The scale of the store is such that there's even a small train helping young, gleeful shoppers on their commute between the stuffed animals and superhero action figures.

Although most of these stores are new kids on the block, **Mode Laliberté,** 595 rue St-Joseph Est (☎ 418-525-4841), has been in this neighborhood through thick and thin. It is a longstanding, local, family-run department store. It's not as high fashion as the rest of the boutiques on the street, but, for affordable furs, it is a good place to look.

Tons of food outlets are on rue St-Joseph — and not all of them are sit-down and formal. **De Blanchet,** 435 rue St-Joseph Est (☎ 418-525-9779), is a brightly lit bakery and gourmet shop that stands out for its modern décor and long display case of cheese. This is an excellent place to pick up a sampler of Québec's different varieties. The smaller **La Boîte à Pain,** 289 rue St-Joseph (☎ 418-647-3666), is an artisan bakery with long lines spilling out the door. It makes innumerable kinds of bread, some of which are only available on Fridays and Saturdays (so that's the time to go). **Camellia Sinensis,** 624 rue St-Joseph Est (☎ 418-525-0247), named after the scientific name for tea, has an astounding variety of leaves from around the world. There is a small sitting area for tastings, and the knowledgeable staff can help you make an intriguing choice.

Rue St-Joseph used to have a roof covering the whole street. The easternmost portion still does. Passing through the doors, you enter what amounts to a gloomy and run-down mall. Actually, this is what the whole strip used to be like before the city demolished most of the roof to initiate the neighborhood's renewal. Still, chocolate lovers who venture into this less scenic part will be glad they did when they eventually find **Champagne Le Maitre Confiseur,** 783 rue St-Joseph Est (☎ **418-652-0708**). It's on the right. This candy factory makes all sorts of chocolate and treats. Empty boxes are waiting to be filled with truffles from the display case. For something out of the ordinary, try the *larme du diable* ("the devil's tear"), a chocolate with zing, made with hot peppers. Peek through the door into the large kitchen in the back — it's a scene straight out of *Charlie and the Chocolate Factory.*

Chapter 21

Living It Up after Dark: Québec City Nightlife

. . . .

In This Chapter

▶ Hitting Québec City's best dance floors
▶ Hearing live music acts throughout the city
▶ Finding neighborhood spots filled with locals

. . . .

*I*n the end, Québec City is quite a small town, and staunchly French. This limits the cultural opportunities, to a large extent, for English-speaking visitors. Mimicking Montréal, there's a yearlong festival schedule with diverse programming. I cover the main highlights in Chapter 3. Québec City also lacks a homegrown performing arts scene, in part, because the most talented artists move to big-time Montréal, the province's largest city. Culture vultures would be wise to follow this migration to satisfy cravings such as opera, ballet, symphony, cirque theater, as well as other forms of performance and spectacle. See Chapter 15 for my recommendations after you get there.

However, for a place its size, Québec City has a booming nightlife. Inside the walls of the **Haute-Ville,** the scene has a resortlike feel, like a mis-placed Yesterdayland from a Disney theme park. Numerous watering holes line the maze of main streets within the walls. The majority of them are small, dimly lit, and intimate places, often with acoustic acts and flickering candles, exposed stone walls, and wooden beams. Folk music of all sorts suits the setting and is, indeed, the norm.

The **Grande-Allée** is Québec City's most popular nightlife strip, with clubs and bars on a larger scale. Many occupy more than one floor of the converted town houses where they often dwell, which seem to sway to the music spilling out of their windows. Most places offer a DJ and dance floor, but a few showcase live music.

Basse-Ville offers lots of action, but it's spread out, extending to the west along the cliffside and into the blue-collar neighborhood of **St-Roch.** Because the rents are cheaper, it's where many of Québec City's edgier, more interesting bars have popped up — away from the colonial razzle-dazzle of the tourist areas. Rue St-Joseph, in St-Roch, is the site of a major urban renewal project, which already boasts several essential destinations.

In this chapter, I tell you about Québec City's most popular nightlife destinations; some lesser known, but equally great spots; and some places frequented only by locals. Some are outside the main tourist districts but are definitely worth checking out. Of course, I do point out the best spots in the Upper and Lower cities, as well as along the Grande-Allée.

On the whole, you spend less money going out in Québec City than in Montréal. Drinks are cheaper, distances between hot spots shorter, and cover charges less frequent. Last call is at 3 a.m., most places don't get going until 11 p.m., and the night peaks at 1 a.m. The legal drinking age is 18. Because of Québec City's quaint size, the dress code is less cosmopolitan than in Montréal. Lots of clubbers dress in jeans and comfy sweaters, but don't let that stop you from looking your best. Ideally, you want to wear something that gets you through a variety of settings, from a cozy pub to a swinging dance club.

Finding Out What's Going On

Unfortunately, Québec City's free nightlife listings magazines are in French. But you don't really need to know French to decipher event listings, so if you want to find something in particular, go ahead and take a look. *Le Soleil* and the *Journal du Québec* are the two French dailies, and their Arts and Entertainment sections may prove helpful. *Le Guide Québec Scope* is a free cultural magazine, partially in English, with restaurant reviews, neighborhood profiles, theater, shopping, and nightlife features, as well as event and show listings. Québec City also has an edition of *Voir,* a free weekly that comes out on Thursdays, and probably has the most comprehensive coverage of the city's cultural calendar.

When deciphering French listings, know that they appear, more often than not, in the 24-hour clock notation. An easy technique is to subtract 12 if the number is over 12h (noon). So 8h30 is 8:30 a.m., but 20h30, is 8:30 p.m. Also, the days of the week are listed in French. They are:

- ✔ *dimanche* (Sun)
- ✔ *lundi* (Mon)
- ✔ *mardi* (Tues)
- ✔ *mercredi* (Wed)
- ✔ *jeudi* (Thurs)
- ✔ *vendredi* (Fri)
- ✔ *samedi* (Sat)

Checking Out the Scene

"No coats; no cover" sums up the action in the winter. Shivering teens scurry between the city's nightlife destinations, dressed merely in scant club-wear and no coats. Many of the bars and clubs have no cover charge, so many of these brazen partygoers opt to leave their warmer gear behind, despite the sub-zero temperatures. This way, they avoid the hassle of coat check at the front door and can head straight to the dance floor or the bar and bop between as many places as they choose. Other spots around town offer a more authentic and less rowdy experience, like neighborhood spots where clamorous patrons talk and laugh over the music and pints of locally brewed draft beer.

Musically speaking, you hear more songs played by live bands than dance music tracks spun by DJs. You're likely to hear lots of live blues, rock, Celtic, and French folk music. In the city's popular *boîtes a chanson* (literally, singing boxes), you hear Québec folk songs in the *chansonier* (or folk) tradition.

For each place in this chapter, if you have to pay a cover charge, I tell you how much, but these clubs are few and far between. I also include the opening nights for an establishment, if they're not open all week long.

Dancing the Night Away: Québec City's Best Clubs

Although your choices may be limited, most clubs play a mix of Top 40, hip-hop, R&B, techno, and all the requisite anthems from the '70s and '80s. Here are my top picks to get you moving:

✔ **Boudoir,** 441 rue de l'Église (☎ 418-524-2777), is, hands down, the city's hottest nightlife destination. Other places are somewhat quaint, but Boudoir feels jet-set and plugged into global culture. During the summer months there's a sprawling terrace out front with heavy mingling action. The main room offers the sharply dressed and smart-looking clientele several seating arrangements in warmly lit, Zen décor, with Buddhist and Far East influences. The downstairs dance-club portion features a vibrating floor. Open: Daily 3 p.m.–3 a.m. Cover: None.

✔ **Cartier de la Lune,** 799 av. Cartier (☎ 418-523-4011), attracts a 30-plus crowd, who cut loose and rock out to retro-classics Wednesday through Saturday nights. Everyone gets down without any pretense or even a second thought. Attitude? Who needs it? Sunday evenings are a popular blues night. Open: Daily 2 p.m.–3 a.m. Cover (includes coat check): Fri–Sat C$2 (US$1.70); blues evenings C$7 (US$6).

- **Chez Dagobert,** 600 Grande-Allée Est (☎ 418-522-0393), is Québec City's most famous nightclub and always a good bet. Le Dag has a stage on the main floor for live performances. Upstairs, an immense steel dance floor is enveloped by pounding bass, blinding lasers, and swiveling, colored spotlights. The whole setup is really quite elaborate. Open: Daily 9 p.m.–3 a.m. Cover: None.

- **Chez Maurice Night Club,** 575 Grande-Allée Est (☎ 418-640-0711), has a main room with several bars that surround a dance floor packed with a dapper clientele that's between 18 and 30 years old. During the summer, there's plenty of action on the front terrace, which is right on the Grande-Allée. Open: Tues–Sun 8:30 p.m.–3 a.m. Cover: Wed–Sat around C$5 (US$4.25).

- **Le Beaugarte,** 2600 bd. Laurier (☎ 418-659-2442), in Ste-Foy, is a cab ride away from Québec City's historic downtown in the suburb of Ste-Foy. If you're looking for that frenzied disco feel with a more mature crowd, it's worth the trip. This is the city's mega-club for 30-somethings and up. Open: Tues–Fri 11:30 p.m.–3 a.m. Cover: None.

- **Le Soñar,** 1147 av. Cartier (☎ 418-640-7333), a basement tapas bar with a small dance floor, is an intimate but decidedly modern lounge. The bar glows like a white cube and is the centerpiece in an otherwise dark setting; the DJ spins a variety of electronic beats, ranging from ambient to deep house. Le Soñar is a refreshing change from the otherwise large spaces, indistinguishable décor, and music of Québec City's other dance clubs. Open: Daily 5 p.m.–3 a.m. Cover: Occasionally Fri–Sat about C$5 (US$4.25).

- **Turf Pub,** 1179 av. Cartier (☎ 418-522-9955), is where many 20-somethings stake out some territory and engage in elaborate mating rituals. By night, the main floor of this pub is a disco — and a bit of a meat market. A sports bar is downstairs in the finished basement. Open: Daily 9 p.m.–3 a.m. Cover: None.

Grooving to Live Music: Where to Catch Québec City's Best Acts

Live music seems to be Québec City's raison d'être in terms of nightlife, especially within the confines of the Haute-Ville. The scale and mood of the establishments seem best fit for lone balladeers and their guitars or small acoustic acts. On most nights, you can find rock, blues, and folk, but not much jazz.

- **Bistro Scanner Multimédia,** 291 rue St-Vallier Est (☎ 418-523-1916), is a bar with oodles of street-cred and plenty of urban edge. Local indie-rock acts play on a small stage up front and a central bar divides the room. At the back, you'll find a pool table and a

Québec City Nightlife

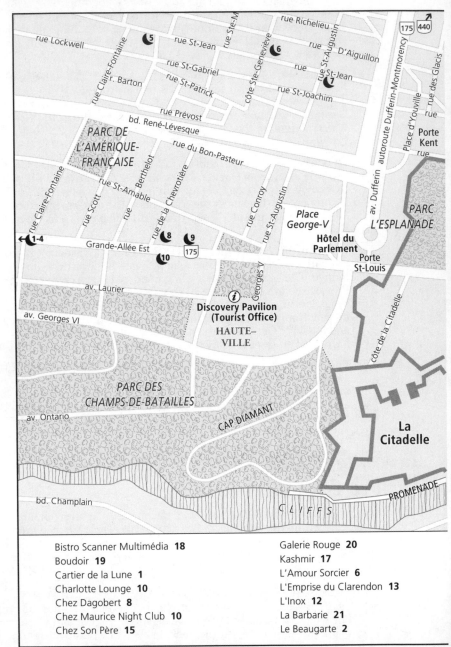

Bistro Scanner Multimédia **18**	Galerie Rouge **20**
Boudoir **19**	Kashmir **17**
Cartier de la Lune **1**	L'Amour Sorcier **6**
Charlotte Lounge **10**	L'Emprise du Clarendon **13**
Chez Dagobert **8**	L'Inox **12**
Chez Maurice Night Club **10**	La Barbarie **21**
Chez Son Père **15**	Le Beaugarte **2**

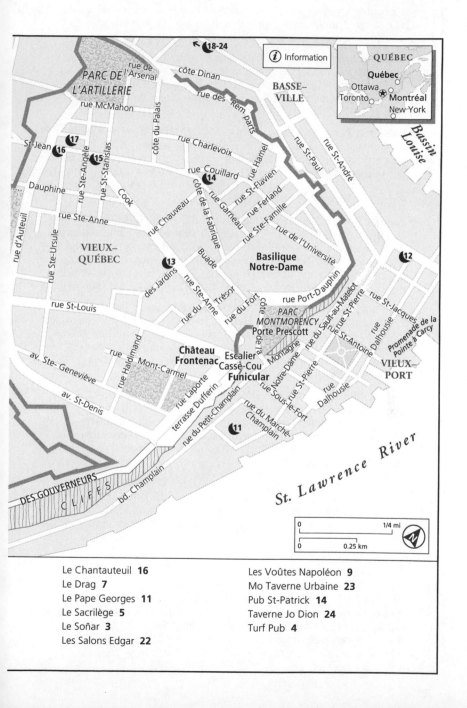

Le Chantauteuil **16**
Le Drag **7**
Le Pape Georges **11**
Le Sacrilège **5**
Le Soñar **3**
Les Salons Edgar **22**
Les Voûtes Napoléon **9**
Mo Taverne Urbaine **23**
Pub St-Patrick **14**
Taverne Jo Dion **24**
Turf Pub **4**

computer terminal with free Internet access. Upstairs has more seating and pool tables. Open: 3 p.m.–3 a.m. Cover: None.

✔ **Charlotte Lounge,** 575 Grande-Allée Est (☎ 418-640-0711), above the main room of Chez Maurice Night Club, has live music most nights. Wednesday, Friday, and Sunday feature a Latin band. On Thursday, it's a '70s rock cover band. But on Saturday, a DJ takes to the decks. Open: Tues–Sun 8:30 p.m.–3 a.m. Cover: C$3–C$4 (US$2.50–US$3.50).

✔ **Chez Son Père,** upstairs at 24 rue St-Stanislas (☎ 418-692-5308), is one of the more popular *boîtes à chansons,* where solo guitarists belt out ballads from a traditional Québec repertoire, as well as the occasional Bob Dylan cover. The *chansonier* takes the stage nightly at 9 or 10 p.m. The crowd sings, sways, and dances along. Open: 8 p.m.–3 a.m. Cover: None.

✔ **Galerie Rouge,** 228 rue St. Joseph Est (☎ 418-688-4777), is in a run-down space with a bric-a-brac bar that serves a pared-down drink selection, but none of the artsy and eclectic types seem to mind. Most come for the live acts in the large room at the rear, which stages up-and-coming bands as well as DJs. Open: Wed–Sun noon–3 a.m. Cover: Occasionally C$5–C$15 (US$4.25–US$12.75).

✔ **Kashmir,** 1018 rue St-Jean (☎ 418-694-1648), near the Porte St-Jean, within the walls of the Haute-Ville, is a popular venue among 20- to 30-year-old Québeckers. It has erratic programming, which ranges from hip-hop and electronica to alt-rock and punk. Open: Wed–Sun 9 p.m.–3 a.m. Cover: Usually between C$5 and C$10 (US$4.25–US$8.50).

✔ **Le Chantauteuil,** 1001 rue St-Jean (☎ 418-692-2030), has been a venue for traditional folk singers and pub-theater since 1968. This low-key spot attracts an artsy clientele of writers, musicians, painters, poets, and photographers, who gather to commiserate over pints of beer. Open: Daily 11 a.m.–3 a.m. Cover: Occasionally C$5–C$10 (US$4.25–US$ 8.50).

✔ **L'Emprise du Clarendon,** 57 rue Ste-Anne (☎ 418-692-2480), off the lobby of the snazzy Hôtel Clarendon, is the one spot where hep-cats can swing to live jazz six days a week (closed Mon). It is a small space, with the seating arranged around a grand piano, which also accompanies two or three other musicians sitting in for the set. Open: Daily 11 a.m.–3 a.m. Cover: None.

✔ **Le Pape Georges,** 8 rue du Cul-de-Sac (☎ 418-692-1320), is a small place with a tiny terrace in the Basse-Ville, serving a menu that features many reds and whites by the glass, cheeses, and cold-cuts. It closes early during the week (at 9 p.m.), but on the weekend, blues, cabaret, and folk performers play late into the night. Open: Daily noon–3 a.m. Cover: None.

✔ **Les Voûtes Napoléon,** 680 Grande-Allée Est (☎ **418-640-9388**), this *boîte à chansons,* set in a downstairs cellar, is very popular for its warm and friendly atmosphere and entertainers who get the crowd singing along. Open: Daily 8:30 p.m.–3 a.m. Cover: None.

Drinking In the Local Flavor: Québec City's Neighborhood Bars and Pubs

The following are the neighborhood watering holes where you're likely to find Québeckers — lots of local flavor and character, but not many tourists:

✔ **La Barbarie,** 310 rue St-Roch (☎ **418-522-4373**), a brewpub operated as a co-op, makes its own beers. You can get a sampler of eight fine brews, each glass held in a special slot of a wooden carousel. It is a small, cozy pub, with dangling Christmas lights around the bar. Open: Daily noon–1 a.m. Cover: None.

✔ **Le Sacrilège,** 447 rue St-Jean (☎ **418-649-1985**), is a neighborhood bar along rue St-Jean but outside the gates, to the west of the walled Haute-Ville. It is a long and narrow establishment with a beautiful and verdant back terrace during the summer. It's crowded — groups of friends sit down wherever there's space. Sometimes, this means joining another table and meeting new people. No worries, though; everyone is very friendly. Open: Daily noon–3 a.m. Cover: None.

✔ **Les Salons Edgar,** 263 rue St-Vallier Est (☎ **418-523-7811**), is larger than a typical neighborhood bar, frequented by a young and hip clientele. It has two rooms with extremely high ceilings. The front room has different seating options, along with a long deconstructed bar where patrons mill about. The back room has five pool tables, which you can rent on an hourly basis. Open: Daily 4:30 p.m.–3 a.m. Cover: None.

✔ **L'Inox,** 37 quai St-André (☎ **418-692-2877**), is a Québec City brewpub that makes about a dozen beers. There is plenty of seating in the bar and outside on the terrace May through September. This establishment enjoys a steady flow of regular patrons and hardcore beer lovers. Open: Daily noon–3 a.m. Cover: None.

✔ **Mo Taverne Urbaine,** 810 bd. Charest Est (☎ **418-266-0221**), is a good spot for after-work drinks among a crowd of young urban professionals relaxing in this updated tavern décor. In an interesting twist, there are beer taps at each table. Patrons serve themselves and pay by the ounce. There's a tapas menu which offers small snacks to accompany your drinks. Open: Mon–Sat 11 a.m.–3 a.m. Cover: None.

✔ **Pub St-Patrick,** 45 rue Couillard (☎ **418-694-0618**), a former muni-tions store during the French colonial period, has a warm atmos-phere, made so by the stone hearth and Celtic musicians who almost sit among the clientele as they play. This pub has more than a dozen varieties of beer on tap. If you're feeling homesick, this may be a good place to hear some slurred English. Ah, that's better. Open: Daily 11:30 a.m.–3 a.m. Cover: None.

✔ **Taverne Jo Dion,** 86 rue St-Joseph Ouest (☎ **418-525-0710**), located in working-class St-Roch, is the oldest tavern in the city. You know you're in Deep Québec by the bright fluorescent lighting, the moose-head trophy above the bar, other dated memorabilia, and the stern-faced regulars. Currently, this place is enjoying a revival in popularity among the younger crowd, as the rest of the neighborhood becomes an increasingly hip nightlife destination. Open: Daily 8 a.m.–3 a.m. Cover: None.

Being Out and Proud in Québec City

The first few blocks of rue St-Jean, to the west of the walled city, just after crossing Côte d'Abraham, is Québec City's Gay Village. Along with gay-run cafes, restaurants, and shops, you also find a growing number of nightlife establishments, which also cater to a gay clientele. Two of the best are the following:

✔ **L'Amour Sorcier,** 789 Côte Ste-Geneviève (☎ **418-523-3395**), started out as a lesbian bar, but is now popular for gay men, too. Whatever your orientation, check your attitude at the door. This bar is comfortable and unpretentious. It has two rooms, one decid-edly more modern and minimalist, finished with corrugated metal as trim. Open: Daily 2 p.m.–3 a.m. Cover: None.

✔ **Le Drag,** 815 rue St-Agustin (☎ **418-649-7212**), is Québec City's largest gay club with two stories, a drag show, and a dance floor from Thursdays to Sundays. Something for everyone, really. Men cram into the main bar to take in the performances, featuring lip-syncing transvestites. Those who cannot squeeze in can watch the proceed-ings on closed-circuit TV monitors in the establishment's other rooms. Open: Daily 10 a.m.–3 a.m. Cover: Around C$3 (US$2.50).

Part V
The Part of Tens

The 5th Wave
By Rich Tennant
WHEN TO USE THE WORD VOILÀ!
©RICHTENNANT
WHEN TAKING A SOUFFLE OUT OF THE OVEN
VOILÀ!
WHEN PULLING A DOVE FROM YOUR TOP HAT
VOILÀ!
WHEN NOT TO USE THE WORD VOILÀ
AFTER GETTING SICK ON BAD SHELLFISH
VOILÀ!
AFTER PUTTING ON YOUR SOCKS
VOILÀ!
AFTER YOUR DOG DOES HIS BUSINESS
VOILÀ!
AFTER A PARTICULARLY LONG BELCH
VOILÀ!

In this part . . .

It's just *le fun* to end with Top Ten lists. *Le fun* is a catchall expression — a cute mix of French and English meaning "good times" — and is a major phrase in Québec. In fact, it's so widely used that its meaning is somewhat vague — like "cool" in English. Go ahead, try it in a sentence, drop it on a local. They'll know exactly what you mean. Saying English words in a French accent seems to inevitably change them somehow. This part lists some essential items that are *le fun* to seek out during your visit.

Chapter 22

Ten *Terroir* Ingredients and Local Specialties to Look for on Your Plate

● ●

In This Chapter

▶ Figuring out when the sap flows from the maple trees

▶ Sipping microbrewery beers and ice cider

▶ Playing Duck, Duck, Duck . . . Lamb!

▶ Seeking the best and most authentic versions of *tourtière* and *poutine*

● ●

*Q*uébec is passionate about its food. This mania probably comes from the province's French roots. By now, numerous other immigrant communities have also made their mark on the culinary landscape, evidenced by the dazzling array of restaurants in both cities and the large inventory of exotic ingredients available from Montréal's independent grocers.

However, Québec produces many delicacies of its own, from cheeses and berries to seafood and game. This bountiful land is filled with different specialty ingredients that you'll want to fill up on during your stay — if you're adventurous.

Instead of having to trek out into the woods and fetch dinner yourself (the way it was done around here until not so long ago), Québec has an increasing number of restaurants specializing in cooking with local ingredients. Some of them call this type of menu "market cuisine." Going to the markets yourself is another way to get your hands on, and mouth around, Québec's *terroir*. Buying locally is an often-overlooked part of the eating-organic and "slow-food" activism.

Maple Syrup

Although many in Québec don't care much for the maple leaf on the Canadian flag as a national symbol, this province is the world capital of maple syrup production. Ironic, eh? During the great spring thaw, sap flows in the maple trees, which sugar bush farmers tap and boil down into this liquid gold. There are sugar bushes all over Québec, but the maples are thickest in the region of Montérégie, southeast of Montréal. In March and April, packs of urbanites trek to sugar shacks for a traditional maple-syrup-bathed feast. It's a rite of spring known as "sugaring off."

Unpasteurized Cheese

Part of what makes Québec distinct from the rest of Canada is the province's laissez-faire attitude. This is a good thing when it comes to cheese — and Martha Stewart would agree. Québec has an outstanding variety of local, specialty cheeses. Many of the best are made from unpasteurized milk, giving them extra flavor and richness. This encourages small dairy farmers to make new varieties from the milk of a single herd — a practice taboo in the rest of Canada because of food-safety concerns. So, *vive la difference!* Some of Québec's more notable unpasteurized varieties include: Pied de Vent from the Îles de la Madeleine and Chateau Mailloux from Charlevoix. Riopelle cheese from Île-aux-Grues, named after Québec's late contemporary artist who was most often compared to Jackson Pollock, is the most recent variety to create a buzz among foodies here.

Microbrewery Beer

Although Molson and Labatt are the two major Canadian beer companies, locals in Montréal and Québec City often opt for microbrewery products instead. There are a number of these beers in the province of Québec, available on tap in bars and in bottles from stores. Unibroue makes several popular kinds, including Blanche de Chambly and Fin du monde. The latter has a high alcohol volume of 9 percent. Its name means, "The end of the world." McAuslan brews Griffon, St-Ambroise, and also an Apricot Wheat Ale. The Brasseurs du Nord make Boreal, which is probably the most popular microbrew province-wide.

Cidre de Glace

Unable to match "ice wine" from Ontario, Québec's beverage industry recently answered by producing "ice cider" from apples. This remarkably similar golden and syrupy alcoholic beverage is also meant to accompany cheese or dessert. It's gaining in popularity, mainly as a cheaper alternative to ice wine, which is very trendy at the moment.

Québec's harsh climate makes it a hostile land for vineyards and producing a palatable wine. Most of the ice cider comes from the Montérégie, a region rich with orchards.

Duck from Lac Brôme

Lake Brôme ducks are shipped around the world. The lakefront duck farm is the oldest in the country. Started in 1912, it remains one of the largest employers in the region. They breed Peking ducks, which have delicious meat. In Montréal, there are a large number of restaurants that have duck, usually a *confit de canard* or a *magret de canard*. If Lac Brôme is not mentioned on the menu, ask the waiter where the kitchen gets its ducks.

Lamb

Québec has two regions that are renowned for their lamb. On Île-Verte, in the lower St. Lawrence River, the lambs are "pre-salted," because they graze on marshes flooded by brackish water. This makes their meat extra tasty. In Charlevoix, the government granted the lamb producers of this region a special designation for their meat. It is the first agricultural product in the province to be protected in such a way. For producers to be able to label their lamb as *de Charlevoix,* they must abide by strict rules for raising their small herds.

Blueberries from Lac St. Jean

After maple syrup, blueberries from Lac St. Jean are perhaps the second-most-famous agricultural crop in Québec. Blueberries are loaded with antioxidants and make excellent pies. They're in season in August. You'll see two kinds in the Québec's markets: wild and farmed. The most worthwhile are the smaller, wild blueberries, intense and flavorful. The people from this region are renowned for their warm hospitality — the region is seen as the province's heartland of sorts.

Strawberries from Île d'Orléans

The St. Lawrence River widens beyond Québec City. Just downriver, lies the Île d'Orléans, an island filled with fields, wooded glades, and rural farming communities. It's said to be the birthplace of French America, because it's where the explorers first settled. The island is also referred to as "Québec City's garden," because it supplies the capital with much of its seasonal fruits and vegetables. Visitors can go fruit picking all summer long; many come for the strawberries, in mid-July, which are particularly delicious.

Tourtière

Nutmeg, clove, allspice, and pepper are the four essential seasonings for this traditional meat pie, a recipe that dates back to 17th-century France. The name refers to a special pot with legs used for baking the pie over the embers of an open fire. There are as many different versions of *tourtière* as there are willing cooks in Québec. A lively province-wide debate rages on between entire regions and extended families about whose *tourtière* is best.

Poutine

Two cities in Québec, Drummondville and Victoriaville, claim to be the birthplace of *poutine*. This local fast-food delicacy, consisting of French fries, brown gravy, and cheese curds, is a favorite at snack bars across the province. Fancier restaurants make upscale versions, with seared foie gras and the like.

Chapter 23

Ten (or So) T-Shirts with Tons of Montréal Street-Cred

● ●

In This Chapter

▶ Wearing a T-shirt as a fashion statement

▶ Picking popular tees out of the crowd

▶ Discovering different local designers

▶ Digging up memorabilia of defunct sports franchises

● ●

*M*ore so for men, but in general, today, it seems you can get "dressed up" merely by wearing your best T-shirt. As a fashion item the tee is often about making a statement, which shows that the wearer is somehow "in the know."

So, if you're looking to take souvenirs back home, but you want to do better than a T-shirt from the Hard Rock Cafe ("ho-hum") or something generic from a souvenir shop on rue Ste-Catherine ("blah"), this chapter offers some creative suggestions.

These tees are locally designed or inspired, and they're all the rage on Montréal's busy streets. They're the T-shirts that stand out if you look at the streaming crowds long enough. For different reasons, each has attained a level of cult status among locals.

Fidel Clothing

These fashion tees by a local designer are iconic in Montréal. Everyone seems to have one, and over the course of a night out you're likely to spot at least two or three people wearing theirs. Fidel makes several different series, including a Zodiac series with one of the 12 signs emblazoned across the chest in one of four colors. The jury's still out as to whether a Zodiac tee makes for a good icebreaker. But Fidel's so popular among the high-cheekboned, boulevard St-Laurent crowd that visitors may wonder if they're standard issue.

Plateau

A group of friends from this uber-trendy neighborhood came up with these in response to the rash of "Brooklyn" T-shirts that were somewhat of a North American fad a couple of years ago. Montréal needed to do its own thing, they thought. Now, their T-shirts come in several color combos, with just "Plateau" across the front in cursive writing. Many wear it to "represent." More than just a neighborhood, it's representative of a mentality and lifestyle. You can say, "Oh, that's very Plateau," and people will know exactly what you mean.

Nordiques/Expos

For local sports fans, there's a ton of nostalgia wrapped up in wearing T-shirts or other memorabilia from Québec's now defunct professional sports teams: the Québec Nordiques (hockey) and the Montréal Expos (baseball). For those keeping score, these sports franchises are now the Colorado Avalanche in the National Hockey League and the Washington Nationals of Major League Baseball.

Baseball fans are rabid for any Expos shirt with 27 on it — it was the number worn by star player Vladimir Guerrero. A Québec Nordiques equivalent would be Joe Sackic's number 19.

McGill/Concordia

A T-shirt from one of Montréal's two English universities also makes for an out-of-the-ordinary souvenir. It's the red and white of the McGill Redmen versus the burgundy and gold of the Concordia Stingers. A wide selection of styles is available at the bookstores of each university on their centrally located downtown campuses. An increasing number of U.S. students are enrolling in these schools, due in part to their low tuition fees. McGill also has quite a reputation: In 2005, it cracked *Playboy* magazine's list of the top ten party schools.

Piknic Electronik

Every Sunday from May to September there's an outdoor dance party on Île Ste-Hélène in Parc Jean-Drapeau featuring some of Montréal's most innovative electronic music producers and DJs. They play under a gargantuan statue — *Man*, by Alexander Calder — with stunning views of the city's skyline. It's an idyllic setting that draws a mixed crowd in various states of leisure: from bouncing revelers to groups of friends lounging in the grass to young families. There's a T-shirt for the event, and some revelers have such a good time that they feel compelled to buy one. You can spot an increasing number of people wearing them about town — testament to the event's growing popularity.

Bily Kun

This bar at the main crossroads of the Plateau is also emblematic of this neighborhood's signature brand of cool. An evening there will immediately expose you to a variety of shabby-chic characters who like to drop by this lively den. The name means "White Horse" in Czech, after the local microbrewery they seem to favor on tap. They also serve absinthe, imported direct from Prague. It's a special place. The T-shirt is for its most ardent fans.

Wolf Parade

At the end of 2005, Wolf Parade was the latest local band to make a splash on the alt-rock music scene. Other acts as of late include Arcade Fire, the Sam Roberts Band, the Stills, the Dears, and the High Dials. Earlier in 2005, *Spin* magazine dubbed the Montréal scene as a next-Seattle of sorts. You'll find the T-shirt of your favorite Montréal group at one of the many "head-shops" that sell rock paraphernalia. Several of these shops are located along rue Ste-Catherine between rue Almyr and avenue de Blurry. Farther east, another concentration of similar storefronts is located between boulevard St-Laurent and rue St-Denis.

St-Viateur Bagels

Fresh, steaming bagels usually get devoured in seconds. They just don't last as long as a T-shirt. Perhaps you'll want to remember the experience of eating one of these fresh out of the oven bagels with a T-shirt from this Mile End bakery. Although the other tees on this list intend to be fashionable, one from St-Viateur bagel is completely unselfconscious, retro without meaning to be, pure kitsch.

Onetop.ca

Onetop.ca is an annual design competition for Québec illustrators, graphic designers, and other visual-media artists. A jury selects 40 winners from among the submissions, and the designs show on T-shirts in a gallery for two months during the summer (June–July-ish). They're slightly more expensive than something store-bought, but a good cut of the price goes to the artists. So, you can look good in a new T-shirt and feel comfortable that you've done your share in supporting the local arts scene.

Montrealite.com

The people behind Montrealite.com have really taken the T-shirt-as-a-blank-canvas idea to heart. This site is the source of many of the cool images you see on tees around town, inspired by different peculiarities including the well known Métro/Retro design, which is an apt parody of the symbol for the '70s-looking subway system.

Three Monkeys

At this street-couture boutique, located in Cours Mont-Royal, the souvenir T-shirt and the fashion tee become one. Three Monkeys commissions Montréal artists to design graphics for their "local series." The T-shirts feature landmarks and icons from the city's streets and skyline, like Habitat '67; the rooftop, milk-bottle, water tank somewhere downtown; the sign above the Five Roses flour mill; and the Biosphere. All of these urban snapshots are indeed a part of Montréalers' collective imagination.

Appendix

Quick Concierge

· ·

Fast Facts

AAA

Canada's affiliate is the CAA. In Montréal their office is downtown at 1180 rue Drummond (☎ 514-861-5111; www. caaquebec.com). It's open Monday through Friday, 9 a.m. to 6 p.m., Thursdays until 8 p.m. The toll-free, emergency, road service number for members is ☎ 800-222-4357.

Québec City's branch of the CAA is located at 444 rue Bouvier (☎ 418-624-8222). Business hours are Monday through Wednesday 9 a.m. to 5:30 p.m., Thursday and Friday 9 a.m. to 8 p.m., and Saturday 10 a.m. to 4 p.m. The emergency road service number for Québec City is ☎ 800-222-4357.

If you're a member of AAA, you can pick up maps, tour books, and traveler's checks at these offices at no extra charge; you can also make travel arrangements here.

American Express

In Montréal, offices of the American Express Travel Service are located at 1141 bd. de Maisonneuve Ouest (☎ 514-284-3300), near rue Stanley.

In Québec City, the nearest office is located at 2700 bd. Laurier (☎ 418-658-8820), in Ste-Foy. It's open Monday through Friday 9 a.m. to 5 p.m.

Area Code

The area code on the Island of Montréal for downtown Montréal is 514. For suburbs around Montréal, the area code is 450.

The area code for Québec City and Ste-Foy is 418.

ATMs

Automatic Teller Machines or *guichets (guee-shea)* are ubiquitous throughout the province of Québec. You can find ATMs in the heart of downtown and throughout the suburban areas. The Bank of Montréal, Banque Nationale, Royal Bank, and Scotia Bank use the Cirrus network. The Caisse populaire and CIBC use the Plus network. For further information, the toll-free numbers for these major banking networks are ☎ 800-424-7787 (Cirrus) and ☎ 800-336-8472 (PLUS), respectively. For a list of ATMs that accept MasterCard or Visa, ask your bank or go to www.mastercard.com or www.visa.com.

Baby Sitters

Most major hotels have someone on staff who can look after your children or can make arrangements for child care if you need it. Be sure to advise them of your child's special needs well in advance.

Montréal YMCA, downtown on rue Stanley (☎ 514-849-8393, ext 777; www.ymca.ca), offers educational day care for kids 18 months to 5 years.

Business Hours

Similar to elsewhere in North America, stores generally open at 9 or 10 a.m. and close at 5 or 6 p.m., Monday through Wednesday and Saturday. Thursdays and Fridays, most stores open at the same time but stay open until 9 p.m. Most stores are also open on Sundays from noon to 5 p.m.

Montréal banks are usually open Monday through Friday, from 8 or 9 a.m. to 4 p.m.

In Québec City, banks are usually open from 10 a.m. to 3 p.m. Monday through Friday, but may also have evening hours on Thursday and Friday.

Camera Repair

In downtown Montréal, AFC Camera Service, 1015 Beaver Hall (☎ 514-397-9505), repairs cameras, as does Camera Technic Company, 1218 Union (☎ 514-866-2223).

In Québec City, Service Camera Pro, 2042 bd. Père-Lelievre (☎ 418-527-0880), repairs every kind of camera on-site: film, digital, and camcorders. Also try Camera Test, 51 bd. René-Levesque (☎ 418-529-2803).

Car Rentals

See Chapter 7 for information on car rentals in Montréal and Québec City.

Convention Centers

Montréal's Palais des Congrès, near Vieux-Montréal and Chinatown, sits between rue Viger and rue St-Antoine and runs west for several blocks starting at the corner of rue Jeanne Mance until rue McGill (☎ 800-268-8122 or 514-871-3170). Métro: Place-d'Armes or Square-Victoria, Place-des-Arts.

Québec City's Centre des Congrès is located at 1000 bd. René-Levesque Est,

just outside the walls of Vieux-Québec and to the right of the Hôtel du Parlement (☎ 888-679-4000 or 418-644-4000).

Credit Cards

To report lost or stolen credits cards, contact the following: American Express (☎ 800-268-9824); Diners Club (☎ 800-336-8472); Discover (☎ 800-DISCOVER); MasterCard (☎ 800-826-2181); or Visa (☎ 800-336-8472).

Currency Exchanges

Banks and *bureaux de change* (exchange offices) almost always offer better exchange rates than hotels, restaurants, and shops — which you should only use in emergencies. You'll also find windows where you can exchange currency at airports and train stations.

In Montréal, the majority of currency exchange offices are Downtown or in Vieux-Montréal. There's one in the Infotouriste office on Dorchester Square, 1255 rue Peel, and several others nearby. There's Bureau De Change IFX, 1134 rue Ste-Catherine Ouest (☎ 514-868-9555), or try Calforex, 1250 rue Peel (☎ 514-392-9100). In Vieux-Montréal, look for Notre-Dame Bureau De Change, 55 rue Notre-Dame Ouest (☎ 514-282-9442).

In Québec City, a *bureau de change* office is in the tourist information office near the Château Frontenac at 12 rue Ste-Anne (☎ 418-694-1014). There's another at the bottom of the steps in Basse-Ville at 46 rue du Petit Champlain (☎ 694-0011).

Customs

Canada Border Services Agency has a toll-free line called the Border Information Service (☎ 800-461-9999). The number for the U.S. Customs and Border Protection office in Montréal is ☎ 514-636-3875.

Dentists

Montréal has a hot line for dental emergencies at ☎ 514-288-8888 and a 24-hour dental clinic at ☎ 514-342-4444.

Québec City has two hot lines that refer callers to available dentists. Call ☎ 418-653-5412 any day or ☎ 418-524-2444 Monday through Saturday.

Doctors

All major hotels should have a doctor on call or be able to call one for you. Embassies and consulates maintain lists of physicians with good reputations. See "Embassies and Consulates," later in this section.

Driving Rules

See Chapter 8.

Electricity

Canada uses the same electricity (110 volts, 60 Hz) as the United States and Mexico, with the same flat-prong plugs and sockets.

Embassies and Consulates

All embassies are in Ottawa.

In Montréal, the American Consulate General is located at 1155 rue St-Alexandre (☎ 514-398-9695). The United Kingdom has a Consulate General at 1000 rue de la Gauchetière Ouest, Suite 4200 (☎ 514-866-5863).

In Québec City, the U.S. Consulate is located near the Château Frontenac, facing Jardin des Gouverneurs, at 2 terrasse Dufferin (☎ 418-692-2095).

Emergencies

Dial **911** for the police, firefighters, or an ambulance.

Holidays

Québec celebrates the following public holidays: New Year's Day (Jan 1); Good Friday and Easter Monday (the Mon following Easter); St-Jean-Baptiste Day (June 24); Canada Day (July 1); Labor Day (first Mon in Sept); Thanksgiving (second Mon in Oct); Remembrance Day (Nov 11); Christmas Day (Dec 25); Boxing Day (Dec 26). Banks and shops are likely to be closed on these days, although museums and restaurants usually stay open.

Hospitals

The following downtown Montréal hospitals have emergency rooms: Montréal General Hospital, 1650 rue Cedar (☎ 514-937-6011); the Royal Victoria Hospital, 687 av. des Pins Ouest (☎ 514-842-1231); the Hôtel Dieux, 209 av. des Pins Ouest (☎ 514-843-2611); and the Hôspital Notre-Dame, 1560 rue Sherbrooke Est (☎ 514-281-6000).

In Québec City, the centrally located Hôtel Dieu is at 11 Côte du Palais (☎ 418-691-5151).

Hot Lines

In Montréal: Alcoholics Anonymous (☎ 514-376-9230); Depressed Anonymous (☎ 514-278-2130); Gay Line (☎ 514-866-0103); Gambling Help and Referral (☎ 514-527-0140); Kids-Help, for children in crisis (☎ 800-668-6868); Parents Line (☎ 800-361-5085 or 514-288-5555); Sexual Assault Line (☎ 514-934-4504); Spousal Abuse Line (☎ 514-873-9010); Suicide Action Montréal (☎ 514-723-4000); Tel-Jeunes, for children or teenagers in crisis (☎ 514-288-2266); Youth Protection (☎ 514-896-3100); Gas Odor Detection (☎ 514-598-3111).

In Québec City: Alcoholics Anonymous
(☎ 418-529-0015); Health Info (☎ 418-648-
2626); Tel-Aide, for emotional distress
(☎ 418-686-2433).

Information

Montréal's Infotouriste Centre (☎ 877-
266-5687 or 514-873-2015; www.bonjour
quebec.com) is located at 1001
Dorchester Square St., one block south
of rue Ste-Catherine Ouest, between
rue Peel and rue Metcalf. June through
early September, the center is open daily
8:30 a.m. to 7:30 p.m. Mid-September
through May, it operates daily 9 a.m. to
5 p.m.

Québec City's main Tourist Information
Centre is located at 12 rue Ste-Anne, just
opposite the Château Frontenac at Place
d'Armes (☎ 877-266-5687). It's open June
through Labor Day 8:30 a.m. to 7:30 p.m.,
and Labor Day through June 9 a.m. to
5 p.m.

Internet Access and Cybercafes

Most large hotels have in-room Internet
access for your computer, via a high-
speed cable. And an increasing number
offer hot spots for wireless laptops.

You can find cybercafes throughout
Montréal. One good, centrally located
option is Virus Café at 3672 bd. St-Laurent
(☎ 514-842-1726). In Chinatown, there's
Café SinoNet, 71A rue de la Gauchetière
Ouest (☎ 514-878-0572). And Netopia,
1737 av. St-Denis (☎ 514-286-5446), is
open 24 hours in the Quartier Latin.

In Québec City, Cybar-Café is at 353 rue St-
Joseph and is open 24/7 (☎ 418-529-5301).
Across the street, Bibliothèque Gabrielle-
Roy, 350 rue St-Joseph Est (☎ 418-641-
6789), has free Internet but is not open
as late. Also, the Musée de la Civilisation,
85 rue Dalhousie (☎ 418-643-2158), has

computers with free Internet access in its
visitor's lounge on the second floor, but
you have to pay C$7 (US$6) admission to
enter.

Language

Québec's official language is French,
which is spoken by 85 percent of the
population.

Liquor Laws

You must be 18 or over to legally drink in
Québec. Beer and wine are sold in restaurants, bars, lounges, and taverns. You can
also purchase alcohol at the government-
controlled Société des alcools du Québec
(SAQ). There are two convenient downtown locations in Montréal: 677 rue Ste-
Catherine Ouest between rue Université
and McGill College (☎ 514-282-9445) and
440 bd. de Maisonneuve Ouest (☎ 514-
873-2274). Also downtown, at 1250 rue
Ste-Catherine Est, there's an SAQ
"Express," which has a smaller selection
but is open until 10 p.m. (☎ 514-521-0184).

Québec City also offers two central locations: in the concourse of the Château
Frontenac, 1 rue des Carriéres (☎ 418-
692-1182), and near the train station at
400 bd. Jean-Lesage (☎ 418-643-4339).

Throughout Québec, beer and a limited
selection of wine are available in grocery
and convenience stores until 11 p.m.

Mail

Postage for mailing letters within Canada
costs C50¢ (US43¢). Letters to the U.S. cost
C85¢ (US72¢) and letters overseas cost
C$1.45 (US$1.25).

Montréal's main post office *(bureau de
poste)*, at 1250 rue Université, near rue
Ste-Catherine (☎ 514-846-5401), is open
Monday through Friday 8 a.m. to 5:45 p.m.
In Vieux-Montréal, the post office is at 157

rue St-Antoine Ouest, between rues Jeanne-Mance and De Bleury (☎ 514-393-1664). Some large convenience stores throughout the city have small post offices located at the back of the store. Look for the red and white Postes Canada logo in the window, or check out the "Find a Post Office" feature on www.canadapost.ca.

Québec City's main post office is located in the Basse-Ville at 300 rue St-Paul (near rue Abraham-Martin) near the port (☎ 418-694-6175). Hours are Monday through Friday 8 a.m. to 5:45 p.m. Another post office is near the Château Frontenac at 3 rue de Buade (☎ 418-694-6102) with the same hours.

Maps

City maps are available for free from city tourist offices, in the Yellow Pages, and perhaps at the front desk of your hotel. To find out where specific buildings or sites are located, you can also use Canada's online directory assistance, www.canada411.com, which provides small maps of locations along with the usual listing information.

In Montréal, the Infotouriste office is at Dorchester Square (see "Information," earlier in this section). You can also find maps at bookstores like Chapters, 1171 rue Ste-Catherine Ouest (☎ 514-849-8825); Indigo, 1500 av. McGill College (☎ 514-281-5549); or Paragraphe Bookstore, 2220 av. McGill College (☎ 514-845-5811). If you want a very thorough street map of Montréal, look for the large yellow books published by MapArt Publishing, widely available in bookstores and convenience stores across the city.

In Québec City, you can pick up free city maps at the Tourist Information office at 12 rue Ste-Anne, just opposite the Château Frontenac at Place-d'Armes. You can also find maps at Archambault, 1095 rue St-Jean (☎ 418-694-2088), and at the Maison de la Presse Internationale, 1050 rue St-Jean (☎ 418-694-1511).

Newspapers/Magazines

Montréal's English-language daily paper is the *Montréal Gazette,* which provides good coverage of city news and arts and entertainment listings, as well as some world news. Canada has two national newspapers, the *Globe & Mail* and the *National Post,* which cover Canadian and world news. You can find these papers at convenience stores throughout the downtown area. English-language papers are harder to find outside the downtown area.

For arts and entertainment coverage exclusively, pick up one of Montréal's weekly alternative publications: the *Hour* or the *Mirror.* Both are available in convenience stores and at the entrance of bars, cafes, and some restaurants downtown, in the Plateau neighborhood, and throughout the city.

In Québec City, major Canadian and American English-language newspapers and magazines are sold in the newsstands of the large hotels, at vending machines on tourist corners in the Vieux-Québec, and at Maison de la Presse Internationale, 1050 rue St-Jean. For events listings, look for the free-press publications *Québec Scope,* a monthly magazine, and *Voir,* a weekly paper. (Both are in French.)

Pharmacies

Québec's major drugstore chain is Pharmacie Jean Coutu, which has a downtown Montréal location in the Ailes de la Mode complex, 677 rue Ste-Catherine Ouest (☎ 514-289-0800), and another big store at 974 rue Ste-Catherine Ouest (☎ 514-866-7791). The other big chain is Pharmaprix, which has a big store at

450 rue Ste-Catherine Ouest (☎ 514-875-7070), open 24 hours.

In Québec City, the Louis Philippe et Jacques Royer pharmacy is located in the Basse-Ville at 57 rue Dalhousie (☎ 418-694-1262).

Police

Dial **911** for emergencies. There are three types of officers in Québec: the municipal police, the Sûreté du Québec (comparable to state police or highway patrol), and the RCMP (like the FBI) that handles cases involving federal laws. RCMP officers are required to speak English. The Montréal and Québec City police provide service in English.

To reach the Sûreté du Québec in Montréal, dial ☎ 514-310-4141. In Québec City, call ☎ 800-461-2131.

Radio Stations

CISM (89.3 FM) is the University of Montréal's radio station, while CKUT (90.3) is McGill University's. The two offer a wide variety of community-based programming and are great sources for hearing about upcoming events in the immediate future.

CJAD (AM 800), an English-language talk-radio station, covers news, sports, weather, and traffic. Canada's National Public Radio equivalent is the CBC (Canadian Broadcasting Corporation). Their Radio One (88.5 FM) is mainly news, while CBC Radio Two (93.5 FM) plays classical music and has various shows on arts, news, and current events. For popular music, try Mix 96 at 95.9 FM, or CKOI at 96.9 FM.

Restrooms

You can find clean restrooms in hotel lobbies, museums, and shopping malls.

In Montréal, that includes Centre Eaton, 705 rue Ste-Catherine Ouest; Cours Mont-Royal, 1455 rue Peel; Les Promenades de la Cathédrale, corner of rue Université and rue Ste-Catherine Ouest; and Les Ailes de la Mode, 677 rue Ste-Catherine Ouest. There are public washrooms at La Baie department store, 585 rue Ste-Catherine Ouest.

In Québec City, the Tourist Information Centre, 12 rue Ste-Anne, has clean and spacious washrooms in the basement.

Safety

Montréal is much safer than many U.S. cities of the same size. However it does have its seedy parts, like around the red-light district on rue Ste-Catherine Est, between boulevard St-Laurent and rue St-Denis. It doesn't mean you can't go there, just stay alert to your surroundings, and use the usual urban precautions that are part of city life.

Québec City, still under a million people, is a small town by comparison. The main guideline here is to avoid leaving valuable possessions in full view in your car. They're best "out-of-sight-out-of-mind" in a trunk.

Smoking

As of May 31, 2006, smoking indoors in public places became illegal throughout Québec. Now, smokers have to go outside.

Taxes

Canada's Goods and Services Tax (*Taxe de produits et services* or TPS in Québec) is 7 percent and applies to everything but alcoholic beverages. Québec's *Provincial Sales Tax* (TVQ) is 7.5 percent, calculated on the price plus the GST.

Taxis

In Montréal, you'll find taxis lined up in front of downtown hotels and busy street corners. At all times, you can hail one passing by. You can also call a taxi company directly and usually have a ride within five to ten minutes. Two major companies are Taxi Co-op (☎ 514-725-9885) and Taxi Diamond (☎ 514-273-6331).

In Québec City, hailing a cab is somewhat more difficult; however, most businesses will be happy to call one for you. If you need to do so yourself, Québec City's two main taxi companies are Taxi Coop (☎ 418-525-5191) and Taxi Québec (☎ 418-525-8123).

Telephone

Bell Canada operates the phone system in Québec. To get the operator, dial 0 (the operator will answer in both French and English). For information or directory assistance, call 411.

Pay phones require C25¢ for a local call, and you can use any combination of coins (except pennies). Pay phones are usually located in glass telephone booths on busy streets, in grocery stores, or in hotel lobbies. Shopping centers usually have pay phones near the restrooms.

Time Zone

Montréal, Québec City, and the daytrip destinations mentioned in Chapter 14 are all in the Eastern time zone. Daylight saving time is observed from late April through late October.

Tipping

The standard for waiters is 15 percent. Cabbies seem to expect 10 percent, even if you don't have any luggage. For bellhops, tip C$1 or C$2 (US85¢–US$1.70) per bag. For hotel housekeeping, count C$1 (US85¢) per person per day. For valet parking, tip C$1 or C$2 (US85¢–US$1.70).

Transit Information

In Montréal, call the STM *(Société de transport de Montréal)* (☎ 514-786-4636) for information about the Métro, city buses, or parabuses for disabled passengers. For airport transportation, call L'Aérobus (☎ 514-931-9002).

Québec's transit authority is the RTC (☎ 418-627-2511).

Toll-Free Numbers and Web Sites

Airlines flying into Montréal

Air Canada
☎ 888-247-2262
www.aircanada.com

Air France
☎ 800-667-2747
www.airfrance.com

Air Transat
☎ 877-872-6728
www.airtransat.com

American Airlines
☎ 800-433-7300
www.aa.com

Atlantic Coast Airlines
☎ 800-361-1970
www.atlanticcoast.com

Atlantic Southeast Airlines
☎ 800-361-1970
www.delta-air.com

Austrian Airlines
☎ 888-817-4444
www.aua.com

British Airways
☎ 800-247-9297
www.british-airways.com

Continental Airlines
☎ 800-231-0856
www.continental.com

Delta Airlines
☎ 800-361-1970
www.delta.com

Japan Air Lines
☎ 800-525-3663
www.japanair.com

KLM Royal Dutch Airlines
☎ 800-225-2525
www.klm.com

Lufthansa
☎ 800-563-5954
www.lufthansa.com

Mexicana
☎ 800-531-7923
www.mexicana.com

Northwest Airlines
☎ 800-225-2525
www.nwa.com

PSA Airlines
☎ 800-428-4322
www.psaairlines.com

Royal Air Maroc
☎ 800-361-7508
www.royalairmaroc.com

Swiss International Airlines
☎ 877-359-7947
www.swiss.com

United Airlines
☎ 800-241-6522
www.ual.com

Airlines flying into Québec City

Air Canada
☎ 888-247-2262
www.aircanada.com

Air Canada Tango
☎ 800-315-1390
www.flytango.com

American Eagle Airlines
☎ 800-433-7300
www.aa.com

Continental Express
☎ 800-231-0856
www.continental.com

Northwest Airlines
☎ 800-225-2525
www.nwa.com

Québecair Express
☎ 877-871-6500

Major hotel and motel chains

Best Western International
☎ 800-528-1234
www.bestwestern.com

Clarion Hotels
☎ 800-CLARION
www.clarionhotel.com

Comfort Inns
☎ 800-228-5150
www.hotelchoice.com

Days Inn
☎ 800-325-2525
www.daysinn.com

Delta Hotels
☎ 877-814-7706
www.deltahotels.com

Econolodge
☎ 877-424-6423
www.hotelchoice.com

Fairmount Hotels
☎ 800-257-7544
www.fairmount.com

Gouverneur Hotels
☎ 888-910-1111
www.gouverneur.com

Hilton Hotels
☎ 800-HILTONS
www.hilton.com

Holiday Inn
☎ 800-HOLIDAY
www.basshotels.com

Howard Johnson
☎ 800-654-2000
www.hojo.com

Hyatt Hotels & Resorts
☎ 800-228-9000
www.hyatt.com

Marriott Hotels
☎ 800-932-2198
www.marriott.com

Novotel
☎ 800-359-6279
www.novotel.com

Radisson Hotels
☎ 800-333-3333
www.radisson.com

Ramada Inns
☎ 800-2-RAMADA
www.ramada.com

Sheraton
☎ 800-325-3535
www.sheraton.com

Travelodge
☎ 800-255-3050
www.travelodge.com

Wyndham Hotels and Resorts
☎ 800-822-4200
www.wyndham.com

Major car-rental agencies

Avis
☎ 800-831-2874
☎ 800-TRY-AVIS in Canada
www.avis.com

Budget
☎ 800-527-0700
www.budgetrentacar.com

Discount
☎ 800-263-2355
www.discountcar.com

Dollar
☎ 800-800-3665
www.dollar.com

Hertz
☎ 800-654-3131
www.hertz.com

Sauvageau
☎ 800-463-8800
www.sauvageau.qc.ca

Thrifty
☎ 800-847-4389
www.thrifty.com

Where to Get More Information

Local tourist information offices

I mention Montréal's and Québec City's main tourism offices throughout this book, but for a quick reference, I include them here, as well: **Centre Infotouriste Montréal**, 1001 Square Dorchester (☎ **877-266-5687** or

514-873-2015; www.bonjourquebec.com); **Tourist Information Centre of Old Montréal,** 174 rue Notre-Dame Est (www.tourisme-montréal.org); **Centre Infotouriste Québec City,** 12 rue Ste-Anne (☎ 877-266-5687; www.bonjourquebec.com); **Greater Québec Area Tourism and Convention Bureau** (Québec City), 835 av. Laurier (☎ 418-649-2608; www.quebecregion.com).

Newspapers and magazines

You can find up-to-the-minute listings of shows, exhibitions, and concerts by visiting the free Web sites of the following English-language publications in Montréal: the *Hour* (www.hour.ca), the *Mirror* (www.montrealmirror.com), and the *Montréal Gazette* (www.montrealgazette.com).

Other sources of information

Several Internet sites list shows, restaurants, and hotels and offer travel information. My favorites include: **DiscoverMontreal.ca** (www.discovermontreal.ca), **MadeinMTL Tourism** (www.madeinmtl.com), **Montreal.com** (www.montreal.com), **MontrealPlus.ca** (http://english.montrealplus.ca), **QuebecCityTourism.ca** (www.quebeccitytourism.ca), **QuebecPlus.ca** (www.quebecplus.ca), **QuebecWeb** (www.quebecweb.com/tourisme/), and **Tourisme Montréal** (www.tourisme-montreal.org).

To find the address or phone number of an establishment not listed in this book, try www.canada411.com, the online version of the phone books.

If you need to check transit information before you leave home, you can find it by visiting the following Web sites: **Access to Travel** (www.accesstotravel.gc.ca), **Montréal transit** (www.stcum.qc.ca), **Québec City transit** (www.stcuq.qc.ca), **Jean Lesage International Airport in Québec City** (www.aeroportdequebec.com), and **Montréal-Trudeau Airport** (www.admtl.com).

Index

See also separate Accommodations and Restaurant indexes at the end of this index.

General Index

• A •

AAA, 91, 285
AARP, 37, 53, 91
accommodations. *See also*
accommodations (Montréal);
accommodations (Québec City);
Accommodations Index,
Montréal; Accommodations
Index, Québec City
bed-and-breakfasts (B&Bs),
90, 211–212
best, 11
boutique hotels, 89
budget for, 33–34
chain hotels, 90
contact information, 292–293
cost-cutting tips, 37
dollar-sign rating, 2–3
Eastern Townships, 185
gay and lesbian travelers, 57
Internet access, 211
kid-friendly, 100, 220–221, 223–224
with kitchen, 37, 110
Laurentian Mountains, 184
luxury hotels, 89–90
Montréal, 89–103
Ottawa, 181
Québec City, 215–226
rack rate, 2, 91, 94
rates, 90–94, 214–215
reservations, 91–93
tipping, 36, 291
without reservations, 93

accommodations (Montréal). *See also*
Accommodations Index, Montréal
bed-and-breakfasts (B&Bs), 90
best room at best rate, 90–93
boutique hotels, 89
chain hotels, 90
independent hotels, 90
kid-friendly, 100
kitchen in, 90, 99
luxury hotels, 89–90
map, 96–97
rates, 90–94
reservations, 91–93
without reservations, 93
accommodations (Québec City). *See also* Accommodations Index,
Québec City
bed-and-breakfasts (B&Bs), 211–212
Internet access, 211
kid-friendly, 220–221, 223–224
map, 216–217
rates, 214–215
airlines. *See also* airports
carry-on luggage, 70, 72
contact information, 291–292
fares, 44–45
lost luggage, 65–66
reservations, 45–46
security measures, 69–70
airports. *See also* airlines
currency exchange and ATMs, 78
Jean-Lesage International Airport
(Québec City), 43, 44, 207–208
Pierre Elliott Trudeau International
Airport (Montréal), 43–44,
78–79, 208
transportation from, 46–47, 78–79

Alouettes (football team), 148–149
American Express, 285
Amtrak (train service), 47
amusement park (Montréal), 138
antiques
  Montréal, 153, 159–160
  Québec City, 257, 260
April, 24, 29
area code, 285
art galleries
  Montréal, 153, 160
  Québec City, 257, 260
arts and crafts (Montréal), 160
Assemblée nationale du Québec
      (Québec City), 249
ATMs, 39–40, 78, 285
attractions. *See also* attractions (kid-
      pleasing); attractions (Montréal);
      attractions (Québec City); day
      trips; guided tours
  budget for, 35
  Eastern Townships, 185–187
  Laurentian Mountains, 181–184
  Ottawa, 178–181
attractions (kid-pleasing)
  Basilique Notre-Dame, 132–133
  Biodôme de Montréal, 133
  Centre des Sciences de Montréal, 144
  Centre d'Interprétation de la
      Côte-de-Beaupré, 247
  Ferry Ride, 247
  Festival de la Gastronomie de
      Québec, 29
  Fête des Neiges (snow festival), 23
  Galeries de la Capitale, 259
  Geordie Theatre Productions, 189
  Great Pumpkin Ball, 28
  IMAX Theatre, 144
  Insectarium de Montréal, 144
  La Biosphère, 144–145
  La Fête des enfants de Montréal, 27
  La Ronde (amusement park), 138
  Lachine Rapids, 138
  Montréal, 143–145
  Musée de Cire (Wax Museum), 248
  Musée McCord d'Histoire
      Canadienne, 141
  Observatorie de la capitale, 248

Parc Aquarium de Québec, 248
Parc de la Chute-Montmorency,
      248–249
Parc Jean-Drapeau, 141–142
Planetarium de Montréal, 145
Québec City, 247–249
Santa Claus Parade, 28
for teenagers, 250–251
Terrasse Dufferin, 249
attractions (Montréal)
  churches, 147–148
  Downtown, 134–135
  East Montréal, 139
  five-day itinerary, 166–168
  guided tours, 149–151
  kid-pleasing, 143–145
  maps, 134–135, 137, 139
  museums, 145–147
  spectator sports, 148–149
  three-day itinerary, 161–166
attractions (Québec City)
  historical, 249–250, 253–256
  kid-pleasing, 247–249
  map, 242–243
  military, 249–250
  strolling streets, 251–252
  for teenagers, 250–251
Atwater Market (Montréal), 128, 160
August, 26–27, 30
Avenue Cartier (Québec City), 262–263
avenue de l'Esplanade (Montréal), 175
avenue Laurier (Montréal), 175

● *B* ●

babysitting services, 52, 285
bagels, 83, 126
Baldwin Barmacie (Montréal), 200
ballet (Montréal), 190
Bank of Canada (Web site), 38
Barfly (Montréal), 197–198
Barraca Rhumerie & Tapas
      (Montréal), 202
bars and clubs (Montréal)
  about, 190–191
  brewpubs, 203
  cafes and bars, 199–201

comedy clubs, 204
concert venues, 199
dance clubs, 195–197
gay and lesbian, 57, 204
live music, 197–199
lounges, 201–202
neighborhood, 202–203
pool halls, 203–204
bars and clubs (Québec City)
dance clubs, 268–269
live music, 269, 272–273
neighborhood, 273–274
baseball team (Montréal Expos), 282
Basilique Notre-Dame (Montréal),
132–133
Basilique Notre-Dame-de-Québec
(Québec City), 241, 255
Basse-Ville (Lower City) (Québec City)
described, 207, 209
nightlife, 266–267
restaurants, 232
bed-and-breakfasts (B&Bs)
Montréal, 90
Québec City, 211–212
beer, 25, 278
Benjo (Québec City), 264
bicycling, 86, 213
Bike Fest (Féria du vélo de
Montréal), 25
Bily Kun (Montréal), 170, 202, 283
Biodôme de Montréal, 133, 165
Bistro Scanner Multimédia (Québec
City), 269–270
Black and Blue Festival (Montréal),
28, 57
Blizzart (Montréal), 195
Blue Metropolis (Montréal literary
festival), 24
blueberries from Lac St. Jean, 279
boat tours and cruises
Montréal, 47, 150–151
Québec City, 47
Bonjour Québec (Web site), 71
books, recommended, 17–18
bookstores
Montréal, 153, 156, 160
Québec City, 257–258, 260, 261
Boudoir (Québec City), 268

Boulevard St-Laurent (Montréal),
133, 158–159
boutique hotels, 89
Brasserie Dieu Du Ciel! (Montréal), 203
brasserie (French cuisine), 116
breakfast, 110, 127–128
Breakneck stairs (Québec City), 256
brewpubs, 203
Bring Your Own Bottle (BYOB)
restaurants, 130–131
brunch, 109
brunch, tams-tams, and beyond
itinerary, 173–176
Brutopia (Montréal), 203
bucket shops (consolidators), 44–45
budget for trip. *See also* money
accommodations, 33–34
ATM withdrawal charges, 40
attractions, 35
cost cutting tips, 36–37
dining, 34–35
hidden expenses, 35–36
nightlife, 35
shopping, 35
taxes, 35–36
tipping, 36
transportation, 34
burgers
Montréal, 125, 126
Québec City, 239
bus service
to Eastern Townships, 185
Greyhound Lines, 47, 55
to the Laurentian Mountains, 182
in Montréal, 85–86
to Montréal, 47
Montréal to Québec City, 80–81
in Québec City, 212
to Québec City, 47, 208
from Trudeau Airport, 79
bus tours
Montréal, 150
Québec City, 253
business hours, 152, 258, 286
BYOB (Bring Your Own Bottle)
restaurants, 130–131
ByWard Market (Ottawa), 180

• C •

cabanes à sucre (sugar shacks), 29
Cabaret à Mado (Montréal), 204
Cactus (Montréal), 196–197
cafes, Montréal, 199–201
Cafeteria (Montréal), 200
calendar of events
  Montréal, 23–28
  Québec City, 29–30
camera repair, 286
Canada Border Services Agency (Web
    site), 78
Canada Customs (Web site), 36
Canada-U.S. border, driving from, 78
Canadian currency, 37–39
Canadian Museum of Civilization
    (Ottawa), 180
Canadian Museum of Contemporary
    Photography (Ottawa), 180
Canadiens (hockey team), 148, 167
car, driving
  from Canada-U.S. border, 78
  to Eastern Townships, 185
  from Jean-Lesage airport, 208
  to Laurentian Mountains, 182
  in Montréal, 84–88
  to Montréal and Québec City from the
      south, 46
  Montréal to Québec City, 80, 208
  Ontario to Montréal, 80
  to Ottawa, 178
  parking and, 62, 85, 87–88, 213, 291
  in Québec City, 213
  to Québec City, 208
  rules of the road, 62, 87
  from Trudeau Airport, 79
car rental
  agencies, 293
  budget for, 34
  discounts, 63
  gasoline, 34, 87
  insurance, 63–64
  Jean-Lesage airport, 208
  Trudeau airport, 79
Carnaval de Québec (Québec City), 29

Carrefour international de theatre
    (Québec City), 29
carry-on luggage, 70, 72
Cartier de la Lune (Québec City), 268
Casa Del Pololo (Montréal), 198
cash, carrying, 39–40
Casino de Montréal (Montréal casino),
    133, 135–136, 167
Casino du Lac Leamy (Ottawa), 181
Casse-Crêpe Breton (Québec City), 240
cellphones, 66–67, 111
Centaur Theatre Company
    (Montréal), 189
Centre Canadien d'Architecture
    (Montréal), 136
Centre des Sciences de Montréal, 144
Centre d'Histoire de Montréal, 146
Centre d'Interprétation de la Côte-de-
    Beaupré (Québec City), 247
Centre Infotouriste Montréal, 293–294
Centre Infotouriste Québec City,
    209, 212
chain hotels, 90
Champagne Le Maitre Confiseur
    (Québec City), 265
Changing of the Guard, 12, 178
Chantecler ski resort (Laurentian
    Mountains), 182
Chapelle Notre-Dame-de Bonsecours
    (Montréal), 147
Chapelle/Musée des Ursulines (Québec
    City), 244
Charlotte Lounge (Québec City), 272
Château Frontenac (Québec City),
    244, 262
Château Ramsey (Montréal), 163
cheese, unpasteurized, 278
Chez Dagobert (Québec City), 269
Chez Maurice Night Club (Québec
    City), 269
Chez Son Père (Québec City), 272
children. *See also* attractions
    (kid-pleasing)
  accommodations, 100, 220–221,
    223–224
  babysitting services, 52
  French language and, 52
  passport for, 61

restaurants, 124, 236
 shopping with, 259
 traveling with, 51–53
Chinatown (Montréal), 82
chocolate, 240, 261, 265
Chocolatier Cupidon Château (Québec
    City), 240
Choco-Musée Erico (Québec City), 240
Christ Church Cathedral
    (Montréal), 147
churches, Montréal, 147–148
cidre de glace, 278–279
Cirque du Soleil (Montréal), 189
City Hall (Hôtel-de-Ville)
    (Montréal), 163
classical music (Montréal), 190
climate
 children and, 52
 fall, 22–23
 overview, 19–20
 spring, 21–22
 summer, 22
 temperature and precipitation, 21
 winter, 16–17, 23
clothing
 for dining, 110
 for nightlife, 191, 267
 packing for trip, 71–72
 T-shirts, 281–284
clothing stores
 Montréal, 153, 160
 Québec City, 257, 258, 261, 263–264
Club 123 (Montréal), 195
Club 737 (Montréal), 200
clubs and bars (Montréal)
 about, 190–191
 comedy, 204
 concert venues, 199
 dance clubs, 195–197
 live music, 197–199
clubs and bars (Québec City)
 dance clubs, 268–269
 live music, 269, 272–273
Cobalt (Montréal), 202
coffee cafes, 131, 238–239
comedy clubs, Montréal, 204
Comedy Nest (Montréal), 204
Comedyworks (Montréal), 204

concert venues, Montréal, 199
Concordia University (Montréal), 282
consolidators (bucket shops), 44–45
consulates and embassies, 287
convention centers, 286
cost-cutting tips, 36–37, 110
credit cards, 40, 41–42, 286
crêpes, 240
cruises (Montréal), 47
cuisine
 bagels, 126
 brasserie (French cuisine), 116
 breakfast, 110, 127–128
 brunch, 109
 chocolate, 240
 crêpes, 240
 overview, 15
 pizza and burgers, 125–126, 239
 poutine, 170, 280
 sandwiches, 126–127
 terroir (local foods), 108–109, 129,
    277–280
currency exchange, 37–39, 78, 286
customs regulations, 75, 78, 286
cybercafes, 67, 288

• *D* •

dance clubs
 Montréal, 195–197
 Québec City, 268–269
dance performance, 190
day trips
 Eastern Townships, 185–187
 Laurentian Mountains, 182–184
 Ottawa, 178–181
days of the week, in French, 267
dentists, 287
department stores, 154–155, 258
design competition (Onetop.ca),
    283–284
Directory Assistance, 84, 294
disabilities, travelers with, 54–56
The Divers/Cité Festival (Montréal), 26
doctors, 287
Downtown Montréal
 attractions, 134–135
 described, 81–82

Downtown Montréal *(continued)*
  maps, 96–97, 112–113, 134–135, 157, 192–193
  nightlife, 192–193
  restaurants, 112–113
  rue Ste-Catherine, 81
  shopping, 155–156, 158
  Underground City, 143, 155, 157
dress code. *See also* clothing
  nightlife, 191, 267
  restaurant, 110
driving. *See* car, driving; car rental
drum-circle (tam-tams), 173, 176
duck from Lac Brôme, 279
duty-free goods, 154, 258

• *E* •

East Montréal, 139
Eastern Townships, day trip, 185–187
Ecole de Danse Swing Cat's Corner (Montréal), 197
Edgar Hypertavern (Montréal), 200
electricity, 287
Else's (Montréal), 202
e-mail access, 67–69
embassies and consulates, 287
emergencies
  doctor and dentist, 287
  hotlines, 287–288
  lost passport, 60
  police, 287, 290
  stolen/lost wallet, 41–42
English establishment itinerary, 171–173
Envol et Macadam (Québec City), 30
escorted tour, 47–48, 49–50
etiquette for dining, 110–111
events calendar
  Montréal, 23–28
  Québec City, 29–30
exchange rate, 38–39, 286

• *F* •

fall, 22–23
families, with children, 51–53. *See also* children

Familyhostel, 52
Fantasia Film Festival (Montréal), 26
Féria du vélo de Montréal (Bike Fest), 25
Ferry Ride (Québec City), 247
Festival de cinéma des 3 Amériques (Québec City), 29
Festival de la Gastronomie de Québec/Coupe des nations (Québec City), 29
Festival de théâtre des amériques (Montréal), 24
Festival des Troubadours et Saltimbanques (Québec City), 30
Festival d'été de Québec (Québec City), 30
Festival International Nuits d'Afrique (Montréal), 26
festivals, 15. *See also* calendar of events
Fête des Neiges (snow festival) (Montréal), 23
Fidel clothing, 281–282
films, recommended, 18
five-day itinerary (Montréal), 166–168
football team (Alouettes), 148–149
Formula One Grand Prix (Montréal), 25
Fortifications de Québec (Québec City), 250, 255
FrancoFolies (French-language music festival), 15
French breakfast, 110
French language
  children and, 52
  days of the week, 267
  overview, 14
  street terminology, 3
French roots itinerary, 168–171
Frommer's (Web site), 46
Funkytown (Montréal), 195

• *G* •

Galerie Rouge (Québec City), 272
gasoline, 34, 87
gay and lesbian travelers, 56–58
Gay Pride Parade (Montréal), 26–27, 57

Gay Village (Montréal)
   accommodations, 57
   described, 82
   map, 194
   nightlife, 57, 194, 204
   restaurants, 57
Geordie Theatre Productions
      (Montréal), 189
Go Go Lounge (Montréal), 201
Goods and Services (Taxe de Produits
      et Services, TPS), 36, 64, 111, 290
Grand Masquerade (Halloween
      celebration) (Montréal), 28
Grand Prix (Montréal), 25
Grande-Allée (Québec City)
   described, 209
   nightlife, 266
   restaurants, 230
Great Pumpkin Ball (Montréal), 28
Greater Québec Area Tourism and
      Convention Bureau, 212, 294
Greyhound Lines (bus service), 47, 55
guided tours
   boat, 150–151
   bus, 150, 253
   escorted, 47–48, 49–50
   horse-drawn carriage, 151, 253
   Montréal, 149–151
   package, 48–50
   Québec City, 252–253
   river cruises, 253
   walking, 149–150, 252–253

• *H* •

Halloween celebration (Grand
      Masquerade) (Montréal), 28
Haute-Ville (Upper City) (Québec City)
   described, 207, 209
   nightlife, 266
high season, 90, 214
historical attractions
   Québec City, 249–250, 254
   Vieux-Québec (Old Québec), 253–256
history of Québec, 13–14
hockey teams
   Canadiens, 148, 167
   Québec Nordiques, 282

holidays
   overview, 287
   St. Patrick's Day, 24
   St-Jean-Baptiste Day, 29–30
horse-drawn carriage, 151, 253
hospitals, 287
Hôtel-de-Ville (City Hall)
      (Montréal), 163
hotlines, 287–288

• *I* •

identity theft, 41–42
illness
   doctor, 287
   medical insurance and, 65
   staying healthy, 66
The Illuminated Crowd (sculpture), 172
Image+Nation (gay and lesbian film
      festival), 57
IMAX Theatre (Montréal), 144
Impact (soccer team), 149
independent hotels, 90
Infotouriste Centre
   Montréal, 83–84, 93, 288, 293–294
   Québec City, 209, 212
Insectarium de Montréal, 144, 165–166
insurance
   luggage, 65–66
   medical, 65
   rental car, 63–64
   travel, 48
   trip cancellation, 64–65
International Festival of Films on Art
      (Montréal), 24
International Volleyball Federation
      World Cup (Montréal), 26
Internet access, 67, 211, 288
itineraries. *See also* day trips
   brunch, tams-tams, and beyond,
      173–176
   connecting with your French roots,
      168–171
   English establishment, 171–173
   Montréal in five days, 166–168
   Montréal in three days, 161–166

• J •

January/February, 23–24, 29
Jardins Botanique (Montréal), 136, 138, 165
Java U (Montréal), 201
Jazz Festival, 25–26, 70
Jean-Lesage International Airport (Québec City), 43, 44, 207–208
Jello Bar (Montréal), 201
July, 26, 30
June, 25–26, 29–30
Just for Laughs Comedy Festival (Montréal), 26, 70, 204

• K •

Kashmir (Québec City), 272

• L •

La Baie, Québec City, 258
La Barbarie (Québec City), 273
La Biosphère (Montréal), 144–145
La Citadelle (Québec City), 244–245
La Fête des enfants de Montréal, 27
La Maison du Jazz (Montréal), 198
La Ronde (Montréal), 138
La Salsatheque (Montréal), 197
Lac Memphrémagog (Eastern Townships), 185
Lachine Rapids (Montréal), 138
L'Agora de la Danse (Montréal), 190
Laika (Montréal), 201
lamb, 279
L'Amour Sorcier (Québec City), 274
Laurentian Mountains, day trip, 182–184
Le Beaugarte (Québec City), 269
Le Chantauteuil (Québec City), 272
Le Cheval Blanc (Montréal), 203
Le Divan Orange (Montréal), 198
Le Drag (Québec City), 274
Le Pape Georges (Québec City), 272
Le Petit Champlain (Québec City), 251, 256, 261–262
Le Petit Château (Québec City), 240
Le Quai des Brumes (Montréal), 198
Le Reservoir (Montréal), 203

Le Sacrilège (Québec City), 273
Le Soñar (Québec City), 269
Le Ste-Elisabeth (Montréal), 203
L'Emprise du Clarendon (Québec City), 272
Les Ballets Jazz de Montréal, 190
Les FrancoFolies de Montréal, 25
Les Grands Ballets Canadiens de Montréal, 190
Les grands feux (Québec City), 30
Les journées de la culture (Montréal), 27–28
Les Pierrots Boite à Chansons (Montréal), 198
Les Salons Edgar (Québec City), 273
Les Voûtes Napoléon (Québec City), 273
L'Inox (Québec City), 273
liquor laws, 267, 288
literary festival (Blue Metropolis) (Montréal), 24
Little Italy (Montréal), 83, 166
local foods (terroir), 108–109, 129, 277–280
L'Opera de Montréal, 190
L'Orchestre Symphonique de Montréal (OSM), 190
lounges, 201–202
luggage
  carry-on, 70, 72
  insurance, 65–66
  packing, 71–72
luxury hotels, 89–90

• M •

magazines/newspapers, 70–71, 267, 289
Magic of Lanterns festival (Montréal), 27
Magog (Eastern Townships), 185
Manifestation international d'art de Québec (Québec City), 29
maple syrup, 24, 278
maps. *See also* maps (Montréal); maps (Québec City)
  brunch, tams-tams, and beyond itinerary, 174
  Eastern Townships, 186

Laurentian Mountains, 183
obtaining, 289
Ottawa, 179
maps (Montréal)
accommodations, 95, 96–97
attractions, 134–135
Downtown Montréal, 96–97, 112–113,
134–135, 157, 192–193
English establishment itinerary, 172
French Roots itinerary, 169
Gay Village, 194
greater Montréal, 76–77
Mile End, 115, 194
nightlife, 192–194
Plateau, 115, 194
restaurants, 112–113, 115
Underground City, 157
Vieux-Montréal (Old Montréal),
95, 112–113, 137
maps (Québec City)
accommodations, 216–217
attractions, 242–243
historical attractions, 254
neighborhoods, 210–211
nightlife, 270–271
restaurants, 228–229
Vieux-Québec (Old Québec), 254
March, 24, 29
Marché Bonsecours (Montréal),
139–140, 162
Marché Jean Talon (Montréal), 83, 166
markets (Montréal), 128–129
Mason, Raymond (sculptor), 172
May, 25, 29
McGill University (Montréal),
164–165, 282
meat pie (tourtière), 280
medical insurance, 65
menus, 110–111
Métro (Montréal subway), 85–86
microbrewery beer, 278
Mile End Bard (Montréal), 195
Mile End (Montréal)
described, 83
maps, 115, 194
nightlife, 194

restaurants, 115, 194
shopping, 158
military 24-hour time, 267
military and historical attractions
(Québec City), 249–250
Mo Taverne Urbaine (Québec City), 273
Mocha Dance (Montréal), 197
Mois de la photo (Montréal), 27
Mondial de la bière (World Beer
Festival, Montréal), 25
money. *See also* budget for trip; taxes
Canadian currency, 37–39, 286
cash, carrying, 39–40
credit cards, 40, 41–42, 286
emergency cash, 41
exchange rate, 38–39, 289
lost or stolen wallet, 41–42
traveler's checks, 41
Montréal casino (Casino de Montréal),
133, 135–136, 167
Montréal Expos (baseball team), 282
Montréal Fringe Festival (Montréal), 25
Montréal High Lights Festival, 24
Montréal Highland Games, 27
Montréal Indy, 27
Montréal International Festival of New
Cinema and New Media, 28
Montréal International Fireworks
Competition, 26
Montréal International Jazz Festival,
25–26, 70
Montréal YMCA, 52
Montrealite (Web site), 284
Mont-Tremblant (Laurentian
Mountains), 184
mountain biking festival (Verlirium)
(Québec City), 30
Musée Château Ramezay
(Montréal), 146
Musée d'Archéologie et d'Historie de
Montréal, 140
Musée d'Art Contemporain de
Montréal, 140
Musée de Cire (Wax Museum) (Québec
City), 248
Musée de la Civilisation (Québec
City), 245

Musée de l'Amérique Française
    (Québec City), 245
Musée des Beaux-Arts de Montréal,
    141, 164
Musée des Ursulines (Québec
    City), 244
Musée du Fort (Québec City), 249
Musée McCord d'Histoire Canadienne
    (Montréal), 141
Musée national des beaux-arts du
    Québec (Québec City), 245–246
Musée Naval de Québec (Québec
    City), 250
Musée Redpath (Montréal), 146
Musée Stewart (Montréal), 147
Museum Day (Montréal), 25
music stores (Montréal), 154, 156
MUTEK (Montréal), 25

● *N* ●

National Gallery of Canada
    (Ottawa), 180
National Passport Information
    Center, 61
neighborhood bars
    Montréal, 202–203
    Québec City, 273–274
neighborhoods (Montréal). *See also*
        Downtown Montréal; Plateau
        (Montréal); Vieux-Montréal (Old
        Montréal)
    best, 10
    Chinatown, 82
    East Montréal, 139
    ethnic, 16
    Gay Village, 82, 194
    Little Italy, 83, 166
    map, 76–77
    Mile End, 83, 115, 158, 194
    Quartier Latin, 82
    shopping by, 155–160
    Westmount, 160
neighborhoods (Québec City). *See also*
        Basse-Ville (Lower City) (Québec
        City); Vieux-Québec (Old Québec)
    best, 10–11
    Grande-Allée, 209, 230, 266

Haute-Ville (Upper City), 207, 209, 266
    maps, 210–211
    shopping by, 259–265
New France Festival, Québec City, 30
newspapers/magazines, 70–71, 267, 289
Newtown (Montréal), 200
nightlife (Montréal)
    about, 15–16
    bars and clubs, 190–191, 202–203
    best, 12
    brew pubs, 203
    budget for, 35
    cafes and bars, 199–201
    classical music and opera, 190
    comedy clubs, 204
    cost of, 191
    dance clubs, 195–197
    dance performance, 190
    dress code, 191
    gay and lesbian, 204
    hours for, 191
    listings, 188
    live music, 197–199
    lounges, 201–202
    map, 192–194
    neighborhood bars, 202–203
    pool halls, 203–204
    theater, 189
nightlife (Québec City)
    about, 266–268
    bars and pubs, 273–274
    best, 12
    budget for, 35
    cost of, 267, 268
    dance clubs, 268–269
    dress code, 267
    gay and lesbian, 274
    hours, 267
    listing information, 267
    live music, 269, 272–273
    map, 270–271
    neighborhood bars, 273–274
North Hatley (Eastern Townships),
    185, 187
November, 28
Nuits d'Afrique (Nights of Africa
    Festival) (Montréal), 26

• O •

Observatorie de la capitale (Québec City), 248
off-season, 36
Old City (Québec City). *See* Vieux-Québec (Old Québec)
Onetop.ca (design competition), 283–284
opaque fare service, 45–46
opera (Montréal), 190
Oratoire St. Joseph du Mont Royal (Montréal), 148
OSM (L'Orchestre Symphonique de Montréal), 190
Ottawa, day trip, 178–181
outdoor dance party (Piknic Electronik), 282–283

• P •

package tours, 48–50
packing for trip, 71–72
Parc Aquarium de Québec (Québec City), 248
Parc Aquatique du Mont-St-Sauveur (Laurentian Mountains), 182
Parc de la Chute-Montmorency (Québec City), 248–249
Parc de l'Artillerie (Québec City), 250
Parc des Champs-de-Bataille (Québec City), 246
Parc Jean-Drapeau (Montréal), 141–142
Parc Lafontaine (Montréal), 145
Parc Maisonneuve (Montréal), 145
Parc Mont-Royal (Montréal), 142
Parc National du Mont Orford (Eastern Townships), 185
parking
  Montréal, 62, 85, 87–88
  in Québec City, 213
  valet, 291
Parliament Hill (Ottawa), 178
passport, 59–62, 78
pastry shops (Montréal), 131
performing arts (Montréal), 189–190
pharmacies, 289–290

picnics, 110, 128–129
Pierre Elliott Trudeau International Airport (Montréal), 43–44, 78–79, 208
Piknic Electronik (outdoor dance party), 282–283
pizza, 125, 239
Place Jacques-Cartier (Montréal), 162
Place-Royale (Québec City), 246, 251, 256, 261–262
Planetarium de Montréal, 145
planning trip. *See also* budget for trip; itineraries
  accommodation reservations, 91–93
  airline reservations, 45–46
  cellphone and e-mail access, 66–69
  with children, 51–53
  package tours, 48–50
  packing luggage, 71–72
  passport, 59–62, 78
  seasons and, 20–23
  staying healthy and, 66
  transportation, 34
Plateau (Montréal)
  described, 82
  maps, 115, 194
  nightlife, 194
  restaurants, 115
  shopping, 158–159
  T-shirts from, 282
police, 287, 290
pool halls, Montréal, 203–204
Pop Montréal, 28
Porte St-Louis (Québec City), 255
post office, 288–289
poutine, 170, 280
Pride Parade (Montréal), 26–27
Promenade de la Pointe à Carcy (Québec City), 252
Provincial Sales Tax (TVQ), 64, 111, 290
Pub Quartier Latin (Montréal), 202
Pub St-Patrick (Québec City), 274

• Q •

Quartier Latin (Montréal), 82
Québec City International Festival of Military Bands, 30

Québec City Winter Carnival, 20
Québec Festival of Devotional
    Music, 30
Québec Nordiques (hockey team), 282
Québec Plus (Web site), 71

• *R* •

rack rate, 2, 91, 94
radio stations, 290
rainfall, 21
Rencontres internationales du
    documentaire de Montréal, 28
rental car. *See also* car, driving
  agencies, 293
  budget for, 34
  gasoline, 34, 87
  insurance, 63–64
  Jean-Lesage airport, 208
  Trudeau airport, 79
reservations
  accommodations, 91–93
  airline, 45–46
  arriving without, 93
  restaurant, 70–71, 111, 230
restaurants. *See also* Restaurant Index,
    Montréal; Restaurant Index,
    Québec City; restaurants
    (Montréal); restaurants (Québec
    City)
  best, 11–12
  breakfast, 127–128
  Bring Your Own Bottle (BYOB),
    130–131
  brunch, 109
  cost-cutting tips, 110
  dining etiquette, 110–111
  Eastern Townships, 187
  gay and lesbian, 57
  Laurentian Mountains, 184
  menus and, 110–111
  Montréal, 111–125
  Ottawa, 181
  Québec City, 230–240
  reservations, 70–71, 111, 230

  smoking and, 111
  supper clubs, 109–110
  tipping, 36, 111, 291
  vegetarian, 129–130, 240
restaurants (Montréal). *See also*
    Restaurant Index, Montréal
  bagels, 126
  breakfast, 127–128
  Bring Your Own Bottle (BYOB),
    130–131
  coffee and pastry, 131
  dollar-sign rating, 111, 114
  kid-friendly, 124
  maps, 112–113, 115
  pizza and burgers, 125–126
  sandwich shops, 126–127
  vegetarian, 129–130
restaurants (Québec City). *See also*
    Restaurant Index, Québec City
  coffee cafes, 238–239
  crêpes, 240
  kid-friendly, 236
  map, 228–229
  pizza and burgers, 239
  price range, 230
  reservations, 230
  vegetarian, 240
restrooms, 290
Rideau Canal (Ottawa), 180
river cruises (Québec City), 253
rue Crescent (Montréal), 156, 158
rue du Trésor (Québec City), 252,
    255–256
rue Notre-Dame (Montréal), 159–160
rue Sherbrooke Ouest (Montréal),
    81, 160
rue St-Denis (Montréal), 159
rue Ste-Catherine (Montréal), 81, 82,
    155–156
rue St-Jean (Québec City), 250–251, 261
rue St-Joseph (Québec City), 251,
    263–265
rue St-Paul (Montréal), 160, 162
rue St-Paul (Québec City), 251, 260
rules of the road, 62, 87

• S •

safety of city streets, 85, 290
Saidye Bronfman Centre for the Arts
    (Montréal), 189
Saint-Sauveur-des-Monts (Laurentian
    Mountains), 182
sales tax, provincial (TVQ), 64, 111, 290
Salon Daome (Montréal), 195–196
sandwich shops (Montréal), 126–127
Santa Claus Parade (Montréal), 28
seasons, 20–23
senior travelers, 53–54
September/October, 27–28, 30
Shakespeare-in-the Park (Montréal), 26
shopping malls (Québec City), 258–259
shopping (Montréal)
    antiques, 153, 159–160
    art galleries, 153, 160
    arts and crafts, 160
    bookstores, 153, 156
    budget for, 35
    business hours, 152, 286
    clothing, 153, 160
    department stores, 154–155
    duty-free goods, 154
    home décor, 153
    by merchandise, 153–154
    music stores, 154, 156
    by neighborhood, 155–160
    rue Crescent, 156, 158
    rue Ste-Catherine, 155–156
    sales tax, 154
    specialty foods and liquor, 153
    T-shirts, 281–284
shopping (Québec City)
    antiques, 257, 260
    art galleries, 257, 260
    bookstores, 257–258, 260, 261
    budget for, 35
    business hours, 258, 286
    chocolate, 240, 261, 265
    clothing, 257, 261, 263–264
    department stores, 258
    duty-free, 258
    kid-friendly, 259

    by neighborhood, 259–265
    shopping malls, 258–259
    souvenirs, 261, 262
    toy stores, 264
sightseeing. See attractions (Montréal);
    attractions (Québec City)
Simons (Québec City), 258
Sky Complex (Montréal), 204
smoking laws, 111, 290
soccer team (Impact), 149
Sociéte de Transport de Montréal
    (STM), 85, 86
Society of Art and Technology
    (Montréal), 196
Sofa (Montréal), 198–199
souvenirs, 261, 262
Sparks Street (Ottawa), 180
specialty foods and liquor,
    Montréal, 153
spectator sports, 70, 148–149
spring, 21–22
St. Patrick's Day Parade (Montréal), 24
Stade Olympique (Montréal),
    142–143, 165
stamps, 288–289
Ste-Agathe des Monts (Laurentian
    Mountains), 182
St-Henri (Montréal), 159–160
St-Jean-Baptiste Day (Québec City),
    29–30
St-Jovite (Laurentian Mountains), 184
STM (Sociéte de Transport de
    Montréal), 85, 86
strawberries from Ile d'Orléans, 279
street terminology (French), 3
St-Viateur Bagels, 283
subway (Métro, Montréal), 85–86
sugar shacks (cabanes à sucre), 29
Sugaring-Off time (Montréal), 24
summer, 22
supper clubs, 109–110

• T •

tam-tams (drum-circle), 173, 176
Tangante (Montréal), 190

Tango Libre (Montréal), 197
tapas, 109
Taverne Jo Dion (Québec City), 274
taxes
  Provincial Sales Tax (TVQ), 64, 111, 290
  refund for non-Canadians, 36
  Taxe de Produits et Services (TPS), 36, 64, 111, 290
taxi cab
  fares, 88
  from Jean-Lesage airport, 207–208
  in Montréal, 88, 291
  phone numbers, 291
  in Québec City, 212, 291
  tipping, 78, 291
  from Trudeau Airport, 78, 79
teen-friendly attractions (Québec City), 250–251
telephone, 84, 291
temperature, average, 21
Tennis Masters Canada (Montréal), 27
Terrasse Dufferin (Québec City), 249
terroir (local foods), 108–109, 129, 277–280
theater (Montréal), 189
Three Monkeys (Montréal boutique), 284
three-day itinerary (Montréal), 161–166
time (military 24-hour), 267
Time Supper Club (Montréal), 196
time zone, 291
tipping
  accommodations, 36, 291
  restaurants, 36, 111, 291
  taxi cab, 36, 78, 291
  valet parking, 291
Tour de l'Ile (Montréal), 25
tourist information
  Eastern Townships, 185
  Laurentian Mountains, 182
  Montréal, 83–84, 288
  Ottawa, 178
  Québec City, 209, 212, 288
  Vieux-Montréal (Old Montréal), 84, 294
  Web sites, 294

Tourist Information Centre of Vieux-Montréal, 84, 294
tours. *See* day trips; guided tours
tourtière (meat pie), 280
toy stores (Québec City), 264
TPS (Taxe de Produits et Services), 36, 64, 111, 290
train travel
  to Montréal, 46–47, 80
  Montréal to Québec City, 81
  to Québec City, 46–47, 208
transportation
  bicycling, 86, 213
  budget for, 34
  contact information, 291
  cruise ships, 47
  to Eastern Townships, 185
  from Jean-Lesage airport, 207–208
  Métro (Montréal subway), 85–86
  in Montréal, 84–88
  to Montréal, 46–47, 78–80
  in Québec City, 212–213
  to Québec City, 46–47, 207–208
  from Trudeau airport, 78–79
travel insurance, 48
traveler's checks, 41
trip cancellation insurance, 64–65
t-shirts, 281–284
Turf Pub (Québec City), 269
TVQ (Provincial Sales Tax), 64, 111, 290
24-hour clock, 267

• *U* •

Underground City (Montréal)
  attractions, 143
  map, 157
  shopping, 155
Unity II (Montréal), 204
Upstairs (Montréal), 199
U.S. Customs and Border Protection, 286
U.S. Department of State, 59

● *V* ●

valet parking, 291
vegetarian restaurants
  Montréal, 129–130
  Québec City, 240
Verlirium (mountain biking festival)
  (Québec City), 30
Versus (Montréal), 200–201
Via Rail (passenger train), 47, 55
Vieux-Montréal (Old Montréal)
  accommodations, 95
  attractions, 137, 143
  described, 15, 81
  maps, 95, 112–113, 137
  restaurants, 112–113
  shopping, 160
  tourist information, 84, 294
Vieux-Québec (Old Québec)
  dining, 227, 230, 255
  historical attractions, 253–256
  map, 254
visitor information
  Eastern Townships, 185
  Laurentian Mountains, 182
  Montréal, 83–84, 288
  Ottawa, 178
  Québec City, 209, 212, 288
  Vieux-Montréal (Old Montréal),
    84, 294
  Web sites, 294

● *W* ●

walking
  Montréal, 85
  Québec City, 212, 251–252
  street safety and, 85
walking tours
  Montréal, 149–150
  Québec City, 252–253
wallet, lost or stolen, 41–42
Wax Museum (Musée de Cire) (Québec
  City), 248
weather
  children and, 52
  fall, 22–23
  overview, 19–20
  spring, 21–22
  summer, 22
  temperature and precipitation, 21
  winter, 16–17, 23
Western Union, 41
Westmount (Montréal), 160
WiFi (wireless fidelity), 68–69
winter, 16–17, 23
Wolf Parade (local band), 283
World Beer Festival, Montréal (Mondial
  de la bière), 25
World Film Festival (Montréal), 27

● *Z* ●

Zoobizare (Montréal), 196

Accommodations Index, Montréal

Auberge Bonaparte, 94, 98
Auberge de La Fontaine, 98
Auberge du Vieux Port, 98
Auberge Les Passants du Sans
  Soucy, 98–99
Best Western Hotel Europa, 99
Crowne Plaza, 99
Delta Centre-Ville, 99
Fairmont The Queen Elizabeth, 100
Hilton Montréal Bonaventure, 100
Holiday Inn Select Montréal
  Centre-Ville, 100
Hotel de la Montagne, 100–101
Hôtel Gault, 101
Hôtel Godin, 101
Hôtel Le Germain, 102
Hôtel Le St-James, 102
Hôtel Nelligan, 102
Hotel Omni Mont-Royal, 103
Hotel Place d'Armes, 103
Hôtel St-Paul, 103
Hotel XIXe Siècle, 103–104
Hyatt Regency Montréal, 55
Le Centre Sheraton Hotel, 104
Le Saint-Sulpice Hôtel Montréal, 104

Loews Hotel Vogue, 104–105
Meridien Versailles Montréal, 105
Montréal Marriott Château
    Champlain, 105
Novotel Montréal Centre, 105
Ritz-Carlton Montréal, 106
Sofitel Montréal, 106
W Montréal, 106–107

Accommodations Index, Québec City

Au Château Fleur De Lys Hôtel, 218
Auberge du Quartier, 215, 218
Auberge St-Pierre, 218
Château Bellevue, 218
Château Cap-Diamant, 219
Château de Pierre, 219
Château Laurier, 219
Chez Hubert, 219–220
Couettes et Café Toast, 220
Delta Québec, 220
Fairmont Le Château Frontenac,
    220–221
Gite Côte de la Montagne, 221
Hilton International Québec, 221
Holiday Inn Select, 221–222
Hôtel Belley, 222
Hôtel Clarendon, 222, 255
Hôtel Dominion 1912, 222–223
Hôtel du Vieux-Québec, 223
Hôtel Le St. Paul, 223
Hôtel Loew's Le Concorde, 223–224
Hôtel Royal William, 224
Le Krieghoff B&B, 224
Le Priori, 224–225
Maison Ste-Ursule, 225
Manoir Lafayette, 225
Manoir Victoria, 225
Relais Charles-Alexandre, 226

Restaurant Index, Montréal

Au Pied de Cochon, 114
Beaver Club, 114, 116

Buona Notte, 116
Café du Nouveau Monde, 116, 117
Cafe Santropol, 129
Casse-Croûte La Banquise, 129
Chez Clo, 128, 129
Chez Cora, 128
Chez L'Épicier, 116
Cobalt, 127
Cosmos Snack Bar, 128
Cube, 117
Eggspectations, 128
Euro Deli, 117
Fondumentale, 118
Golden Curry House Restaurant, 118
Il Piatto Della Nonna, 118
Isakaya, 119
La Binerie Mont-Royal, 129
La Colombe, 131
La Croissanterie, 119
L'Avenue, 127
Le Cartet, 127
Le Commensal, 129
Le Continentale, 119–120
Le P'tit Plateau, 131
Le Reservoir, 127
Le Roi du Plateau, 120
Le Vaudeville, 120
L'Express, 120–121
L'Orchidée de Chine, 121
Moishe's Steak House, 121
Mont-Royal Hot Dog, 128
Ouzeri, 121–122
Patati Patata, 122
Philinos, 122
Piton de la Fournaise, 131
Pushap Sweets, 130
Restaurant Lafleurs, 129
Rosalie, 122–123
Rôtisserie Italienne, 123
Rumi, 123
Schwartz's, 124
Spirite Lounge, 130
Taquéria Mexicaine, 124
Toqué!, 124
Trattoria Trestevere, 125
Yoyo's, 130–131

Restaurant Index, Québec City

Asia, 231
Aux Anciens Canadiens, 231
Buffet de l'Antiquaire, 231
Café de la Paix, 231–232
Café du Monde, 232
Casse-Crêpe Breton, 232
Conti Caffe, 232–233
Initiale, 233
L'Ardoise, 233
Largo, 233–234
L'Astral, 234

Laurie Raphaël, 234
Le Commensal, 240
Le Continental, 235
Le Momento, 235
Le Paris-Brest, 235
Le Saint-Amour, 236
L'Echaudé, 234–235
Les Frères de la Côte, 236
L'Utopie, 236
Péché Véniel, 236–237
Poisson d'Avril, 237
Sushi Taxi, 237
Voodoo Grill, 237–238
Yuzu Sushi, 238

Notes

BUSINESS, CAREERS & PERSONAL FINANCE

0-7645-5307-0

0-7645-5331-3 *†

Also available:
- Accounting For Dummies †
  0-7645-5314-3
- Business Plans Kit For Dummies †
  0-7645-5365-8
- Cover Letters For Dummies
  0-7645-5224-4
- Frugal Living For Dummies
  0-7645-5403-4
- Leadership For Dummies
  0-7645-5176-0
- Managing For Dummies
  0-7645-1771-6

- Marketing For Dummies
  0-7645-5600-2
- Personal Finance For Dummies *
  0-7645-2590-5
- Project Management
  For Dummies
  0-7645-5283-X
- Resumes For Dummies †
  0-7645-5471-9
- Selling For Dummies
  0-7645-5363-1
- Small Business Kit For Dummies *†
  0-7645-5093-4

HOME & BUSINESS COMPUTER BASICS

0-7645-4074-2

0-7645-3758-X

Also available:
- ACT! 6 For Dummies
  0-7645-2645-6
- iLife '04 All-in-One Desk Reference
  For Dummies
  0-7645-7347-0
- iPAQ For Dummies
  0-7645-6769-1
- Mac OS X Panther Timesaving
  Techniques For Dummies
  0-7645-5812-9
- Macs For Dummies
  0-7645-5656-8
- Microsoft Money 2004 For Dummies
  0-7645-4195-1

- Office 2003 All-in-One Desk
  Reference For Dummies
  0-7645-3883-7
- Outlook 2003 For Dummies
  0-7645-3759-8
- PCs For Dummies
  0-7645-4074-2
- TiVo For Dummies
  0-7645-6923-6
- Upgrading and Fixing PCs
  For Dummies
  0-7645-1665-5
- Windows XP Timesaving
  Techniques For Dummies
  0-7645-3748-2

FOOD, HOME, GARDEN, HOBBIES, MUSIC & PETS

0-7645-5295-3

0-7645-5232-5

Also available:
- Bass Guitar For Dummies
  0-7645-2487-9
- Diabetes Cookbook For Dummies
  0-7645-5230-9
- Gardening For Dummies *
  0-7645-5130-2
- Guitar For Dummies
  0-7645-5106-X
- Holiday Decorating For Dummies
  0-7645-2570-0
- Home Improvement All-in-One
  For Dummies
  0-7645-5680-0

- Knitting For Dummies
  0-7645-5395-X
- Piano For Dummies
  0-7645-5105-1
- Puppies For Dummies
  0-7645-5255-4
- Scrapbooking For Dummies
  0-7645-7208-3
- Senior Dogs For Dummies
  0-7645-5818-8
- Singing For Dummies
  0-7645-2475-5
- 30-Minute Meals For Dummies
  0-7645-2589-1

INTERNET & DIGITAL MEDIA

0-7645-1664-7

0-7645-6924-4

Also available:
- 2005 Online Shopping Directory
  For Dummies
  0-7645-7495-7
- CD & DVD Recording For Dummies
  0-7645-5956-7
- eBay For Dummies
  0-7645-5654-1
- Fighting Spam For Dummies
  0-7645-5965-6
- Genealogy Online For Dummies
  0-7645-5964-8
- Google For Dummies
  0-7645-4420-9

- Home Recording For Musicians
  For Dummies
  0-7645-1634-5
- The Internet For Dummies
  0-7645-4173-0
- iPod & iTunes For Dummies
  0-7645-7772-7
- Preventing Identity Theft
  For Dummies
  0-7645-7336-5
- Pro Tools All-in-One Desk
  Reference For Dummies
  0-7645-5714-9
- Roxio Easy Media Creator
  For Dummies
  0-7645-7131-1

SPORTS, FITNESS, PARENTING, RELIGION & SPIRITUALITY

0-7645-5146-9

0-7645-5418-2

Also available:
- Adoption For Dummies
  0-7645-5488-3
- Basketball For Dummies
  0-7645-5248-1
- The Bible For Dummies
  0-7645-5296-1
- Buddhism For Dummies
  0-7645-5359-3
- Catholicism For Dummies
  0-7645-5391-7
- Hockey For Dummies
  0-7645-5228-7

- Judaism For Dummies
  0-7645-5299-6
- Martial Arts For Dummies
  0-7645-5358-5
- Pilates For Dummies
  0-7645-5397-6
- Religion For Dummies
  0-7645-5264-3
- Teaching Kids to Read
  For Dummies
  0-7645-4043-2
- Weight Training For Dummies
  0-7645-5168-X
- Yoga For Dummies
  0-7645-5117-5

TRAVEL

0-7645-5438-7

0-7645-5453-0

Also available:
- Alaska For Dummies
  0-7645-1761-9
- Arizona For Dummies
  0-7645-6938-4
- Cancún and the Yucatán
  For Dummies
  0-7645-2437-2
- Cruise Vacations For Dummies
  0-7645-6941-4
- Europe For Dummies
  0-7645-5456-5
- Ireland For Dummies
  0-7645-5455-7

- Las Vegas For Dummies
  0-7645-5448-4
- London For Dummies
  0-7645-4277-X
- New York City For Dummies
  0-7645-6945-7
- Paris For Dummies
  0-7645-5494-8
- RV Vacations For Dummies
  0-7645-5443-3
- Walt Disney World & Orlando
  For Dummies
  0-7645-6943-0

GRAPHICS, DESIGN & WEB DEVELOPMENT

0-7645-4345-8

0-7645-5589-8

Also available:
- Adobe Acrobat 6 PDF
  For Dummies
  0-7645-3760-1
- Building a Web Site For Dummies
  0-7645-7144-3
- Dreamweaver MX 2004
  For Dummies
  0-7645-4342-3
- FrontPage 2003 For Dummies
  0-7645-3882-9
- HTML 4 For Dummies
  0-7645-1995-6
- Illustrator CS For Dummies
  0-7645-4084-X

- Macromedia Flash MX 2004
  For Dummies
  0-7645-4358-X
- Photoshop 7 All-in-One Desk
  Reference For Dummies
  0-7645-1667-1
- Photoshop CS Timesaving
  Techniques For Dummies
  0-7645-6782-9
- PHP 5 For Dummies
  0-7645-4166-8
- PowerPoint 2003 For Dummies
  0-7645-3908-6
- QuarkXPress 6 For Dummies
  0-7645-2593-X

NETWORKING, SECURITY, PROGRAMMING & DATABASES

0-7645-6852-3

0-7645-5784-X

Also available:
- A+ Certification For Dummies
  0-7645-4187-0
- Access 2003 All-in-One Desk
  Reference For Dummies
  0-7645-3988-4
- Beginning Programming
  For Dummies
  0-7645-4997-9
- C For Dummies
  0-7645-7068-4
- Firewalls For Dummies
  0-7645-4048-3
- Home Networking For Dummies
  0-7645-42796

- Network Security For Dummies
  0-7645-1679-5
- Networking For Dummies
  0-7645-1677-9
- TCP/IP For Dummies
  0-7645-1760-0
- VBA For Dummies
  0-7645-3989-2
- Wireless All In-One Desk Reference
  For Dummies
  0-7645-7496-5
- Wireless Home Networking
  For Dummies
  0-7645-3910-8

HEALTH & SELF-HELP

0-7645-6820-5 *†

0-7645-2566-2

Also available:
- Alzheimer's For Dummies
  0-7645-3899-3
- Asthma For Dummies
  0-7645-4233-8
- Controlling Cholesterol For
  Dummies
  0-7645-5440-9
- Depression For Dummies
  0-7645-3900-0
- Dieting For Dummies
  0-7645-4149-8
- Fertility For Dummies
  0-7645-2549-2

- Fibromyalgia For Dummies
  0-7645-5441-7
- Improving Your Memory
  For Dummies
  0-7645-5435-2
- Pregnancy For Dummies †
  0-7645-4483-7
- Quitting Smoking For Dummies
  0-7645-2629-4
- Relationships For Dummies
  0-7645-5384-4
- Thyroid For Dummies
  0-7645-5385-2

EDUCATION, HISTORY, REFERENCE & TEST PREPARATION

0-7645-5194-9

0-7645-4186-2

Also available:
- Algebra For Dummies
  0-7645-5325-9
- British History For Dummies
  0-7645-7021-8
- Calculus For Dummies
  0-7645-2498-4
- English Grammar For Dummies
  0-7645-5322-4
- Forensics For Dummies
  0-7645-5580-4
- The GMAT For Dummies
  0-7645-5251-1
- Inglés Para Dummies
  0-7645-5427-1

- Italian For Dummies
  0-7645-5196-5
- Latin For Dummies
  0-7645-5431-X
- Lewis & Clark For Dummies
  0-7645-2545-X
- Research Papers For Dummies
  0-7645-5426-3
- The SAT I For Dummies
  0-7645-7193-1
- Science Fair Projects For Dummies
  0-7645-5460-3
- U.S. History For Dummies
  0-7645-5249-X

Get smart @ dummies.com®

- Find a full list of Dummies titles
- Look into loads of FREE on-site articles
- Sign up for FREE eTips e-mailed to you
  weekly
- See what other products carry the
  Dummies name
- Shop directly from the Dummies bookstore
- Enter to win new prizes every month!

* Separate Canadian edition also available
† Separate U.K. edition also available

Available wherever books are sold. For more information or to order direct: U.S. customers
visit www.dummies.com or call 1-877-762-2974.
U.K. customers visit www.wileyeurope.com or call 0800 243407. Canadian customers visit
www.wiley.ca or call 1-800-567-4797.